The Oxford Dictionary of
English
Grammar

SECOND EDITION

BAS AARTS

SYLVIA CHALKER

EMUND WEINER

Bas Aarts is Professor of English Linguistics at University College London. He has published many books and articles on English grammar, most recently the *Oxford Modern English Grammar*.

The late **Sylvia Chalker** was the author of several grammar books, including *Current English Grammar* and the *Little Oxford Dictionary of English Grammar.* She was also a contributor to the *Oxford Companion to the English Language*.

Edmund Weiner is Deputy Chief Editor of the *Oxford English Dictionary* and co-author (with Andrew Delahunty) of the *Oxford Guide to English Usage*.

 SEE WEB LINKS

This is a web-linked dictionary. There is a list of recommended web links in the Appendix, on page 454. To access the websites, go to the dictionary's web page at www.oxfordreference.com/page/enggram.

OXFORD
UNIVERSITY PRESS

Great Clarendon Street, Oxford, OX2 6DP,
United Kingdom

Oxford University Press is a department of the University of Oxford.
It furthers the University's objective of excellence in research, scholarship,
and education by publishing worldwide. Oxford is a registered trade mark of
Oxford University Press in the UK and in certain other countries

First edition published 1994
First issued as an Oxford University Press paperback 1994
Reissued, with corrections, in new covers 1998
Second edition published 2014

Published in the United States of America by Oxford University Press
198 Madison Avenue, New York, NY 10016, United States of America

British Library Cataloguing in Publication Data

Data available

ISBN: 978-0-19-965823-7

Printed in Great Britain by
Clays Ltd, Elcograf S.p.A.

Contents

Contents

Preface to the First Edition

Grammar, etymologically speaking, is related to *glamour*. Though few people might claim that grammar is glamorous in the modern sense, there is considerable interest in English grammar today and no shortage of grammar books, ranging from small basic books aimed at children or elementary-level foreign learners, through more advanced manuals to large scholarly works. The trouble is—they may be about the same language, but they do not always speak the same language. The very range of the grammar books on offer presents problems.

There are many ways of describing grammar, and a wealth of terminology. Some of it strikes the layman as jargon (*disjunct, matrix, pro-form, stative*); other words appear ordinary enough but conceal specialized meanings (*comment, focus, specific*). Worse, the same terms, old or new—*comparison, formal, pronoun, reported speech, root, stress*—are used by different grammarians with different meanings.

Such difficulties are not entirely avoidable. Any subject of study needs specialist words. Different grammarians are entitled to analyse language in different ways, and fresh viewpoints may call for new terms. But while grammarians sometimes explain what they mean by a new or unusual term, it is rarer for them to point out that they are using an existing term in a different way. This is a cause of real confusion. Another problem is that new terms may in the end turn out simply to be alternatives for an old concept—a synonym in fact (e.g. *progressive, continuous*).

We have tried in this dictionary to indicate the range and variety of meanings that may lie behind a single term. The main emphasis is on the terminology of current mainstream grammar, but we have also included a considerable number of entries on the related areas of speech and meaning—more grandly known as phonetics and semantics. Users will also find some terms from Generative Grammar, which has greatly influenced mainstream grammar in recent years—but some of the more theoretical terminology of linguistics and semantics is excluded. We have also on the whole excluded outdated grammatical terminology, apart from a few traditional terms which may be familiar to the general reader.

The authors would like to thank Professor Flor Aarts, of the Katholieke Universiteit, Nijmegen, who read an early draft of the book: his comments, we believe, have led to many improvements, but the authors are alone responsible for any blemishes that remain. We would also like to thank our families for their support, encouragement, and, at times, forbearance.

SC
ESCW

London, Oxford 1993

Preface to the Second Edition

Students of English are faced with an ever-expanding list of terms when studying the grammar of present-day English. The *Oxford Dictionary of English Grammar* offers help by defining current terminology clearly with the help of numerous example sentences and quotations from the scholarly linguistic literature. Where the same terminology is used differently by linguists, these differences are explained, and where different terminology is used in the same way, this is also clearly signalled.

This new edition of the *Oxford Dictionary of English Grammar* differs from the first edition in many ways:

- All entries have been completely revised and updated.
- There are many new entries covering recent terminology, for example from *The Cambridge Grammar of the English Language*.
- There are new short entries on the most important grammars of English published since the beginning of the twentieth century.
- Usage advice is given where appropriate, though it is never prescriptive.
- Advice is sometimes given regarding the use of terminology that most linguists would agree is best avoided.

Readers familiar with the first edition will notice that the entries on English phonetics have been removed. The reason for this is that it is very unusual for phonetics to be covered under the heading of 'grammar', and this terminology is best dealt with elsewhere.

The term 'grammar' is conceived of in this dictionary as encompassing syntax and morphology, and the aim is to cover terminology that is used in the current literature on English grammar. The dictionary also has entries on related fields of study, such as corpus linguistics, historical linguistics, lexicology, (lexical) semantics, sociolinguistics, stylistics, and so on, but only when this terminology is broadly relevant to grammar. Terms from theoretical frameworks are also covered to some extent, especially those from Generative Grammar and Systemic Grammar, though for a fuller treatment the reader is referred to Peter Matthews's *Concise Oxford Dictionary of Linguistics*.

I am grateful to the late Sylvia Chalker and to Edmund Weiner for their excellent work on the first edition of this book, and to Rebecca Lane and Jamie Crowther at OUP for their support during the writing process. Finally, thanks are due to Jill Bowie for her meticulous copy-editing and to Donald Watt for proofreading.

BAS AARTS
University College London

Organization

1. Entries are strictly alphabetical. Thus:

   agent
   agentive
   agentless passive
   agent noun

2. *Cross-references* to other entries are signalled by an asterisk when they occur in running text, e.g.

   Aktionsart
   The lexical expression of *aspect...

3. In formal cross-references, the entry referred to is indicated in small capitals, e.g.

   focusing subjunct See FOCUSING ADVERB.
   A cross-reference to a phrase listed within an entry is given in a mixture of small capitals (for the entry headword) and italics (for the remainder of the phrase), e.g. COMPLEX *sentence.*

4. When a cross-reference relates to a particular numbered sense in another entry, the number of the relevant sense is indicated, e.g. *base (2) or BASE (2).

5. Where a word is not a grammatical term in itself, but forms part of a *phrase* which is dealt with elsewhere, this is indicated, e.g.

   act See SPEECH ACT.

6. Where a term is dealt with at the entry for some larger term, this is indicated, e.g.

   formulaic subjunctive See SUBJUNCTIVE.

7. Where two or more terms are *synonyms*, the definition appears under the preferred term, usually with a reference to the alternative term, e.g.

   folk etymology
   ...Also called **popular etymology**.

   and the other term is cross-referenced with an asterisk, e.g.

   popular etymology
   The same as *folk etymology.

8. Where two or more terms are in a *contrastive* relationship, this is stated at the beginning of both entries, e.g.

   abstract...
   ...Contrasted with *concrete.

   concrete...
   ...Contrasted with *abstract.

9. *See (also)* at the end of (part of) an entry indicates that further information will be found at the entry indicated. Sometimes the user is referred to a closely related word, e.g.

   coordinate...
   ...*See also* COORDINATION.

   At other times the reference is to a 'background' concept, e.g.

   discord...
   ...*See* AGREEMENT.

10. *Compare* at the end of (part of) an entry indicates that although the entry is complete, it may be useful to read entries for related or overlapping terms, or terms with which this term could be confused, e.g.

abbreviated ...

... *Compare* BLOCK LANGUAGE; REDUCED CLAUSE.

These particular entries show that certain types of language that might reasonably be described as *abbreviated* are in fact given special labels.

11. Words are marked with *word class labels* (*n.* = noun, *adj.* = adjective, *v.* = verb, etc.) only when they can belong to more than one class.

12. Where word class labels are conjoined (e.g. *n. & adj.*), the definition is framed so as to cover both uses, with parentheses surrounding the part of the definition that applies to only one of the two uses, e.g.

countable

(*n. & adj.*) (Designating) a noun with singular and plural forms.

which is equivalent to:

(*n.*) A noun with singular and plural forms.

(*adj.*) Designating a noun with singular and plural forms.

13. In certain entries, words and phrases quoted as examples are given *abbreviated dates* indicating their earliest known recorded appearance in English. In these, the number is that of the century and the preceding E, M, L mean 'early', 'mid', and 'late': 'E19' means '1800–1829', 'M19' means 1830–1869', and 'L19' means '1870–1899'. OE means 'Old English' (before 1150), ME 'Middle English' (1150–1349), and LME 'late Middle English' (1350–1469).

14. In many entries, quotations from works on language and linguistics are given in order to illustrate the use of the word being defined. Only the author's name and the date of the work are cited: fuller details are given in the References section.

15. Meanings are signalled by single inverted commas: e.g. *Wherever you go, you'll be covered by this insurance* ('No matter where you go . . . ').

16. *Derivatives* of a headword are listed at the end of the entry and indicated by a single preceding dot. They are undefined if their meaning is plain once that of the parent word is known, and if they are not found in 'extended terms' (special phrasal combinations). For example, at the end of the entry for **syntax** we have:

• **syntactic, syntactically**.

17. *Extended terms* are listed alphabetically at the end of the entry following any derivatives, and indicated by two preceding dots. They are given brief definitions or fuller discussion as appropriate. For example, in the entry for **modifier** we have:

•• **modifier clause**: a clause that postmodifies a head, e.g. a *relative clause.

•• **sentence modifier**: a modifier that modifies a complete sentence or clause.

Notational Conventions

*	An asterisk used before a citation of a linguistic form indicates an impossible structure, i.e. a structure that does not conform to the grammatical rules of English. Example: *They likes to read. In this example the third person <u>plural</u> subject *they* is followed by a verb with a third person <u>singular</u> inflectional ending.
?	A question mark used before a citation of a linguistic form indicates a structure that is of doubtful acceptability. Example: ?*Give it me*.
Ø	This symbol is used to indicate an implicit subject. Example: *I want [Ø to read it]*.
arrows	These indicate movement, For example, in *What did you see?* the pronoun *what* functions as the direct object of the verb *see* and has been moved to the beginning of the sentence to form an interrogative structure:

What did you see_?

The underscore symbol is explained below.

brackets [. . .]	Brackets are used: (1) to indicate words that together form a constituent phrase, clause, etc. A *labelled bracketing* includes a subscript indicator of the syntactic status of the constituent. Example: *[$_{NP}$ Cats][$_{VP}$ eat [$_{NP}$ fish]]*; (2) to indicate that a lexical item, usually a verb, is followed by a complement which contains a particular word. Example: *have [to]* indicates that the verb *have* is followed by a complement that contains the word *to*, e.g. *I have <u>to</u> leave*.
co-indexing	Items that are co-referential can be co-indexed, i.e. bear the same subscript letter, usually an 'i'. Example: *He$_i$ shaves himself$_i$ twice every day*.
italics	These are used: (1) to cite words, sentences, etc. as linguistic forms; (2) to indicate words, phrases, etc. that require highlighting. For underlined italics, see below.
<u>*underlined italics*</u>	Within italicized citations of linguistic forms, underlining is used to highlight particular words (or other elements) for attention.
underscore ('_')	This symbol indicates a 'gap' in the clause with which a displaced element is associated. For example, in *What did you see _ ?* the pronoun *what* has been moved to the beginning of the sentence from the position indicated by '_' to form an interrogative structure.

Abbreviations

A/AP (or Adj/AdjP)	adjective/adjective phrase
Adv/AdvP	adverb/adverb phrase
AmE	American English
BrE	British English
CaGEL	*The Cambridge grammar of the English language*, by Rodney Huddleston, Geoffrey K. Pullum, et al. Cambridge: Cambridge University Press, 2002.
CGEL	*A comprehensive grammar of the English language*, by Randolph Quirk, Sidney Greenbaum, Geoffrey Leech, and Jan Svartvik. London: Longman, 1985.
D/DP	determinative/determinative phrase (or determiner/determiner phrase)
det	determinative (or determiner)
DO	Direct Object
IO	Indirect Object
N/NP	noun/noun phrase
OMEG	*Oxford Modern English grammar*, by Bas Aarts. Oxford: Oxford University Press, 2011.
P/PP	preposition/prepositional phrase
S	sentence
V/VP	verb/verb phrase

A *Adverbial as an *element of *clause structure.

The symbol is used in some modern analyses of clause structure (e.g. CGEL). *See* ADVERBIAL (1).

Compare C; S; O; V.

See also ADJUNCT.

A-bar category *See* X-BAR SYNTAX.

abbreviated Shortened or contracted so that a part stands for the whole.

This term is used to designate language (a clause, phrase, word, etc.) in which words inessential to the message are omitted and the grammar sometimes deviates from standard rules. It is a very general term, since individuals will vary in how severely they abridge, and exactly how they do it when writing diary entries, notes, etc.

Abbreviated sentences of a more predictable kind are a frequent feature of informal writing (e.g. text messages, handwritten notices) and conversation. Here the subject and part of the verb are often omitted.

Having a wonderful time here

See you soon

All news then

Back at 5

More tea? (= Would you like . . . ?, Do you want . . . ?)

Abbreviated language overlaps with *ellipsis, but is less subject to constraints. For example, there is no need for the 'missing words' to be 'recoverable'.

Labels and printed instructions, too, often use abbreviated language; and here not only subjects but objects also are typically omitted, e.g.

Contains natural herb extracts

Avoid getting into the eyes

Other forms of abbreviated language appear in titles and newspaper headlines.

•• **abbreviated clause**: the same as *reduced clause.

•• **abbreviated form**: the same as *contraction (2).

Compare BLOCK LANGUAGE; REDUCED CLAUSE.

See also ABBREVIATION.

abbreviation A shortened form of a *word or *phrase, standing for the whole.

This term is applied in three different ways.

1. A string of letters—often spoken as such—formed from the initial letters of the (main) words of a phrase. Also called *initialism, e.g.

BBC	(British Broadcasting Corporation)
CBI	(Confederation of British Industry)
ERM	(Exchange Rate Mechanism)
OTT	(over the top)
PC	(personal computer)
UK	(United Kingdom)

Sometimes the letters represent syllables of a word:

ID	(identity or identification card)
TB	(tuberculosis)

2. A word (sometimes called a *clipping) standing for the whole, retaining at least one syllable of the original word.

ad	(advertisement) (M19)
demo	(demonstration) (M20)
flu	(influenza) (M19)
pub	(public house) (M19)
phone	(telephone) (L19)
sitcom	(situation comedy) (M20)

Clippings vary in their level of formality; *mike* (microphone) and *wellies* (wellington boots) are at the informal end of the scale. Other abbreviations are acceptable in formal contexts, e.g. *bus* (omnibus), *maths* (US *math*) (mathematics); or their origin may even be virtually forgotten, e.g. *mob* (from Latin *mobile vulgus*).

3. A written convention which is unpronounceable in its shortened form. This includes abbreviations of personal titles, e.g. *Col.*, *Dr*, *Mrs*, *Sgt.*, etc.

Also:

St.	(street)	*etc.*	(etcetera)	*MS*	(manuscript)
Fr.	(French)	*kg*	(kilogram)		
Gk	(Greek)	*rpt*	(repeat)		

There are a few special written conventions for plurals:

pp   (pages)   *MSS* or mss (manuscripts)
ff.   (following pages)

Written Latin abbreviations are sometimes read out in their English equivalents, but some are only pronounced as letter strings, e.g.

e.g.   (*exempli gratia*) ('for example', /ˌiːˈdʒiː/)
i.e.   (*id est*) ('that is', /ˌaɪ ˈiː/)
cf.   (*confer*) ('compare', /ˌsiː ˈef/)
a.m. and *p.m.*   (*ante meridiem* and *post meridiem*: /ˈeɪ ˌem/, /ˈpiː ˌem/).

Chemical formulae and other symbols can be regarded as a special type of abbreviation:

H_2O (water)   *Fe* (iron)   & (and)
–   (minus)   + (plus)

Compare ACRONYM; BLEND; CONTRACTION; INITIALISM.

ability One of the semantic categories used in the classification of *modal verbs.

The term is particularly applied to the *dynamic (2) meaning of *can* and *could*. It contrasts with other meanings of these verbs such as *permission and *possibility.

See also MODAL; MODALITY.

ablative (*n. & adj.*) (In older grammar.) (A case) that expresses meanings such as 'by N', 'with N', or 'from N' (where N = *noun).

This case, occurring and originally named in Latin, is not relevant to English, where such meanings are expressed by *prepositional phrases. The corresponding semantic categories include *agent, *instrument, and *means. The nearest equivalent in English to the **ablative absolute** of Latin (*ablativus absolutus*) is the *absolute clause.

Compare CASE.

absolute

1. (*n. & adj.*) (Designating) the *unmarked *degree (1) in the three-way system of comparing *adjectives and *adverbs (e.g. *kind, soon*), in contrast to the *comparative forms (*kinder, sooner*) and the *superlative forms (*kindest, soonest*). Also called **plain grade** or **positive**.

2. Non-gradable. *See* GRADABLE.

3. Used for *possessive *pronouns that can stand on their own (*mine, yours, his, ours, theirs*), contrasted with *my, your*, etc. which are placed before nouns (the latter being variously analysed as pronouns or as determinatives (1)). Also called **independent possessive pronouns**.

4. (In older usage.) Designating an *adjective or *verb which occurs in certain unusual constructions or syntactic relationships, e.g.

(i) an adjective used without a following noun (e.g. *the poor*);
(ii) a normally transitive verb used intransitively (e.g. *Have you eaten?*); and
(iii) a comparative or superlative form of an adjective used without the specific mention of a relationship (e.g. *I only want the best*).

> 1931 G. O. CURME The absolute comparative is not as common as the absolute superlative . . . *higher* education; a *better*-class cafe.

See also ABSOLUTE CLAUSE.

● **absolutely** (in older usage, as 4(i) above.)

> 1884 *New English Dictionary* In 'the public are informed', 'the young are invited', *public* and *young* are adjectives used absolutely.

absolute clause A *non-finite or *verbless *clause containing its own subject, attached to a sentence from which it is separated by a comma (or commas), and not introduced by a subordinator. Also called **absolute construction**.

A verb, if used, can be an *-ing* or an *-ed/-en* form. Examples:

> The fight to board the train—*the women crushed against the doors, the children desperately clutching their mothers*—repeated itself at this provincial station
>
> *The platform empty once more*, I settled down for the night

Except for a few set phrases (*weather permitting, present company excepted*) absolute clauses tend to be formal and written. If the subject is a pronoun it must be in the *nominative (i.e. the subjective (1)), not the *accusative (i.e. the objective (1)), case (e.g. *I refusing to go, Nicholas went alone*), so absolute clauses are sometimes called **nominative absolutes**. (This contrasts with the *ablative absolute of Latin grammar, where the comparable noun is in the ablative case.)

See also SMALL CLAUSE.

absolutive case *See* ERGATIVE.

abstract Used mainly of *nouns that denote an action, idea, quality, or state; contrasted with *concrete.

The traditional division of common nouns into abstract and concrete nouns is semantic. It therefore cuts across the more strictly grammatical classification into *uncount and *count nouns. It is unsatisfactory as a way of trying to deal with syntactic differences: the abstract label does fit many uncount nouns (e.g. *Everybody needs advice/fun/luck*; not **an advice/*

*funs/*two lucks*), but abstract nouns also include count nouns (e.g. *We had an idea/another quarrel/better solutions*; not **We had idea/quarrel/ better solution*). Other abstract nouns have both count and uncount uses (e.g. *several important discoveries/an important discovery*; *a voyage of discovery*).

•• **abstract case**: *see* CASE.

acceptability Of a language form or an utterance: the quality of being judged by native speakers as normal or possible.

Native speakers may disagree over whether a particular *utterance is grammatically acceptable or not. An individual's judgement of acceptability may be affected by personal, regional, or social background, by perceptions of 'correctness', and so on. For example, judgements differ over the acceptability of:

? You ain't seen nothing yet
? She was realizing there was a problem
? The house was building for three years
? We convinced them to go
? Either Monday, Tuesday, or Wednesday would suit me

Linguists make a distinction between acceptability and *grammaticality, since sentences may be grammatically correct according to the *rules, but unacceptable for some other reason. For example, a properly constructed, grammatically correct sentence could be so long that it becomes unacceptable because it is virtually impossible to understand. In this sense, acceptability is related to actual performance, while grammaticality is a feature of (more idealized) *competence.

Acceptability can extend to *word formation. Thus, although the suffix *-ish*, with the meaning 'somewhat like', 'somewhat', combines with concrete nouns (e.g. *foolish, snobbish, kittenish*) and adjectives (e.g. *coldish, pinkish*), there could be degrees of acceptability as regards words newly formed with this suffix (e.g. *?yuppyish, *idiotish, ?trendyish, ?*aquamarinish*).

• **acceptable**.

> 1988 R. QUIRK Characters in Dickens can use *an't* or *ain't* for 'isn't' without any hint that such forms are other than fully acceptable.

accidence (In older grammar.) The part of grammar that deals with the *inflections of words; the way words change to indicate different grammatical roles.

This category traditionally contrasts with *syntax. For example, the differences between:

drive, *drives*, *driving*, *drove*, and *driven*

or between:

driver, *driver's*, *drivers*, and *drivers'*

would come under the heading of accidence in a traditional grammar. In more modern grammar the term has been superseded by *inflection, which, together with *derivation, is dealt with under *morphology.

Apparently *accidence* was an alteration of *accidents* (plural), used around 1600 to mean 'the changes to which words are subject in accordance with the relations in which they are used', translating the Latin neuter plural *accidentia*; although it is possible that the latter was misunderstood as a feminine singular noun and rendered *accidence*.

accusative *See* OBJECTIVE (1).

acquisition *Linguistics.* The process of learning a language.

The term **child language acquisition** is used in descriptions of how children develop the ability to speak a language.

See also LANGUAGE ACQUISITION DEVICE.

acrolect *Sociolinguistics.*

1. A term used to describe varieties of a language in a *creole continuum. Specifically, in a particular community the acrolect is the variety that is nearest to the standard.

Compare BASILECT; HYPERLECT; MESOLECT.

2. More generally, the most prestigious or 'highest' social variety of a language.

The term is sometimes used in connection with mother-tongue English speakers. Thus standard British English spoken with a standard accent may be considered an acrolect (*see also* HYPERLECT). It is also used of varieties of English in regions where English is a second (or third) language.

> 1977 J. T. PLATT I feel that in the case of Singapore English . . . a very distinct non-British English acrolect is gradually emerging.

• **acrolectal**.

acronym *Morphology.*

1. Strictly, a *word formed from (i) the initial letters of other words, or from (ii) a mixture of initials and syllables, e.g.

(i) *AFAIK* (=as far as I know)
    NATO (=North Atlantic Treaty Organization)
    NIMBY (=not in my back yard)

(ii) *radar* (=radio detection and ranging)
    yuppie (=young urban professional + diminutive ending)

Sometimes included in the general term *abbreviation.

2. More loosely, an *abbreviation pronounced as a string of letters, especially letters that stand for the name of an organization or institution, e.g. *BBC, USA*.

This usage may be due to the fact that the specific term for this type of abbreviation (*initialism) is not widely known.

act *See* SPEECH ACT.

action The process of acting or doing, expressed by a *verb.

Many transitive verbs used in the active *voice are said to 'act upon' their objects, which are given the *semantic role of *patient. However, not all such verbs imply actors, actions, or patients in any meaningful way (e.g. *I heard screams, He contracted hepatitis*).

Traditionally and loosely the term is used of *any* verb, but this is best avoided.

1884 NEW ENGLISH DICTIONARY *Action of a verb, verbal action*: The action expressed by a verb; properly of verbs which assert *acting*, but conveniently extended to *the thing asserted by a verb*, whether action, state, or mere existence, as I *strike*, I *stand*, I *live*, I *am*.

See also CASE (1); CASE GRAMMAR; SEMANTIC ROLE.

actional passive *See* PASSIVE.

action verb A *verb (also called an **event verb**) describing a *situation that occurs over a limited period of time which has a beginning and an end, e.g. *arrive, make, listen, walk*. Contrasted with a *state verb.

The terms *action and **event**, used to describe verbs, are popular equivalents for *dynamic (1). (Similarly, **state verb** is popularly substituted for **stative verb**.) The alternative labels are not, however, strictly synonymous, since the main verb in *I am growing old*, as part of a *progressive construction, must be described as dynamic, but less obviously denotes either an action or an event.

Compare DYNAMIC; STATIVE.

active (*adj.*) Of a *verb, *clause, *construction, etc.: designating an exponent of the grammatical *category of *voice whereby the grammatical

*subject is the *agent of the action denoted by the verb. Contrasted with
*passive.

(*n.*) A construction (verb phrase, clause, sentence) in which the referent
of the grammatical *subject typically carries out the action expressed by
the verb (i.e. is its *agent). Contrasted with passive.

The term is sometimes applied to the verb itself such that the verbs in
the following examples are said to be in the active voice:

> The bird *caught* the worm
> The sun *rises* in the east

Many verbs, e.g. intransitive verbs, can occur only in the active.

> 1985 R. QUIRK et al. There are greater restrictions on verbs occurring in the
> passive than on verbs occurring in the active.

•• **active verb**: (in older usage) the same as *action verb.

See also AGENT; *BY*-PHRASE; DOUBLE PASSIVE; *GET*-PASSIVE; PATIENT;
PSEUDO-PASSIVE; SEMANTIC ROLE; SEMI-PASSIVE; VOICE.

activo-passive *See* MEDIOPASSIVE.

actor *See* AGENT.

adj-bar category *See* X-BAR SYNTAX.

adjectival (*n. & adj.*) Loosely, (a *word, *phrase, or *clause) behaving
like an *adjective (including single-word adjectives); e.g. in *a damp cloth*,
the word *damp* is an adjectival element.

The term is also used for examples like the following:

> *guide* price
> the *greenhouse* effect
> the man *in the white suit*
> an *I'm-all-right-Jack* attitude

Some writers informally use the word *adjectival* to describe all of the
italicized strings (or even say that they are adjectives), but this is
infelicitous, since *form and *function are being confused: the first two
examples involve nouns as *modifiers; the third example involves a
*prepositional phrase; and the final example has a clause as modifier.

Note that the terms *adjectival* and *adverbial* are not entirely comparable. *Adverbial* can denote one of the main *elements (1) in clause
structure (the others being *subject, *verb, *object, and *complement); it is
then a function label. Adjectivals operate at a lower level, often as part of a
noun phrase (which itself may function as subject or object). An adjectival
may in some instances be the sole realization of a complement (e.g. *You*

look hungry), but the adjectival as such is not a functional element in clause structure.

• **adjectivally**: in an adjectival manner, as an adjective.

•• **adjectival clause**: the same as *adjective clause (1).

•• **adjectival noun**: (in older usage) an adjective that behaves like a noun, e.g.

> the *poor*
> the *old*
>
> Compare ABSOLUTE (4).

•• **adjectival passive**: the same as *pseudo-passive and statal *passive.

adjectivalization *Morphology.* The conversion of a member of another *word class into an *adjective; the use of such a word in an adjectival function.

The commonest way of forming an adjective from another part of speech is by adding an *affix (e.g. *wealth/wealthy; fool/foolish; hope/hopeful*).

A well-known feature of English is the use of *nouns in attributive position to modify other nouns (e.g. *greenhouse effect, holiday camp, wind instrument*). This usage is sometimes called adjectivalization, but it is best avoided; *see* ADJECTIVAL.

adjective A major *word class, traditionally (i.e. *notionally) defined as containing 'describing' words, or 'words that tell us something about a noun'.

In modern grammar adjectives are usually defined in *morphosyntactic terms. Formally, a *central adjective meets four grammatical conditions. It can

(i) be used *attributively in a noun phrase (e.g. *an old man*)

(ii) follow *be* or another *copular verb, and thus occur in *predicative position (e.g. *He looks old*)

(iii) be premodified by *intensifying words such as *very* (e.g. *He's very old*)

(iv) have *comparative and *superlative forms (e.g. *an older person, the oldest person in the group*)

In addition, some adjectives take *un*-as a *prefix, e.g. *unhappy, unusual*.

However, not all adjectives comply with all these criteria. Adjectives with an *absolute (2) meaning (i.e. ungradable adjectives) fail criteria (iii) and (iv) (e.g. **very unique, *more unique than . . .*), whereas adjectives which are restricted to *predicative uses (e.g. *afraid*) or to *attributive uses (e.g. *utter*) fail criteria (i) and (ii) respectively.

Adjectives other than attributive-only adjectives can sometimes be *postpositional:

> people *impatient* with the slow progress of the talks

For a few adjectives this position is obligatory:

> the president *elect*
>
> the body *politic*
>
> the harbour *proper*

Adjectives used with *indefinite compound pronouns must follow these pronouns:

> nothing *special*, someone *silly*

Some adjectives are used with *the* in noun phrases. When referring to people, the meaning is 'people of that sort':

> the *great* and the *good*
>
> the *poor*
>
> the *disadvantaged*

but note *the Almighty*. (A few participles can also, exceptionally, have singular meaning, e.g. *the accused, the deceased*.) *See also* ABSOLUTE (4).

Other adjectives prefaced by *the* refer to abstract qualities, e.g.

> the *bizarre*, the *grotesque*, the *occult*

In a number of set expressions the 'adjective' takes a plural ending, e.g. *Olympic hopefuls*, though arguably this is a noun converted from an adjective.

> Some are used in set phrases:
>
> in *public*
>
> in *short*
>
> for *better* or *worse*

Historically, adjectives were once called **noun adjectives** because they named attributes which could be added to a **noun substantive** (Latin *adjectivus* from *adjicere* 'to add') to describe it in more detail, the two being regarded as varieties of the class **noun** or 'name'.

> 1612 J. BRINSLEY *Q*. How many sorts of Nouns have you? *A*. Two: a Noun Substantive, and a Noun Adjective. A noun adjective is that cannot stand by itself, without the help of another word to be joyned with it to make it plain.

•• **numeral adjective**: *see* NUMERAL.

•• **phrasal adjective/phrasal-prepositional adjective**: terms used in CGEL:

> 1985 R. QUIRK et al. We could moreover identify 'phrasal adjectives' (derived from participial forms of phrasal verbs) such as *run down*

('exhausted, depressed') and 'phrasal-prepositional adjectives' such as *fed up* (*with*).

See also DEMONSTRATIVE ADJECTIVE; QUALITATIVE ADJECTIVE.

adjective clause

1. Commonly, another name for *relative clause.

1932 C. T. ONIONS Adjective Clauses are introduced by Relative Pronouns.

This term is dated and a misnomer, because it confuses *form and *function. As such it is best avoided.

See also ADJECTIVAL; ADJECTIVALIZATION.

2. An adjective phrase (a *verbless or *small clause without an overt subject in some analyses) functioning as *adverbial.

Keen to take part, he volunteered his services

The crowd, *angry now*, charged at the police

adjective complement
A *phrase or *clause that is *licensed by an *adjective.

Adjective complements can be *realized as (i) prepositional phrases or (ii) various kinds of clauses, e.g.

(i) They were innocent *of the crime*

   She is brilliant *at chess*

(ii) I am sorry *that you don't like it*

   We were not very clear *why we had been asked*

   You were mad *to tell them*

   I've been busy *answering letters*

Such complementation may be obligatory, e.g.

   She is fond *of Swiss cheese* (*She is fond)

or optional, e.g.

   I am so glad (*that you got the job*)

adjective order
The order in which *adjectives are placed in *attributive position within *noun phrases.

When two or more adjectives premodify a noun, there is usually a 'natural' or a 'preferred' order for them. Thus *your wonderful new cream woollen jumper* is *acceptable, but *your woollen new cream wonderful jumper* is not. It has proved difficult to formulate comprehensive and satisfactory rules to describe the ordering, and there are often alternative possibilities, but in general the order is related to the semantic properties of the adjectives. One ordering principle that has been observed is that adjectives that express inherent characteristics (e.g. *woollen, Welsh*) are closer to the noun than those that express subjective judgements (e.g. *wonderful*). Similarly, size adjectives precede age and colour adjectives; thus *a big old yellow bus* is fine, but *?a yellow big old bus* sounds odd.

adjective pattern *See* PATTERN.

adjective phrase (AP/AdjP) A *phrase with an *adjective as *head. Such phrases can occur in *attributive and *predicative position, and can contain *modifiers and/or *complements, e.g.

Dan is *happy*

Fran seems *very lazy*

You make some *highly dubious* assumptions

She is *very difficult to understand*

That's *simple enough*

Compare ADJECTIVAL; ATTRIBUTIVE; PREDICATIVE.

AdjP An abbreviation for *adjective phrase. Also: **AP**.

adjunct

1. (In older usage and in some modern theoretical frameworks.) Any *word, *phrase, or *clause expanding the clause or phrase of which it forms a part with grammatically optional material.

The term has been variously used for words, phrases, or clauses considered to be of secondary importance from the point of view of meaning, including e.g. vocatives and adjectives modifying nouns.

Adjuncts in this sense are marginal to clause and phrase structure, and therefore omissible. Thus in *Sadly, my neighbour moved two months ago*, both *sadly* and *two months ago* can be omitted, leaving a still grammatical, meaningful sentence.

Adjuncts are not *licensed by a *head in the way that *complements are, and do not have a *semantic role to play in the *proposition expressed.

This usage is also common in some theoretical frameworks (e.g. *X-bar syntax), where adjuncts can operate at phrase level (e.g. *silly* in *a silly person*) as well as at clause level.

In Jespersen's terminology *adjunct* describes the functional role of a *secondary joined to a *primary by *junction.

1933b O. JESPERSEN A secondary can be joined to a primary in two essentially different ways, for which we use the terms **Junction** and **Nexus**. As separate names for the secondary in these two functions we shall use the terms **Adjunct** and **Adnex** respectively.

2. Sometimes used to mean the same as *adverbial.

3. (In CGEL and related frameworks.) A particular subclass of *adverbial, contrasted with *conjunct, *disjunct, and *subjunct.

In this categorization, only adverbials functioning as an *element of clause structure (represented as 'A') are adjuncts. By this definition, *with gusto* is an adjunct in the first sentence below, but *evidently* in the second is not:

He spoke *with gusto*
Evidently, I was wrong

Adjuncts of this special type often refer to place, time, or process (including 'manner', 'means', 'instrument', and the *agentive *by*-phrase used in passive clauses), and are integrated into clause structure to some degree. Thus, they can, for example, be in the *focus position of a *cleft construction:

It was *with gusto* that he spoke (cf. *It was *evidently* that I was wrong)

Typically, these adjuncts come in end position, after the verb (and object, if any). But other positions are also possible; thus *frequency adjuncts* usually come in mid position, e.g.

They *usually* arrive late

Adjuncts are sometimes divided on functional grounds into *predication adjuncts and *sentence adjuncts.
• **adjunction:** *see* ADJUNCTION.
•• **linking adjunct**: *see* LINKING WORD.
•• **predicative adjunct**: *see* PREDICATIVE.

See also ADNEX; JUNCTION; PRIMARY; SECONDARY; SENTENCE ADJUNCT; VIEWPOINT ADJUNCT.

adjunction A process whereby one element (*affix, *word, *phrase, etc.) is adjoined to another.
•• **Chomsky adjunction:** a special type of adjunction in which a category B is linked to a category A first by making B a sister of A, and then by making A and B taken together daughters of a copy of the original node A:

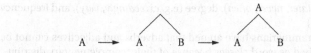

adnex (In Otto Jespersen's terminology.) The functional role of a *secondary (3) when joined in a clause through **nexus** to a *primary (2), which is typically a verb or some other part of the predication.

1933a O. JESPERSEN *The dog runs*, nexus: *runs* . . . is adnex to *dog*.

1933b O. JESPERSEN The adnex may be any word or combination of words which can stand as a predicative ... e.g. a prepositional group. Could she have believed herself in the way?

The term is not in general use today.

See also ADJUNCT; JUNCTION; PREDICATION ADJUNCT; PRIMARY; SECONDARY; SENTENCE ADJUNCT.

adnominal (n. & adj.) (A *word or *phrase) attached to, i.e. *modifying, a *noun. Adnominals can precede or follow the head noun, and with it they form a noun phrase, e.g.

our wonderful new home
a country cottage
my parents' flat
somewhere *to live*
a place *of one's own*

●● **adnominal relative clause**: an ordinary *relative clause, whether *defining or *non-defining (so called because it functions in the same way as other adnominals):

houses *that we've looked at*
Sandringham House, *which we visited*

The label is not common, but is used to distinguish this type of clause from *free relative clauses.

adposition A cover term for *postpositions (2) and *prepositions.

adverb Items belonging to this *word class typically function as the *head of an *adverb phrase which *modifies a *verb (e.g. *spoke quietly*), an adjective (e.g. *really awful*), another adverb (e.g. *very quietly*), or, more rarely, a noun (e.g. *?his almost victory, the events recently*).

Adverbs form a notoriously mixed word class. Traditionally they are divided into various meaning-related categories, such as manner (e.g. *hurriedly, sideways, thus*), modality (e.g. *perhaps, probably, certainly*), time (e.g. *later, never, often*), degree (e.g. *exceedingly, very*), and frequency (e.g. *daily*).

Some grammarians have argued that adverbs and adjectives cannot be distinguished as word classes because of their *complementary distribution, and hence belong to a single class, but others have disputed this.

2010 J. PAYNE, R. HUDDLESTON & G. K. PULLUM Complementarity between adjectives and adverbs is often used in support of a further claim, periodically espoused by a variety of linguists from Kuryłowicz (1936) to Baker (2003), that adjectives and adverbs are effectively inflectional variants of a single major

category ... [W]e argue not only that complementarity as defined does not
hold, but that distribution *per se* is irrelevant to the issue of whether adverbs
are inflectionally related to adjectives.

In CaGEL many words traditionally regarded as adverbs are reassigned to
the class of prepositions, e.g. *downstairs, here, inside, there*; and other
words are reassigned to the class of nouns, e.g. *yesterday, today*.

Loosely, in popular grammar, the term *adverb* is often used to cover
*adverb phrases and *adverbials in general. More strictly, where the latter
terms are used, *adverb* can be restricted to a single word functioning as
the head of an adverb phrase.

•• **adverbial of degree, adverb of degree, degree adverb, degree
adverbial**: *see* DEGREE.

•• **adverbial of manner, adverb of manner, manner adverb, manner
adverbial**: *see* MANNER.

See also ADJUNCT; ADVERBIAL; ADVERB PHRASE; CONJUNCT; DISJUNCT;
PREDICATION ADJUNCT; SENTENCE ADVERB; SUBJUNCT.

adverb clause *See* ADVERBIAL CLAUSE.

adverbial

1. (*n.*) (In some modern grammar frameworks, e.g. CGEL.) One of
the five *elements of *clause structure, symbolized by A, comparable to
*subject (S), *verb (V), *object (O), and *complement (C).

Unlike subjects, verbs, and complements, which are usually essential,
adverbials are optional elements of clause structure that can be *realized
by phrases or by clauses (*adverbial clauses), e.g.

You've done that [$_{AdvP}$ *very well*]: SVOA
Paul visited [$_{NP}$ *last night*]: SVA
[$_{clause}$ *When you've quite finished*], we can begin: ASV
[$_{clause}$ *Though disappointed*], she said nothing: ASVO

2. (*adj.*) Of or pertaining to an *adverb.

1872 R. MORRIS In Elizabethan writers we find the adverbial *-ly* often omitted,
as '*grievous* sick', '*miserable* poor'.

• **adverbially**.

•• **adverbial clause**: *see* ADVERBIAL CLAUSE.

•• **adverbial conjunction**: *see* CONJUNCTION.

•• **adverbial group**: a term used in *Systemic Grammar, corresponding to
*adverb phrase. *See* GROUP (1); WORD GROUP.

•• **adverbial of means**: *see* MEANS.

•• **adverbial particle**: *see* PARTICLE.

•• **adverbial phrase**: the same as *adverb phrase. This usage is to be
avoided since *form and *function terminology are mixed.

adverbial clause Any *clause (*finite, *non-finite, or *verbless) functioning as an *adverbial. (Also called **adverb clause**, but this is to be avoided because two *form (3) labels are used.)

> They succeeded *because they persevered*
> Don't do it, *unless you're sure*
> I'll come *when I'm ready*
> *Although injured*, he struggled on
> *While travelling*, he contracted jaundice
> Make it Thursday, *if possible*

In more traditional usage, only the finite clauses (i.e. the italicized portions in the first three examples) would be included here.

Adverbial clauses are often classified on semantic grounds into such categories as clauses of *time, *place, *condition, *concession, *purpose, *reason, *result, *comparison, *manner, and *comment.

In some frameworks (e.g. CaGEL, OMEG) most of the clauses above are regarded as prepositional phrases in which a preposition (*because, unless,* etc.) takes a clause as complement.

adverbialization The *derivational process of forming an *adverb from another part of speech.

Adding *-ly* to an adjective is the most obvious example of this process (e.g. *bad/badly, pretty/prettily*). Another affix with the same result is *-wise* (e.g. *jobwise*: 'as regards jobs or a job').

adverb particle See PARTICLE.

adverb phrase (AdvP) A *phrase headed by an *adverb which typically functions as an *adverbial in *clause structure, e.g.

> He speaks *quickly*
> We were *often* able to use the pool
> The store *happily* exchanged the unwanted gifts

Adverb phrases can also function as *modifiers inside phrases, e.g.

> [AdvP [AdvP *quite*] *miraculously*]
> [AdjP [AdvP *extremely*] *competent*]

affected *Semantics*. Influenced, acted upon: used to describe the typical *semantic role of the *direct object.

The *direct objects in the following are said to have an affected role:

> I hugged *Lucy*
> Ken hit *his head*

*Goal, *objective (3), and *patient are sometimes used in this way, but distinctions are often made.

In some theories about semantic roles, the subjects of *copular verbs, and even of *intransitive verbs, are said to have an affected role, e.g.

Lucy was in the garden

Her hat lay on the seat beside her

Compare RECIPIENT.

affective The same as *attitudinal and *emotive.

affirmative (form)
   1. Of a *sentence or *clause: stating that a *proposition is true. Contrasted with *negative. (Also sometimes applied to verbs that are not negated.)
   In some grammars the term *positive is used with the same meaning.
   2. The same as *assertive.
   Compare POLARITY.

affix *Morphology*. An addition to the *root (or *base (2) form) of a word, or to a *stem, in order to form a new *lexeme or a new form of the same word.

An affix added before the root is a *prefix (e.g. *un*-natural, *over*-weight); one added at the end is a *suffix (natural-*ness*, weight-*less-ness*). Affixes can be *derivational (*garden* > *gardener*) or *inflectional (*garden* > *gardens*).

Some non-European languages also have **infixes**. These are additions that are inserted within the base of a word. In English perhaps marginal examples of this phenomenon are the plural -*s* inserted in the middle of some compounds (e.g. *hangers-on*), or in a few cases swearwords inserted within a word (e.g. *abso-bloody-lutely*).

See also DERIVATION; FORMATIVE; INFLECTION; MORPHEME.
   • **affixation**: the joining of an affix or affixes to (the root or stem of) a word.

agent A *semantic role label applied to a *phrase that refers to the logical 'instigator' or 'doer' of an action or event denoted by a *verb, particularly a *dynamic (1) verb, i.e. the phrase that refers to the person, or other *animate being, that carries out the action denoted by the verb. (Sometimes called *agentive, e.g. in *Case Grammar.)

Broadly, the term can be used in relation to both *transitive and *intransitive verbs. It is applied to the subject of an active transitive verb and to the *by-phrase of a corresponding *passive sentence. Thus *the old lady* is the agent both in *The old lady swallowed a fly* (which can be described in terms of actor-action-goal), and in *The fly was swallowed by the old* *lady*. The term can also be applied to the subject of an intransitive verb (e.g. *Little Tommy Tucker* sings for his supper).

The term clearly makes more sense when restricted to a 'doer' who, in a real sense, initiates an action, than when applied to the subject of some 'mental process' verb (e.g. *She didn't like it*) or of a verb of 'being' (e.g. *She was old*). Some analysts therefore restrict the term, and would not apply it to the noun phrase *the old lady* if her action was unintentional and involuntary.

In popular grammar, *agent* contrasts principally with *instrument and *means.

The label *agent* is often used interchangeably with **actor**, though a distinction is sometimes made:

> 1997 R. VAN VALIN & R. J. LAPOLLA The generalized AGENT-type role will be termed **actor** and the generalized PATIENT-type role will be called **undergoer**. Accordingly, in an active sentence in English, the actor is the subject, which, with a certain kind of verb, would be an AGENT, and with another kind of verb would be an EXPERIENCER, and with yet another kind of verb would be a POSSESSOR, and so on.

•• **agent noun**: a noun whose referent is the person, entity, etc. which carries out the action denoted by a verb, and which is formed by adding the suffix *-er* or *-or* to a verb; e.g. *actor, instructor, manufacturer, teacher, worker*. Some agent nouns are inanimate (e.g. *computer, shocker*), and some have no independent *base (e.g. *author, butcher*).

agentive

1. (*n. & adj.*) (Designating) a *noun, *suffix, or *semantic role that indicates an *agent.

In the sentence *This great ceiling was painted by Michelangelo*, *Michelangelo* is the agent and *by Michelangelo* is an agentive phrase.

In the words *doer, farmer*, and *lover* there is an agentive suffix, *-er*, which contrasts with the *comparative suffix *-er* in *kinder, nicer*.

> 1964 J. VACHEK The comparative suffix *-er* does not imply the change of the word-category of the basic word, while the agentive *-er* necessarily does so.

Verbs in context can be described as agentive or **non-agentive**. An **agentive verb** posits an animate instigator of the action. Contrast:

> The postman banged on the door (agentive verb)
> The door was banging in the wind (non-agentive verb)

2. In *Case Grammar the **agentive case** is defined semantically (together with *objective (3), *dative (2), etc.), and so the subject of an active verb is frequently (though not always) agentive (the agent). This is a specialized use.

1968 C. J. FILLMORE The cases that appear to be needed include: *Agentive* (A), the case of the typically animate perceived instigator of the action identified by the verb.

agentless passive *See* PASSIVE.

agent noun *See* AGENT.

agglutinative *See* ANALYTIC.

aggregate noun A *noun that is 'plural-only' in form (e.g. *outskirts*, *remains*), or functionally plural-only, though lacking an -*s* (e.g. *people*, *police*).

A few aggregate nouns can take singular or plural verbs (e.g. *the works is/are in* Birmingham).

Compare COLLECTIVE NOUN; PLURALE TANTUM; SUMMATION PLURAL.

agree Be in *concord; take the same *number, *gender, *person, etc. (as another element in the clause or sentence).

See AGREEMENT.

agreement A *morphosyntactic phenomenon whereby two (or more) elements in a clause or sentence are harmonized in terms of the *shape they take, e.g. with regard to *person, *number, or *gender. Also called **concord**.

In English, the most generally recognized agreement is that between a subject and a verb. As verbs have few *inflections, this mainly affects the third person singular of the *present tense of lexical verbs, where the -*s* ending contrasts with the other persons of the singular, and with the plural (e.g. *He* or *she works*, but *I, we, you, they work*). The verbs *be* and *have* as main verbs, and as auxiliaries in the *progressive, *passive, and *perfect constructions (*I am working, They were telephoned, She has worked*), also agree with their subjects, as does *do* when used as a main or auxiliary verb (e.g. *Tom does his homework at night; Does she support your plans?*).

Prescriptivists favour strict grammatical agreement. But **notional concord**, where agreement follows the meaning, is a common feature of English, and acceptable to most grammarians:

Everybody knows this, don't they?
Neither of them approve (more strictly: *approves*)
The committee have decided... (*has decided*...)
£10 is all I have

A minor type of verb agreement, called **proximity agreement** (or **proximity concord**), is the agreement of a verb with a closely preceding noun, instead of with the noun head that actually functions as subject of the sentence in question. Such agreement may be marginally acceptable when it supports notional concord, but is generally considered ungrammatical:

?No one except my parents care what happens to me

??A parcel of books have arrived for you

Number agreement also normally exists between a subject and a *subject-related predicative complement (e.g. *She* is *a pilot*; *They* are *pilots*), and between a direct object and an *object-related predicative complement (e.g. *I consider her a brilliant pilot*, *I consider them brilliant pilots*).

Number and gender agreement affects *pronouns and *determinatives (1), e.g.

He has lost *his* umbrella

There were *many* problems and *much* heartsearching

I borrowed *those books* (**this books*) from the library

She blames *herself* (**himself*)

Aktionsart The lexical expression of *aspect; the expression of various types of *situations (actions, processes, etc.) by *lexical items (often in association with their *dependents) as opposed to by grammatical means (e.g. the *progressive construction). This term is usually spelt with a capital letter, since it is a German noun which literally means 'kind or type of action'. (Also called **lexical aspect** and **situation aspect**.)

alethic (Pronounced /əˈliːɪk/.) Necessarily and logically true.

The term, taken from *modal logic, comes from the Greek word *alētheia* 'truth', and is concerned with the necessary truth of *propositions. It is sometimes used in the analysis of modal verbs, though most grammarians include this meaning under *epistemic *modality. The distinction between alethic and epistemic modality, when it is made, is that alethic modality is concerned with logical deduction (e.g. *If she's a widow, her husband must have died*), whereas epistemic modality, relates to confident inference (e.g. *They were married over fifty years—she must miss him*).

allograph A particular printed or written form of a letter of the alphabet (or more technically of a *grapheme).

Thus a lower-case ⟨a⟩, a capital ⟨A⟩, an italic ⟨*a*⟩, and a scribbled letter *a* are all allographs of the same grapheme.

Compare GRAPH; MORPHEME (1).

allomorph *Morphology.* An alternant of a *morpheme (1); any form in which a (meaningful) morpheme is actually realized. (Also called **morphemic variant**.)

This label includes both phonologically *conditioned alternants (e.g. plural /s/, /z/, and /ɪz/, as in *cats* /kæts/, *dogs* /dɒgz/, and *horses* /ˈhɔːsɪz/) and grammatical alternants such as *–ed/-en* (as in *heated, frozen*) for the *past participle *morpheme. We can also talk of a **zero allomorph** in *sheep* (plural), and various irregular allomorphs in *mice, geese,* and so on.

• **allomorphic**: of or pertaining to an allomorph.

Compare FORMATIVE; MORPH.

alternant

1. Any of the possible variants of a particular *category, *feature, etc. of the language.

2. *Morphology.* Another word for *allomorph.

• **alternance, alternation**: the existence of alternants and the relationship between them.

• **alternate**: vary between alternants.

> 1935 J. R. FIRTH Vowel alternance is also a very important morphological instrument in the strong conjugation of verbs. There are thirty vowel alternances for our babies to learn.

> 1991 P. H. MATTHEWS [D]ifferent inflections mark the same category: thus *e* in *men* and the *-s* in *seas* both mark Plural. We will say that the inflections **alternate**.

alternative conditional-concessive clause (In CGEL.) A type of
*conditional clause with an element of *concessive meaning that contains the sequence *whether . . . or (whether) . . .*, e.g.

> *Whether Sue comes or whether she phones us* is immaterial
> *Whether Liam likes it or not,* he will have to attend the meeting

In CaGEL this is a type of **exhaustive conditional**.

See also UNIVERSAL CONDITIONAL-CONCESSIVE CLAUSE; CONDITION; CONDITIONAL.

alternative question *See* QUESTION.

ambient *it* *See* DUMMY.

ambiguity The phenomenon whereby a *word, *phrase, *clause, or
*sentence has more than one meaning.

•• **lexical ambiguity**. Ambiguity can be due to a word having more than one meaning; e.g. *I don't seem to have a chair.* Was the speaker complaining that she had nothing to sit on, or that there was nobody to introduce her at a speaking event?

•• **grammatical ambiguity** (or **structural ambiguity**). This can be caused in many different ways, for example by ellipsis (or uncertainty whether there is ellipsis) within a *noun phrase:

> He was wearing new red socks and boots (Were the boots new and red too?)
>
> They are advertising for teachers of French, German, and Russian (Is this about separate teachers of these three languages, or people capable of teaching all of them?)
>
> Visiting relatives can be tedious (Is the speaker talking about relatives who are making a visit or about making the visit themself?)

Because *prepositional phrases can appear in different kinds of structures, for example as *modifiers in noun phrases or as *adverbials in clause structure, there is often considerable doubt as to what material they relate to. Thus in *These claims have been dismissed as mere bravado by the police* the context will make clear that the meaning is 'dismissed by the police', but it is also possible to interpret *mere bravado by the police* as a noun phrase.

Similarly, *to*-infinitive clauses, which can have a multiplicity of functions, may be ambiguous:

> Railmen defy union order to stop coal shipments (This means either that the railmen defied the union order, so as to stop the shipments, or they continued the shipments in defiance of an order to stop them.)

Ellipted clauses of comparison are another frequent cause of ambiguity:

> I had better taste in films than friends (Was the speaker's taste in films better than his taste in friends, or did he have better taste in films than his friends had?)

In complex sentences, ambiguity can arise when not just a phrase, but a whole finite clause is open to more than one interpretation. (Intonation will disambiguate if the sentences are spoken.)

> I didn't go because it was my birthday (Did the speaker not go at all, or did they go, but for some reason other than it being their birthday?)
>
> He said he wouldn't lend me the money and I couldn't go (Did he say that I wouldn't be given any money and also that I couldn't go, or could I not go as a consequence of not being lent the money?)
>
> He'll tell you when they arrive (Does this mean that he will inform you of the time of their arrival, or that he will tell you something after they arrive?)

A further type of ambiguity is caused by the fact that many English words can be interpreted as belonging to more than one word class. Headline English is a rich source of such ambiguity:

> Juvenile court to try shooting defendant (Will there be an attempt to use guns in court, or will the defendant in a shooting case be tried?)

> Peking bars escape from 'terror' purge (Was the Chinese government taking measures to prevent (*bar*) someone from escaping, or had the city's drinking venues escaped some harsh new decree?)

> American ships head to Libya (Did someone send a head on a ship, or did some ships set out on a journey?)

● **ambiguous**: displaying ambiguity.

ambilingual (*n. & adj.*) (Designating) a person who has complete mastery of two languages.

> 1959 J. C. CATFORD In everyday speech the word 'bilingual' generally refers to a person who has virtually *equal* command of two or more languages. If a special term is required for such persons of equal linguistic skill (which is very difficult to measure) I should prefer to call them 'ambilinguals'. Ambilinguals are relatively rare.

● **ambilingualism**.
Compare BILINGUAL.

amplifier *See* INTENSIFIER.

anacoluthon (Pronounced /ænəkəˈluːθɒn/. Plural **anacoluthons**, **anacolutha**.) Syntactic discontinuity within a *clause or *sentence; a clause or sentence which either breaks off while incomplete, or switches part-way through to a different syntactic structure; *discontinuity of this kind as a general phenomenon.

Informal spoken language often contains anacoluthon, much of which may pass unnoticed by the listener, e.g.

> One of my sisters—her husband's a doctor and he says if you take aspirin your cold will go in a week, but if you do nothing it will take seven days

> It's a course which I don't know whether it will be any good

> I thought that you were going—well, I hoped that you were going to help

> Why don't you—it's only a suggestion—but you could walk

The term was formerly used in rhetoric, but has been adopted into linguistics. In rhetoric, the general phenomenon was called *anacoluthia* and an individual instance *anacoluthon*.

Compare the *rhetorical (1) term **aposiopesis**: the abrupt ending of an utterance or speech, as in this extract:

... No, you unnatural hags,
I will have such revenges on you both,
That all the world shall—I will do such things,—
What they are, yet I know not; but they shall be
The terrors of the earth! You think I'll weep;
No, I'll not weep.
Shakespeare, *King Lear*, II, iv, 270–275

• **anacoluthic, anacoluthically**.

analogy The replication or imitation of the *inflections, derivatives, and
*constructions of existing words in forming the inflections, derivatives,
and constructions of other words.

Analogy normally governs the patterns of *word-formation. Recent
years have, for example, seen numerous new *verbs with the *prefixes *de-*
(e.g. *deselect*) and *dis-* (e.g. *disinvest*) and *nouns beginning with *Euro-*
(e.g. *Eurocrat, Eurosceptic, Eurospeak, Eurozone*). Other new nouns have
been formed with such well-established *suffixes as *-ism* (e.g. *endism,
handicapism*). New verbs almost always inflect regularly (e.g. *faxing, faxes,
faxed*), by analogy with regular verbs.

In *historical linguistics, the term *analogy* is used in connection with the
tendency for *Irregular forms to become *regular (e.g. *shape, shove*: past
tense *shaped, shoved*, in the 14th century *shoop, shofe*; *past participle
shaped, shoved, in the 14th century *shopen, shoven*). Interestingly, irregular patterns are sometimes spread by analogy: for example, the historical
*past tense form of the verb *dive* is the regular *dived*, but the irregular *dove*
arose in British *dialects and American English during the nineteenth
century; similarly *scarves, hooves*, and even *rooves* have tended to replace
the historical and regular *plurals *scarfs, hoofs*, and *roofs*.

Analogy probably accounts for the recently developed pronunciation of
covert (traditionally /ˈkʌvət/) to rhyme with *overt*, and *dissect* (traditionally
/dɪˈsekt/) to rhyme with *bisect* (each pair of words has a certain amount of
shared meaning).

Over-regularization by analogy is seen in the early efforts at speaking
English of both young children and foreign learners, who may well say *He
goed, mouses, sheeps*, and so on.

Compare OVERGENERALIZATION.

analysable Capable of being analysed; particularly used of words that
can be broken down into constituent *morphemes. Contrasted with
unanalysable.

Compare *dis-interest-ed-ness* with *interest*, which cannot be analysed further into morphemes, although *in-* or *inter* are meaningful elements in other words, such as *inborn, incurable, interfaith*.

analyse Distinguish the grammatical elements of a *word, *phrase, *clause, *sentence, *construction, etc. in a particular context, and how they relate to other such elements.

There are many ways in which words, phrases, clauses, sentences, constructions, etc. can be analysed. A word can be analysed into its *root (or *base) and *affixes (e.g. *dis-interest-ed-ness*). Simple sentences and clauses can be analysed into *subject, *predicator, *predicate, *object, *adverbial, etc. *Complex and *compound sentences are often analysed into different types of clauses, e.g. *coordinate clause, *subordinate clause, *relative clause, and so on.

analysis The process of breaking up *words, *phrases, *clauses, *sentences, *constructions, etc. into their *constituent parts.

See also ANALYSE; COMPONENTIAL ANALYSIS; CONTRASTIVE *analysis*; DISCOURSE *analysis*; DISTRIBUTION; IMMEDIATE CONSTITUENT *analysis*; MULTIPLE *analysis*.

analytic

1. *Morphology*. Designating a language without (or with few) *inflections. (Also called **isolating**.)

In an analytic language, word (or *constituent) order plays an important role in establishing *meaning. In extremely analytic languages most words consist of single *morphemes. Analytic languages contrast with *synthetic (1) languages, which rely heavily on changing the form of words, and **agglutinative** languages, in which words are 'welded' together from smaller words or units, each contributing a bit of grammatical meaning.

English, having few inflections, is more analytic than, say, Latin or German, but it has some synthetic characteristics (e.g. *happy/happier/happiest*; *time/times*) and some agglutinative features (e.g. *mis-under-stand-ing, in-contest-able*).

By analogy, the contrast between analytic and synthetic is sometimes applied to syntactic features of English. Thus *multi-word verbal *constructions (e.g. perfect *have taken*) and *periphrastic *adjective *comparisons (e.g. *more unusual, most unusual*) are analytic, whereas corresponding single-word forms (e.g. *took*; *odder/oddest*) are synthetic.

•• **analytic mood**: the grammatical manifestation of *mood, not by means of verbal inflections, but by means of a construction, specifically the combination of a *modal auxiliary with a *lexical verb, e.g. *will take, must go*.

2. *Semantics.* Designating a *proposition that is necessarily true by virtue of the meaning of the words contained in it, without reference to a particular situation or to particular circumstances, in contrast to *synthetic (2).

For example, *Jim is a boy. Therefore, Jim is male* is analytically true.

anaphor

1. A *word or *phrase that refers back to an earlier word or phrase.

In *My cousin said he was coming to see me, he* is a personal *pronoun used as an anaphor for *my cousin* (which is its *antecedent). But more usually *he* would be described as a *pro-form substituting for *my cousin*. (Notice that *he* could also refer to some other male individual in this example.)

2. zero anaphor, **null anaphor**: an anaphor that is non-overt; e.g. in *Government-Binding Theory the sentence *I want to leave* is analysed as involving a null anaphor pronoun **PRO** (called 'big PRO'):

I_i want [PRO_i to leave] (The subscript 'i' indicates *co-reference.)

PRO is contrasted with **pro** ('little pro'), which is posited as a null subject in languages that typically drop overt subjects, e.g. Italian, Spanish, and Greek.

anaphora

1. The use of a *word or words as a substitute for a previous linguistic unit when referring back to a person, thing, event, etc., denoted by the latter.

*Pronouns and other *pro-forms are frequently used anaphorically to avoid repetition, e.g.

I called *John* because I wanted to ask *him* something

Sometimes a *noun is repeated, and then the identity of reference is usually shown by a marker of *definiteness (*the, that*, etc.) in the later (*anaphoric*) reference. Consider the following nursery rhyme:

Old Mother Hubbard
went to the cupboard
to get her poor dog a bone;
But when *she* got *there*,
the cupboard was bare,
and so *the* poor dog had none.

She and *there* (line 4) refer back to *Old Mother Hubbard* (line 1) and *the cupboard* (line 2). *The cupboard* (line 5) and *the poor dog* (line 6) refer back to *the cupboard* and *her poor dog* in lines 2 and 3.

The term anaphora is sometimes extended to include more indirect reference, e.g.

I've still got a book of nursery rhymes I had as a child, but *the cover* is torn

Obviously *the cover* refers to the cover of the book that was mentioned earlier.

2. Loosely, a *hypernym for both anaphora (1) and *cataphora.

When the term is so used, the two types are then distinguished as **backwards anaphora**, **backward-looking anaphora**, or **unmarked order anaphora** (= (1) above), and **forwards anaphora**, **forward-looking anaphora**, **anticipatory anaphora**, or **marked order anaphora** (=cataphora).

● **anaphoric**: involving anaphora.

● **anaphorically**.

> 1909–49 O. JESPERSEN *The little one* is used anaphorically if it means 'the little flower' or whatever it is that has just been mentioned.

●● **anaphoric ellipsis**: *see* ELLIPSIS.
Compare ANTECEDENT.

and-relationship A *syntagmatic relationship. Contrasted with **or-relationship** (i.e. *paradigmatic relationship).
See also CHAIN; PARADIGM; SAUSSUREAN; SYNTAGMATIC RELATIONSHIP.

Anglo-Saxon The same as *Old English.

animate Denoting a living being.
The term is particularly used in the classification of *nouns. Animate nouns (e.g. *girl*, *tiger*, etc.) refer to persons and animals, in contrast to **inanimate** nouns (e.g. *happiness*, *zoo*), which refer to things, ideas, situations, etc. In English this distinction is almost entirely a matter of meaning, not grammar, although there is a rough correspondence in some *personal and *relative *pronouns: *he*, *she*, and *who* usually have animate *reference, whereas *it* and *which* are mainly used in connection with inanimate referents.

anomalous Not conforming to the *rules of a particular system, grammar, etc.
●● **anomalous finite**: a *finite *verb form which forms the *negative by adding -*n't*, and forms *interrogatives through *inversion.
This category includes all the *modal verbs; all uses of *be*; *do* as an *auxiliary verb; and some uses of *have* (e.g. *I haven't enough money*, but not, for example, forms using *do-support: *I don't have enough money*).
This is a somewhat dated term for dealing with the characteristic syntactic behaviour of *be*, *do*, and *have*, which, in most frameworks, can be *main verbs or *auxiliary verbs.
Compare DEFECTIVE; IRREGULAR.

answer *See* RESPONSE.

antecedent A unit to which a particular *word or *phrase refers back grammatically.

Typically antecedents are *noun phrases to which *pronouns can refer, e.g. in *My brother telephoned to say that he'd be late* the noun phrase *my brother* is the antecedent of *he* (though *he* could also refer to some other male individual).

Such a grammatical relationship can exist even when the pronoun refers back, not to the identical person or thing, but to a previous linguistic form, e.g.

I've lost *my umbrella* and will have to get a new *one*

Less obviously *do, so, do so, there, then,* and a few other *pro-forms can refer back to antecedents which may be verbal, adverbial, or clausal, e.g.

I *cried* more than I'd ever *done* before in my life

You could *buy a yearly season ticket*, but I don't advise *doing so*

'*Petrol prices are going up again.*' 'Who told you *that*?'

Loosely, despite the meaning of the word, the term *antecedent* is sometimes extended to refer to phrases that come later than their pro-forms, e.g.

If you see *her*, will you give *Mary* a message for me?

Compare ANAPHOR; ANAPHORA; CATAPHORA; PRO-FORM.

anterior time A time that precedes some other point in time, referred to by means of *tense, or in another way.

The term is sometimes used to describe the meaning of the *perfect construction. For example, in

(i) You're too late. They *have left*

(ii) This time next week, he *will have forgotten* all about it

(iii) I realized I *had lost* my key

the italicized *perfect constructions indicate a time before points in the present (i), the *future (ii), and the *past (iii). The third type of anterior time, as in (iii), is commonly called **before-past**.

● **anteriority**.

See also PAST; PAST PERFECT; TENSE.

anticipated dislocation *See* DISLOCATION.

anticipation *Psycholinguistics*. A slip of the tongue by which a linguistic element is used earlier than it should be.

This is a term used by some psycholinguists for part of what many people would call a **spoonerism**, e.g.

The cat popped on its drawers (i.e. the cat dropped on its paws)

anticipatory Anticipating the logical *subject (1) or (more rarely) *object, when the latter are *postponed until later in the *sentence or *clause by *extraposition.

In the first sentence below, *it* is an **anticipatory subject** (the grammatical subject), and in the second sentence *it* is an **anticipatory object**:

> *It* is better *to have loved and lost* than never to have loved at all
>
> I take *it that you agree with me*

There is considerable confusion in the usage of the terms available to describe the various functions of the word *it*. For some grammarians, **anticipatory *it*** (used with extraposition) and **preparatory *it*** are identical, but they distinguish this usage from *dummy *it* (or empty *it* or prop *it*), as in e.g. *It is raining*. Others use all or some of these terms differently, or use one of them as an umbrella term.

See also IMPERSONAL; INTRODUCTORY; SUBJECT.

•• **anticipatory anaphora**: *see* ANAPHORA.

antonym *Semantics*. A word opposite in *meaning to another. Contrasted with *synonym.

For example, *good, thick, few*, and *life* are antonyms of *bad, thin, many*, and *death*. More accurately we should talk of a word that is opposite in some of its meanings to other words. For example, the antonym of some meanings of *old* is *young*, and of others it is *new*.

Some linguists distinguish different types of opposite meaning, and reserve the term *antonym* for *gradable opposites (e.g. *good/bad*), excluding both *complementary terms (e.g. *life/death*) and relational *converses (e.g. *buy/sell, teach/learn, husband/wife*).

• **antonymous**: that is an antonym.

• **antonymy**: the relationship of opposite meaning that exists between words (this word is itself the opposite of *synonymy).

Compare BINARY; COMPLEMENTARY; COMPLEMENTARITY.

See also HETERONYM; HOMONYM; HOMOPHONE; HYPONYM; MERONYM; POLYSEME; POLYSEMY; SYNONYM.

AP An abbreviation for *adjective phrase. Also: **AdjP**.

aphaeresis (Pronounced /æˈfɪərəsɪs/. Plural **aphaereses**.)

1. The omission of a sound at the beginning of a word, regarded as a morphological development.

The now unpronounced sounds at the beginning of *gnat, knight, psyche* are examples of this phenomenon.

2. The omission of letters, or a syllable, at the beginning of a word, as routinely occurs in contractions, e.g.

I'll (= I will), you've (= you have), he'd better (= he had)

or in *clippings, e.g.

(omni)bus, (tele)phone

This phenomenon is now dealt with under *contraction, clipping, and so on. The term is derived from rhetoric via historical linguistics.

Compare APOCOPE.

apocope (Pronounced /əˈpɒkəpɪ/.) The omission of a syllable or syllables at the end of a word. *Compare* APHAERESIS.

This has happened historically with the loss, since *Old English times, of many verb inflections (e.g. OE *we lufodon*, ME *we loveden, we lovede*, ModE *we loved*; OE *sungen*, ModE *sung*). Today it happens as a type of *clipping, e.g. *auto(mobile), des(irable) res(idence), long vac(ation), spag (hetti) bol(ognese), trad(itional)*.

Like aphaeresis, apocope is an old term from diachronic linguistics.

apodosis (Pronounced /əˈpɒdəsɪs/. Plural **apodoses**.) The *matrix clause, as opposed to the *if-clause in a *conditional *construction, e.g.

I would be upset if they found out

I feel that if you tell her now *she'll be upset*

Contrasted with *protasis.

apo koinou (Pronounced /ˈæpəʊ ˈkɔɪnuː/.) A term from the Greek *apo koinou* 'in common' to denote an unusual *construction which consists of two *clauses which have a word or phrase that is syntactically shared.

In *There's a man outside wants to see you*, *a man* can be regarded as the *postponed *subject of *-'s* (=*is*) and as the subject of *wants*.

The term is not in general use today; such a construction would be called a *blend or treated as deviant. But *see* CONTACT CLAUSE.

apostrophe The sign ⟨'⟩ which is used to indicate (i) the omission of a letter or letters, as in *don't, 'cause*, the *'90s*; and (ii) the modern *genitive *case (2), as in *boy's, men's*.

The apostrophe is rarely used in abbreviations that are no longer felt to be contractions (e.g. *(in)flu(enza)*) or in colloquial abbreviations (e.g. *info(rmation)*). *O'clock* (= *of the clock*) is an obvious exception.

The *possessive apostrophe originally marked the omission of *e* in writing (e.g. *fox's, James's*), and was equally common in the nominative plural, especially of proper names and foreign words (e.g. *folio's = folioes*).

It was gradually disused in the latter, and extended to all possessives, even where *e* had not been previously written, as in *man's*, *children's*, *conscience' sake* (though the latter is somewhat dated, and is often replaced by *conscience's*).

In modern English the use of the apostrophe to mark ordinary *plurals (e.g. *potato's*, *ice-cream's*) is generally regarded as illiterate, and is disparagingly referred to as the *greengrocer's apostrophe. It is usually acceptable with the less usual plurals of letters and dates, e.g.

Mind your *p's* and *q's*

That is what people did in the *1960's*/*1960s*

The current rules for possessive apostrophes are:

Add *'s* to a singular word (e.g. *the boy's statement*, *an hour's time*, *Doris's husband*, *her boss's team*)

Also add *'s* to plural words that do not end in -*s* (e.g. *the men's action*, *the people's will*)

With plural words ending in -*s* only add an apostrophe at the end (e.g. *ladies' shoes*, *the Lawsons' house*).

Names from ancient times ending in *s* do not necessarily follow these rules (e.g. *Socrates' death*).

It is an error to use the apostrophe with possessive pronouns (e.g. *hers*, *its*, *ours*, *theirs*, *yours*). *It's* means 'it is' or 'it has'. For 'belonging to it', the correct form is *its* (e.g. *The cat hasn't eaten its food*).

appellative

1. (In older grammar.) (*n.*) A common noun used as a *name, particularly when addressing someone, e.g. *Mother*, *Sir*, *Doctor*.

In modern grammar, dealt with as a *vocative.

2. (*adj.*) Of a word, especially a *noun: designating a class, not an individual; common, in contrast to *proper.

1755 S. JOHNSON As my design was a dictionary, common or appellative, I have omitted all words which have relation to proper names.

applied linguistics *See* LINGUISTICS.

apposition A relationship of two (or more) units, especially *noun phrases, such that the two units are normally grammatically parallel, and have the same referent, e.g.

Our longest reigning monarch, Queen Victoria, reigned from 1837 to 1901

The third edition of *OUP's biggest dictionary, the Oxford English Dictionary*, is being published online

a

Grammarians vary in how widely they apply the term *apposition*. In the narrowest definition (**full apposition**), both parts are noun phrases which are identical in reference (i.e. in an **equivalence relationship**), and either part could be omitted, as in the examples above, without affecting the grammaticality or the essential meaning of the sentence.

> 2002 R. HUDDLESTON & G. K. PULLUM et al. Appositive dependents are ones which when substituted for the matrix NP in a declarative clause systematically yield a clause which is an entailment of the original.
> 1. a. *She sang in* [*the opera 'Carmen'*]. b. *She sang in 'Carmen'*.
> 2. a. *It was founded in* [*the year 1850*]. b. *It was founded in 1850*.
> 3. a. [*The verb 'use'*] *is transitive.*   b. *'Use' is transitive.*

More loosely, apposition may include pairs of units where not all these conditions apply (**partial apposition**). One part may be a clause (an **appositive clause**, see below). Or the relationship may be one of example, not identity, e.g.

> *A monarch, for example a twentieth-century monarch*, may have limited powers

Alternatively, the omission of one part may result in an ungrammatical sentence, e.g.

> *A very important person* is coming—*the Queen* (we could not say **is coming— the Queen*)

Apposition is predominantly *non-restrictive (the second part adds information but is not essential), although *restrictive apposition is possible (e.g. *the author Graham Greene*).

Grammarians also disagree about whether structures such as the following are cases of apposition or not:

> the number thirteen
> my sister Mary
> the expression 'greenhouse effect'
> the city of Oxford
> that fool of a man

•• **appositive clause:** a *finite *clause, often introduced by *that*, which complements (*postmodifies in some models) the content of a *noun (phrase). Also called **appositional clause.** Example:

> They had the <u>idea</u> *that everything would be all right in the end*

This can be paraphrased as follows: *The idea is that everything would be all right in the end.* Here is a similar but non-defining clause:

> They ignored Wendy's very sensible <u>suggestion</u>, *(namely) that the police should be told*

Such clauses are grammatically distinct from *relative clauses. The word *that* is a *conjunction, not a *pronoun, so these clauses have their own *subject (and *object, where applicable), and *which* is never possible. The preceding noun is an abstract noun, such as *belief, fact, idea*.

The term appositive clause can be extended to non-finite clauses, e.g.

The <u>request</u> *to send money* shocked us

My <u>work</u>, *looking after these old people*, is rewarding

appositional Of or pertaining to *apposition.
●● **appositional clause**: the same as **appositive clause** (*see* APPOSITION).
●● **appositional compound**: a compound which, semantically, is a hyponym of both of its constituent words, e.g. *manservant, drummer boy, oak tree*.

appositive (*n. & adj.*) (An element) standing in a relation of *apposition to another element.

appositive clause *See* APPOSITION.

appropriacy *Sociolinguistics*. The quality of being suitable for a given social situation.

The concept of appropriacy is linked to those of *formal versus *informal, *register, and so on.
● **appropriate**.

approximate negator *See* SEMI-NEGATIVE.

arbitrary Lacking any physical or principled connection.

Most language use is arbitrary in this sense, however systematic its grammar. There is no inherent reason why a dog should be called *dog* in English, *chien* in French, *Hund* in German, *perro* in Spanish, and *cane* in Italian.

Compare ICONIC; ONOMATOPOEIC.

archaic Of a *word or grammatical structure: no longer in ordinary use, though retained for special purposes.

archaism
1. The use of words or grammar characteristic of an earlier period of the language.
2. An instance of such usage.

Some archaisms survive in special registers, such as legal or religious language; others are fixed locutions, phrases, etc. familiar from literature, proverbs, and so on. Archaisms include:

(i) individual words, e.g.

methinks
perchance
thou/thine/thee/thy
whence
whereat ye

(ii) verbal *inflections, e.g.

goeth
knowest

(iii) some grammatical structures, e.g.

Our Father, *which art* in heaven (= who is)
He who hesitates is lost (= Anyone who)
All that glitters is not gold (= Not everything that . . . is . . .)
We *must away* (= must go/leave/be off)
Would that I could help (= I wish)
So be it
If it please your lordship
He has come but once in *these two years past*

argument *Semantics.* An element that is assigned a *semantic role in a *proposition.

The term is used technically in **predicate calculus** (also called **predicate logic**), as a part of *logical semantics. Generally speaking, an argument is a person, other animate being, or inanimate entity that is (actively) involved in a particular *situation denoted by a *verb.

> 1984 R. HUDDLESTON Semantic predicates may be classified according to the number of arguments they take. Thus 'love' (the semantic predicate expressed by **love**) takes two; 'sleep' (as in *Ed was sleeping*) takes one; 'give' (as in *Ed gave me the key*) takes three.

In mainstream grammar the phenomenon is often dealt with in terms of *intransitive, *transitive, *ditransitive, etc. verbs.

•• **argument structure:** a specification of the number and types of arguments that a *predicate takes.

•• **external argument**: the argument that is outside the *verb phrase (or *predicate (1)) in a clause, i.e. the *subject.

•• **internal argument**: the argument(s) of a verb that is (are) internal to the *verb phrase.

See also VALENCY.

article An umbrella word class label for *the* (**definite article**) and *a/an* (**indefinite article**).

The articles are sometimes classified as a distinct *word class. In modern grammar they are regarded as a subclass of *determinatives (1).

Some grammarians, even later ones, wrongly considered the articles to be a special kind of *adjective.

> 1711 J. GREENWOOD There are two *articles*, *a* and *the*. These are really Nouns Adjective, and are used almost after the same Manner as other Adjectives. Therefore I have not made the Article (as some have done) a distinct Part of Speech.

See also DETERMINER; ZERO ARTICLE.

artificial language A specially invented language, usually intended as a means of international communication.

Esperanto is perhaps the best known artificial language, but many others have been invented.

ascriptive Attributing a property to a person or entity. Thus in e.g.

> Jim is *rich*
> My tea is *cold*

the properties of 'being rich' and 'being cold' are ascribed to an individual named Jim and to a beverage, respectively.

•• **ascriptive *be***: the verb *be* as used in the examples above.

See also IDENTIFY; SPECIFYING *BE*.

aspect A category of grammar used to describe how a *situation, as expressed by a *verb, or by a verb in combination with its *arguments, unfolds over time.

English is often considered to have two aspects: *progressive aspect, as in:

> I am/was writing to Robert

which expresses a situation that is regarded as being in progress (or an incomplete situation); and *perfect aspect (sometimes less felicitously called *perfective aspect*), as in the example below which expresses a completed situation in the past:

> I have/had written to Robert

The analysis of the perfect *construction as involving aspect is disputed. For one, it is only the *present perfect that can be said to express aspectual meaning in relating a past situation to the present time (by conveying *current relevance). The other perfect constructions (the *past perfect, *perfect infinitive, etc.) merely express *anterior time. Some grammars (e.g. CaGEL) regard the perfect construction as a (secondary) *tense.

See also PHASE (3).

Traditionally, and often to this day in English language teaching contexts, both aspects are treated as part of the tense system in English, and mention is made of tenses such as the **present progressive** (e.g. *We are waiting*), the **present perfect progressive** (e.g. *We have been waiting*), and the **past perfect progressive** (e.g. *We had been waiting*), with the latter two combining two aspects. There is a distinction to be made, however, between tense and aspect. Tense is concerned with how time is encoded in the grammar of English, and is often based on morphological form (e.g. *write, writes, wrote*); aspect is concerned with the unfolding of a situation, and in English is a matter of syntax, using the verb *be* to form the progressive, and the verb *have* to form the perfect. For this reason combinations like those above are nowadays referred to as constructions (e.g. the *progressive construction*, the *present perfect progressive* construction).

- **aspectual**: of or pertaining to an aspect or aspects.
- **Aspects Model, Aspects Theory**: *see* STANDARD THEORY.
- **aspectual lexical verb**: *see* ASPECTUALIZER.
- **lexical aspect**: *see* AKTIONSART.
- **situation aspect**: *see* AKTIONSART.

aspectualizer A *verb that carries a meaning that pertains to *aspect, e.g. *begin, cease, continue, discontinue, finish, keep, proceed, quit, start, stop*. (Also called **aspectual lexical verb**.)

aspectual lexical verb See ASPECTUALIZER.

assertion A *statement, declaration, etc. that something is (believed to be) true.

In general, assertions tend to be made in grammatically *positive (1) *declarative sentences. Nevertheless, *assertion* is a pragmatic rather than a grammatical category, and other syntactic structures can make assertions, e.g.

Isn't it hot today? (= 'it is hot today')

Wrong number! (= 'you have dialled/I got a wrong number')

If you believe that, you'll believe anything (= 'you cannot possibly believe that')

See also ASSERTIVE (FORM); CLAUSE TYPE; SPEECH ACT.

assertive (form) A class of forms that tends to be restricted to positive contexts. Some linguists prefer *affirmative (form)):

> 2002 R. HUDDLESTON & G. K. PULLUM et al. We prefer 'affirmative' as it suggests the two most important features: positive in contrast to negative (an affirmative answer is a positive one) and declarative in contrast to interrogative (to affirm is to state, not to ask).

Certain *determinatives (1), *pronouns, and *adverbs which, by reason of their meaning, are more usual in positive contexts are replaced by a corresponding set of *non-assertive forms (also called **non-affirmative forms** or **negative polarity items**) in *negative, *interrogative, and *conditional contexts. Assertive forms (also called **affirmative forms** or **positive polarity items**) include the *some* series of words (e.g. *some, somebody, someone, something, somewhere*) and adverbs such as *already*, which contrast with the non-assertive *any*-series (e.g. *any, anybody, anyone, anything, anywhere*) and adverbs such as *yet*. Compare, for example:

> I've *already* planted *some* spring bulbs

with:

> I haven't planted *any* bulbs *yet* (negative clause)
> Have you planted *any* bulbs *yet*? (interrogative clause)
> If *anyone* has planted *any* bulbs, let me know (conditional clause)

The demarcation between assertive and non-assertive is not rigid. Although non-assertive forms are often impossible in positive statements (e.g. **I've already planted any*), assertive forms may be possible in negative and interrogative clauses, where they suggest a markedly positive meaning (e.g. *Have you planted <u>some</u> bulbs already?*). Non-assertive forms occasionally occur in positive statements (e.g. *<u>Any</u> small bulbs would be suitable*).

●● **assertive context/territory**: a term applied to the whole *predication (1) in positive clauses, an area where assertive forms may be expected.

Similarly, the predication of negative clauses, interrogatives, and conditionals is a **non-assertive context/territory**.

Compare NEGATIVE.

● **assertiveness**: the fact of being assertive.

asyndetic Not connected by *conjunctions. Contrasted with *syndetic.

The term is particularly applied to the *coordination of *words, phrases, *clauses, etc. without an overt *coordinator, as in:

> I like cheese, bread, olives, pastries
> Sad, white, frightened, her face was the picture of misery

Such coordination is less usual than coordination with a conjunction, and is therefore stylistically marked.

Compare PARATAXIS.

See also ASYNDETON.

asyndeton (Chiefly used as a *rhetorical (1) term.) The omission of a *conjunction, e.g.

I came, I saw, I conquered

See also ASYNDETIC; COORDINATION.

atelic *Semantics*. A *verb, *construction, *situation, etc. which does not express an inherent end point or goal, e.g.

It is raining

The children are watching TV

Compare CONCLUSIVE; DURATIVE; IMPERFECTIVE (2); PERFECTIVE (2); PUNCTUAL.

See also TELIC.

attachment rule A 'rule', sometimes called the **subject-attachment rule**, which stipulates that the unexpressed *subject of a *subordinate clause has the same referent as the subject of an associated *superordinate clause. In the following example it's the people referred to by the *phrase *the monks* in the *matrix clause who are selling fruit, and who are making use of a network of salespeople:

Making use of a network of salespeople, the monks were selling fruit between one province and another

There are exceptions to the rule where it need not apply, but failure to observe it often results in absurd *misrelated constructions or *hanging participles.

See also CONTROL.

attitudinal *Semantics*. Relating to attitude, or conveying an attitude.

As a category of meaning, **attitudinal meaning** is contrasted with *cognitive or *referential meaning. Comparable terms sometimes used are *affective and *emotive.

A speaker or writer's choice of words may be affected by his or her attitude to the listeners or readers addressed. Thus **attitudinal varieties** of language (e.g. formal, informal, neutral, casual, slangy) contrast with regional or social varieties (determined largely by the speaker's origins), and with varieties affected by the 'field of discourse' (such as the journalistic, the literary, and so on). Attitudinal meaning is also conveyed by intonation in spoken English.

Compare COMMUNICATIVE; CONNOTATIVE; EMOTIVE; INTERPERSONAL; PROPOSITIONAL MEANING; REFERENTIAL MEANING.

Many individual words are neutral as regards attitudinal meaning, but some are not. Compare *offspring, child, kiddy,* and *terrorist, insurgent, guerilla, freedom fighter.*

•• **attitudinal disjunct**: the same as content *disjunct.

•• **attitudinal past**: the *past (2) tense used to express a speaker's attitude, usually a tentative one, rather than to refer to past time, e.g.

Did you want something?

I was hoping you could help

•• **attitudinal prefix**: a *prefix that primarily describes an attitude, e.g. *anti*-social, *pro*-American.

attraction The same as proximity *agreement.

attribute

1. An *adjective phrase or *noun phrase typically preceding a noun in a noun phrase, and describing or expressing a characteristic of the noun; e.g. *new* in *the new library* or *power* in *power struggle. Compare* MODIFIER.

2. An adjective phrase or noun phrase functioning as *complement of a verb, and ascribing a property to the subject (**subject attribute**) or object (**object attribute**); e.g. *capable* in *She seems capable,* or *a capable person* in *We find her a capable person.* Other grammatical labels used for this function are *subject-related predicative complement and *object-related predicative complement.

The second meaning is less general than the first, and also potentially confusing, although etymologically, the sense is 'a word or phrase denoting an attribute of a person or thing', however that may be expressed within a sentence.

See ATTRIBUTIVE; PREDICATIVE.

attributive

1. Designating (the position taken by) a *noun phrase, *adjective phrase, etc. functioning as an *attribute (1); contrasted with *predicative.

Some adjectives can only occur in attributive position (e.g. *former, inner, mere, lone, main, indoor, utter*). Nouns used attributively cannot normally be transferred to predicative use (*the effect is greenhouse, *this holiday is bank*), though a small number of predicative uses of nouns may be the historical result of such a transfer (e.g. *She is frightfully county; So Regency, my dear*).

Attributive adjectives are sometimes classified in more detail according to *meaning. Subclasses include *intensifying adjectives (e.g. _pure invention_, _utter madness_, _total stranger_), *restrictive adjectives (also called *limiting or *limiter adjectives; e.g. _a certain person_, _the main trouble_), and adjectives related to nouns (_the criminal code_, _medical students_).

2. (In *Systemic Grammar.) Designating any relationship in which an attribute is ascribed to an entity.

This may be a quality (e.g. _sensible_ in _She is sensible_), a circumstance (e.g. _in the garden_ in _She is in the garden_), or a possession (e.g. _a lovely garden_ in _She has a lovely garden_).

• **attributively**.

autonomous syntax The view propounded in *Generative Grammar (2) that syntax is independent of other *levels of grammar, and that semantic (logical), phonetic, etc. representations are derived from syntactic representations. This view was disputed by proponents of *Generative Semantics, and by many other linguists working in non-generative frameworks.

autosemantic _Semantics._ (_n. & adj._) (A *word or *phrase) that has meaning outside a context or in isolation.

> 1962 S. ULLMAN Full words are 'autosemantic', meaningful in themselves, whereas articles, prepositions, . . . and the like are 'synsemantic', meaningful only when they occur in the company of other words.

Since most lexicographers manage to ascribe meanings to all words, and not merely to 'full' words, and even many full words change meaning according to context, the term is obviously somewhat relative.

Compare FULL _word._

auxiliary (_n. & adj._) (A *verb) principally used in combination with one or more other verbs, including a *main (lexical) verb, to form *constructions that indicate *tense, *aspect, *voice, etc., such as the *progressive construction, *perfect construction, and *passive construction. In older grammar called **helping verb**.

The verbs used for this purpose in English include _be_, _do_, and _have_, and the *modal auxiliary verbs (also called the **modals**).

An auxiliary cannot function as the only verb in a complete sentence. Apparent exceptions to this principle are examples of ellipsis or substitution (e.g. _He won't do it, will he_?). Auxiliaries thus contrast functionally with *main verbs.

On formal grounds an auxiliary can be defined as a member of a class that is grammatically distinct from other verbs by conforming to the *NICE properties. For example, auxiliaries form *interrogative clauses by *inversion of the subject and the verb (e.g. *Are you ready?*, *Can you help?*; but not **Want you to help?*), and negative clauses simply by adding *-n't* (e.g. *They aren't, We mustn't, She doesn't*; but not **She wantn't*). Auxiliary verbs thus contrast with *lexical verbs (full verbs), which form interrogatives and negatives with the auxiliary *do* (*dummy *do*).

The verbs *be, do*, and *have* can be used both as auxiliaries and as main verbs. *Do* and *have* as main verbs typically use *do*-support for interrogatives and negatives (e.g. *Did you do the washing? I don't have a car*), unlike *be*.

In some grammatical models the terms auxiliary and main are reserved for the functional role of verbs in sentence structure, and other terms are used for the formal classifications.

> 1985 R. QUIRK et al. We shall find good grounds for distinguishing 'auxiliary' and 'main', as functional terms, from the terms which define classes of word. Of these, there are three: modal verbs . . . always function as auxiliaries; full verbs . . . always function as main verbs; and primary verbs . . . can function either as auxiliaries or as main verbs.

In CaGEL the verb *be* is always an auxiliary:

> 2002 R. HUDDLESTON & G. K. PULLUM et al. It follows from our syntactic definition that *be* is an auxiliary verb not only in examples like *She is working* or *He was killed* but also in its copula use, as in *They are cheap* (cf. *They are not cheap* and *Are they cheap?*).

See also SEMI-AUXILIARY.

a-word A *word beginning with the syllable *a* and belonging to a class of words (some more like adjectives, others more like adverbs) that mainly function *predicatively.

Grammarians have variously classified *a*-words as *adjectives and as *adverbs, but few, even among the adjective-like ones, can be used in *attributive position, e.g.

> The children were *afraid/alone/ashamed/awake*

but not:

> *An *afraid/alone/ashamed/awake* child was crying

Some of the more adjective-like words can be used attributively when they are *modified, e.g.

> You see before you a *very ashamed* person

and some can be modified by *much* (which typically goes with verbs), e.g.

> I am *very much afraid* that . . .

The more adverb-like *a*-words can follow verbs of motion, e.g.

They've gone *abroad/aground/away*

Some *a*-words can be classed as *adverbs and as *prepositions, e.g. *aboard, above, across, along, around*, etc., as in:

We hurried *along* (adverb)

We hurried *along* the road (preposition)

(However, some grammarians would argue that both instances of *along* are prepositions in these examples.) There are also some words beginning with *a*- which are prepositions only (e.g. *amid, among*), but prepositions are usually excluded from the *a*-word category.

back-formation *Morphology*. The formation of a new *word by the removal of (real or apparent) *affixes, etc. from an existing word; a word that is an instance of this.

A back-formation is revealed by the fact that the date of its first use is later than that of the word it was derived from. The majority of back-formations in English are verbs. Examples:

burgle (L19)	from *burglar* (M16)
caretake (L19)	from *caretaker* (M19)
housekeep (M19)	from *housekeeping* (M16)
liaise (E20)	from *liaison* (M17)
reminisce (E19)	from *reminiscence* (L16)
scavenge (M17)	from *scavenger* (M16, from earlier *scavager*)
shoplift (E19)	from *shoplifting* (L17)

backshift (*n.*) The changing of a *present tense form of a *verb to a *past tense form in a *subordinate clause under the influence of a past tense in the *superordinate clause, e.g.

I didn't apply for the job, although I *was* female and *had* the right degree

Here logically present tenses would be possible, and would make more sense, since the speaker's sex hasn't changed and she still has a degree.

When using the past tense of a reporting verb (e.g. *say, think, remark*) it is common to shift the tense of the words spoken or thought into past tenses too. Thus:

'I am sorry I haven't asked them yet, but I will.'

may (with backshift) become:

Mark said he *was* sorry he *hadn't* asked them yet, but he *would*.

Analogously, a past tense ('*I asked them*') can be backshifted to a *past perfect (*He said he* had asked *them*). However, backshift (sometimes known as the **sequence of tense rule**) is not automatic. Importantly, if the time frame of the speaker is the same

as that of the speaker whose words are being reported, the tenses do not
need to change:

He said he won't
He said he wouldn't } be around in the year 2050.

(*v.*) Change (a tense) in this way.

1985 R. QUIRK et al. The past subjunctive . . . or hypothetical past . . . is backshifted to hypothetical past perfective if there is a change in time reference.

Compare FREE INDIRECT SPEECH.

backwards anaphora *See* ANAPHORA.

bahuvrihi *Morphology*.

1. Of a *compound *noun: having the meaning 'a person or thing
possessing a certain characteristic'. Also called *exocentric compound and
possessive compound.

The term is derived from a Sanskrit word, formed from *bahu* 'much' and
vrihi 'rice', and literally means 'having much rice'. In English grammar it is
usually applied to compounds with a non-literal meaning that cannot be
deduced from the literal meaning of the separate parts. It is particularly
used of somewhat pejorative words, in which some unflattering attribute
stands for the person alleged to possess it. English compounds of this type
include:

blockhead (M16)	hunchback (E18)
butterfingers (M19)	lazybones (L16)
egghead (E20)	loudmouth (M20)
fathead (M19)	paleface (E15)
highbrow (L19)	scatterbrain (L18)

2. The term is sometimes used in a wider sense to include other
compounds in which the head element cannot be equated with the whole.
For example, just as an *egghead* or a *scatterbrain* is a person, not a kind of
head or brain, so a *hardback* is not a type of back, but a book with this
characteristic.

•• **extended bahuvrihi compound**: a bahuvrihi compound in which a
suffix is added to the second part, e.g.

egg-head<u>ed</u>, military-industri<u>al</u>.

Compare ENDOCENTRIC; EXOCENTRIC.

bare coordinate (In CaGEL.) The part of a *coordination structure preceding the *coordinator, e.g. _homes and offices_.

bare existential clause *See* EXISTENTIAL.

bare infinitive The *infinitive form of a *verb without a preceding *particle (2) _to_.

Bare infinitives are thus identical with the *base (1) form of the verb. They are used after:

(i) the core *modal verbs, e.g. _I must go, he will return_, and can occur with *marginal modals, e.g. _You needn't bother_

(ii) *dummy _do_ in questions and negatives, e.g. _Does he know? They didn't say_

(iii) verbs of perception, e.g. _We saw/heard them go, I felt it bite me_ (these verbs can also be followed by -_ing_ forms)

(iv) the verbs _make_ and _let_, e.g. _Make/let them wait_

(v) a few fixed expressions, e.g. _make do, make believe, (live and) let live, let go_

and in various other patterns, e.g. _I'd rather try than do nothing_.

Some of the listed verbs listed require a *_to-infinitive_ when used in the *passive construction, e.g.

We were made to wait

A bare infinitive is rarely interchangeable with a _to_-infinitive, although the verb _help_ is unusual in this regard because both the bare infinitive and the _to_-infinitive are often possible, e.g.

Please help me (to) do the washing-up

However, the version with _to_ is more common in British English, and there is a subtle difference in meaning between these variants according to some grammarians.

•• **bare infinitive clause:** a *clause whose verb phrase contains as its *head a bare infinitive form of a lexical verb, i.e. without a preceding *particle (2) _to_, e.g.

They made us _drink warm orange juice_

(In some analyses the postverbal NP is part of the bare infinitive clause.)

bar level category *See* X-BAR SYNTAX.

base _Morphology_.

1. (Of a *verb.) The basic or uninflected form. Also called **base form**.

Go, like, and _sing_ are bases or base forms, in contrast to _went, likes, sang_, which are not.

The base form of a verb is used:

(i) *non-finitely:

as an *infinitive (e.g. *You must go*);

(ii) *finitely:

as an *imperative (e.g. *Listen!, Be quiet, Have a biscuit*)

as a *present tense form for all persons other than the third person singular (e.g. *I always listen* as opposed to *He always listens*; the verb *be* is an exception to this.)

as the so-called present *subjunctive (*They insisted that he listen*).

2. An element in word structure to which a process (e.g. affixation) can apply. Also called **base morpheme**.

Usually the base is an element to which one or more *affixes can be attached; e.g. *sing* + *-s* = *sings*, *great* + *-er* = *greater*, *great* + *-ly* = *greatly*; *walk* + *-ed* = *walked*. *Fearless* consists of a base *fear* + a suffix *-less*; *indiscreet* consists of the negative *prefix *in-* + the base *discreet*.

Various problems arise, however, in the analysis of some less simple words, which sometimes do not consist merely of a core with one or more affixes attached to it. For example, *unanswerable* consists of the negative prefix *un-*, the *root *answer*, and the *suffix *-able*. But we do not have a word **unanswer*; we can only attach *un-* to *answerable*. So what is the status of the latter form?

A related problem is that we can sometimes analyse a word as containing an affix, but what remains when the affix is removed is not recognizable as a core word. *Gratuitous* apparently has the *adjective suffix *-ous* (compare *pompous, monstrous, outrageous*), just as *gratuity* has a noun suffix *-y*, but we do not recognize *gratuit-* as a word.

Some frameworks (e.g. CGEL) reserve the term base for units of these two types (*answerable* in the context of *unanswerable*, and the incomplete form *gratuit-*). They then refer to units such as *answer, sing, great* (core words to which additions can be made as in 1 above) as *stems or *roots. Thus *base* may be less 'basic' than root or stem.

This is, however, an area where terminology is confused, as the quotations below demonstrate.

1985 R. QUIRK et al. To capture what is common to *pole, desire, jeal-* and *pi-* [as in *depolarization, desirous, jealous* and *pious*], therefore, we obviously cannot use 'word' and we shall speak instead of STEM. We can then say that stems *desire* and *jeal-* combine with the affix *-ous* to yield the adjectives. But a further distinction is necessary, as this is inadequate when we want to describe *depolarization*, since if we said that the affixes *de-, -ar, -ize,* and *-ation* are combined with the stem this might imply that *de-* can combine with *pole* or *polar,* to yield the words **depole,* **depolar.* In fact, it is with the verb *polarize* or the deverbal noun *polarization* that *de-* can combine. We need to distinguish a unit that may be neither STEM nor WORD but of which we can say that it is with this unit that a particular affix is combined. We shall call this unit the BASE.

[I]n some linguistic descriptions the minimal unit in morphology and word formation is called 'morpheme', with the further distinctions 'inflectional morpheme' (*eg* plural *-s*), 'free morpheme' or 'minimal free form' (*eg: pole*), 'bound morpheme' (*eg: un-, jeal-*), with the latter necessarily further subdivided between 'affixal morpheme' (*eg: un-*) and 'stem morpheme' (or 'root' or 'lexical morpheme', eg: *jeal-*). What we are calling BASE might in this framework be termed 'base morpheme'. It should be noted that linguists differ in their terminology for these distinctions, some reversing our use of STEM and BASE, others using 'root' for what in this book is called 'stem'.

2002 R. HUDDLESTON & G. K. PULLUM et al. The two main morphological categories that figure in the structure of words are **bases** and **affixes**. In English bases are characteristically **free** while affixes are normally **bound**. An alternative for 'base' is 'stem' (though the latter is also used in other senses); and 'root' is commonly used for a simple base. We allow the term 'base' to apply to words as well as to parts of words in order to achieve greater generality.

●● **base component:** *see* CATEGORY.

●● **compound base:** a base made up of two simple bases.

●● **derivative base:** a base with an affix.

2002 R. HUDDLESTON & G. K. PULLUM et al. *Gentleman* is therefore a *compound base,* but *gentlemanly* and *ungentlemanly* are derivative bases; *gentle* and *man* are simple bases. Compound and derivative bases are defined by their internal structure, and simple bases by their lack of any such structure.

●● **lexical base:**

2002 R. HUDDLESTON & G. K. PULLUM et al. [O]ne that is not part of a larger base formed by a process of lexical word-formation.

Basic English A variety of the English language, comprising a select vocabulary of 850 words, invented by C. K. Ogden, of Cambridge, and intended for use as a medium of international communication.

The word *basic* was an acronym for *British American Scientific International Commercial (English).* Ogden's book, *Basic English,* was published in 1931, and the idea enjoyed some vogue. But the language produced tended to be unnatural and un-English, an artificial language rather than simplified English.

Basic English is not to be confused with the computer language called BASIC, or Basic, an acronym for *Beginners' All-purpose Symbolic Instruction Code.*

basilect *Sociolinguistics.*

1. A term used to describe varieties of a language in a *creole continuum. Specifically, in a particular community the basilect is the variety that is furthest away from the standard language.

Compare ACROLECT; HYPERLECT; MESOLECT.

2. More generally, the least prestigious variety of a language. The term can be used to describe the dialects of people speaking English as their mother-tongue, and can also be applied in communities where English is used as a second or third language.

• **basilectal**: of, pertaining to, or characteristic of a basilect.

basis of comparison *See* COMPARISON.

BBC English *Standard English, as supposedly spoken by professional broadcasters working for the British Broadcasting Corporation.

In its early days the BBC encouraged a standard non-regional 'educated' accent among its broadcasters. The policy was established by the first managing director, John Reith, who sought 'a style or quality of English that would not be laughed at in any part of the country', and was implemented by the Advisory Committee on Spoken English, established by Reith in 1926 and succeeded, during the Second World War, by the BBC Pronunciation Unit. BBC policy has been considerably modified since the 1950s, and 'BBC English' is now only one of the accents heard from newsreaders, announcers, and other programme presenters.

See also KING'S ENGLISH.

before-past *See* ANTERIOR TIME; PAST PERFECT.

beneficiary *Semantics.* (*n. & adj.*) (Indicating) the *semantic role assigned to a *noun (or noun phrase) referring to a person or animal that is intended to benefit from the action expressed by the verb. Also called **benefactive**. Contrasted with *recipient.

In an inflected language such as Latin, beneficiary could describe the meaning of the *dative (2) case. In English the meaning of 'intended recipient' is often indicated by a *for*-phrase. In the following examples *her*, *you*, *the poor dog*, and *himself* carry beneficiary meaning:

I bought her a present

I bought this for you

She got the poor dog a bone
He found himself a job

Some grammarians call objects that allow a prepositional construction
with *for* **beneficiary objects**. Thus they distinguish between *her* in *I gave
her a present* (recipient role) and *her* in *I bought her a present*
(beneficiary role).

Compare DATIVE (2).

bilingual

(*adj.*)

1. Able to speak two languages fluently.

2. Spoken or written in two languages (e.g. *a bilingual dictionary*).

(*n.*) A person who speaks two languages fluently.

• **bilingualism**, (rarely) **bilinguality**.

Compare AMBILINGUAL.

binary Designating, or relating to, a pair of *features in a language which
are mutually exclusive, or the opposition between them.

Binary (dichotomous) contrasts are a notable feature of the *lexicon,
which contains many pairs of words of opposite meaning. The phenomenon is often dealt with under *antonymy. Antonyms, however, include, or
may be restricted to, *gradable pairs (e.g. *good/bad, high/low*), whereas
binary opposition, strictly speaking, characterizes pairs with an ungradable, all-or-nothing contrast (sometimes called *complementaries), such
as *alive/dead, married/single, human/non-human* (contrast the gradable
inhuman). *Converse relations (e.g. *buy/sell, husband/wife*) can also be
considered binary.

In theoretical linguistics syntactic, semantic, and phonological binary
contrasts are recognized. Nouns, for example, can be characterized as
[± animate] and [± abstract], and clauses can be considered as [± finite]
(where in each case '±' stands for '+ or −'). The system has considerable
limitations, since by no means all of the lexicon or syntax lends itself to
this kind of either/or analysis.

Compare COMPONENTIAL ANALYSIS.

•• **binary noun**: the same as *summation plural. *See also* PLURALE
TANTUM.

binding *See* BOUND; GOVERNMENT-BINDING THEORY.

binomial A phrase containing two parallel units joined by a conjunction,
in which the order is relatively fixed. Sometimes called **irreversible
binomial**. Examples:

blood and thunder   ladies and gentlemen
heaven and hell   one and all
highways and byways   thick and thin
knife and fork

Compare FIXED PHRASE; IDIOM.

blend A *word, *phrase, or *construction which is formed by merging parts of linguistic elements, units, etc.

1. *Morphology*. Examples of **lexical blends** (also called **blend words**, **word blends**) are:

bit (= binary + digit) (M20)
brunch (= breakfast + lunch) (L19)
camcorder (= camera + recorder) (L20)
fantabulous (= fantastic + fabulous) (M20)
smog (= smoke + fog) (E20)
televangelist (= television + evangelist) (L20)
motel (= motor + hotel) (E20)

Note that while most blends are formed by joining a pair of words at the point where they have one or more letters or sounds in common (e.g. mo̲to̲r + ho̲tel > motel), a few are not formed in this way (e.g. *brunch, camcorder*).

2. *Syntax*. **Syntactic blends** include such structures as:

I would have liked to have done it (*I would have liked to do it* + *I would like to have done it*)
Neither claim impressed us, nor seemed genuine (*Neither claim impressed us or seemed genuine* + *The claims neither impressed us nor seemed genuine*)
I do not dare refuse (*I dare* (modal) *not refuse* + *I do not dare* (lexical verb) *to refuse*)

This is a general term covering various types of structures, which could be regarded as merely stylistically awkward, or as grammatically dubious or *anacoluthic. A dated term for a particular type of blend is *apo koinou.
● **blending**: the process by which a blend is formed.
    Compare CONTAMINATION; GRADIENCE.

block language A type of language that differs from canonical linguistic structures in being reduced or compacted in various ways, so as to convey a message economically. It is used especially in notices and newspaper headlines.

Block language often consists of single *noun phrases (e.g. *No exit*, *Essex's snappy reply to a negative image*), or displays an abbreviated *clause structure with *articles, *auxiliary verbs, or other minor words omitted, e.g.

Tanks met by rain of stones
19 dockers dismissed unfairly
Jailed racing driver's bail request rejected

Bloomfieldian (*n.*) An adherent of the work of the American linguist Leonard Bloomfield (1887–1949).

(*adj.*) Of, pertaining to, or characteristic of Bloomfield or his work.
Bloomfield's *Language* (1933) became an influential textbook, particularly in the United States. The approach is associated with *structural linguistics and with theories of behaviourist psychology.

1990 R. H. ROBINS 'Bloomfieldian linguistics' can reasonably be treated as a unity; and because, during this period (1933–1957), linguistics as an auton-omous discipline became more firmly established and more widely repre-sented in universities in the United States than elsewhere, Bloomfieldian influences were felt over the whole learned world in linguistic studies.

*Generative Grammar (2) was in part a reaction against Bloomfieldian linguistics in the 1950s and 1960s.

See also POST-BLOOMFIELDIAN; STRUCTURALISM.

borrow Take (and often adapt) (a *word, structure, etc.) from another language.

borrowing The process of taking over a *word (or sometimes structure) from a foreign language; a word so borrowed (also called a *loanword).

The term is somewhat misleading, since 'borrowed' words usually become a permanent, not a temporary, part of the borrowing language. Many borrowings are modified to bring them into line with the phonological rules of their new language.

As has often been remarked, the richness of the English *vocabulary is in large part due to borrowing from many other languages of the world, sometimes in such a way as to allow fine *denotative, *connotative, or *stylistic distinctions between semantically related or nearly synonymous words to emerge.

Loanwords attain different degrees of assimilation into the language. Some are totally assimilated to the native word-stock, and are phonetically and orthographically integrated (e.g. *butter, fail, gas, umbrella*). Others are fully part of the English vocabulary, but retain traces of their foreign origin in their pronunciation, spelling, or inflection (e.g. *addendum*, *phenomenon, genre, faux pas*). A third group may be well assimilated in their form, but remain semantically tied to a foreign context (e.g. *matador, rajah, sampan, samurai, tundra*). Finally, there is a category of words (into which all loanwords must initially fall) which have not yet achieved general currency but occur in very limited contexts, such as during an English-speaker's stay in a foreign country, in news and current affairs, or in travel writing, books on foreign cuisine, anthropological works, etc. Examples would vary from one person's vocabulary to another's, but might include *aficionado, intifada, peshmerga, tiramisu*, and *Waldsterben*.

Surprisingly few words have been borrowed into English from the neighbouring Celtic languages (Welsh, Gaelic, and Irish). *Bannock* and *crag* are among the few early borrowings from Old British; *coracle* and *flannel* came from Welsh later; *clan, slogan*, and *whisky* from Gaelic; and *banshee, galore*, and *shamrock* from Irish.

Borrowing from Latin has been constant from the very earliest times, and has always included quite central vocabulary items, such as *cheese, kiln, pillow*, and *tile*, borrowed before Old English was recorded. Later Latin loans tended to originate in a learned context, but many have since become general (e.g. *focus, inflate, orbit*). Many Latin loanwords have entered the language, virtually unchanged, through the intermediary of French (e.g. *condition, oracle, superior*), and in the same way, many borrowings from ancient Greek have come through Latin (e.g. *abyss, cemetery, history*), although some are direct loans (e.g. *acme, kudos, rhizome*).

The Scandinavian settlement in late Old English times had a marked effect on the English vocabulary: Danish- and English-speaking communities lived side by side for some time, so that penetration was deep and all-pervasive. Even form words, such as *they, them, their, though*, and *near*, were borrowed. Nearly all early Scandinavian loanwords are central items such as *cast, egg, law, take*.

French has contributed more than any other language to the English vocabulary, starting with the earliest post-Conquest loanwords (e.g. *castle, prison, war*). Borrowing at all levels of vocabulary was especially heavy during the later Middle Ages, greatly affecting the core vocabulary (e.g. *age, blue, chase, front, people, search*, and so on); more recent borrowing has been mostly at the learned and cultured level (e.g. *avant-garde, surrealism*).

Other important European sources of loanwords have been Dutch (e.g. *brandy, deck, hoist*), Low German (e.g. *hawker, smuggle*), Italian (e.g. *motto, semolina*), and Spanish (*alligator, mosquito*).

Loanwords from outside Europe tended, in the earlier period of exploration, to come through other languages such as Dutch and Portuguese.

As English-speaking settlements emerged, first in North America and then in other parts of the world, and as Britain imposed its political and commercial domination during the nineteenth century, direct borrowings came from a large number of other languages, e.g. *sheikh* (Arabic), *boomerang*, *kangaroo* (Australian Aboriginal), *lychee* (Chinese), *taboo* (Tongan), *moccasin*, *skunk* (Algonquian), *judo*, *tycoon* (Japanese), *caddy*, *rattan* (Malay), *thug* (Hindi), *bungalow* (Gujarati), etc.

Owing to migration, ease of travel, mass communication, and similar factors, words of foreign origin abound in present-day English speech and writing, particularly in the fields of cookery, the arts, and politics. It is difficult to predict whether any given word will become part of the vocabulary in the long term.

bound

1. *Morphology*. Of a *morpheme, *root, etc.: not *free; normally occurring only in combination with another (bound or free) form.

Bound morphemes (or **bound forms**) include *inflections such as -*s*, -*ing*, –*ed*, and *affixes such as *de*-, *dis*-, *un*-, and -*ly*.

See also BASE.

2. Of a *clause: *subordinate.

In some grammatical theory, a **bound clause** is roughly the same as a *subordinate clause or *dependent clause, although the latter terms are much more common.

3. In theoretical grammar, **binding** is concerned with the relationship of *anaphors, *pronouns, and *referring expressions to their antecedents, or to their referents in the outside world. *See* GOVERNMENT-BINDING THEORY.

bounded Of the referent of a *noun: capable of being conceived of as a separate unit.

> 1984 R. HUDDLESTON In *another cake*, *cake* has a bounded or **individuated** interpretation: it is conceived of or perceived as a unit, a discrete entity; in *so much cake* it has an unbounded or **mass** interpretation: we are simply concerned with the substance as such rather than some bounded unit consisting of that substance.

● **boundedness**.

This terminology is not very general, but is intended to address the problem that many *count nouns (e.g. *difficulty*) can also be interpreted as *mass nouns.

> 1984 R. HUDDLESTON An uncountable noun... cannot sustain an individu-ated interpretation; the converse, however, does not hold. As the examples with *cake*... show, particular instances of countable nouns can receive mass interpretations. It is precisely for this reason that I have treated countability

and boundedness as distinct concepts. Such a treatment differs from that commonly found in grammars of English, where a single contrast of mass noun versus count noun is recognised.

When nouns are divided into either *count or *uncount (usually the same as *mass), it is common to describe nouns that belong to both categories in terms of overlap, or in terms of *conversion.

bracketing A method for visualizing the internal structure of *sentences, *clauses, *phrases, etc. using pairs of (square) brackets. When *form labels are appended (in subscript form) to the left-most bracket of each pair, we speak of **labelled bracketings**.

As an example we might contrast the alternative analyses assigned by different grammars to the sentence *He believes the calculations to be wrong* using labelled bracketings:

He believes [$_{NP}$ the calculations][$_{clause}$ to be wrong]

He believes [$_{clause}$ the calculations to be wrong]

In the first analysis the verb *believe* takes a *noun phrase and a *clause as its *complements, whereas in the second analysis there is only one complement in the form of a clause.

Labelled bracketings can also be used to visualize structural *ambiguities. Thus *He saw the people on the ship* is ambiguous between a reading in which the people referred to were on the ship when they were seen, and a reading in which the speaker was on the ship when he made his observation:

He saw [$_{NP}$ the people [$_{PP}$ on the ship]]

He saw [$_{NP}$ the people] [$_{PP}$ on the ship]

For complicated sentences which involve many instances of brackets within brackets the representations can become difficult to read. For such cases *tree diagrams are often preferred.

Compare BRANCHING.

branching (*n. & adj.*) This term refers to the connections between a unit (*clause, *phrase, etc.) and its *constituent parts, which are represented by lines ('branches', like the branches of a tree) within a *tree diagram. For example, the following representation of a *verb phrase (2) is a branching structure in which the lines that run from VP to V and NP are branches:

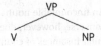

The word sometimes occurs with *prefixes, e.g. **left-branching, right-branching**, and **mid-branching** (also called **medial branching** or *nesting). The structure above is a right-branching structure in which the *head precedes its *complement. Initial *subordinate clauses (*When I came home* it was dark) are left-branching, whereas final subordinate clauses are right-branching (*It was dark when I came home*).

Briticism A *word or *phrase that is of distinctively (modern) British origin, particularly in contrast to a different American equivalent.

British English (BrE) The *variety of English used in Great Britain, as contrasted with varieties used in other English-speaking areas.

broad negative A *word which is *negative in import and in its grammatical effect, or a word that is mainly used in a negative context.

   The term is not in general use. It includes not only *adverbs that are normally classified as *semi-negative (such as *barely, hardly, scarcely, seldom, rarely*, etc.), but also words such as *bother* and *necessarily* which normally appear in negative contexts and which some grammarians call *non-assertive items.

   Compare SEMI-NEGATIVE.

by-form A collateral and sometimes less frequent form of a *word.

   This is an old-fashioned term from *philology. It is generally used for a word form which has essentially the same origin as a related word, but a distinct pronunciation and spelling, and which has had significant currency among speakers and writers of *Standard English. Examples in the *Oxford English Dictionary* include:

   chaw (LME) besides *chew* (OE)
   clift (LME) besides *cliff* (OE)
   commonality (LME) besides *commonalty* (ME)
   harrow (as in *the Harrowing of Hell*) (ME) besides *harry* (OE)

The by-form may be regarded as a subcategory of *doublet.

   Compare HETERONYM (2).

by-phrase In a *passive *construction: an optional *prepositional phrase introduced by the *preposition *by* which takes as *complement a *noun phrase that typically carries the *semantic role of *agent; e.g.

   The fire stations in the centre were closed *by the mayor* last year

   See also ACTIVE; VOICE.

C *Complement as an *element in *clause structure.

calque (*n.*) The same as *loan translation.

(*v.*) Form (a *word or expression) as a loan translation (on a foreign word or expression).

> 1958 A. S. C. ROSS M[oder]n E[nglish] *That goes without saying* is a translation-loan of (better, is calqued on) M[oder]n French *cela va sans dire.*

Cambridge Grammar of English A pedagogical *grammar published in 2006, written by Ronald Carter and Michael McCarthy.

Cambridge Grammar of the English Language, The (CaGEL)

A large reference *grammar published in 2002 by Cambridge University Press, written by a team of linguists whose principal authors are Rodney Huddleston and Geoffrey K. Pullum. Along with *A *Comprehensive Grammar of the English Language* this is a standard modern reference grammar of English.

canonical

1. Representing a typical exemplar or *realization of a *category. For example, canonical *nouns denote people, places, or entities, and the canonical realization of a *direct object in English is a *noun phrase.

2. Representing a typical *pattern of *formal or *functional elements. For example, [*determinative (1) + noun] represents a basic canonical noun phrase pattern, and *subject-*predicator-*object represents a canonical *clause pattern.

3. The same as *kernel.

See also ELEMENT.

cardinal number A *word denoting quantity (*one, two, three,* etc.), in contrast to an *ordinal number (*first, second, third,* etc.). Also called **cardinal numeral**.

See also NUMBER; NUMERAL.

case

1. An *inflection of *nouns (or noun phrases), including *pronouns, the *realization of which is *conditioned by grammatical function.

Unlike Latin, which has six cases, English distinguishes only between the overtly marked *subjective, *objective, and *genitive cases.

English pronouns in particular show distinctions between subjective case, objective case, and genitive case; e.g.

I, me, my/mine
you, you, your/yours
he, him, his/his
she, her, her/hers
we, us, our/ours
they, them, their/theirs
who, whom, whose/whose

The genitive case inflection (*boy's*, *boys'*) is strictly speaking not added to a word, but to a noun phrase, which may not even end in a noun; e.g.

[the King of Spain]'s daughter
[the man opposite]'s car

Some grammars prefer to use the classical terminology:

2002 R. HUDDLESTON & G. K. PULLUM et al. The classical terms 'nominative' and 'accusative' are quite opaque, and some modern grammars have replaced them by the more transparent 'subjective' and 'objective' respectively. The view taken here, however, is that the correlation between case and syntactic function is so complex that these new terms run the risk of creating confusion, and we have therefore preferred to retain the traditional terms—which also have the advantage that they are much more widely used in the grammars of other languages.

•• **absolutive case:** *See* ERGATIVE.

•• **plain case** (also called **common case**): an unmarked case carried by non-pronominal nouns. For example, the nouns *cats* and *milk* in the sentence *Cats like milk* are in the plain case.

2. Spelt with a capital 'c' (**Case**), this term refers to the various conceptions of this notion in *Government-Binding Theory, e.g. **abstract Case**, **inherent Case**, **structural Case**.

3. (In *Case Grammar.) The *semantic role of a noun or noun phrase in relation to other words in the *clause or *sentence.

Case Grammar A model of grammar developed in the late 1960s by the American linguist Charles Fillmore (1929-2014), which pays special attention to cases, understood as *semantic roles. The theory, along with other developments in *Generative Grammar (2), grew to some extent out of a dissatisfaction with the earlier *Standard Theory.

In this framework, case is not a *morphosyntactic *category (as in traditional grammar; *see* CASE (1)) but a category of *meaning. Thus, in *The burglars broke the door down* the grammatical *subject is an *agent, but in *The knife cut the bread easily* it is an *instrument. By contrast, in *The neighbours heard nothing* the subject is a *dative (2), whereas in *The whole place was a mess* it is a *locative (2).

The original six cases recognized were *agentive (2), *instrument (1), *dative (2), *factitive (2), *locative (2), and *objective (3). Subsequent adaptations and revisions introduced the *experiencer case (formerly dative), *result (formerly factitive), *source, *goal (2), and *patient, among others.

Case Grammar made a major contribution to the study of the relationships between grammar and meaning, but has no active practitioners.

> 1986 F. J. NEWMEYER Despite the lack of success of case grammar itself, most generative syntacticians would agree today that any adequate theory must include a characterization of semantic cases (or, as they are more commonly termed, 'thematic roles') and relate them to other aspects of syntactic patterning.

See also SEMANTIC ROLE.

catachresis (Plural **catachreses**.) The (perceived) erroneous use of a term applied to a concept.

> 1926 H. W. FOWLER Wrong application of a term, use of words in senses that do not belong to them.

An old-fashioned term, originally rhetorical. Examples given by Fowler were the 'popular' use of *chronic* = 'severe', *asset* = 'advantage', *conservative* (as in *conservative estimate*) = 'low', *annex* = 'win', and *mutual* = 'common'.

> 1589 G. PUTTENHAM Catachresis, or the Figure of abuse . . . if for lacke of naturall and proper terme or worde we take another, neither naturall nor proper and do vntruly applie it to the thing which we would seeme to expresse.

• **catachrestic**, **catachrestically**.

cataphora The use of a *pronoun or other *pro-form to point forward to a later *word, *phrase, or *clause; an example of this process. Sometimes called **forwards anaphora**, but usually contrasted with *anaphora (1).

Examples:

What I want to say is *this*: please drive carefully.

If you see *him*, will you ask Bob to telephone me?

Here is *the news*. In the House of Commons, the Government had an
overwhelming majority...

- **cataphoric**: of or involving cataphora.
- ● **cataphoric ellipsis**: *See* ELLIPSIS.

category A group of items that share a set of characteristics; a class.
This is a very general term, used in different ways by different grammarians. In most analyses *nouns, *verbs, *adverbs, etc. (i.e. the *word
classes) and their associated *phrases are regarded as linguistic categories,
but there is somewhat less agreement as to whether notions such as
*subject, *predicate, *tense, *agreement, *aspect, *mood, *gender, and
*person should also be regarded as such.

> 1968 J. LYONS [T]here is very little consistency or uniformity in the use of the
> term 'category' in modern treatments of grammatical theory.

Linguistic categorization is heavily influenced by the Aristotelian conception of categories, which regards them as sharply delimited, and not
allowing for *gradience.
- **categorical** (or **categorial**): relating to categories.
- ● **categorial component**: in early *Generative Grammar (2) this component (also called **base component**) is the set of *phrase structure rules
(also called **categorial rules**) that is instrumental in forming basic (*kernel) grammatical structures.

catenative (*n. & adj.*) (A *verb) that can form a chain with one or more
subsequent verbs, e.g.

> *want* to *go*
> *hate* to *tell* you
> *begin walking*
> *go shopping*

The *construction may involve a *direct object, e.g.

> She *wanted* them to *go*
> He *made* us *laugh*
> I *watched* him *paint/painting* the door

Chance juxtapositions are not catenative constructions. Contrast:

> We stopped to talk to the old man ('in order to talk')
> You only helped me to satisfy your own conscience ('in order to satisfy')

with

> We *stopped talking* to the old man (catenative)
> You *helped* me to *answer* one question (catenative)

The grammatical analysis of sentences like those above is controversial.

2002 R. HUDDLESTON & G. K. PULLUM et al. The term 'catenative' reflects the fact that this construction is recursive (repeatable), so that we can have a chain, or concatenation, of verbs followed by non-finite complements, as in *She intends to try to persuade him to help her redecorate her flat*. The term 'catenative' is applied to the non-finite complement, and also to the verb that licenses it.

•• **catenative complement**: (in CaGEL) a *function (1) label assigned to a *non-finite clause which is *licensed by a catenative verb. In the examples below, the highlighted clauses function as catenative *complements:

They believe the event *to be fictitious*
She seems *to enjoy food*

•• **catenative verb**: a verb that takes a *catenative complement.
See also CATENATIVE-AUXILIARY ANALYSIS; COMPLEX CATENATIVE CONSTRUCTION; DEPENDENT-AUXILIARY ANALYSIS.

catenative-auxiliary analysis (In CaGEL.) In this analysis (preferred by the authors of CaGEL) *auxiliary verbs are not regarded as being *dependent on a *main verb, as in the traditional *dependent-auxiliary analysis in which auxiliaries are seen as 'helping verbs', but as *catenative verbs that take their own *complements, namely *catenative *complements.
See also DEPENDENT-AUXILIARY ANALYSIS; LEXICAL VERB; MAIN VERB; VERB.

causal *See* CAUSATIVE.

causative (*n. & adj.*) *Semantics.* (a word, especially a verb) expressing cause, causation, or reason. (Also called **causal**.)
The term is particularly used in connection with *verbs. In classic semantic theory, the verb *kill* is a causative verb, meaning 'cause to die'. Other causatives include verbs of motion such as *place* or *put*, i.e. 'cause (something) to be (in a place)', and more general verbs that express the notion of 'result', e.g. *elect*, as in *They have elected my brother as chairman*.
Other causative verbs include *get* and *have*, as in *Get your hair cut* or *We've had the house painted*.
The term is also applied to other linguistic units, e.g. *clauses:

Because you're not ready, we have to leave without you
I won't be able to send you the transcript *since you didn't send me your CV*

The string *because of* can be described as a causative (complex) *preposition in *We left because of the rain*, and in *She died of a fever*, the *prepositional phrase *of a fever* carries causative meaning.
• **causatively**.
Compare CONATIVE.
See also ADVERBIAL CLAUSE; CAUSE.

cause The event, circumstance, condition, reason, etc. which gives rise to a particular *situation, considered as one of the semantic categories used in the classification of *verbs, *phrases, *clauses (especially *adverbial clauses), etc.

See also CAUSATIVE.

causer A *semantic role associated with an entity (person, animal, etc.) that brings about an event, *situation, etc., e.g.

> *The builders* damaged the wooden floor

central

1. Of, at, or forming, the centre.

●● **central determiner**: (in CGEL) defined positionally as a *determiner (2) that follows a *predeterminer (such as *all*, *both*, *such*), if present, and precedes a *postdeterminer (such as a number), if present.

Among the most frequent central determiners are *a/an* and *the*, *possessives (*my*, *your*, *his*, *her*, *its*, *our*, *their*), and *demonstratives (*this*, *these*, *that*, *those*); e.g.

> such *a* nuisance
> all *our* yesterdays
> *my* two left feet
> both *those* two criminals

2. Conforming to all or most of the (morphosyntactic) criteria that define a particular *word class, *phrase, *function (1), etc. The same as *prototypical.

●● **central adjective**: an *adjective that conforms to all or most of the *morphosyntactic criteria that define the class of adjectives, e.g. occurring in *attributive and/or *predicative positions, being *gradable, and taking the prefix *un-*. Contrasts with *marginal adjective.

●● **central coordinator**: *see* COORDINATOR.

●● **central modal**: a *modal verb that conforms to all or most of the *morphosyntactic criteria that define the class of modal verbs, e.g. conforming to the *NICE properties, having no *third person singular *-s *inflection, and having no *non-finite form. Also called **core modal**. Contrasts with *marginal modal.

●● **central noun**: a *noun that conforms to all or most of the *morphosyntactic criteria that define the class of nouns, e.g. the ability to be preceded by *the*, taking a plural *-s inflection. Contrasts with *marginal noun.

•• **central passive**: a *passive construction that has a regular *active counterpart, in contrast to a *semi-passive or *pseudo-passive construction.

•• **central preposition**: a *preposition that conforms to all or most of the *morphosyntactic criteria that define the class of prepositions. Contrasts with *marginal preposition.

•• **central verb**: a *verb that conforms to all or most of the *morphosyntactic criteria that define the class of verbs, e.g. taking a present or past *tense inflection. Contrasts with *defective verb.

3. **central meaning**: See MEANING.

• **centrality**: the fact or quality of being central in one of the above senses.

centre-embedding See EMBEDDING.

chain (Designating) a relationship between two linguistic units in a linear sequence.

•• **chain and choice**: the *syntagmatic and *paradigmatic relationships that exist between linguistic units.

The contrast between chain and choice can be applied at various levels of linguistic analysis. Thus, if we take the words *bat, cat, fat, hat*, etc., the letters *b, c, f*, and *h* are in a chain relationship with *-at*, but in a choice relationship with each other.

At a higher level, if we wish to add one word to complete the sentence *The cat . . . on the mat*, the chain relationship requires a *verb, but the choice is wide (*is, jumped, lay, lies, sat, slept*, etc.).

Compare AND RELATIONSHIP; COLLIGATION; *OR* RELATIONSHIP; PARADIGM (2); PARADIGMATIC; SYNTAGM.

See also CATENATIVE.

choice See CHAIN; SYNTAGM; SYNTAGMATIC RELATIONSHIP.

Chomsky adjunction See ADJUNCTION.

Chomskyan (*adj.*) Of, pertaining to, or characteristic of (the theories of) the American linguist Noam Chomsky (b. 1928).

(*n.*) An adherent of Chomsky's theories.

Chomsky's *Syntactic Structures* (1957) and *Aspects of the Theory of Syntax* (1965) introduced *Generative Grammar (2) and gave a radically new direction to linguistics. Over time he continued to develop his theories and published extensively on phonology (his best-known contribution being *The Sound Pattern of English* in 1968, with M. Halle), on language and the human mind, and also, critically, on American foreign policy and politics. His latest thinking on linguistics forms part of the *Minimalist Program.

See also GENERALIZED PHRASE STRUCTURE GRAMMAR; GENERATIVE; GENERATIVE GRAMMAR (2); GOVERNMENT-BINDING THEORY; GRAMMAR; HEAD-DRIVEN PHRASE STRUCTURE GRAMMAR; PHRASE STRUCTURE GRAMMAR; PRINCIPLES AND PARAMETERS THEORY; STANDARD THEORY; TRANSFORMATIONAL GRAMMAR.

circumfix(ation) See PARASYNTHESIS.

circumstance The state of affairs surrounding and affecting a *situation (action, event, etc.).

The term is sometimes invoked in its general sense in a detailed analysis of *subordinate clauses of *cause or reason. Thus the following sentences may be characterized as showing a relationship of circumstance (before the comma) and consequence (after the comma), rather than (or in addition to) cause/reason plus consequence:

Since you're so clever, why don't you do it yourself?

Seeing it's so late, we'd better take a taxi

• **circumstantial** (n. & adj.): (an element) expressing circumstance.

citation form A *word or other linguistic unit (e.g. a *lexeme) that is being cited in, and for the purpose of, discussion.

1985 R. QUIRK et al. *It ... can only very rarely receive stress, for example when it is used as a citation form: Is this word IT?* [looking at a manuscript]

class A group of linguistic items with shared characteristics; a *category.

See OPEN; CLOSED (1); WORD CLASS.

•• **class noun**: (less generally) the same as *count noun.

•• **dual class membership**: see DUAL (2).

class dialect See DIALECT.

classical plural See FOREIGN PLURAL.

classifier

1. An *affix which shows the subclass to which a *word belongs.

The term is not in general use in English grammar, but is sometimes applied to *affixes, e.g. *un-* meaning 'not', 'the opposite of' (e.g. *unkind, unintentional*); *de-*, *dis-* and *un-* (reversing an action, e.g. *decontaminate, disconnect, untie*); *-let*, 'small' (e.g. *piglet*). The term is more useful with reference to a language such as Chinese, which has a system for marking semantic classes. *Noun classifiers in such languages may indicate shape ('long', 'thin', 'sticklike'), size and colour, whether the referent is *animate, etc.

2. A word (typically in *attributive position) which has the role of identifying the class or kind of the following noun; in contrast to an *epithet.

Classifiers include both *adjectives (also called *classifying adjectives) and nouns, e.g.

a *medieval* castle, a *thatched* cottage, a *country* house
See also CLASSIFYING.

classifying Designating the use of *a/an* or the *zero article to indicate membership of a class.

In describing the meaning and usage of the *articles many grammars contrast *specific and *generic (in addition to the better-known distinction between *definite and *indefinite). However, although *the* + a singular count *noun can clearly have generic meaning and refer to a class as a whole, as in *The black rhino is in danger of extinction*, the indefinite article cannot have this meaning (**A* black rhino is in danger of extinction). Some grammars therefore prefer the label *classifying*, rather than *generic*, for the use of *a/an* or the zero article with various non-specific meanings:

A black rhino can be very dangerous
We cannot afford *a new car*
More people should train as *engineers*

•• **classifying adjective**: a term used in some analyses to describe a subgroup of *adjectives:

1990 COLLINS COBUILD ENGLISH GRAMMAR **Classifying adjective**, an adjective used to identify something as being of a particular type; EG *Indian*, *wooden*, *mental*. They do not have comparatives or superlatives. Compare with qualitative adjective.

•• **classifying genitive**: a genitive which classifies the head *noun, rather than indicating 'possession'. (Also called *descriptive genitive.) Examples:

a women's college
child's play
a moment's thought
a stone's throw

clausal negation *See* NEGATION.

clause A unit of grammar which typically involves a *subject–*predicate (1) relationship, and which operates at a level lower than a *sentence, but higher than a *phrase.

In traditional grammar, a clause has its own *subject and a *finite *verb, and is part of a larger sentence. Thus *We left when the film finished* consists of a *main clause (*We left*) and a *subordinate clause (*when the film finished*).

Some modern grammar uses the *clause, rather than the sentence, as the basis of structural analysis, so that in some instances clause and sentence are coterminous. Under this view, the example above *We left when the film finished* is a *main clause which contains a subordinate clause (*when the film finished*), though usage differs (*see* MAIN CLAUSE).

We should distinguish *non-finite and *verbless clauses, such that the following example, even though it contains only one finite verb (italicized), has four clauses (bracketed):

[My father *travels* by bus [to get to work on time], [leaving home at 5.00 a.m.], and [usually returning after 10.00 p.m.]]

A clause-based analysis allows a functional analysis into five elements of English clause structure: *subject, *verb, *object, *complement, and *adverbial, with the verb element as the most essential, and the *adverbial optional and the most mobile.

• **clausal**: of or relating to a clause.

•• **clause complex**: (in *Systemic Grammar) a *compound or *complex sentence, viewed as a 'composite' of clauses.

See also ADVERBIAL CLAUSE; COMPLEMENT CLAUSE; FREE RELATIVE CLAUSE; NOMINAL CLAUSE; RELATIVE CLAUSE; *THAT*-CLAUSE; *WH*-CLAUSE.

clause fragment *See* NON-SENTENCE.

clause type (Also called **sentence type**.) This refers to one of the ways in which *clauses can be categorized syntactically. Typically four types are distinguished: *declarative, *exclamative, *imperative, and *interrogative.

The classification applies to *main clauses and *subordinate clauses (except for imperatives, which cannot occur as subordinate clauses).

Each of the clause types has a typical use. Thus, declaratives are typically used to make *statements; exclamatives are typically used to utter *exclamations; interrogatives are typically used to ask *questions; and imperatives are typically used to issue *directives.

When a particular clause type is used in a non-typical way (e.g. a declarative used as a question), we speak of indirect *speech acts.

Considerable confusion is caused when statement, question, exclamation, and directive are used as both syntactic and semantic categories, which is why some grammarians are careful to use declarative, exclamative, imperative, and interrogative as syntactic categories, and statement, question, exclamation, and directive as categories of *usage.

Compare MINOR SENTENCE.

See also MOOD.

cleft construction A *sentence or *clause formed from another by dividing the latter into two clauses, each with its own *finite *verb, so as to place emphasis on a particular component (the *focus) in the original sentence. The formulaic structure of cleft constructions is as follows:

It + form of the verb *be* + *FOCUS + *relative clause (*who(m)/that/Ø/which . . .*)

For example, the following sentence:

Bob always plays golf on Sundays

can be reworded as any of the following cleft sentences (with the focused element in small caps):

It is BOB who always plays golf on Sundays (i.e., not his brother)

It is GOLF (that) Bob always plays on Sundays (not tennis)

It is ON SUNDAYS that Bob always plays golf (not Mondays)

In these sentences the focus comes after the verb *be* in the *main clause (the first clause), and the relative clause contains information which is assumed to be 'known', and is therefore less important. A *verb phrase cannot be the focus of a cleft sentence.

Another type of structure, sometimes included under cleft, is more carefully distinguished as the **pseudo-cleft construction** (also called ***wh*-cleft**). It contains a *free relative clause, introduced by a ***wh*-relative item (usually *what*), as *subject. Formulaically pseudo-clefts can be represented as follows:

What (or *where/when*) + . . . + form of the verb *be* + FOCUS

The focus comes at the very end. It identifies what the *wh*-clause specifies as needing identification, e.g.

What they like is A LONG LUNCH

Unlike the cleft sentence, the pseudo-cleft can have a verb phrase in the focus position, e.g.

What Bob does on Sundays is (TO) PLAY GOLF

In a **reverse pseudo-cleft** construction the order of the clauses is inverted:

A LONG LUNCH is what they like

• **clefting, pseudo-clefting**

See also INFORMATION STRUCTURE.

cline A continuum, a series of gradations between linguistic elements, *constructions, etc.

A term applied in various areas of grammar where there are no clear-cut contrasts.

See also GRADIENCE.

clipping *Morphology*. The formation of a new *lexical item by shortening an existing one; an example of this. A type of *abbreviation. Examples:

omnibus > bus	examination > exam
influenza > flu	telephone > phone

Compare REDUCTION.

clitic *Morphology*. (*n. & adj.*) (A form) pronounced with very little emphasis, usually shortened, and typically phonologically attached to a host word.

There is some debate in the literature as to whether clitics are *words or *affixes.

> 2012 A. SPENCER & A. R. LUÍS English, then, has elements which behave phonologically like affixes because they have to be attached to some host, but which don't behave morphologically like affixes given that they attach to words of any category. Furthermore, they have the function and meaning of words and may even correspond to a full word form, but they don't have the autonomy of words.

The term is abstracted from the words denoting the two main kinds of clitic: *enclitic (dependent on a preceding word) and *proclitic (attached to, or dependent on, a following word).

Enclitics include abbreviated *verbs, as in *He's here, I'm leaving*. Although the *articles (*a/an, the*) are arguably proclitics, and so is *do* when reduced to a consonant only in *d'you know?*, the term proclitic is little used with reference to English grammar.

closed

1. Of a *word class: to which new words are rarely or never added; in contrast to *open (1).

The closed classes—also called **closed systems**—in English are the *pronouns, *determinatives (1) (which include the *articles), *modal verbs, *prepositions, and *conjunctions. Very occasionally a new word may be added to a closed class: thus *plus* (once only a preposition and a *noun) began to be used colloquially as a conjunction in the mid-twentieth century, e.g. *He's handsome plus he's rich*. But, on the whole, closed classes do not allow newcomers, even though sometimes it may be desirable. For example, it would be useful for English to possess a singular unisex pronoun. However, none of the many words suggested has become part of ordinary usage.

Contrast **minor** and **major word class** (*See* MAJOR).

2. Of a conditional clause or sentence: *See* CONDITION; CONDITIONAL.

closed interrogative *See* INTERROGATIVE.

closed question *See* QUESTION.

code

1. *Sociolinguistics.* (A general term for) a language, *dialect, or speech *variety. *Code* can also mean any of two or more distinct languages (in a situation where more than one is available to a speaker). For example, a *bilingual Welsh/English speaker can be said to have two codes. The term is particularly favoured by those wishing to avoid the possibly pejorative overtones of the word *dialect.* Thus a person who frequently changes from, say, a regional variety of English to *Standard English is said to be operating with two codes.

A sociological theory put forward in the early 1970s contrasted an **elaborated code** and a **restricted code**. Speakers of the former, it was claimed, used more complicated *sentence structures and a larger *vocabulary, and conveyed meaning more explicitly than people operating with a restricted code. The two codes were said to characterize middle-class and working-class speech. The theory aroused both interest and argument.

●● **code-switching**: this occurs when a speaker changes from one language code to another, according to where they are, who they are talking to, which *speech community they identify with, and so on.

2. The 'C' in the acronym NICE refers to code. *See* NICE PROPERTIES.

cognate

1. (*n. & adj.*) (A *word or language) related in form to another word or language by virtue of the fact that both are derived by direct descent from the same source.

Latin *mater*, German *Mutter*, and English *mother* are cognate words or cognates. French, Italian, and Spanish are cognate languages: they are all derived from Latin.

2. cognate object: an *object related in form and meaning to the *verb it *complements, e.g.

fight the good *fight*
sing a *song* of sixpence
smile a shy *smile*

cognitive *Semantics*. Of *meaning: relating objectively to facts, and to the denotations of *words outside of a particular *context of utterance, in contrast to *attitudinal meaning.

The analysis of different types of meaning is far from simple, and different semanticists make different distinctions. Cognitive meaning is similar to *descriptive (3) or *referential meaning, in contrast to *interpersonal meaning.

Compare DENOTATIVE; IDEATIONAL.

See also COMMUNICATIVE MEANING; CONATIVE; CONNOTATION; DE-SCRIPTIVE; EMOTIVE; ILLOCUTIONARY MEANING; INTERPERSONAL MEAN-ING; REFERENTIAL MEANING.

•• **Cognitive Grammar:** see COGNITIVE GRAMMAR.

•• **Cognitive Linguistics:** see COGNITIVE LINGUISTICS.

Cognitive Grammar A term coined by R. Langacker, referring to the study of grammar using the insights and methodology of *Cognitive Linguistics.

Cognitive Linguistics A cover term for a number of different *usage-driven and meaning-driven linguistic frameworks in which language is viewed as being part of general human cognition, rather than being autonomous, as in *Chomskyan linguistics.

coherence The set of relationships within a *text that link sentences by *meaning. The term contrasts with *cohesion.

Coherence often depends on (shared) knowledge, implication, or inference. The following mini dialogue shows coherence:

A: You weren't at the meeting yesterday.

B: My daughter's ill.

A's statement can be understood as a *question, and B's statement can be understood as an explanation. But if B had replied with a rather different statement, e.g. 'Marmalade is a kind of jam', the conversation would lack coherence.

cohesion

1. The set of relationships within a *text that link *sentences through grammar or *lexis. The term contrasts with *coherence. In the following dialogue *there* grammatically substitutes for *at the meeting*, and the pronoun *it* refers to *the meeting*.

A: You weren't at the meeting yesterday.

B: No, I'm sorry I wasn't *there*. How did *it* go?

1976 M. A. K. HALLIDAY & R. HASAN Cohesion occurs where the INTERPRE-TATION of some element in the discourse is dependent on that of another. The one PRESUPPOSES the other, in the sense that it cannot be effectively decoded except by recourse to it. When this happens, a relation of cohesion is set up, and the two elements, the presupposing and the presupposed, are thereby at least potentially integrated into a text.

See also COHESIVE.

2. The 'uninterruptability' of *words.

It is a defining characteristic of words in English that normally no elements can be inserted within them. There are some exceptions. Thus an expletive can be inserted into some words, e.g. *abso-bloody-lutely*.

Compare TMESIS.

cohesive Having the property of grammatically linking different parts of a *text or *utterance.

For example, when *pronouns and other *words are used to refer backwards or forwards to other words, *phrases, etc. in a text, they are sometimes described as **cohesive devices**.

• **cohesively**
• **cohesiveness**: another name for *cohesion.

Compare ANAPHORA; CATAPHORA.

co-hyponym *See* HYPONYM.

coinage *See* NEOLOGISM; NONCE; WORD FORMATION.

collective Short for *collective noun.

collective noun

1. A *noun that refers to a group of individual people or animals, and which in the *singular can take either a singular or *plural *verb. Examples include *army, audience, committee, family, herd, majority, parliament, team*.

The choice of singular or plural verb—and corresponding *pronouns and *determinatives (1)—depends on whether the group is considered as a single unit or as a collection of individuals, e.g.

The audience, *which was* a large one, *was* in *its* place by 7 p.m.

The audience, *who were* all waving *their* arms above *their* heads, *were* clearly enjoying *themselves*

Notice that even when followed by a plural verb, such nouns still take a singular determinative; e.g.

This family are all accomplished musicians

The use of a plural verb with a grammatically singular noun of this type is more common in British English than in American English.

2. Loosely (notionally defined), any noun referring to a group—including nouns that can only (in the sense used) take a plural verb: *cattle*, *clergy*, *people*, *police*.

See AGGREGATE; GROUP NOUN; PLURALE TANTUM.

colligation A grouping of *words that occur in the same type of syntactic *constructions, in contrast to a grouping of words that are regularly in an individual (semantic) relationship with each other, which is called a *collocation. The term was introduced by the British linguist J. R. Firth.

As an example, *verbs of perception such as *hear*, *notice*, *see*, and *watch* enter into *colligation* with an *object (shown in italics below), and either the *bare infinitive or the *-*ing* form of a verb (underlined below), e.g.

We heard *the visitors* leave/leaving
They noticed *him* walk away/walking away
She heard *Pavarotti* sing/singing
I saw *it* fall/falling

The term is far less general than the contrasting term *collocation*.

• **colligate** (cause to) be in colligation (with another word).

Compare CONSTRUCTION; CO-OCCURRENCE; PATTERN.

See also CHAIN; SYNTAGMATIC.

Collins Cobuild English Grammar A grammar written by the late John Sinclair and associates using data from the Collins Cobuild Corpus.

See also NEO-FIRTHIAN.

collocable Of a *word or *phrase: typically able to *collocate with another word or phrase.

1961 Y. OLSSON Although '*have* a look' and '*take* a look' are both collocable with *at*, '*have* a look' is alone in collocating with *for*.

• **collocability**.

collocate (*v.*) (Pronounced /ˈkɒləkeɪt/.) (Cause to) co-occur with (another *word) so as to form a *collocation.

1951 J. R. FIRTH In the language of Lear's limericks ... *person* is collocated with *old* and *young*.

(*n.*) (Pronounced /ˈkɒləkət/.) A word that collocates with another.

All words are to some extent restricted in their usage by virtue of both their *word class and their *meaning. But many are much more restricted, and can occur only with one other word or with a limited set of other

words, or be used only in a particular type of structure. For example, the
*prepositions that are used with certain *nouns, *adjectives, and *verbs are
often fixed; e.g.

account for	adherence to	by chance
consist of	inconsistent with	long for
on foot	rely on	similar to
under the auspices of		

Here we can say that *adherence* collocates with *to*, and *account* collocates
with *for*, and that *adherence* and *to*, and *account* and *for* are collocates.

collocation The habitual juxtaposition of two or more particular *words
(such that these words are then said to be *collocated); an instance of such
a juxtaposition.

The technical sense in linguistics was introduced by the British linguist
J. R. Firth, although the word had been loosely applied in linguistic
contexts previously.

Collocation is a type of *syntagmatic relationship typically between
individual elements (words, *phrases) that consistently occur together,
e.g. *smoked salmon, comb my hair*. Two kinds should be distinguished:

•• **grammatical collocation**: a type of *construction where a *verb, *adjective, etc. must be followed by a particular *preposition (e.g. *account for,
afraid of*), or a *noun must be followed by a particular form of the verb
(e.g. *the foresight to do it*, rather than **the foresight of doing it*).

•• **lexical collocation**: a type of construction in which particular nouns,
adjectives, verbs, *adverbs, etc. form predictable connections with other words.
For example, we can say *cancel an engagement* ('call off an appointment')
or *break off an engagement* ('call off a marriage'), but not normally
**withdraw/*revoke/*discontinue an engagement*. This is a **collocational
restriction**. Compare also such collocations as *take advantage of*.

Special cases of collocation (e.g. *come a cropper, kith and kin*), in which
the elements are mutually predictable, can be analysed as *idioms or
*fixed phrases.

• **collocational**: relating to collocations, e.g. **collocational differences**
(between American and British English), **collocational possibilities**,
collocational range.

Compare SEMANTIC RESTRICTION.

colloquial Belonging or proper to ordinary conversation; not formal or
literary. *Compare* INFORMAL.

In ordinary everyday language, especially between speakers who know
each other well, a casual style of speech is both frequent and appropriate.
Are you doing anything tomorrow evening? as a preliminary to an

invitation is probably more suitable than *Have you an engagement for tomorrow evening?* Colloquial speech is not substandard, nor is it the same as *slang.

   Compare REGISTER.

• **colloquialism**: a colloquial *word or *phrase; the use of such words or phrases.

• **colloquially**: in the language of ordinary conversation.

colon *See* PUNCTUATION.

combination A (loose) *syntagmatic relationship between *words, or other language units, as opposed to a *paradigmatic or contrastive relationship; an instance of this.

   For example, at word *level, a combination can denote a frequently occurring sequence of two (or occasionally more) words. At word level some usage restricts the term to a sequence that functions virtually as a single word (e.g. *oak tree, prime minister*), usually in contrast to a *collocation, which may be discontinuous and *phrasal (e.g. *advantage* was *taken of* him). In other usage the terms are virtually interchangeable.

   Compare COMPOUND; CONSTRUCTION.

combinatorial Able to combine with other linguistic units.

> 1968 J. LYONS In general, any formal unit can be defined (i) as being distinct
> from all other elements which contrast with it, and (ii) as having certain
> combinatorial properties.

combinatory Relating to a *combination, or combinations; *collocational.

•• **combinatory coordination**: *coordination in which the coordinated units have a joint meaning, in contrast to *segregatory coordination.

   Henry and Margaret met is an example of combinatory coordination, since the only possible interpretation is that they met each other. The sentence cannot be segregated into two coordinated *clauses: *Henry met and Margaret met.*

combining form A *bound (1) form used in conjunction with another linguistic element in the formation of a *word, especially a *neoclassical compound.

   The term is usually used in a narrower sense than bound *morpheme to refer to forms that contribute to the particular sense of words, e.g.

> *arch-* ('chief', 'pre-eminent'):   *archduke, arch-enemy*
> *geo-* ('earth'):   *geography, geology*

| -(o)cracy ('rule'): | *meritocracy, theocracy* |
| -(o)logy ('study of'): | *archaeology, zoology* |

Combining forms contrast with *prefixes and *suffixes that adjust the sense of a *base (2) (e.g. *un-*, *ex-*) or change the *word class of the base (e.g. *-ation*, *-ize*).

•• **initial/final combining form:** *See* NEOCLASSICAL COMPOUND.

comitative Having the meaning 'in company with' or 'together with'.

The term is primarily useful in the description of languages that have a particular *case (1) for this meaning, but it is sometimes applied to English phrases on the *pattern *with* + animate *noun. In *I went there with my cousin, with my cousin* has a comitative sense.

comma *See* PUNCTUATION.

command *See* DIRECTIVE; IMPERATIVE.

comment *Semantics.* That part of a *sentence which says something about the *topic.

Also called *focus or *rheme by some linguists. The comment often coincides with the *predicate (1).

Compare TOPIC.

comment adjunct (In some models.) A subcategory of *adjunct (*adverbial), sometimes called *disjunct, including items such as *frankly, no doubt,* expressing an observation, etc. on what is said in the containing clause.

The category also overlaps with *comment clause (e.g. *to be frank*).

See also MODAL ADJUNCT.

comment clause A parenthetical *clause, often only containing a *subject and verb, which is loosely connected syntactically with the rest of the *sentence, and functions pragmatically to offer a comment, viewpoint, etc. on what is being said.

Comment clauses may be *finite or *non-finite, and include many clichés and conversation *fillers (2), e.g.

(as) you know	they say
I think/suppose	generally speaking
you see	as I said
to be frank	so it seems

See also DISCOURSE MARKER.

common General, *unmarked; in which a (usual) distinction is not made.

•• **common case**: *see* CASE (1).

•• **common core**: the basic grammar and *vocabulary shared by all varieties of the English language (a rather vaguely delimited concept).

•• **common gender** (occasionally called **common sex**): the characteristic shared by many *animate nouns which make no distinction of *gender (examples are *baby, person, horse, sheep*). Occasionally the term refers more narrowly to *nouns which denote *animate beings when sex is irrelevant, and which can be referred to using *it* or *which* (e.g. *A baby cannot feed itself*). *See also* GENDER; FEMININE; MASCULINE. *Compare* DUAL GENDER.

•• **Common Germanic**: *See* GERMANIC.

•• **common noun**: a noun which is not the name of any particular person, place, thing, etc.; contrasted with *proper noun. Common nouns are further classified grammatically into *count and *uncount nouns, and semantically into *abstract and *concrete nouns.

communicative

1. Of or pertaining to communication.

•• **communicative competence**: a practical kind of social competence which denotes a speaker's ability to understand the implications of utterances, to appreciate what type of language use is appropriate in different situations, etc.; in contrast to the notion of *grammatical competence developed in *Generative Grammar (2).

•• **communicative dynamism**: variation in the importance or prominence of different parts of an *utterance in conveying information. The concept was developed in the *Prague School.

Compare COMMENT; GIVEN; INFORMATION STRUCTURE; NEW; RHEME; THEME; TOPIC.

•• **communicative meaning** (or **function**): the *illocutionary meaning of an utterance, whatever its *form. Thus an *interrogative clause may have the communicative function of an *exclamation (e.g. *Isn't it a lovely day?*).

See also ATTITUDINAL; CONATIVE; CONNOTATION; DENOTATIVE; DE-SCRIPTIVE; EXPRESSIVE; INTERPERSONAL; PROPOSITIONAL MEANING; REF-ERENTIAL MEANING; SPEECH ACT.

2. Of a teaching method, etc.: that emphasizes *functions (2) and *meaning, rather than grammatical forms alone.

Communicative teaching methods have led in some quarters to learners developing fluency in talking ('communication') at the expense of grammatical accuracy, but this was not the intention of the early proponents of the approach, and there has been a shift of emphasis back towards grammar.

Communicative Grammar of English, A A book written by Geoffrey Leech and Jan Svartvik, first published in 1975, which seeks to describe English grammar from the point of view of how the patterns of English can be used to achieve certain communicative aims.

comparative

1. (*adj.*) Of a *gradable *adjective or *adverb (or a *construction containing one): expressing a higher degree of the quality or attribute denoted by the *absolute (1) form, whether through *inflection (essentially, by the addition of -*er* to the absolute form) or *periphrasis (by the use of *more*), e.g.

better, happier, sooner, more beneficial, more energetically

•• **comparative degree**: the middle degree of *comparison, between absolute and *superlative.
•• **comparative element**: (in CGEL) the unit in a *matrix clause which expresses the standard of *comparison, e.g.

It was *colder/more exhilarating* than we expected

(*n.*) (An adjective or adverb that is in) the comparative degree.

2. *Linguistics*. The term **comparative linguistics** usually refers to a branch of linguistics that is concerned with the historical similarities and differences between languages or varieties of languages. This discipline made great advances in the nineteenth century. Related terms are **comparative grammar, (comparative) philology**, and *historical linguistics.

The term can also refer to the study and comparison of two (modern) languages, but this is often distinguished as *contrastive linguistics.

comparative clause A *clause expressing a *comparison.

There is considerable variation in the labelling of different kinds of clauses and sentences that express the notion of comparison. Narrowly, the term *comparative clause* can be applied to a clause following a comparative form (underlined in the examples below; called the *comparative element in CGEL), e.g.:

It was <u>colder</u> *than we expected*
It was <u>more expensive/less expensive</u> *than last year*

Usually clauses expressing *equivalence, beginning with *as* (and following *as* or *so* + a positive *adjective or *adverb), are included, e.g.

It was (not) <u>as cold</u> as it was last year

In popular grammar, a comparative clause is a type of *subordinate clause; in more formal models, it is a clause that *postmodifies a preceding adjective or adverb.

Comparative clauses are *elliptical, sometimes with nothing but the *conjunction and one *word remaining, e.g.

It's not <u>as cold</u> *as* (it was) *yesterday*
You know them <u>better</u> *than I* (do)

Interestingly, not only do some comparative clauses lack a *subject, but in some no subject can be inserted, e.g.

It was much <u>more expensive</u> *than was anticipated*

In CaGEL *than* and *as* in the second part of the comparative *construction are not part of the comparative clause.

See also COMPARE.

comparative element *See* COMPARATIVE CLAUSE.

comparative grammar *See* COMPARATIVE.

comparative philology *See* COMPARATIVE.

compare Form the *comparative and *superlative degrees of (an *adjective or *adverb).

Compare GRADABLE.

See also COMPARATIVE CLAUSE; COMPARISON.

comparison
1. The act or instance of comparing one thing with another. This very general term can be used to cover any grammatical means of comparing things.

In *comparative clauses introduced by *than* or *as*, whatever is represented by the *adjective, *adverb etc. that functions as the comparative element is sometimes called the **standard of comparison**, and the **basis of comparison** is whoever or whatever is being compared in the comparative clause. Thus in

Pete is happier than Paul

the standard of comparison is happiness, and the basis of comparison is Paul.

Comparison may include expressions of 'sufficiency' or 'excess', e.g.

They did not arrive *early enough* to help
They arrived *too late* to help

•• **comparison of equality/inequality**: the former is exemplified by *Jack is as competent as Greg*; the latter by *Jack is less competent than Greg*.

•• **scalar/non-scalar comparison**: with the former the comparison is on a scale (*hot–hotter–hottest*), but with the latter this is not the case (e.g. *This book's cover is the same as that one's*).

2. The action of forming the comparative (or comparative and *superlative) form of an adjective or adverb.

The three **degrees of comparison** are *absolute (1), *comparative, and *superlative.

comparison clause A *clause containing some kind of *comparison.

This label may include *comparative clauses, and also clauses introduced by *as if/as though*:

He looked as if/as though he'd seen a ghost.

Alternatively, it may exclude comparative clauses, and be used in contrast with them. (Clauses introduced by *as if* and *as though* are also often analysed as clauses of *manner.)

competence *Linguistics*. The internalized knowledge of the *rules of a language that native speakers possess; contrasted with their actual **performance**.

The distinction between competence and performance is due to Noam Chomsky, and forms an important part of *Generative Grammar (2). Native speakers' competence enables them to generate an infinite number of grammatical sentences, make *grammaticality judgements, detect *ambiguities, etc. By contrast, performance, what a speaker actually says (i.e. the use they make of their competence), may at times be *ungrammatical or confused—and is also subject to constraints, such as *utterance length, that do not affect idealized competence.

Compare COMMUNICATIVE COMPETENCE; LANGUE.

complement

1. A *constituent (*phrase, *clause, etc.) that is *licensed by a *head, e.g. a *verb, *noun, or *adjective.

The complements of verbs include phrases and clauses, e.g.

She bought *a new laptop*
We think *that the rain will stop by 4 p.m.*

In most models the *subject is not regarded as a complement of the verb; CaGEL is an exception.

The constituents following nouns that are related to verbs are often analysed as complements, e.g.

They were annoyed by her <u>refusal</u> *to answer* (cf. She refused to answer)
His <u>allegation</u> *that she will resign by Friday* is unfounded (cf. He alleged that...)

But other kinds of abstract nouns can also take complements, e.g.

His <u>reluctance</u> *to write a reference for me* (cf. He is reluctant...)
The <u>fact</u> *that the story was made up* didn't bother me

The italicized clause in the second example is often regarded as *appositive, and analysed as a complement in some models but as a *postmodifier in others.

The label *complement* can be useful when a noun is incomplete by itself (compare *They deplored her lack of remorse* and **They deplored her lack*).

Complements of adjectives include *prepositional phrases and clauses, e.g.

<u>fond</u> *of chocolate*
I'm <u>sorry</u> *that you are ill*
We're <u>sad</u> *to hear your news*

Complements of *prepositions (also called *objects of prepositions) are usually *noun phrases or prepositional phrases, e.g.

<u>in</u> *the bag*
<u>over</u> *the moon*
<u>out of</u> *order*

In some frameworks (e.g. CaGEL and OMEG), words that are traditionally regarded as subordinating *conjunctions are analysed as prepositions that take clausal complements, e.g.

We watched the film <u>after</u> *she left*
He wore a thick coat <u>although</u> *it was hot*

Predicative complements are *adjective phrases, noun phrases, etc. which ascribe a property to the referent of another phrase. These are labelled in more detail as:

(i) **subject complement** (in CGEL, abbreviated C_s), **subjective predicative complement** (in CaGEL, abbreviated PC^s), **subject-related predicative complement** (in OMEG), e.g.

She is *a lawyer*
All my students seem *very clever*

Typically complements of this type 'complete' the verb *be* or another *linking verb.

(ii) **object complement** (in CGEL, abbreviated C_o), **objective predicative complement** (in CaGEL, abbreviated PC^o), **object-related predicative complement** (in OMEG), e.g.

They called me *a fool*

I consider tranquillizers *dangerous*

A **predicative oblique** (a term used in CaGEL) is an object-related *predicative phrase that occurs after a preposition, typically *as*, e.g.

We regarded them as *interlopers*

The entire *as*-phrase is then called a **marked predicative complement**. In CGEL the term **prepositional object complement** is used for the NP alone.

•• **complement clause**: a clause that functions as complement (called a *catenative complement in CaGEL), e.g. We wanted *to help him*.

•• **core complement**: (in CaGEL) typically a *noun phrase directly licensed by a verb. Compare *non-core complement* below.

•• **external complement**: the *subject (in frameworks that regard the subject as a complement of the verb).

•• **internal complement**: the complements of a verb that are part of the *verb phrase (2) in a clause or sentence, e.g. the *direct object, *indirect object, etc.

•• **non-core complement**: (in CaGEL) typically a prepositional phrase which contains a noun phrase that is indirectly licensed by a verb. Compare *core complement* above. *See also* OBLIQUE.

 2. More narrowly, one of the five *elements of clause structure, along with subject, verb, object, and adverbial.

complementarity *Semantics*. A relationship of oppositeness between pairs of *words, such that to deny one is normally to assert the other, and vice versa; e.g. *dead/alive*.

See also COMPLEMENTARY.

complementary (*n. & adj.*) (Designating) a *word which, with another word, forms a pair of mutually exclusive opposites.

Such complementaries (sometimes considered a type of *antonym) are usually ungradable either-or terms, e.g. *alive/dead*, *married/single*.

See also BINARY; CONTRADICTORY.

complementary distribution *Morphology* and *syntax*. Two forms are in complementary distribution if they have a different shape in a particular morphological or syntactic environment, and can hence be said to represent the same item at some *level of representation; e.g. *a* and *an* placed before nouns.

> 2003 I. PLAG The idea of complementary distribution is used not only in science, but also in everyday reasoning. For example, in the famous novel *The Strange Case of Dr. Jekyll and Mr. Hyde*, both men are the surface realizations of one underlying schizophrenic personality, with one realization appearing by night, the other by daylight. Dr. Jekyll and Mr. Hyde are complementarily distributed: in morphological terms they could be said to be allomorphs of the same morpheme.

complementation

1. The *licensing of a *complement by a *verb, *noun, *adjective, etc. that functions as a *head.

For most linguists this is a syntactic concept, but note the semantic perspective in the quotation below.

> 1985 R. QUIRK et al. We reserve the term complementation (as distinct from *complement*) for the function of a part of a phrase or clause which follows a word, and completes the specification of a meaning relationship which that word implies.

●● **complementation pattern**: a particular grammatical structure that a verb (or noun, adjective) licenses, e.g. verb + *indirect object + *direct object.

●● **complex intransitive complementation**: *See* COMPLEX INTRANSITIVE.

●● **complex transitive complementation**: *See* COMPLEX TRANSITIVE.

●● **ditransitive complementation**: *See* DITRANSITIVE.

●● **intensive complementation**: *See* INTENSIVE.

2. The same as *complementary distribution (a rare use).

> 1948 E. A. NIDA The forms *I* and *me* generally occur in complementation: *I* occurs in preverbal subject position, *me* in postverbal object position and after prepositions.

complementizer
A word that introduces a clause (regarded in *Generative Grammar (2) as a **complementizer phrases**) which functions as *complement to a verb or some other *head. The items *that, whether, if* (in interrogative clauses), and *for* belong to this class.

The term is particularly used in Generative Grammar (2). It is narrower in meaning than *subordinating conjunction or *subordinator.

> 1994 L. HAEGEMAN Complementizers such as *whether, if, that* and *for* introduce a sentence (IP): C selects an IP-complement. The choice of the type of IP is determined by the choice of C. The complementizers *that* and *if* select

a finite clause as their complement; *for* selects an infinitival clause and *whether* selects either type.

complementizer phrase (CP) A *phrase which has a *complementizer as its *head. *See* COMPLEMENTIZER; FUNCTIONAL CATEGORY; HEAD.

complete sentence A *sentence that does not lack any of its major components, such as *subject, *predicate, etc.; one that is not *elliptical. *Compare* KERNEL.

complex (*adj.*) Consisting of two or more parts; often in contrast to either *simple or *compound.

•• **complex catenative construction**: *See* COMPLEX CATENATIVE CONSTRUCTION.

•• **complex conjunction**: a two- or three-word *conjunction (e.g. *in that, providing that, as soon as*).

•• **complex infinitive**: *see* INFINITIVE.

•• **complex intransitive**: *see* COMPLEX INTRANSITIVE.

•• **complex preposition**: a two- or three-word *preposition (e.g. *out of, because of, prior to, on behalf of*), in contrast to an ordinary one-word preposition (e.g. *from, before*). *See also* COMPOUND PREPOSITION.

•• **complex sentence**: a *sentence containing at least one *subordinate clause, in addition to one or more *matrix clauses, e.g. *When you've quite finished, we can begin. Compare* COMPOUND SENTENCE.

•• **complex stem**: *See* STEM.

•• **complex transitive**: *see* COMPLEX TRANSITIVE.

•• **complex verb phrase**: a *verb phrase (1) which, in addition to a *main verb, includes one or a combination of *modal, *perfect, *progressive, and *passive auxiliaries (e.g. *can leave, will have forgotten, must have been being investigated*), but excludes any *complements.

•• **complex word**: generally, a word consisting of at least two parts, usually a *base and one or more *bound morphemes. Thus *impolite* and *rudeness* contrast both with unanalysable words, long or short, e.g. *dog, hippopotamus*, and with *compound words. However, there is very considerable variation in the way different linguists deal with morphology, and usage of terminology is correspondingly fluid. The word *blackboard*, for example, which is a *compound in many definitions, is classed as a complex word in another model, and even as a compound *stem.

(*n.*) **clause complex**: *See* CLAUSE.

complex catenative construction (In CaGEL.) Typically a *construction in which a *catenative verb is followed by a *noun phrase (called the **intervening NP**) which functions as *direct object, and which is understood as the semantic *subject of a following *non-finite clause which itself functions as a *catenative complement, e.g.

Our boss [wants] [us] [to cycle to work]
I didn't [intend] [the report] [to be published online]

Also regarded as complex catenative constructions are cases where the intervening NP belongs in the *subordinate clause and can take a *genitive case, e.g.

He was [longing] [for *the meeting* to end]
The University would not [authorize] [*his teaching* the students in the park]

complex intransitive A term used to describe a *verb which *licenses a *subject-related predicative *complement—hence **complex intransitive complementation**—or a *pattern or *clause in which a verb licenses a subject-related predicative complement, the latter in the form of a *noun phrase, *adjective phrase, etc, e.g.

Jake is very excited to be here

Also called *intensive.

   Compare COMPLEMENTATION; COMPLEX TRANSITIVE; DITRANSITIVE; INTRANSITIVE; MONOTRANSITIVE; TRANSITIVE.

complex transitive A term used to describe a *verb which *licenses a *direct object and an *object-related predicative *complement—hence **complex transitive complementation**—or a *pattern or *clause in which a verb licenses an object (underlined below) and an object-related predicative complement, the latter in the form of a *noun phrase, *adjective phrase, etc. (italicized below), e.g.

They made <u>him</u> *leader*
Let's paint <u>the town</u> *red*

In the complex transitive pattern, the object noun phrase may or may not be directly 'acted upon' (i.e. carry the *semantic role of *patient). However, the object, and what follows it, are in a semantic (but not grammatical) subject-*predicate relationship (indicated by underlining below), e.g.

They painted <u>the house blue</u>
We watched <u>him leave</u>
I knew <u>him to be a crook</u>
They made <u>him pay</u>
I saw <u>him arrested</u>

There are considerable differences of analysis here: in some frameworks the verbs in these constructions are would be considered ordinary *transitive or *catenative verbs followed by a *direct object and a *complement clause. In other frameworks the underlined strings are clauses.

Compare COMPLEMENTATION; COMPLEX INTRANSITIVE; DITRANSITIVE; INTRANSITIVE; MONOTRANSITIVE; TRANSITIVE.

component

1. Any one of the major parts of the theory of *Generative Grammar.

Different sets of components have been proposed at different times, for example a **categorial component** (*see* CATEGORY), a set of *transformational *rules (the **transformational component**), a **phonological component**, and a **semantic component**. In more recent theory the term **module** is preferred.

See also TRANSFORMATIONAL GRAMMAR.

2. *Semantics.* A small unit of *meaning (*see* *feature (2)) that forms part of the total meaning of a *word, and that can be shared by other words.

See COMPONENTIAL ANALYSIS.

componential analysis
The analysis of linguistic elements, especially *lexical items, into syntactic, semantic, and/or phonological *features (2).

Frequently cited classic examples concern terms for people and animals that can be shown to have, or lack, certain features, and these are often indicated using a *binary notation of plus ('+') or minus ('−') signs. Thus *stallion* or *boar* can be represented as [+male] [+adult] [−human], etc. The combination '±' is also used to indicate that a feature may or may not apply. Thus clauses can be analysed as being [±tensed]. However, the validity of the technique has been criticized.

See also SEMANTIC.

composition

1. An older term for *compounding.

1926 H. W. FOWLER Composition—How words are fused into compounds.

2. The way in which language is composed of units which incorporate other units.

1968 J. LYONS The relationship between the five units of grammatical description . . . is one of *composition.* If we call the sentence the 'highest' unit and the morpheme the 'lowest', we can arrange all five units on a scale of *rank* (sentence, clause, phrase, word, morpheme), saying that units of higher rank are composed of units of lower rank.

compound (*n.*)
A *word formed by combining two or more words (*bases (2) or *lexemes); a compound word.

(*adj.*) Formed by combining two or more units; especially consisting of two or more parts of equal value—hence, e.g. **compound sentence**: a sentence containing two or more *coordinated *main clauses.

Compare COMPLEX *sentence*; SIMPLE (2) *sentence*; and *see* COMPOUND-COMPLEX SENTENCE.

Among compound words, **compound *nouns** and **compound *adjectives** are particularly common, e.g. *bookcase, handlebar, laptop, mind set, windscreen, fact-finding, home-made, south-facing, tax-free*.

Some *adverbs (e.g. *somehow, hereby*) are also described as compound, in contrast to simple adverbs (e.g. *just, only*).

In general, compound words contrast with simple words, and with words formed by *derivation or *inflection. At a more technical level, terminology is by no means agreed, and even the distinction between compound and complex may be blurred.

• **compounding**: the *word formation (2) process of forming compound words by joining at least two independent words (bases, lexemes) together; contrasted with the other main type of word formation, derivation (and sometimes *conversion). Also sometimes called *composition.

•• **compound base**: *See* BASE (2).

•• **compound lexeme**: *See* LEXEME.

•• **compound preposition**: The term is used to refer to *complex prepositions, i.e. *multi-word sequences that behave like simple prepositions, e.g. *in front of, on account of*, but can also be used to describe examples like *into, throughout*. *See also* COMPLEX preposition.

•• **compound stem**: *See* STEM.

•• **compound stress**: In general, compounds have the stress on the first element, whereas *phrases have the stress on the second element; compare ′*blackboard* (compound) with *black* ′*board* (phrase). However, this generalization is not without exceptions.

•• **compound subject, compound object**: now more usually called **coordinated subject, coordinated object**.

•• **compound tense**: *See* PRIMARY; TENSE.

•• **compound verb**: an older term for multi-word verb.

(*v.*) Combine (words, bases) so as to form a compound word.

compound-complex sentence A sentence containing at least two *coordinated *clauses (making it compound), as well as at least one *subordinate clause (making it complex). For example:

[main He told me [subordinate that Fran would fly to Italy]] but [main he told Pete something else]

Comprehensive Grammar of the English Language, A (CGEL)

A large reference *grammar published by Longman in 1985, written by Randolph Quirk, the late Sidney Greenbaum, Geoffrey Leech, and Jan Svartvik. An update of *A *Grammar of Contemporary English*. Along with *The *Cambridge Grammar of the English Language* this is a standard modern reference grammar of English. A shorter version with a pedagogical focus was published as *A Student's Grammar of the English Language* in 1990. Various other grammars have adopted the CGEL grammatical framework, e.g. *A *Communicative Grammar of English* and the *Longman Grammar of Spoken and Written English*.

computational linguistics *See* LINGUISTICS.

conation (As a meaning expressed in language.) 'Trying'.

This term is sometimes applied to a *verb *construction such as *manage (to do)*, *fail (in doing)*.

The term is derived from Latin *conari* 'to try'.

conative (*n.* & *adj.*) *Semantics*. (Designating) language which aims to persuade.

A term used occasionally in theories of *meaning to refer to the use of language which causes or persuades others to do what the speaker wants. **Conative meaning** thus overlaps with the *instrumental (2) function.

The term is derived from Latin *conari* ('to try').

Compare DIRECTIVE.

See also ATTITUDINAL; COMMUNICATIVE; CONATION; CONNOTATION; EMOTIVE; EXPRESSIVE; INTERPERSONAL; PROPOSITIONAL MEANING; REFERENTIAL MEANING.

concession The act, or an instance, of conceding, admitting.

Concession is one of the meaning categories used in the analysis of *adverbial clauses, e.g.

I love cheese, *although I know it contains a lot of fat*

See also CONCESSIVE.

concessive Expressing *concession.

A **concessive *clause** (or **clause of concession**) is usually introduced by a concessive *subordinator, e.g. *although, (even) though, whereas, while,* and, in Scotland, *even although*. These clauses are sometimes classified together with clauses of *contrast, and sometimes distinguished. They include *finite, *non-finite, and *verbless clauses; e.g.

> Although he was angry
> Although feeling angry   } he did not raise his voice
> Although angry

1985 R. QUIRK et al. Concessive clauses indicate that the situation in the matrix clause is contrary to expectation in the light of what is said in the concessive clause.

Concessive *prepositions include *despite, in spite of, for* (obligatorily followed by *all*), *notwithstanding*, e.g.

For all his protestations, nobody believed him

There are also **concessive *adverbs**, including *anyhow, anyway, however, nevertheless, still, though, yet*, e.g.

He was angry; he did not raise his voice, though

conclusive *Semantics.* Of a *dynamic (1) *verb, or its *meaning: implying a resulting change of state, progress towards some goal, or possibly some single action, or transitional action, or event leading to a definite end. Contrasted with **non-conclusive**.

The term is not in popular use.

Compare ATELIC; DURATIVE; PERFECTIVE; PUNCTUAL; TELIC.

concord The same as *agreement.

concrete Of a *noun: denoting a physical object: a person, an animal, or an observable, touchable thing; contrasted with *abstract.

Compare COUNT.

condition A circumstance, situation, action, etc. upon the fulfilment of which another circumstance, situation, action, etc. obtains.

Condition is one of the meaning categories used in the analysis of *conditional clauses. A distinction is often made between **factual conditions** and **counterfactual conditions**.

In a factual condition (also called a **neutral**, **open**, or **real condition**) the condition may or may not be fulfilled, e.g.

If it rains tomorrow, we won't go

If Bob's there already, he will have heard the news

A *counterfactual condition (also called a **closed**, **hypothetical**, **rejected**, **remote,** or **unreal condition**) implies that the speaker does not think that the condition is, will be, or has been fulfilled, and therefore the fulfilment of the *main clause *proposition is either in doubt or will not obtain, e.g.

If he made a bit more effort, he might get somewhere

Most conditional clauses posit a **direct condition**, which means that there is a logical (causal) link between the conditional clause and main clause. An **indirect condition** occurs when there is a logical gap between the two parts of a conditional *construction. For example, the stated outcome in the following examples does not depend on the fulfilment of the *if-clause:

You look tired, if you don't mind my saying so

If you're going in July, it will be raining

See RHETORICAL.

See also ALTERNATIVE CONDITIONAL-CONCESSIVE CLAUSE; UNIVERSAL CONDITIONAL-CONCESSIVE CLAUSE.

conditional (*adj.*) (Used for) expressing a *condition.

(*n.*) A *sentence containing a conditional *clause.

•• **conditional clause**: a clause introduced by a **conditional *conjunction/ *subordinator**, the commonest of which are *if* and *unless*, e.g.

We can't implement this plan *if she is abroad*

If and *unless* can also introduce *non-finite and *verbless clauses, e.g.

If *in doubt,* say nothing, *unless advised otherwise*

Other conditional conjunctions include *on condition (that), providing that, provided (that).*

•• **conditional sentence** (also called **conditional *construction**): a combination of a *main clause and conditional clause. The *if-clause is called the *protasis, and the main clause is the *apodosis. CaGEL's analysis is different:

2002 R. HUDDLESTON & G. K. PULLUM et al. Traditional grammar takes *if* to be a subordinating conjunction, not a preposition, and many modern works follow this analysis; *if* is therefore commonly regarded as forming part of the protasis. We are using 'conditional adjunct' for the constituent including *if*, and protasis just for the subordinate clause . . . Note also that we use 'conditional construction' rather than 'conditional clause', because the latter could be understood as applying to either the subordinate clause or the superordinate one.

Simplified grammar books for foreign learners often classify conditional constructions into three types according to the tense forms used:

(i) **first conditional** (also called the **will-condition**): involves a present tense verb form in the conditional clause, and *will* in the main clause, e.g.

If I *see* them, I *will* tell them

(ii) **second conditional** (also called the ***would*-condition**): involves a past tense verb form in the conditional clause, and *would* in the main clause, e.g. If I *saw* them, I *would* tell them

(iii) **third conditional** (also called the ***would have*-condition**): involves a past perfect in the conditional clause, and *would have* in the main clause, e.g. If I *had seen* them, I *would have told them*

These are ordered in terms of the degree of likelihood that the condition can be fulfilled. This analysis is, however, a misleading oversimplification, as many other combinations are possible, e.g.

If you listen, you learn things

If you had paid attention, you would know

The former, which involves two *present tenses, is sometimes called the **present condition**.

●● **conditional tense**: Traditional grammarians often label *should/would* + *infinitive (e.g. *Should you wish to purchase the item, call us*) and *should/would* + *perfect infinitive (*Should you have done so already, please ignore this message*) as conditional *tenses. But this analysis is out of favour today. This term is also applied to the modal *past forms of *verbs, as in *If he ate it, he would be very ill* (cf. second conditional above), and to the *were* *subjunctive, as in *If he were to come, we would have a party*.

See also ALTERNATIVE CONDITIONAL-CONCESSIVE CLAUSE; CONDITION; UNIVERSAL CONDITIONAL-CONCESSIVE CLAUSE.

conditioning The phenomenon whereby a *modification is brought about in a unit (*word, *phrase, etc.) by virtue of the (grammatical) context. For example, the *indefinite article takes the form *an* when it precedes a word that begins with a vowel, and *pronouns change their *case (1) *inflection depending on their grammatical *function (1) (cf. *I saw him; He saw me*).

When a *variant is not modified in this way it is said to be **unconditioned**.

● **conditioned**.

See also FREE VARIATION; VARIANT.

congruence *Linguistics*. Correspondence between different *levels of linguistic analysis, e.g. the levels of syntax and semantics.

There are many consistent relationships between *form and *meaning. For example, many abstract *nouns are *non-count. However, there are also cases where a direct correspondence is absent. Thus in the following example in many analyses the italicized noun phrase is regarded as the grammatical *direct object of the *verb *expect*, even though semantically it is the *agent of the verb *open*:

I expect *the caretaker* to open the door by 9 a.m.

● **congruent**: exhibiting congruence.

conjoin (*v.*) Join (two or more, usually equal, units); *coordinate.

For grammarians who use this term, **conjoining** roughly corresponds to *coordination. **Conjoined clauses** result in *compound sentences.

(*n.*) (In CGEL.) An item (*word, *phrase, or *clause) coordinated with another, e.g.

boys and *girls*
by hook or *by crook*
We laughed and *we cried*

conjoint (In CGEL.) A *coordinated structure, containing two or more *conjoins. The parts (*conjoins*) are thus distinguished from the whole (*conjoint*).

conjugate Provide the different *inflectional forms of a *verb in a *paradigm.

This traditional term is not now considered applicable to English. It is more commonly used in connection with *inflected languages like Latin or French that have forms varying in accordance with *person and *number to a much greater extent than in English.

See also CONJUGATION.

Compare DECLINE; DECLENSION.

conjugation

1. A connected scheme of all the *inflectional forms of a *verb; a division of the verbs of a language according to the general differences of inflection.

2. The class into which verbs are put according to the exact forms of inflectional variation, usually called first, second, etc. conjugation. Also called **conjugational class** or **verbal inflection class**.

1841 R. G. LATHAM The Praeterite Tense of the Weak Verbs is formed by the addition of *d* or *t* . . . The Verbs of the Weak Conjugation fall into Three Classes.

Neither sense is in current use for English grammar.

See also CONJUGATE; PARADIGM.

Compare DECLINE; DECLENSION.

conjugational class *See* CONJUGATION.

conjunct

1. An *adverbial with a joining (or connective) *function (2), often that of joining a *clause or *sentence to an earlier clause or sentence. Popularly called *connector.

Conjuncts have a variety of meanings, including (i) listing, (ii) reinforcement, (iii) *result, and (iv) *concession, e.g.

(i) *First of all*, I'd like to thank all those people who sent in comments.

(ii) *Moreover* (or *Above all*), I owe a debt of gratitude to my parents.

(iii) I would like, *therefore*, to close this meeting.

(iv) I must, *nevertheless*, point out that it will affect your credit rating.

In some analyses of *adverbials (e.g. CGEL) conjuncts contrast with *adjuncts, *disjuncts, and (sometimes) *subjuncts. In analyses that do not use these labels, or make different distinctions, conjuncts (roughly as defined here) are called **structural conjunctives**, or **conjunctive/connective/discourse/linking adjuncts** (or **adverb(ial)s**).

2. Another word for a *conjoin, i.e. a unit joined to another by a *coordinator.

conjunction

1. A *word used to join words, *phrases, *clauses, or *sentences.

The conjunction is one of the generally recognized *word classes (parts of speech). Two main types are generally distinguished:

Coordinating conjunctions (also called *coordinators) join units of 'equal' status:

free *and* easy

poor *but* honest

speak now *or* forever hold your peace

Subordinating conjunctions (also called *subordinators) introduce *subordinate clauses, e.g. *although, because, if, since, when*, etc.

Conjunctions consisting of two or more words are called *complex conjunctions (e.g. *as if, as soon as, assuming (that), but that, in case, in that*). Those that formally resemble other *word classes are sometimes labelled accordingly, e.g.

adverbial conjunctions: *immediately, now* (e.g. *Immediately I hear, I'll let you know*)

verbal conjunctions: *assuming* (*that*), *granted* (*that*)

nominal conjunctions: *every time, the moment* (e.g. *The moment he comes, I'll let you know*)

2. Joining together, juxtaposition.

This is a very general term, but is sometimes narrowed down and contrasted with *disjunction.

1976 R. HUDDLESTON The term 'conjoining' will sometimes be found in place of coordination; coordination with *and* and *or* are often distinguished as 'conjunction' and 'disjunction' respectively (with 'conjunction' here used in the logician's sense, rather than the traditional grammarian's, for whom it denotes a class of words).

conjunction group (In *Systemic Grammar.) A *word *group consisting of a *conjunction and *modifier(s), e.g. *and so, even if, not until*.

conjunctive

1. (*n. & adj.*) (A *word or *phrase) functioning in the same way as a *conjunction or *conjunct, or having some other similar function.

•• **conjunctive adjunct**: the same as *conjunct. *See also* sense **3.** below.

2. The same as *subjunctive, but mostly used to describe classical languages such as Latin and Greek.

3. In *Systemic Grammar the term refers to a *cohesive word that operates at the textual level.

2014 M. A. K. HALLIDAY & C. MATTHIESSEN [C]onjunctive Adjuncts are textual—they set up a contextualizing relationship obtaining between the clause as a message and some other (typically preceding) portion of text.

connective (*n. & adj.*) (A *word or other linguistic device) serving to link linguistic units.

*Conjunctions and/or *conjuncts are classed as connectives. *Linking (or *copular) *verbs are also sometimes included.

• **connectivity**.

•• **connective adjunct**: *see* CONJUNCT.

•• **connective device**: a linguistic means of binding a *text together; a term covering *coherence and *cohesion.

Compare COORDINATION.

connector The same as *conjunct.

connotation *Semantics*. An additional meaning that a *word (or other linguistic unit) evokes by virtue of personal or cultural associations, in contrast to its *denotation.

Connotation is peripheral compared with 'dictionary meaning', and is considerably dependent on subjective judgement. For example, the connotations of *police* for some people may be 'reliable', 'helpful', 'protectors of law and order', 'the front line against crime', etc. For others, the connotations may be 'harassment', 'breathalysers', 'arrests', 'water cannon', etc.

- **connotational**, **connotative**: pertaining to, or involving, connotation. Connotative meaning is related to *attitudinal meaning.

   See also ATTITUDINAL; COMMUNICATIVE; CONATIVE; DESCRIPTIVE; EMOTIVE; INTERPERSONAL MEANING; PROPOSITIONAL MEANING; REFERENTIAL MEANING.

consecutive Expressing consequence or *result.
** **consecutive clause**: (an older name for) a result *clause.

constative *See* PERFORMATIVE.

constituent A linguistic unit that forms part of a larger structure.

   A very general term, which can cover *morphemes (1), *words, *phrases, and *clauses as parts of larger units.

   See also IMMEDIATE CONSTITUENT.
- **constituency**: the relationship of a linguistic unit to another unit of which it forms a part.
** **constituent order**: the order in which *constituents are arranged in *sentences and clauses. This term is to be preferred to *word order.
** **constituent command (c-command)**: In *Government-Binding Theory this is a technical term to designate a dominance relationship between units in a sentence, related to the traditional notion of *government.

construct (In older grammar.) (*v.*) Combine *words, *phrases, and/or *clauses, etc. grammatically into a larger structure; form into a *construction. For instance, *rely* is constructed with a *prepositional phrase. the *head of which is *on*.

   (*n.*) A rare term variously used for *collocation or *construction.

construction

   1. A conventional pairing of a particular syntactic structure or *pattern with a *meaning. The term is not always defined precisely, and different concatenations of linguistic elements can be said to qualify as constructions:

   *noun + noun (e.g. *wind energy*)
   *determinative (1) + noun (e.g. *the street*)
   *subject + *verb + *direct object (e.g. *I heard her voice*)
   *preposition + *noun phrase + preposition (e.g. *by means of*)
   verb + noun phrase + *to-infinitive (e.g. (*They*) *want me to come*)
   It + be + noun phrase + *who/that-* *clause (e.g. *It was the milkman who rang the doorbell*)

   In some theories, e.g. *Generative Grammar (2), the notion of construction is discarded.

1995 N. CHOMSKY The notion of grammatical construction [can be] eliminated, and with it, construction-particular rules. Constructions such as verb phrase, relative clause, and passive remain only as taxonomic artifacts, collections of phenomena explained through the interaction of the principles of UG, with the values of parameters fixed.

See also CONSTRUCTION GRAMMAR; SYNTAGM.

2. The process of creating constructions as defined in (1).

1755 S. JOHNSON *Construction . . .* the putting of words, duly chosen, together in such a manner as is proper to convey a complete sense.

- **constructional**.
- **constructional relation:** *See* RELATION.

Construction Grammar A cover term for a number of linguistic frameworks in which *constructions, defined as conventionalized pairings of structures with meanings, are *primitive. By contrast, practitioners of *Chomskyan linguistics and some other theoretical frameworks regard constructions as epiphenomenal (*See* CONSTRUCTION).

2006 A. GOLDBERG What makes a theory that allows constructions to exist 'a construction-based theory' is the idea that the network of constructions captures our grammatical knowledge of language *in toto*, i.e. **it's constructions all the way down**. [emphasis in original]

construe (In traditional grammar.)

1. The same as the verb *construct.

1902 *New English Dictionary* All the verbs and adjectives which are or have been construed with *of*.

2. Analyse the syntax of (a sentence).

Neither meaning is common in modern grammar.

contact clause A term introduced in Jespersen (1909–49) to denote a *relative clause joined to a *noun without any connecting word.

1970 B. M. H. STRANG Contact-clauses are ancient structures of independent origin, not just relatives with pronouns left out . . . At the beginning of II [the period 1570–1770] . . . they were still extensively used where the 'relative' had subject function, as in Shakespeare's *I see a man here needs not liue by shifts*. This is ambiguous . . . There was good reason for confining the structure to object relations, where there is no ambiguity (as in Defoe, *the same trade she had followed in Ireland*): since the 18c this limitation has been customary.

1. Normally: a defining *clause in which the relative *pronoun, if it were overt, would function as *object of the *verb, or of a deferred *preposition.

the woman *I love* > the woman *whom I love*
a crisis *we could have done without* > a crisis *that we could have done without*
a problem *you know about* > a problem *which you know about*

Similar contact clauses are possible in which the relative word can also express time, cause, or manner:

The moment *I saw it*, I knew it was mine > The moment *that/when I saw it . . .*
The reason *I asked* was that I needed to know > The reason *that/why I asked . . .*
This is the way *you should do it* > This is the way *that you should do it*

But when the relative word expresses place, the use is possibly non-standard, e.g.

?This is the exact place *Latimer and Ridley were burnt* > This is the exact place *where . . .*

2. More rarely, a relative clause in which the relative pronoun, if it were overt, would function as the *subject; e.g.

Who was it *said 'Inside every fat man there's a thin one trying to get out'*? > Who was it *who said . . .*
There's someone at the door *says you know him* > There's someone at the door *who says . . .*
There's a guy *works down the chip shop swears he's Elvis* (pop song) > There's a guy *who works down the chip shop who swears . . .*

Compare APO KOINOU.

contamination The process by which two more or less synonymous linguistic *forms are blended by accident or through confusion, so as to produce a new form.

The process occurs in speech owing to hesitation between two semantically similar forms. Examples of such words that appear to have arisen spontaneously (though they would now be used, if at all, self-consciously) include *insinuendo* and *portentious*.

The term was first used in English by the translator of Herman Paul's works on language.

1988 V. ADAMS We should perhaps distinguish . . . between the contamination which arises because words are imperfectly known, or unfamiliar, and that resulting from 'slips of the tongue'. The dialectal examples appear to represent the former; it is the latter kind of contamination which Paul is defining.

Compare BLEND.

contemporary English *See* MODERN ENGLISH.

content clause A term introduced by Otto Jespersen which is used in a number of recent grammars of English, e.g. CaGEL and OMEG, to denote certain types of finite *subordinate clauses which are often syntactically similar to *main clauses.

Content clauses introduced by *that* are *declarative content clauses which can function in various ways, e.g. as *subject or *direct object:

> *That he can have simply disappeared* is unbelievable
> I don't believe (*that*) *the police made a thorough search*

The following examples involve *interrogative and *exclamative content clauses:

> I really don't see *what you mean*
> She knows *what a good teacher you are*

In other frameworks (e.g. CGEL) content clauses are analysed as *nominal clauses.

content disjunct An *adverbial that comments on the content of a *proposition, in contrast to a *style disjunct. Also called **attitudinal disjunct**. Example:

> *Regrettably*, nobody bothered to tell them

content word A word with a statable meaning, as listed in a dictionary. Also called **lexical word** or *full word; contrasted with *grammatical word (1).

Content words include most *open (1) class words—*nouns, *verbs, *adjectives, and *adverbs. The distinction between content and grammatical words is blurred, rather than rigid.

See also GRADIENCE.

context

1. The same as *co-text.

2. When reference is made only, or predominantly, to the non-linguistic *situation in which an *utterance is made (who is addressing whom, whether formally or informally, why, for what purpose, when, where, etc.), we speak of the **context of situation** (also called **situational context** or *extralinguistic context). This can be an important factor in interpreting the full *meaning of utterances, as opposed to only the *truth-conditional meaning. Although some 'texts' are complete in themselves, others rely heavily on the extralinguistic situation for the interpretation of *pronouns, *adverbials (e.g. *here, there, now, then, yesterday*), and *tenses. The term context of situation was first used widely in English by the social anthropologist Bronislaw Malinowski.

• **contextual**. *Compare* TEXTUAL.

   See also CONTEXT-FREE; CONTEXT-SENSITIVE.

context-free (In *Generative Grammar.) Applicable in any *context.

   A **context-free rule** is one that is theoretically applicable in all linguistic contexts, with no exclusions or *variants. A **context-free grammar** is a grammar containing rules only of this simple type.

   See also CONTEXT-SENSITIVE.

context-sensitive (In *Generative Grammar.) Applicable only in certain specified *contexts. Also called **context-dependent**.

   Context-sensitive contrasts with *context-free. Rules for the formation of English *noun *plurals need to be context-sensitive, so that plurals with –*es* and such *irregular forms as *men*, *teeth*, etc. are accurately generated.

contingency A *situation (event, state of affairs, etc.) dependent on another situation.

   This term is used in some analyses of the meaning of *adverbials as an umbrella term for *cause, *condition, *concession, *purpose, *reason, and *result.

•• **clause of contingency** (or **contingent clause**): a *clause that expresses contingency.

continuative

   1. A label applied to one of the uses of the *present perfect. (see *continuative* PRESENT PERFECT)

   2. The term is sometimes used to describe elements of a small group of linguistic items that are used to extend a conversation, e.g. *oh, well, right*.

•• **continuative relative clause**: *See* RELATIVE.

   Compare RESTRICTIVE; *sentential* RELATIVE. *clause*

continuous (tense) The same as *progressive (*tense). A term used in the domain of English Language Teaching.

•• **present continuous (tense)**: the same as present progressive (tense).

•• **past continuous (tense)**: the same as past progressive (tense).

contract Shorten (a *word, syllable, etc.) by omitting or combining some elements.

   1884 *New English Dictionary Ain't* . . . A contracted form of *are not*.., used also for *am not*, in the popular dialect of London and elsewhere.

•• **contracted form**: the same as *contraction (2).

contraction

1. The action of shortening a *word, syllable, etc. by omitting and combining elements.

2. A shortened form of a word that can be attached to another word (usually as an *enclitic); the two words together. Also called **abbreviated form**, **contracted form**, or **short form**.

Thus both *'m* and *I'm* are described as contractions. Other contractions in English are:

's (= is/has)   *'re* (= are)   *'ve* (= have)
'd (= had/would)   *'ll* (= will)   *n't* (= not)

Compare CLIPPING; REDUCTION.

contradictory (*n. & adj.*) *Semantics*. The term is applied to *propositions: they are said to be contradictory when they cannot both be true or both be false at the same time, e.g. *My father is older than my mother* and *My father is younger than my mother*.

Two words that are opposite in meaning to another are called contradictories, e.g. *life/death* and *male/female*, though the more usual label is *complementary.

contrafactive Designating either a *verb followed by a *complement clause which expresses a *proposition that is contrary to fact, or a proposition that is contrary to fact. Thus in:

I wish (that) I knew the answer
I'll pretend (that) I know

the verbs *wish* and *pretend* are **contrafactive verbs** (or **contrafactives**), and the propositions following them are **contrafactive propositions**.

Compare COUNTERFACTUAL; FACTIVE; FACTUAL.

contrastive

1. Of *clauses, *conjunctions, *conjuncts, etc.: expressing a discrepancy or contrast, typically between what is expressed in a *main clause and an associated *subordinate clause, or between what is expressed in a particular *sentence and a preceding one.

•• **contrastive clauses** (also called **clauses of contrast**; sometimes classified with *concessive clauses): these are introduced by **contrastive conjunctions** such as *whereas*, *while*, *whilst*, e.g.

I adore jazz, *whereas* my husband prefers classical music

•• **contrastive conjuncts**: these are *conjuncts that express a contrast, such as *alternatively*, *by contrast*, *however*, *rather*, *more accurately*, e.g.

The Germans won four medals. *By contrast,* the Russians won twenty-six.

2. contrastive analysis, contrastive grammar, contrastive linguistics: the comparative study of two or more languages, especially from the point of view of translation or foreign language teaching.

Contrastive analysis is *synchronic.

Compare COMPARATIVE LINGUISTICS; HISTORICAL LINGUISTICS.

• **contrastivity**.

control In *Generative Grammar (2) the unexpressed *subject in the bracketed *subordinate clause of the first example below (indicated by 'Ø') is said to be **controlled** by the subject of the *matrix clause (**subject control**). (The subscript 'i' indicates *co-reference.) In the second example we have **object control**, and in the final example we have **arbitrary control**, i.e. there is no controller present in the linguistic *context. This kind of linkage is regulated by a component of the grammar called **Control Theory**.

I$_i$ tried [Ø$_i$ to leave]

I$_i$ persuaded Dawn$_i$ [Ø$_i$ to leave]

[Ø$_i$ To see Rome in the spring] is a wonderful experience

See also ATTACHMENT RULE.

conversational implicature *See* IMPLICATURE.

conversational maxims The same as the *maxims of conversation.

See COOPERATIVE PRINCIPLE, THE.

Conversational Principle, the The same as the *Cooperative Principle.

converse (*n. & adj.*) *Semantics*. (Designating) one of a pair of relationally opposite *words.

Converses are a particular type of *antonym; e.g. *buy/sell, husband/wife, learn/teach*.

Compare BINARY; COMPLEMENTARY.

conversion A *word formation (2) process by which a word belonging to one *word class is assigned to another word class without the addition of an *affix. (Also called **reclassification** or **functional shift**.) Sometimes regarded as part of *derivation.

Words produced by conversion are mainly *nouns, *verbs, and *adjectives. Conversion is a very old process in English, as the date range of the examples given below shows:

Nouns from verbs: *a bounce* (E16), *a meet* (M19), *a retread* (E20), *a swim* (M16; M18 in current sense)

Verbs from nouns: *to fingerprint* (E20), *to highlight* (M20), *to holiday* (M19), *to mob* (M17), *to necklace* (E18; L20 in current sense)

Adjectives from nouns: *average* (L18), *chief* (ME), *commonplace* (E17), *cream* (M19), *damp* (L16; E18 in current sense), *game* (plucky; E18)

An unusual recent conversion is the use of *plus*, already a *preposition and noun, as a colloquial *conjunction:

10% bonus offer until 31st December, *plus* you'll get a mystery present

Minor types of conversion include conversions of *closed (1) class words (e.g. *the ins and outs, the whys and wherefores*); of *affixes (e.g. *So you've got an ology, isms and wasms*); and arguably even of whole phrases (e.g. *his prolier-than-thou protestations*).

A distinction is sometimes made between **full conversion**, as here, and **partial conversion**. In the latter a word takes on only some of the characteristics of the new word class. Uses of adjectives in *constructions like *the poor, the handicapped* are cited as examples of partial conversion, since they do not permit marking for *plural or *countability (**six poors*, **a handicapped*; but compare *Olympic hopefuls*). However, this analysis is disputed by other grammarians, who prefer to treat such *usage as involving either an adjective functioning as the *head of a *noun phrase, or a noun phrase with an *empty (2) *head.

co-occur Of linguistic units: that are positioned together, though not necessarily adjacent.

This term and *co-occurrence were introduced by the American linguist Zellig Harris (1951).

Compare COLLIGATION.

co-occurrence The *syntagmatic occurrence of two or more linguistic units in juxtaposition (or close proximity), as *licensed by the *rules of grammar and/or the rules of the *lexicon.

For example, a verb like *devour* must be followed by a *direct object: we can say *I devoured a sweet*, but not **I devoured*. Similarly, the grammar of English stipulates that the *perfect auxiliary *have* must occur with a *past participle:

have done, have seen

and not with a *simple past (3) verb form:

**have did, *have saw*

Such limitations are called **co-occurrence restrictions, co-occurrence relations**, or **co-occurrence rules**.

Compare COLLIGATION; SELECTIONAL RESTRICTION.

Cooperative Principle, the *Pragmatics.* An unspoken code of communicative behaviour guaranteeing that speakers are truthful, informative, relevant, and lucid, especially in conversation. (Also called **the Conversational Principle**.)

The concept derives from influential work by the philosopher H. P. Grice (1913–88). He suggested that, in general, speakers cooperate by adhering to four **maxims of conversation**: the **Maxim of Quality**, the **Maxim of Quantity**, the **Maxim of Relevance**, and the **Maxim of Manner**. Of course, speakers sometimes lie or deliberately mislead, but the Cooperative Principle is so strong that people usually try to make sense of what they hear.

See also IMPLICATURE; RELEVANCE THEORY.

coordinate (*v.*) (Pronounced /kəʊˈɔːdɪneɪt/.) Join (linguistic units of equal status), commonly by means of a *coordinator.
• **coordinating correlative**: *See* CORRELATIVE.

(*adj.*) (Pronounced /kəʊˈɔːdɪnət/.) Of a linguistic unit: joined to another of equal status, as in **coordinate clause**; contrasted with *subordinate.

(*n.*) (Pronounced /kəʊˈɔːdɪnət/.) One of the constituent parts of a coordination structure. The same as *conjoin.

See also COORDINATION.

coordinating conjunction *See* COORDINATOR.

coordination The joining together of two or more units, called *conjoins, at the same hierarchical syntactic level, usually by means of a *coordinator. Also called **conjoining**.

The units so joined may be anything from single *words (e.g. *knife and fork, poor but honest, double or quits*) to *clauses (as in *compound sentences).

Some grammarians include under the term coordination structures that lack a coordinator (which could be supplied), called *asyndetic co-ordination (e.g. *juice, tea, coffee, milk*). The more usual type of coordination, with a conjunction, is then termed *syndetic coordination. When several coordinators are used, we speak of **polysyndetic coordination** (e.g. *juice and tea and coffee and milk*).

See also COMBINATORY COORDINATION; CONJUNCTION; MULTIPLE COORDINATION; PSEUDO-COORDINATION; SEGREGATORY COORDINATION; SUBORDINATION.

coordinator Also called **coordinating conjunction**. The main (or *central) coordinators are *and, but,* and *or.* Other items share certain

characteristics with *subordinators and *conjuncts, but differ in other
ways.

See also MARGINAL COORDINATOR.

copula A *verb that links a *subject with a subject-related predicative
*complement, especially the verb *be*. Often used interchangeably with
*linking verb or **copular verb**.
- **copular, copulative**: functioning as a copula.
- ●● **copular verb**: a verb that functions as a copula.
- ●● **copulative compound**: *see* DVANDVA.

core *See* COMMON CORE.

co-refer Of *words: have shared or identical *reference.

> 1980 E. K. BROWN & J. E. MILLER The sentence [i.e. *John thinks that he is
> intelligent*] has two possible readings ... depending on whether *John* and *he*
> are used to refer to the same individual, or co-refer, or refer to different
> individuals.

See also CO-REFERENCE.

co-reference A relationship between two linguistic units such that
they *co-refer, i.e. denote the same *referent in the extralinguistic context.

With co-reference, often indicated by subscript *indices, two
expressions refer to the same person or thing in the world, e.g.

> $Simon_i$ said that he_i would help

(though note that in this example, *he* can also refer to some other male
individual).

Co-reference is often achieved through the use of *pro-forms, but is to
be distinguished from *substitution. In the latter the pro-form stands for
another *word, *phrase, etc., e.g.

> I bought a new laptop, and Leo *did so* too (i.e. and Leo *bought a new laptop*
> too)

Co-reference may have effects on *sentence grammar. For example, a
sentence containing a *reflexive or *reciprocal pronoun as *direct object,
i.e. a direct object which is co-referential with the subject of the sentence,
cannot be *passivized:

> We could hardly see each other in the fog ~ *Each other could hardly be seen
> in the fog

Co-reference is one of the phenomena dealt with under the heading
of *binding in *Government-Binding Theory.
- **co-referential, co-referentiality**.

core modal The same as *central modal.

corpus (Plural corpuses, corpora.) A collection of authentic spoken and/or written *texts.

The study of the English language has been transformed in recent decades by the collection of large quantities of authentic texts in corpora on which grammatical, pragmatic, lexicographic, historical, etc. analyses can be based.

●● **corpus-based**: Research that is corpus-based is deductive in outlook in that it uses (annotated) corpora to test hypotheses about language.

●● **corpus-driven**: Research that is corpus-driven is inductive in outlook and takes unannotated corpus data as the starting point for investigation.

●● **corpus linguistics**: a methodological approach to the study of language by means of corpora, now usually in computerized form.

See also NEO-FIRTHIAN; SURVEY OF ENGLISH USAGE, THE.

'correct' grammar *See* CORRECTNESS.

correctness Grammatical *acceptability according to the *rules.

Traditionally, grammar was thought to be concerned with *prescriptive rules stating what is, and is not, 'correct' usage. Present-day linguists try to provide a *descriptive outlook on grammar, and tend to avoid the term *correctness*. However, this attitude is arguably somewhat disingenuous, since even the most permissive description must be based on some decisions about what to include.

Compare ACCEPTABILITY; GRAMMATICAL.

correlative (*n.*) (One of) a pair of elements that join two similar parts of a *phrase, *clause, or *sentence.

(*adj.*) That is a correlative; made up of, or joined by, correlatives.

●● **coordinating correlatives**: these include:

both . . . and
either . . . or
neither . . . nor
not only . . . but also

●● **subordinating correlatives**: these include:

hardly . . . when
if . . . then
so/such . . . that
less/more . . . than

correspondence A systematic syntactic relationship between two structures, which is matched by a *meaning relationship.

A correspondence of this kind exists between an *active sentence containing a *direct object (e.g. *Everyone watched the eclipse*) and its *passive counterpart with the former object now the *subject (e.g. *The eclipse was watched by everyone*).

cosubordination A term used to describe a *subordinate clause which is *dependent in some sense (e.g. it cannot stand on its own), but not *embedded. The italicized clause in the following example instantiates the phenomenon:

If Leigh likes the food, he can come for lunch next week

See also GRADIENCE; SUBORDINATION.

co-text The larger *text in which another (portion of) text appears without reference to the circumstances, location, *situation, etc. in which the larger text is used, i.e. without reference to the *context of situation.

count Designating a *noun that can be used with numerical values.
•• **count noun** (also called *countable noun): contrasts with *uncount, **uncountable**, or **non-count noun**.

Count nouns usually have different *singular and *plural forms (*book/ books*, *child/children*), and when used in the singular must be preceded by a *determinative (1): *a/this/that book*; not * *I bought book*.

In the plural, count nouns have the potential for combining with certain determinatives (1), some of them exclusive to the plural, e.g. *few, many, these*.

The binary division of *common nouns into count and uncount poses a few problems: some nouns belong to both categories, whereas others do not neatly fit either category.

See MASS; PLURAL.

countable (*n. & adj.*) (Designating) a *noun with *singular and *plural forms. *See also* COUNT.

A term introduced by Otto Jespersen.
• **countability**.

counterfactual Of a *conditional *construction: relating to an unreal or hypothetical situation (i.e. one contrary to fact), in contrast to a real condition. Thus

If Henry had been on that plane, he would have been killed

is counterfactual, since the person referred to as Henry was not on the plane and was not killed.

Compare CONTRAFACTIVE.
See also FACTUAL.

counter-intuitive Contrary to what would be expected intuitively.

A term sometimes used in (grammatical) analysis. For example, it is counter-intuitive to suppose that *active clauses are derived from *passive ones, or that *affirmative clauses are derived from *negative ones.

The term was introduced in by Noam Chomsky.

courtesy subjunct *See* SUBJUNCT.

covert subjunctive *See* SUBJUNCTIVE.

creativity The ability of the native speakers of a language to produce and to understand an infinite number of *sentences of their language, many of which they have never produced or heard before.

creole *Sociolinguistics*. A *pidgin that has become a mother tongue.

Though definitions vary, a creole is typically the first language of a speech community, and so has greater lexical and syntactic complexity than a pidgin.

> 2008 J. SIEGEL Like any other vernacular language, a creole has a full lexicon and a complex set of grammatical rules, and is not at all restricted in use, having a complete range of informal functions.

As with any language, there are usually several varieties, but they can generally be distinguished according to their closeness to the language on which they are based. *See* ACROLECT; BASILECT; HYPERLECT; MESOLECT.

Most creoles have developed from contact between a European language (especially English, French, or Portuguese) and another (often African) language. But the process of *creolization is not straightforward, and most English-based creoles and pidgins contain certain words of Portuguese origin, such as West African *palava* 'trouble' from Portuguese *palavra* 'word'.

English-based creoles are found in the Caribbean—the most widely spoken being Jamaican Creole—and in other ex-colonial territories.

creolize Make into a creole.

● **creolization**.

> 1980 R. A. HUDSON There is no research evidence of changes which have happened during creolisation which cannot be matched by changes to a pidgin without native speakers.

●● **creolized language**: a *creole.

cumulative exponence *See* EXPONENCE.

current *See* LINKING VERB.

current relevance A concept often invoked in explaining the *meaning of the present *perfect in contrast to the *past tense.

For example, *My employer has raised my salary* might be uttered in preference to *My employer raised my salary* in a situation in which the rise in salary has only just become known. Similarly, *My grandmother has lived in Oxford all her life* means that she is still alive and living in Oxford. (Compare: *She lived in Oxford all her life*.) The concept, however, is not easy to pin down, and certainly past tenses can also have present effects or results (e.g. *I crashed the car yesterday—so I can't drive over to see you today*).

dangling modifier The same as *hanging participle.

dangling participle The same as *hanging participle.

dative (*n. & adj.*)

1. (Designating) a *case (1) *inflection carried by *nouns and *pronouns (*noun phrases) that function as *indirect object, or express a *recipient role in some languages. English does not have a dative case inflection.

2. (In *Case Grammar.) (Expressing) the *semantic role taken by the noun (or noun phrase) referring to the person or other *animate being 'affected' by the action expressed by the *verb. The *referent may be the grammatical *subject or *object of traditional grammar. For example, in Case Grammar, *Tom* is a dative in both the following sentences:

Tom was attacked by the dog

We forced Tom to listen

In some formulations of Case Grammar it is said that in a phrase such as *Tom's chin*, Tom has a dative role (because the chin 'belongs to' Tom). The dative case was later renamed *experiencer. The dative of Case Grammar is not equivalent to the semantic role carried by an indirect object, which is *recipient or *beneficiary.

•• **ethic(al) dative** (or **dative of advantage**): a dative that refers to a person or entity that has an interest in the meaning expressed by a verb.

de-adjectival Of a *word: derived from an *adjective.

De-adjectival *nouns are common, e.g. *falsehood* (ME) from *false*, *kindness* (ME) from *kind*, *subsidiarity* (M20) from *subsidiary*.

declaration

1. An *utterance that makes a *statement.

2. An utterance which by the mere virtue of being said brings about a result (also called *performative). This is a specialist term from *speech act theory for a particular type of *illocutionary act, e.g. *I declare the meeting closed; You're fired.* *Verbs in such utterances are called *performative verbs.

See also ILLOCUTION.

declarative

(*n.*)

1. A *clause type with an unmarked *word order in which the *subject precedes the *verb, typically used for making *statements. Declarative is a formal syntactic category, whereas statement is a category of *usage (though in some frameworks it is the other way round). Clauses that are declarative in form can be used not only to make (pragmatic) statements, but also to ask *questions (*You understand what you're doing?*) or to give orders (*You will report back to me tomorrow*). These are examples of indirect *speech acts.

2. (*n.*) (In *speech act theory.) A verb that makes a *declaration (2).

(*adj.*)

1. Of a clause: that is formally a declarative.

•• **declarative mood**: an alternative term for *indicative mood.

•• **declarative question**: *see* INTERROGATIVE; QUESTION.

Compare EXCLAMATIVE; IMPERATIVE; INTERROGATIVE.

See also DECLARATION.

2. Of or pertaining to a *declaration (2), or to the verb used in making one.

1990 D. VANDERVEKEN The primitive declarative verb is 'declare', which names the illocutionary force of declaration. 'Declare'... also has an assertive use, but in its declarative use it exemplifies the characteristic features of the set in that the speaker purely and simply makes something the case by declaring it is so.

declarative clause A clause that is formally a *declarative.

See also CLAUSE TYPE.

declarative question *See* INTERROGATIVE; QUESTION.

declension

1. The *variation (2) of the form of a *noun, *pronoun, or *adjective to show different *cases (1), such as *nominative, *accusative, and *dative, in the *singular and *plural.

2. The class into which such words are put according to the exact forms of this variation, usually called first, second, etc. declension. Also called **declensional class** or **nominal inflection class**.

The term is applicable to a language such as Latin, where nouns, pronouns, and adjectives are declined in this way, but not to English, where only six words (five *personal pronouns and *who*) show any case distinctions.

See also DECLINE.

Compare CONJUGATE; CONJUGATION; PARADIGM.

declensional class *See* DECLENSION.

decline *Inflect a *word (typically a *noun) through different *case (1) forms; supply the case forms of an element in the form of a *paradigm.

See also DECLENSION.

Compare CONJUGATE; CONJUGATION.

deep structure In earlier versions of *Generative Grammar (2) the deep structure of a *sentence is an (abstract) representation of its syntactic *structure, reflecting its *meaning (to various degrees, as the theory developed). It can be transformed into a *surface structure. In some cases the deep and surface structures are identical; in other cases one or more *transformations are applied.

Deep structures can be used to explain the way in which sentences are interpreted. A classic example from the early theory was an *ambiguous sentence such as *Visiting aunts can be boring*, which was said to have two different deep structures depending on whether it means 'going to visit one's aunts can be boring' or 'aunts who visit (or when visiting) can be boring'. Each of these two interpretations was supposed to have its own syntactic representation in deep structure. Similarly, two sentences with identical surface structures such as *John is eager to please* and *John is easy to please* have different deep structures. Conversely, an *active and *passive pair of sentences, with different surface structures, were said to have the same deep structure, e.g.

The dog bit the man

The man was bitten by the dog

Later versions of Generative Grammar (2) used the related, but not identical, concepts of **D-Structure** and **S-Structure**. In the current *Minimalist Program the levels of deep and surface structure have been abandoned.

More loosely, deep and surface structure are often used as terms in a simple binary opposition, with the deep structure representing meaning, and the surface structure being the actual sentence we see.

defective Of a *noun, *verb, etc.: incomplete, lacking a complete set of forms.

The *modal verbs in English can be described as being defective: they have only one form each (or at most two, if the pairs *will/would, can/could*, etc. are treated as belonging to the same *lexeme), since they lack *third person *singular and *non-finite forms.

Another defective verb is *beware*, which is used only as an *imperative, or as a *to*-infinitive:

Beware of the dog

I warned him to beware of the dog

See also PERIPHRASIS.

deferred preposition *See* STRANDED PREPOSITION.

defining Of *modification or a *modifier: that identifies or restricts
the meaning of the modified *head. Also called **restrictive**, **integrated**.
Contrasted with *non-defining (or *non-restrictive).

Various kinds of linguistic unit, including *adjectives and different kinds
of *postmodification, can have a defining or restrictive function. For
example, in *my blind friend*, the adjective may well be understood to
identify uniquely one particular friend. But in *my blind mother*, the
adjective is non-defining, because it merely adds some information about
my mother. Similarly, in the examples below the *non-finite clause and
the *prepositional phrase define the man in question:

The man *wearing a military uniform* is my uncle

The man *with all the gold braid* is my uncle

By contrast, the postmodification in the following examples is non-defining:

The British troops, *wearing bright red uniforms*, were an easy target

The Duke, *resplendent in his uniform*, led his army to victory

The terms defining and non-defining are, however, primarily applied to
*finite *relative clauses.

●● **defining relative clause** (also called **identifying relative clause**,
integrated relative clause, **restrictive relative clause**): a finite clause that
postmodifies a *noun and restricts its meaning:

News is not what a person *who doesn't care much about anything* wants to read

All the news *that's fit to print*

There are only two posh papers on a Sunday—the one *you're reading* and this
one

A defining relative clause is typically not separated from the noun it
modifies by a comma, and may sometimes, as in the third example, be
a *contact clause.

Compare ADNOMINAL, APPOSITIVE CLAUSE.

definite Of a linguistic form: having, or indicating, identifiable particular
or exclusive *reference. Contrasted with *indefinite.

● **definiteness**.

●● **definite article**: the *determinative (1) *the*, which is typically used
in a *noun phrase whose *referent has either just been mentioned (or
is implied), or is assumed to be familiar or uniquely identifiable in
some way.

I had to call a taxi. *The* driver couldn't find *the* house

The sun is out at last

I heard it on *the* radio

See also INDEFINITE ARTICLE.

*Determinatives (1) other than *the* can also make a noun phrase definite, e.g. *demonstrative *this* and *that*. All these items can collectively be labelled **definite determinatives** or **definite identifiers**. *Proper nouns are inherently definite (at least in context), and so are the *personal pronouns (*he*, *she*, etc.), in contrast to indefinite *somebody*, *something*.

Compare SPECIFIC.

•• **definite frequency**: *see* INDEFINITE.

•• **past definite** and **past indefinite**: these labels, as applied to *tense, are rarely used in English grammar, but in fact the simple *past tense does usually imply some definite point or period in the past, whereas some uses of the *present perfect have a more indefinite meaning.

I have spoken to my bank manager. In fact, I *spoke* to him again yesterday

degree

1. Each of the three points on the scale by which gradable *adjectives and *adverbs are compared; this scale as a feature of an adjective or adverb.

The three degrees are *absolute (1), *comparative, and *superlative:

great, greater, greatest
good, better, best
soon, sooner, soonest

Compare GRADABLE.

2. Indicating greater or lesser intensity, as one category of adverb meaning.

•• **adverb of degree**, **adverbial of degree**, **degree adverb**, **degree adverbial**: (usually) an adverb or *adverbial that expresses a *meaning indicating greater or lesser intensity, e.g. *much*, *quite*, *so*, *too*, *very*.

Degree is one of the traditional semantic categories into which *adverbs are divided, in contrast to *manner, *time (1), and *place, though not all grammarians use the term. Some modern grammarians prefer to use *intensifier more or less as a *synonym. Others make subtle distinctions between degree adverb, intensifier, and *emphasizer, sometimes differentiating them, sometimes making either degree adverb(ial) or intensifier the superordinate term.

See also DEGREE OF MODALITY.

degree of modality
Term referring to the extent to which a *statement, *clause, etc., is **modalized**, i.e. displays *modal meaning. Factual statements (*Today is Friday*) are **unmodalized**, whereas clauses with a clearly

identifiable modal meaning (typically expressed by modal verbs) display a high degree of modality.

See also KIND OF MODALITY; STRENGTH OF MODALITY.

deictic (*n. & adj.*) (A word) designating the semantic property of 'pointing', expressed lexically or grammatically, i.e. having the function of relating a *sentence or *utterance to its *extralinguistic *context (*time* (1), place, etc.).

The four *demonstratives are the prime deictic elements in English, with *this* and *these* pointing to what is *proximal in space or time, and *that* and *those* pointing to what is *distal in space or time. Other words commonly included in this category are *here, there, now, then, today, yesterday, tomorrow*, and the *personal pronouns (*I, we, you*, etc.). Tense is also a deictic category.

See also DEIXIS.

deixis The phenomenon of *lexical items or grammatical *constructions 'pointing' to *extralinguistic circumstances such as *time (1) and *place in relation to an *utterance, or the features of the language collectively that do this.

> 1977 J. LYONS The term 'deixis' . . . is now used in linguistics to refer to the function of personal and demonstrative pronouns, of tense and of a variety of other grammatical and lexical features which relate utterances to the spatiotemporal co-ordinates of the act of utterance.

See also DEICTIC.

deletion The process by which a *constituent in a particular *structure is omitted. Also called *ellipsis.

An example of this would be the deletion (or, perhaps better, omission) of the subject in *imperative clauses, e.g. *Wait here!*

•• **verb phrase deletion**: the deletion of a *verb phrase (2) under identity with a previous instance of it, e.g.

> All the children *enjoyed the outing*, and the parents too

delexical Of a *lexical item: having little or no (*referential) *meaning.

English sometimes uses a *verb + *object construction where a plain *intransitive verb could also be used. For example, instead of saying *I looked*, you can say *I had a look*; instead of *I'll think about it*, you can say *I'll give it some thought*. Verbs used in this way include *do, have, give, make*, and *take*, and when so used they retain little of their usual meaning. The main meaning is carried instead by the object *noun phrase. For this reason such verbs are often called *light verbs.

Compare GRAMMATICAL WORD.

delicacy The *scale determining the degree of detail in a grammatical analysis.

Delicacy is one of the three (or four) scales (*see* SCALE-AND-CATEGORY GRAMMAR) of *Systemic Grammar. At the primary degree of delicacy, clauses can be classified as free (roughly, *main or *superordinate) or *bound (2) (roughly, *subordinate). At the next degree of delicacy, they can be classified to show how distant they are from the *main clause, i.e. whether they are immediately *subordinate, or subordinate to another subordinate clause.

Compare DEPTH; EXPONENCE; RANK.

demonstrative (*n. & adj.*) (Designating) any of a set of *pronouns and *determinatives (1) when used to refer to people, *situations, entities, etc. that are in a particular spatial or temporal relationship with the speaker or writer.

•• **demonstrative adjective**: the traditional label for a *demonstrative determinative. A misnomer.

•• **demonstrative determinative**: any of the determinatives (1) *this*, *these*, *that*, and *those*, expressing either *proximal or *distal meaning, e.g.

We really need to repair *this* leak very soon
Those teachers know nothing about history

•• **demonstrative pronoun**: any of the pronouns *this*, *these*, *that*, and *those*, expressing either proximal or distal meaning, e.g.

This doesn't suit me, but I really like *those*
That was exciting!

In some models *this*, *these*, *that*, and *those* are regarded as belonging to either the pronoun class or to the determinative (1) class in all their uses.

denominal Of a *word: derived from a *noun.

Denominal nouns (nouns derived from other nouns) include many words formed by adding a *suffix to a noun: *booklet* (M19), *childhood* (OE), *gangster* (L19), *lectureship* (M17), *lioness* (ME), *mileage* (M18), *spoonful* (ME), *teenager* (M20), *villager* (L16).

Denominal *adjectives include words with pseudo-*participles, such as *red-eyed* (M17), along with words formed from a noun + suffix, e.g. *childish* (OE), *hopeless* (M16), *friendly* (OE).

Denominal *verbs include those formed with *prefixes and suffixes such as *be-* and *-ize*, e.g. *behead* (OE), *dynamize* (M19).

An older term for this was **denominative**.

denotation *Semantics.*

1. The primary (often literal) meaning of a *word, in contrast to its *connotation.

Denotation relates to generally definable 'dictionary' meanings. Thus the denotation of *(the) police* is 'the civil force of a state that is responsible for maintaining public order'.

● **denotative.**

●● **denotative.** meaning (or **denotational meaning**): this is also called *cognitive, *descriptive, or *referential meaning.

See also ATTITUDINAL MEANING; COMMUNICATIVE MEANING; CONATIVE; EMOTIVE; ILLOCUTIONARY MEANING; INTERPERSONAL MEANING.

Compare REFERENCE; SENSE.

2. The relationship between a word (or other linguistic unit) and its *referent(s), e.g. the relationship between the word *horse* and the set of all horses, or the totality of characteristics that apply to a particular entity (in the case of horses, all characteristics that define that animal). Similar to *extension.

deontic *Semantics*. Of or relating to the notions of *obligation, *permission, prohibition, etc., as applied to the uses and meanings of *modal verbs. Deontic modality is sometimes called **intrinsic modality**, or treated under the broad heading of *root modality, with the latter defined as any type of modality except *epistemic modality. Examples:

You *must* obey your parents

You *may* go now

You *shouldn't* mislead me

In the analysis of modal meaning and use, deontic modality is usually contrasted with epistemic modality. But some analysts make a three-way contrast, the third term being *alethic. Alternatively, the three-way contrast is between deontic, epistemic, and *dynamic (2) modality.

dependency The phenomenon of a linguistic entity being *dependent on another.

●● **dependency relation**: a relation between units where one unit is described as dependent on the other.

●● **dependency grammar**: a grammar or theoretical model that describes dependency relations, e.g. *Word Grammar, *valency grammar.

dependent (*n. & adj.*) (A linguistic unit) that is *subordinate to some other linguistic unit. Contrasted with *independent.

●● **dependent-auxiliary analysis**: a term used in CaGEL to refer to an analysis (not preferred by the authors of that book) of *auxiliary verbs as being dependent on a *main verb, much as in the traditional analysis in which auxiliaries are seen as 'helping verbs'. Contrasted with the *catenative-auxiliary analysis which the authors advocate.

•• **dependent element, phrase, clause**, etc.: any unit other than the *head within a *phrase, e.g. a *modifying phrase inside another phrase (*the dead rat*); a subordinate clause functioning as *complement of a verb (*I think that it's too late for coffee*), etc.

•• **dependent genitive**: *see* GENITIVE.

Compare EMBEDDED.

See also LEXICAL VERB; VERB.

depictive *See* RESULT.

depth In *Systemic Grammar, a scale (*see* SCALE-AND-CATEGORY GRAMMAR) measuring the degree of complexity of the analysis. Depth is sometimes handled as part of the scale of *delicacy.

derivation

   1. *Morphology*. The *word formation (2) process of forming a new *lexeme by adding an *affix to an existing lexeme; contrasted with *compounding (and sometimes *conversion). *See also* INFLECTION. Examples:

   alleviation (from *alleviate*)
   interference (from *interfere*)
   sub-editor (from *editor*)
   unhelpful (from *helpful*)

Derivation produces a new lexeme (e.g. *driver* from *drive*), whereas an inflectional suffix produces another form of the same word (e.g. *driven, driving, drives*).

   2. (In *Generative Grammar (2).) The process by which a *structure of one kind is formed (or *derived*) from another structure through the application of the appropriate *rules. As an example, in early theory a *passive sentence was said to be derived from an *active one (*see* TRANSFORMATION). In later theory both active and passive sentences are derived from more abstract representations.

• **derivational:** pertaining to, used in, or due to derivation.

•• **derivational suffix:** *see* SUFFIX.

See also: DERIVATIVE.

derivative *Morphology*.

   1. (*n. & adj.*). (A *lexeme) formed from another lexeme by a process of *derivation.

   2. (*adj.*) Of an *affix: used in derivation.

• **derivatively**.

•• **derivative base:** *see* BASE.

derive *Morphology*.

1. Of a *word etc.: descend from an earlier word in the same or another language.

Thus the *noun *denim* is derived from 17th-century *serge denim*, from French *serge de Nîmes* ('serge made in the town of Nîmes'); *atonement* derives from the *prepositional phrase *at one* + the suffix *-ment*.

2. Form a *lexeme from another lexeme by a process of *derivation (1).

3. (In *Generative Grammar (2).) obtain one *structure from another by applying certain *rules, *transformations, etc.; *see* DERIVATION (2).

descriptive

1. Of a *word, *phrase, etc.: ascribing a property to an entity.

•• **descriptive adjective**: an *adjective that ascribes a property to the *noun it *modifies, in contrast to a *limiting adjective (1). The latter is an old-fashioned term, since modern grammarians assign most so-called 'limiting adjectives' to a separate class of *determinatives (1).

•• **descriptive genitive**: a *genitive construction in which the genitive phrase has a describing function (also called *classifying genitive). Thus, in *a master's degree, a doll's house, ladies' shoes*, the genitive does not indicate 'possession', but rather describes the noun it modifies (cf. *a doctoral degree, a miniature house*).

•• **descriptive relative clause**: another term for *non-defining or *non-restrictive *relative clause.

•• **descriptive rule**: *see* RULE.

2. Describing the *structure and *usage of a language, usually at a particular point in time, avoiding comparisons with other languages or other historical periods, and free from social valuations. Contrasted with *prescriptive.

•• **descriptive linguistics**: a branch of linguistics that is concerned with describing the structure of a particular language at a particular time, in contrast with *historical or *comparative linguistics. Many modern grammarians aim to describe language as it is used in **descriptive grammars**, and avoid laying down idealized, unrealistic *rules, in contrast to the more *prescriptive aims of usage books.

See also DESCRIPTIVISM; LINGUISTICS; SYNCHRONIC LINGUISTICS.

3. *Semantics*. (In some classifications of *meaning.) **Descriptive meaning** is similar to *denotative, *cognitive, or *referential meaning. Contrasted with *attitudinal and *interpersonal meaning.

Compare IDEATIONAL.

See also COMMUNICATIVE MEANING; CONATIVE; CONNOTATION; EMOTIVE; ILLOCUTIONARY MEANING.

descriptivism An approach to (grammatical) linguistic analysis, characterized by a concern with describing a language objectively. The term is often applied to the American *structuralist school, which preceded *Generative Grammar (2), but also to modern grammatical frameworks.

• **descriptivist**.

descriptor A *word or expression used to describe or identify, often in combination with a *proper noun.

> 1985 R. QUIRK et al. Proper nouns often combine with descriptive words which we will call descriptors, and which also begin with a capital letter, to make composite names like *Senator Morse, Dallas Road.*

desententialization *See* SUBORDINATION.

destination *See* SOURCE (2).

determination The function of specifying what kind of *reference a *noun phrase has; as opposed to a function such as *modification.

> 1985 R. QUIRK et al. Determination. This term may be used for the function of words and (sometimes) phrases which, in general, determine what *kind of reference* a noun phrase has: for example, whether it is definite (like *the*) or indefinite (like *a/an*), partitive (like *some*) or universal (like *all*).

determinative

1. (*n.*) (in CaGEL.) A member of a mainly *closed class of *words that typically precede *nouns (or, strictly speaking, *noun phrase *heads) and limit their *meaning in some way. Determinatives in this sense mainly function as *determiners (1) in noun phrase structure. In CGEL the nomenclature is reversed: the word class label is determiner, whereas the function label is determinative. *See* DETERMINER (2).

Most determinatives are restricted by *number-related meaning as to the category of noun they can occur with, e.g.

many/few apples (*count plural)

but

much/little food (*uncount)

Determinatives can be classified from the point of view of meaning into a large number of categories such as *demonstrative (*this, that*), *degree (*few, little*), *existential (*any, some*), *free relative (*which, whatever*), and *interrogative (*which, what*). There is disagreement about how to analyse certain elements such as *my, your,* and *his* when these are placed before nouns. In some frameworks they are regarded as determinatives, in other frameworks as *pronouns.

Some grammars favour a twofold classification: one model groups all determinatives and *numbers as either *identifiers or *quantifiers (with *definite and *indefinite cutting across these groupings); another divides them, very differently, into general and *specific determinatives. The multiplicity of labels resulting from these different approaches can be confusing.

   2. (*n. & adj.*) (In CGEL.) (A word or *phrase) performing the *function (1) of *determination, typically inside noun phrases.

•• **determinative element**: (in CGEL) an element with a determinative function.

   See also DETERMINER.

determinative phrase (DP) (In CaGEL.) A *phrase headed by a *determinative (1) (conceived of as a *word class). For example, in the noun phrase *almost all people* the word *all* is a determinative which is *premodified by *almost*. These two words together form a DP inside the NP.

   Compare DETERMINER phrase.

   See also DETERMINER.

determiner

   1. (In CaGEL.) A *function (1) label used for a *word or *phrase performing the function of *determination, typically inside *noun phrases.

   2. (In CGEL.) A member of a mainly *closed class of words that typically precede nouns (or, strictly speaking, noun phrase *heads) and limit their *meaning in some way. Determiners mainly function as *determinatives (2) in noun phrase structure. In CaGEL the nomenclature is reversed: the word class label is determinative, whereas the function label is determiner. *See* DETERMINATIVE (1).

   CGEL distinguishes:

   *predeterminers, e.g. *all, both, half; double, twice,* etc.; *one-third,* etc.; *such, what*

   *central determiners, e.g. *a, an, the, this,* etc.; *my, our,* etc.; *every, each, no,* etc. *See also* CENTRAL (1).

   *postdeterminers, e.g. *few, many, much, little,* and the *cardinal and *ordinal numbers.

   The class is not entirely closed, given that, for example, numbers belong to an open-ended set.

   Determiners in this sense are sometimes called *limiting adjectives in traditional grammar. However, not only do they differ from the class of adjectives with regard to the kinds of meaning they convey, but they also differ *distributionally: they must normally precede ordinary adjectives in noun phrase structure, and there cannot normally be more than one determiner in a noun phrase (e.g. *the my book).

3. In some models determiner is used both as a *form (1) and *function (1) label.

See also DETERMINER PHRASE; DETERMINATIVE.

determiner phrase (DP) (In *Generative Grammar (2).) A *phrase headed by a *determiner (2) (conceived of as a *word class). Phrases traditionally analysed as *noun phrases are regarded as DPs in this framework. Thus the phrase *the computer* is a DP headed by *the*, not a noun phrase headed by *computer*.

Compare DETERMINATIVE PHRASE.

See also DETERMINATIVE.

deverbal (*n. & adj.*) (A *word) derived from a *verb.

Examples of deverbal nouns:

dismissal (E19), *driver* (LME), *payee* (M18), *shrinkage* (E19), *starvation* (L18)

Examples of deverbal *adjectives:

arguable (E17), *clingy* (E18), *innovative* (E17), *tiresome* (E16)

A less usual, probably obsolescent, term is **deverbative**.

Compare GERUND; GERUNDIAL NOUN.

deviant Differing from what is 'normal' or expected. The term is used by some linguists as an alternative way of saying that a particular *structure or *usage is (perceived to be) of dubious *acceptability, or (in more *prescriptive works) incorrect.

Deviant sentences are often marked with a question mark (?), and sometimes with an asterisk (*), though the latter is usually reserved for clearly *ungrammatical structures, e.g.

?Looking out of the window, a fire-engine screamed past

?Having lived abroad so long, my outlook has changed (*see* HANGING PARTICIPLE)

*Lived abroad having long so, changed outlook my has

• **deviance**.

Compare GRAMMATICAL; ILL-FORMED.

diachronic *Linguistics.* Concerned with the historical development of (a) language; contrasted with *synchronic.

The study of the changes in pronunciation, grammar, *vocabulary, etc. between an old(er) version of a language and its present-day incarnation is referred to as **diachronic phonology, diachronic syntax**, etc., or, more generally, as **diachronic linguistics** (also called *historical linguistics).

The term is often attributed to Ferdinand de Saussure (1857–1913), who used it in his *Cours de linguistique générale* (1916).

Diachronistic has also been used.

Compare COMPARATIVE (2).

See also SAUSSUREAN.

- **diachronically**.
- ● **diachrony** (somewhat rare): the diachronic method or treatment.

dialect A *variety of a language that is distinct from other varieties in grammar, *vocabulary, and accent.

Dialects may be regional, or based on class differences (they are then usually called **social dialects** or **class dialects**), or a mixture of the two. Although dialects are usually recognizable from a speaker's accent, the term also implies differences of grammar. The following examples show grammatical differences from the structures typical of the *standard variety:

> I likes it (cf. standard *I like it*)
>
> I ain't done it (cf. standard *I haven't done it*)
>
> I didn't have no breakfast (cf. standard *I didn't have breakfast*)
>
> It needs washed (cf. standard *It needs to be washed*)
>
> We got off of the train (cf. standard *We got off the train*)
>
> Look at them cows (cf. standard *Look at those cows*)

Vocabulary may also differ across dialects, e.g. *while* meaning 'until' (*Wait while the lights are green* was allegedly a level-crossing notice in northern Britain confusing to southerners); *learn* meaning 'teach' (as in the book title *Lern yerself Scouse*); *happen* meaning 'perhaps'.

For some the term dialect implies deviation from some standard educated norm, but linguists regard the standard variety as just another dialect. When it comes to global varieties of English, the term dialect is not used; instead *variety is preferred, or terms such as American English or Indian English.

Compare STANDARD ENGLISH.

- **dialectal**: of or pertaining to dialect or a dialect.
- ● **dialect geography**: another term for *dialectology.

dialectology The study of *dialects, particularly regional ones.

dictionary meaning *See* MEANING.

dictionary word *See* LEXEME; WORD.

diglossia *Sociolinguistics*. A term coined by Charles Ferguson in 1959 to describe a situation in which two or more varieties of the same language are used by the same speakers under different conditions.

The term is particularly appropriate when applied to those languages that have distinct 'high' and 'low' varieties, for example, Arabic, which has a 'classical' form and several colloquial forms. It has recently been suggested that a weakened notion could be applied to English, where there are not only many 'high' and 'low' *vocabulary equivalents (e.g. *purchase/buy*; *larceny/theft*; *sufficient/enough*), but where such a concept could account for some alternatives in grammatical usage, for example *whom* versus *who*.

• **diglossic**.

  Compare ACROLECT; CODE-SWITCHING.

dimensions of modality A term used in CaGEL to refer collectively to *degree of modality, *kind of modality, and *strength of modality.

diminutive (*adj.*) Of a derivative *word: denoting a member that is small in size (literally or metaphorically) of the class, *category, etc. which the base word denotes. Of a *suffix: forming diminutive words.

  (*n.*) A diminutive word or suffix.

Some diminutives are stylistically neutral (e.g. *manikin, piglet*), but many are used as a mark of informality (e.g. *bunny, comfy, sweetie*), to show affection (e.g. *auntie*), or to belittle (e.g. *starlet*). Proper names often have diminutive forms: e.g. *Bessie, Betsy, Betty, Lizzie*, and *Lilibet* (for *Elizabeth*), *Dick* (for *Richard*), *Jimmy* (for *James*), and *Teddy* (for *Edward*).

  Compare HYPOCORISTIC.

direct condition *See* CONDITION.

directive

  1. (*n. & adj.*) (A clause) issuing a command or order. In modern grammatical analyses that distinguish *structure and *usage, the noun *directive* is used as a usage label indicating the function of a *clause as issuing a command or order. Contrasted with the syntactic label *imperative.

Because directives (in the sense understood by the layperson) are often expressed syntactically by imperative clauses (e.g. *Speak up! Leave me alone! Stop teasing the cat!*), the terms are often used interchangeably. However, what is in meaning effectively a directive, command, or order can be expressed grammatically in other ways, e.g. by a *declarative or *interrogative clause: *You will do as I say; Could you make less noise?* Conversely, imperative clauses can have other pragmatic functions, such as requests (e.g. *Please give generously*) or invitations (*Have some more coffee*). It is for this reason that many grammarians insist on distinguishing structure and usage, using different terminology for the two domains.

2. (In some theories, with a wider meaning.) (Pertaining to) an *utterance which suggests, requests, or warns that a course of action should be carried out.

direct object (DO, O^d, or O$_d$) A *noun phrase or *clause which is *licensed by a *transitive verb and normally occurs after the *verb, typically carrying the *semantic role of *patient. When a *pronoun is used, it appears in the *objective (1) case. Examples:

Rachel ate *some of those vegetables* (noun phrase)

The police cautioned *him* (pronoun)

He said *that he was not coming* (finite clause)

They wanted *to go to Sweden* (non-finite clause)

Generally the DO of an *active declarative clause can become the *subject of a *passive clause, but there are restrictions on this:

Some of those vegetables were eaten by Rachel

He was cautioned by the police

?That he was not coming was said by him

*To go to Sweden was wanted by them

The direct object is often simply called the *object, unless there is likelihood of confusion with the *indirect object. When an indirect object is present, it is normally placed before the DO (e.g. *They sent us some leaflets*).

Typically the DO is 'affected' or 'acted upon' by the action denoted by the verb, but this is not always the case, as the examples below show:

We've bought *a flat*

We really wanted *a house*

I hope we haven't made *a mistake*

For this reason direct objects are best defined using syntactic rather than semantic criteria.

See also COGNATE OBJECT.

direct question *See* DIRECT SPEECH.

direct speech The reporting of speech by repeating the actual *words used, without making any grammatical changes; an example of this, e.g.

'Is there anybody there?' said the listener

This contrasts with the *indirect speech exemplified in the following:

The listener asked whether there was anybody there

See also FREE DIRECT SPEECH; REPORTED SPEECH.

discontinuity The splitting of a *construction by the insertion of a *word, *phrase, etc., or a particular instance of this.

Examples (not all uncontroversial) might include:

Have you *finished*? (verb phrase)

Look the word *up* (phrasal verb)

That's a *hard* act *to follow* (modification)

There's *a man* outside *who wants to see you* (noun phrase and its modifying relative clause)

The time has come, the Walrus said, *to talk of many things* (noun phrase and its modification)

Discontinuity is very common in sentences containing *comparative clauses, e.g.

I spend *more money* on clothes *than I can really afford*

• **discontinuous**: (of a construction) split into parts by the insertion of a word, phrase, etc.

discord Lack of concord. *See* AGREEMENT.

discourse A connected stretch of language (especially spoken language), usually bigger than a *sentence, and particularly viewed as interaction between speakers, or between a writer and reader(s).

> 1991 M. HOEY Discourse . . . is used in two ways . . . Firstly it refers to all aspects of language organization . . . (whether structural or not) that operate above the level of grammar. Then, more specifically, it refers to the level of description that concerns itself with the structure . . . of (spoken) interaction.

Some users confine the term to spoken language, contrasting discourse with written text.

•• **discourse adjunct**: the same as *conjunct.

•• **discourse analysis**: the analysis of how spoken and/or written stretches of language are structured.

This can include looking at grammatical and semantic connections *between* sentences, just as syntax is the study of such connections *within* a sentence. In this respect discourse analysis is much the same as *text linguistics. But more usually discourse analysis is particularly concerned with sociolinguistic aspects of language, such as the organization of 'turn-taking' in conversation.

> 1991 M. McCARTHY Discourse analysis is concerned with the study of the relationship between language and the contexts in which it is used. It grew out of the work in different disciplines, in the 1960s and early 1970s, including linguistics, semiotics, psychology, anthropology and sociology. Discourse

analysts study language in use; written texts of all kinds, and spoken data, from conversation to highly institutionalised forms of talk.

•• **discourse marker**: *see* DISCOURSE MARKER.

Compare COHERENCE; COHESION.

See also FIELD OF DISCOURSE.

discourse adjunct The same as *conjunct.

discourse marker A *word, *phrase, or *clause that is used to guide, change, terminate, etc. the flow of a conversation or other type of verbal interaction. Also called **pragmatic marker**, **pragmatic particle**, or *filler (2).

The term is somewhat specialized, and not easily defined, but the label generally includes words that are not part of the syntactic structure of a clause or *sentence, e.g. *ah, oh, well, you see, I mean*

See also COMMENT CLAUSE.

discovery procedure *See* LEVEL; STRUCTURALISM.

discrete Separate, not on a *cline or continuum.

In the Aristotelian tradition the *word classes are regarded as discrete and sharply bounded, but in recent decades, especially in *Cognitive Linguistics, it has been claimed that many boundaries between linguistic categories are fuzzy.

Compare GRADIENCE; PROTOTYPE.

disjunct An *adverbial that has a more detached role in *clause or *sentence structure than other adverbials, and functions as a *sentence adverbial.

Disjuncts contrast in some grammars (e.g. CGEL and related frameworks) with *adjuncts (3), *conjuncts (1), and *subjuncts. In other grammars they are called *sentence adjuncts or **sentence modifiers**.

Disjuncts can express the speaker's or writer's attitude to, or observations about, the content of a sentence (*content disjuncts, also called **attitudinal disjuncts**), e.g.

Tragically, the rescue party arrived too late ('it is tragic that the rescue party arrived too late')

or they can signal the speaker's or writer's comments on the way in which an utterance is articulated (*style disjuncts), as in:

Honestly, nobody could have done any better ('if I'm honest . . .')

To be blunt, the whole thing was hopeless ('if I'm blunt . . .')

disjunction *Semantics.* Choice between two possibilities, or an instance of this, typically signalled by the word *or*.

  See DISJUNCTIVE

  Compare CONJUNCTION (2).

disjunctive (*n. & adj.*) (Designating) a *word (especially the *conjunction *or*) or a *construction that expresses alternatives.

  The terms disjunctive and disjunction are taken from logic. Further distinctions can be made. In **exclusive disjunction** the choice is 'one-or-the-other-but-not-both', e.g.

  (Either) the train is late, or it's been cancelled
  He died in (either) 1940 or 1941

With **inclusive disjunction** both alternatives are possible, e.g.

  (Either) the train is late—or my watch is fast (perhaps both)
  They certainly visited us in 1939 or 1940 (maybe both)

With **disjunctive interrogatives**, the presence of *either* allows the possibility that both alternatives are true: *Did you visit (either) Edinburgh or Glasgow?* But where only one of the alternatives can be true, the word *either* is not possible in a question:

  *Have you either passed or failed?
  *Is their eldest child either a boy or a girl?

dislocation The displacement of (typically) a *noun phrase to *clause-initial or clause-final *position, combined with the use of a *pro-form that is *co-referential with the displaced noun phrase.

● **dislocate**.

●● **right dislocation**: dislocation in which the pro-form comes first, and the noun phrase is therefore dislocated to the right in the linear sequence of a clause, e.g.

  He's a good cricketer, *your young son*

This is also called **postponed identification**.

●● **left dislocation**: dislocation in which the noun phrase is moved to the left, and a pro-form is added, e.g.

  Your young son, he's a good cricketer

This is also called **anticipated dislocation**.

  Dislocation is particularly a feature of informal spoken English.
  Compare BRANCHING.
  See also NUCLEUS.

distal Indicating that an entity, person, etc. is (far) away (from the speaker). Contrasted with *proximal; the same as **non-proximal**.

  This label is applied to the *deictic words *that* and *those*.

distribution Every *word or *phrase is limited in some way with regard to the syntactic *contexts in which it can occur, and the set of such contexts is its distribution. For example, the distribution of the *articles *a* and *an* is restricted to use with *singular *count *nouns (e.g. *a knife*, but not **a knives* or **a cutlery*).

In traditional grammar, the *word classes are often defined in *notional terms (e.g. 'a noun is a naming word'). In practice the assignment of a word to a particular *word class depends much more on its possible distribution in the structure of a *clause. The distribution of two units may overlap, giving **overlapping distribution**, or the two may be mutually exclusive (for example, *a* or *an* cannot occur with *the*).

● **distribute**.
● **distributional**: of or involving (syntactic) distribution. Hence **distributional analysis**, distributional *equivalence.
● **distributionally**.

Compare COMPLEMENTARY DISTRIBUTION.
See also SLOT-AND-FILLER.

distributive (*n. & adj.*) (A *word or *phrase) that relates to individual members of a class separately, not jointly.

Words like *each* and *every* are **distributive words**. Phrases like *once a week* and *three times per year* are **distributive expressions**.

Distributive plural concord is common in expressions such as *The children all had such eager faces* (where clearly each child had only one face), but a **distributive singular** is often possible, e.g. *They all had such an eager expression*.

ditransitive (*n. & adj.*) (A verb) that *licenses two *objects (2), namely a *direct object and an *indirect object; hence **ditransitive complementation**, or a *pattern or *clause in which a verb licenses a direct object and an indirect object. Also called **double transitive (verb)**. Examples:

I gave my mother flowers
They told me lies

The following example is not considered to involve a ditransitive verb in recent models, but instead contains a verb that takes a direct object and a further *complement in the form of a *prepositional phrase:

I gave flowers to my mother

Ditransitive complementation is sometimes said to include indirect objects followed by various types of clause, e.g.

She told me (that) she was delighted
I hadn't asked her what she wanted
She urged me to take a holiday

However, it should be noted that grammarians disagree over how to describe verb complementation, and not everyone would agree with the analysis of the examples above as involving a ditransitive pattern.

Compare COMPLEMENTATION; COMPLEX INTRANSITIVE; COMPLEX TRANSITIVE; INTRANSITIVE; MONOTRANSITIVE; TRANSITIVE.

do-insertion *See* DO-SUPPORT.

domain

1. *Sociolinguistics.* The situation or sphere of activity to which an utterance relates, with regard to the way it affects the use of language.

1982 G. LEECH et al. *Domain.* This has to do with how language varies according to the activity in which it plays a part . . . We can thus refer to the domains of chemistry, law, religion, and so on.

As will be seen from this quotation, there is a certain overlap and blurring between 'societal' domains (e.g. home, church) and academic or professional domains (e.g. chemistry, journalism, law).

Domain is sometimes said (as it is by these authors) to be a part of *register, but a distinction can be made between domain as the sphere in which language is used, and register as the kind of language used, which partly depends on the subject matter.

Compare GENRE.

2. The same as (semantic) *field.

1968 J. LYONS In recent years, there has been a good deal of work devoted to the investigation of lexical systems . . . with particular reference to such *fields* (or *domains*) as kinship, colour, flora and fauna, weights and measures, military ranks, [etc.].

dominate (In *Generative Grammar (2).) One *node dominates another if it is placed higher up in a *tree diagram in a direct (but not necessarily uninterrupted) line to the other, lower node.

1994 L. HAEGEMAN Node A dominates node B if and only if A is higher up in the tree than B and if you can trace a line from A to B going only downwards

• **dominance**.

do-support The use of a form of the *auxiliary verb *do* as a *dummy verb (hence **dummy *do***) in *interrogative clauses, *negative clauses, *emphatic clauses, *tag questions, etc. Also called ***do*-insertion**. Examples:

Do you understand?

He *doesn't* understand

You're wrong, he *does* understand!

He *doesn't* understand, *does* he?

The term comes from *Generative Grammar (2).

See also NICE PROPERTIES.

double accusative (In older grammar.) A structure which contains a *direct object and an *indirect object. In recent grammar this is called a *ditransitive structure.

double-barrelled question A *question in which the same *interrogative *word is repeated, as in *Who is who?*

This is an older term, not in general use.

double genitive See GENITIVE.

double marking The use of a redundant grammatical *feature (1) where a grammatical concept is already expressed.

The term is often used of structures such as *I would have liked to have seen it*, where the second *perfect construction is unnecessary if the intended meaning is 'I would have liked to see it' or 'I would like to have seen it'.

Compare BLEND.

double negative The occurrence of two *negative words in a single *clause or *sentence.

It is usually incorrect in *Standard English to negate a clause more than once, e.g.

*I never said nothing

*I haven't got none

In these cases the first negative could be omitted, or the second replaced by a *non-assertive form (e.g. *anything, any*). But the argument, from logic, that 'two negatives make a positive' is unjustified, as many English *dialects and other languages do have mutually reinforcing multiple negation, as did earlier forms of English.

Occasionally a double negative occurs quite legitimately in a single clause where in a sense the two negatives do cancel each other out, e.g.

You can't not worry about it (= 'you have to worry')

Surely nobody has no friends (= 'everybody has some friends')

Notice that these sentences take positive *tags (3):

You can't not worry, *can you*?

Nobody has no friends, *do they*?

The following is not a double negative, because two clauses are involved:

I wouldn't be surprised if the Jacksons didn't come

This is potentially confusing: it can mean that the speaker expects the Jacksons not to come (in which case both negatives are justified), or it can mean 'I wouldn't be surprised if they came'. However, the following example is unambiguous: *I didn't ask him not to go.*

double passive A *clause containing two *passive constructions, the second involving an *infinitive, as in:

*Receipts are not proposed to be issued
Certificates are expected to be despatched next week

*Usage books sometimes warn against all such structures, but their acceptability in fact varies. *Verbs like *expect* in the second example, which are also possible in the pattern verb + *object + passive infinitive (e.g. *We expect certificates to be despatched*), seem grammatical when they occur in the double passive construction. Verbs that do not fit this pattern with a single passive (e.g. *We propose receipts to be issued*) do not happily take a double passive either.

doublet Either of a pair of *words that have developed from the same original word, but are now somewhat different in form, and can be used in different senses.

Examples of doublets that have arisen from a single parent form within English are:

human (M16), *humane* (LME)
metal (ME), *mettle* (M16)
mood (in grammar) (M16), *mode* (LME)
patron (ME), *pattern* (M16)
shade (OE), *shadow* (OE)

Examples of doublets that arose through borrowing from other languages at different times:

faction (L15), *fashion* (ME)
hostel (ME), *hotel* (M17)
ration (M16), *reason* (ME)
See BY-FORM.
Compare HETERONYM (2).

double transitive The same as *ditransitive.

downtoner See INTENSIFIER.

D-Structure See DEEP STRUCTURE.

dual (*n. & adj.*) (A form) expressing two or a pair, in contrast to *singular and *plural.

In some languages dual is an important *category, and there are *inflected dual forms of *nouns, *verbs, etc. In English *both*, and to a lesser extent *either* and *neither*, are the only *grammatical words (1) indicating **dual number**.

•• **dual class membership**: the property of being a member of two classes; said e.g. of nouns that can be both *count and *uncount (e.g. a *cake*, some *cake*).

•• **dual gender (term)**: (a word) that can apply equally to a male or a female individual (e.g. *parent*, *guest*); contrasted with single-*gender terms such as *father*, *hostess*. *See also* GENDER; MASCULINE; FEMININE.

Compare BINARY; PLURALE TANTUM.

dummy Dummy elements (also called *empty elements) are *words which have no intrinsic meaning, but play a role in the grammatical structure of a *clause, *construction, etc.

•• **dummy *do***: a dummy *verb used to form *interrogative, *emphatic, and *negative clauses:

What *does* Liam want? He *didn't* say

•• **dummy *it***: a dummy *pronoun used especially as the *subject in sentences about the weather and time. Also called **ambient *it***, **empty *it***, **formal *it***, **prop *it***, or **unspecified *it***. Examples:

It is five o'clock, and *it* is snowing again

A similarly vague *it* also appears in various idiomatic phrases:

We've made *it*

Beat *it*

Well, that's *it*—let's go

In the following example, which involves *extraposition, *it* is referred to as *anticipatory *it*:

It is clear that the weather won't improve before the end of the week

Compare REFERENTIAL *IT*.

The word *there* in *existential sentences (called existential *there*) is also regarded as a dummy word, and then sometimes called the **dummy pronoun** *there*.

See also DO-SUPPORT; INTRODUCTORY *IT*.

duration Length or span of time, considered as part of the *meaning of a *word.

The term is particularly used in relation to *verbs, *prepositions, and *adverbs in various types of *constructions.

Prepositions and adverbs that are part of *phrases, *clauses, etc. expressing duration include *since, for, from, to*; e.g.

I've been here *for a month*

*Progressive constructions are usually said to imply a temporary state or limited duration, e.g.

I am living in a hostel

durative Of a *situation expressed by a *verb: taking place over a period of time; contrasted with *punctual.

The term is particularly used in relation to *dynamic (1) verbs that describe activities and processes (often of limited duration), which are used especially in *progressive constructions:

It is snowing

She's driving home

I'm cleaning the carpet

Compare ATELIC; CONCLUSIVE; TELIC.

●● **durative aspect**: the same as progressive aspect.

dvandva (*n. & adj.*) (Designating) a *compound consisting of two elements, neither of which is equivalent to the whole, and which could otherwise be syntactically joined by *and*. Also called **copulative compound**.

Examples are very rare in English, except in place names such as *Alsace-Lorraine, Schleswig-Holstein, Bosnia-Herzegovina*, and company names such as *Alcatel-Lucent, Colgate-Palmolive*.

The term is from the Sanskrit, representing a reduplication of the word for 'two'.

dynamic Having a meaning that implies action or change.

1. Of (chiefly verbal) meaning: relating to actions, events, happenings, and processes; e.g.

We *bought* a new car

War *erupted* in 1939

They never *play* our tune

I *worked* hard all my life

Verbal meaning can be seen as either dynamic or *stative. It is common practice to describe *verbs that can be used in *progressive constructions as **dynamic verbs**, in contrast to **stative verbs**, which typically cannot. However, it is more accurate to speak of dynamic and stative *meaning*, since many so-called stative verbs can be used dynamically with a shift in meaning. Compare the following pairs:

I *have* two sisters. We're *having* a party

They *are* hard-working. You *are being* so silly

They *look* alike. My prospects *are looking* good

Compare ACTION VERB.

Less generally, the terms dynamic and stative are applied to other *word classes. *Nouns and *adjectives, for example, are characteristically stative, referring to stable things, or expressing stable qualities, but they may denote temporary, dynamic properties when used in a *progressive construction:

He is being *foolish*

You are being *a nuisance*

*Adverbs, particularly *manner adverbs, often express dynamic meaning in combination with a dynamic verb:

He behaves *foolishly*

2. dynamic modal: In some analyses of the category of *modal verbs, dynamic is added as a third category of meaning, contrasting with *deontic and *epistemic meaning. Dynamic modals express meanings such as 'ability', 'volition', and 'predisposition', as well as 'circumstantial' meanings. Such modals are said to be typically *subject-oriented, rather than *speaker-oriented. Examples:

Nadine *can* read a novel in an evening ('ability' attributed to Nadine)

My cat *will* lie in front of the fire for hours ('volition' attributed to my cat)

There *must* be a solution to this problem ('circumstantial necessity')

Contrast:

You *can't* borrow my pen (deontic)

You *can't* be serious (epistemic)

Unlike modals with deontic or epistemic meaning, the *past tense forms of dynamic modals can refer to past time:

She *could* already read and write when she was four ('ability' in the past)

Even as a small child, she *would* sit reading for hours ('volition' in the past)

Early Modern English A phase in the history of the English language lasting from approximately 1500 to 1700.

echo utterance An *utterance that repeats all or part of what the previous speaker has said.

Echo utterances can take various forms, but function either as *questions:

A: He's a strange man. B: *He's strange?*

A: Yes, he collects beetles. B: *What does he collect?*

or as *exclamations:

A: Beetles. And then he sings to them. B: *He does what?*

A: He sings to them. B: *He sings to them!* You're joking.

-ed clause A *non-finite *clause whose *verb phrase contains a *past participle as its *head. Also called **past participle clause** or **past-participial clause**. Examples:

Jane had *her tonsils removed*

Disgraced by his conduct, the banker lost his knighthood

Notice that the first example contains its own *subject, whereas the second example does not.

In CaGEL the italicized clause in the following example is also an *-ed* clause:

I have *eaten all the sandwiches*

Compare BARE INFINITIVE CLAUSE; -ING CLAUSE; PARTICIPLE CLAUSE; TO-INFINITIVE CLAUSE.

-ed form (A way of referring to) either the *past (2) tense form of any *verb, or the past tense and *past participle forms of a verb. The former use includes both *regular past tenses, which are actually marked by *-ed* (e.g. *look**ed***), and *irregular ones, which are not (e.g. *rang, saw, wrote*).

See also -EN FORM; -ED CLAUSE; PARTICIPLE CLAUSE.

Compare PARTICIPIAL ADJECTIVE.

editorial we The use of *we* by a single writer, perhaps to avoid the more egocentric-sounding *I*.

Compare ROYAL WE.

-ed participle *See* -ED CLAUSE; PAST PARTICIPLE.

effected object The same as *result object.

effective (In *Systemic Grammar.) Of a *verb (or a *clause containing such a verb): describing goal-directed action; contrasted with *descriptive (3).

An effective clause may be *active or *passive, and must either contain an *agent or imply one, e.g.

The intruders smashed the door down

The door was smashed down (by the intruders)

elaborated code *See* CODE.

elaboration *See* EXPANSION.

element

1. Any of the units used in the *functional (1) *analysis of *clauses.

According to a widely used analysis, there are five possible functional units, namely *subject, *verb, *object, *complement, and *adverbial (abbreviated as S, V, O, C, and A), although to avoid mixing *form and *function labels it might be more appropriate to use P (= *predicator) instead of V. Examples are shown in the following table:

SV	Time / will tell
SVO	Not many people / know / that
SVC	The Lake District / is / beautiful
SVA	A funny thing / happened / on the way to the forum
SVOO	The world / doesn't owe / you / a living
SVOC	They / were painting / the town / red
SVOA	I / will forget / my own name / in a minute

In *Systemic Grammar predicator replaces verb (as suggested above), object is included within complement, *adjunct replaces adverbial, and there is a fifth Z element used for nominal groups whose status is indeterminate between subject and complement. Indeterminate status is assigned, for example, to titles, e.g.

A Tale of Two Cities

and elements in which subject and object are said to be fused, e.g.

Jack persuaded *Fiona* to come

2. (More generally.) Any functional part of a larger structural whole.
*Affixes, for example, are elements in *word structure; and a *phrase
consists of an essential element, the *head, along with *determiners (1),
*modifiers, and so on.

See also DUMMY; WH-ELEMENT.

ellipsis Omission from speech or writing of a *word or words that can be
recovered by the hearer or reader from contextual cues.

Words are often omitted from informal speech where they can be
recovered from the situation (*exophoric ellipsis):

(Are you) coming?

(Is there) anything I can do to help?

In more *formal speech and writing, words are often grammatically
recoverable from the text (*anaphoric ellipsis or *cataphoric ellipsis), and
in many cases it is normal to omit words in order to avoid repetition:

We're as anxious to help as you are (anxious to help)

Unless you particularly want to (buy tickets in advance), there's no need to buy
tickets in advance

A: Tom's written to *The Times*.

B: Why (has he written to *The Times*)?

A: I don't know (why he has written to *The Times*). He's always writing letters
and (he is always) complaining about something.

There are, however, grammatical constraints as to what can be omitted.
Thus a *co-referential subject can be omitted in a *coordinated *clause:

I telephoned my aunt and _ told her the news

but cannot always be omitted when the link is between *main (matrix) and
*subordinate clauses:

*I told my aunt the news when _ telephoned her

though compare:

I told my aunt the news when _ telephoning her

Strictly, ellipsis exists only when the missing words are exactly recoverable. But the term is normally extended to include such sentences as:

He wrote a better letter than I could have (written)

and often to looser examples of omission, such as:

You remember that man (who/whom/that) I introduced to you?

- **elliptical**: characterized by, or exhibiting, ellipsis.
  Compare RECOVERABILITY; REDUNDANCY; REFERENCE; SUBSTITUTION.
  See also GAPPING.

ellipt Omit (an element) by *ellipsis.

1990 S. GREENBAUM & R. QUIRK In medial ellipsis medial elements are
ellipted: Jill owns a Volvo and Fred (owns) a BMW.

embed Include (a linguistic unit) within another. *See also* EMBEDDING.
- **embedded**.

1975 T. F. MITCHELL Sometimes the embedded sentence is more apparent
than others. The subject-verb-object pattern of *he'd done it* in *John thought
he'd done it* seems immediately to mark it as sentential.

•• **embedded question**: *see* INDIRECT QUESTION.

embedding The inclusion of a linguistic unit within another linguistic
unit. Embedding contrasts with *conjoining, much as *subordination
contrasts with *coordination. As an example, in the following sentence the
*comparative clause is embedded in an *adjective phrase:

She was [AP gloomier *than she normally was*]

When a unit is embedded in a unit of the same type we speak of **self-
embedding** (also called **centre-embedding**). Thus in the next example
the *prepositional phrases *of the ship from Hong Kong* and *from Hong
Kong* are embedded in higher prepositional phrases:

[PP on the deck [PP of the ship [PP from Hong Kong]]]

In some analyses the notion of embedding seems to be applied only
to *subordinate clauses contained in higher clauses, and typically
functioning as *subject, *complement, etc., e.g.

That she was gloomy was characteristic
They did not believe *that they were doomed*

It is not immediately obvious whether in *Ed liked it, whereas Max thought it
appalling* (an example discussed by R. Huddleston) the subordinate clause
whereas Max thought it appalling is embedded in the sentence as a whole.
In accordance with the definition of embedding above as 'the inclusion of a
linguistic unit in another linguistic unit', we *do* seem to have a case of
embedding here. However, a subordinate clause like this, which is not a
*constituent of a higher clause, is not embedded according to Huddleston:

1984 R. HUDDLESTON The suggestion is that in [*Ed liked it, whereas Max
thought it appalling*] the subordinate clause is an immediate constituent of
the sentence, and in that case it is not embedded . . .

Theoretically the process of embedding can lead to sentences or phrases of indefinite length.

See also INDIRECT QUESTION; RECURSION.

Compare NESTING; PUSHDOWN.

emotive *Semantics*. Arousing feeling, emotion.

In theories of *meaning, *emotive* refers to the kinds of meaning subjectively attached to expressions by particular users (both individuals and communities). It is roughly equivalent to *attitudinal meaning in some of its uses, and contrasts with *cognitive and *referential meaning.

Any words relating to the emotions can be labelled emotive. For example, some grammarians label verbs like *dread, hate, loathe, love*, etc. as **emotive verbs** or **verbs of emotion**.

Various grammatical devices can be used to produce **emotive effects**, such as *exclamations, the use of *do* in *imperatives (e.g. *Do listen!*), stress (e.g. *I AM listening; That WAS stupid*), the use of *emphasizers (e.g. *Really!*; *That was very risky indeed*), or the use of non-*correlative *so* and *such* (e.g. *So risky; Such a stupid thing to do*).

See also COMMUNICATIVE; CONATIVE; CONNOTATION; DENOTATIVE; DESCRIPTIVE; EXPRESSIVE; INTERPERSONAL; PROPOSITIONAL MEANING; PSYCHOLOGICAL VERB.

emotive *should* The same as *putative *should*.

emphasis Special importance or prominence attached to a certain part of a *sentence, *phrase, *word, etc.

The term is used in its general sense. Emphasis is often achieved by marked *focus; by unusual stress (for example, on an *auxiliary verb, as in *I did call you!*); by grammatical devices such as *cleft or *pseudo-cleft sentences, or by the use of *do* in *declaratives or *imperatives (e.g. *I do apologize, Do be sensible*).

emphasizer

1. An *adverb that adds to the expressive force of the *clause, or part of the clause, to which it applies, e.g. *really* in *I really think you might have telephoned*.

Only some grammatical models subdivide adverbs with this level of semantic detail. CGEL has emphasizers as a subcategory of *subjunct.

Also called **emphasizing adverb**.

2. In some grammatical models, a sub species of *intensifying adjective that has a heightening, reinforcing effect (generally only in *attributive use), e.g. *pure* nonsense, a *real* idiot.

Also called **emphasizing adjective**.

emphatic Imparting or expressing emphasis.

•• **emphatic pronoun**: a *reflexive pronoun when used for emphasis, e.g. *himself* in *He admitted himself that the whole thing had been a mistake.*

empty

1. Having no (lexical) meaning; *dummy.

•• **empty *it***: the same as *dummy *it*, though *see also* ANTICIPATORY.

•• **empty word**: the same as *grammatical word (1).

2. Not phonetically realized.

In some versions of *Generative Grammar (2) units that have been *moved leave behind a *trace which is inaudible, and such elements are regarded as examples of **empty categories**, e.g.

[The government]ᵢ was toppled tᵢ (where 't' indicates a trace left behind by the moved subject, and the subscript 'i' indicates *co-reference)

Compare ZERO.

empty category *See* EMPTY (2).

enclitic *Morphology.* (*n. & adj.*) (A form) pronounced with very little emphasis, usually shortened, and attached to a preceding host word. Contrasted with *proclitic.

Common **enclitic forms** include *-n't*, parts of the *verbs *be* and *have* (e.g. *they're*, *he's* = 'is' or 'has', *we've*), *'ll*, and *'s* meaning *us* (as in *Let's go*).

Compare CLITIC and *see* CONTRACTION (2).

end (Situated or occurring in) the last part of a *phrase, *clause, *sentence, etc.

•• **end position**: the same as *final position.

See also FRONT; INITIAL; MEDIAL; POSITION.

end-focus A term used in CGEL to refer to the placing of the most important information in a *sentence or *clause (the *focus) at the end.

Since it is customary to introduce *given information at the beginning of a sentence, and to impart *new information towards the end, end-focus is an *unmarked characteristic of *information structure. This is referred to as the **principle of end-focus**.

In writing, the end of a clause or sentence will normally be taken to be the focus, unless there is some unusual punctuation or other sign (e.g. italics or capital letters); and marked *word order may be used to maintain this focus. In speech, the focus is realized by nuclear pitch, which typically falls on the last stressed syllable, e.g.

Write to the li'BRARian

(There may of course be more than one nuclear pitch in a sentence if it is a long one.) The focus can be moved without changing the word order by moving the nucleus, e.g.

'WRITE to the librarian

Compare END-WEIGHT.

See also CLEFT; GIVEN; INFORMATION STRUCTURE; MARKED; NEW; PSEUDO-CLEFT; RHEME; THEME.

ending An informal label to denote the final part of a *word.

In English the term applies to *inflectional *suffixes such as those used in the *plural forms of *nouns (e.g. *cats*), in the various forms of *verbs (e.g. *looks, looked*), and in the *comparative and *superlative forms of certain *adjectives and *adverbs (e.g. *longer, longest, sooner, soonest*). It also applies to *derivational *suffixes (*-ness, -ity*, etc.).

endocentric

1. Of a *structure: syntactically a *projection (1) of the word which is its *head. Also called *headed. Contrasted with *exocentric.

The following *phrases, with their heads italicized, are all endocentric:

too *dreadful* to contemplate	(adjective phrase)
rather more *surprisingly*	(adverb phrase)
she who must be obeyed	(noun phrase)

1933 L. BLOOMFIELD The forms *John* and *poor John* have, on the whole, the same functions. Accordingly, we say that the English character-substance construction (as in *poor John, fresh milk*, and the like) is an *endocentric* construction.

2. Of a *compound: grammatically and semantically equivalent to one of its parts.

Many compounds belong to the same *word class as their head word and preserve the latter's basic meaning, e.g.

fire alarm (alarm giving warning of fire)
girlfriend (friend who is a girl) } nouns

duty-free (free from duty)
rock hard (hard as a rock) } adjectives

1933 L. BLOOMFIELD Since a *blackbird* is a kind of a *bird*, and a *door-knob* a kind of a *knob*, we may say that these compounds have the same function as their head members; they are endocentric.

endophora *Reference within a text. Contrasted with *exophora.

This is a general term, covering both *anaphora and *cataphora.
● **endophoric**: e.g. **endophoric reference**, which is the same as endophora.

> 1976 M. A. K. HALLIDAY & R. HASAN We shall find it useful in the discussion to have a special term for situational reference. This we are referring to as exophora, or exophoric reference; and we could contrast it with endophoric as a general name for reference within the text ... As a general rule, therefore, reference items may be exophoric or endophoric; and if endophoric they may be anaphoric or cataphoric.

end-weight A term used in CGEL to refer to the tendency of longer (i.e. heavier) units of information to come at the end of a *sentence or *clause. A fuller term also used in CGEL is the **principle of end-weight**.

Since *new information may need more detailed explanation than *given information, end-weight often goes hand-in-hand with *end-focus, e.g.

> The bread industry and nutritionists alike have been trying to get the message across *that a healthy balanced diet should include sufficient bread*

The 'weighty' part of the message here comes naturally at the end. Notice how the word *across* is positioned immediately after *message*, and not at the end of the sentence. Grammatically it could be positioned there, but the sentence would then be harder to process.

See also INFORMATION STRUCTURE.

-en form (A way of referring to) the *past participle of any *verb, including *regular verbs.

The name is based on the fact that many *irregular verbs take this ending in their *past participle (e.g. *broken, chosen, driven, forgotten, taken*), but the label includes all past participles (e.g. *looked, hated, brought, kept, set, known, gone, drunk*).

Because it is restricted, unlike *-ed*, to the participle, it is a useful shorthand way of distinguishing past participles from *past tense forms.

See also -ED FORM; PARTICIPLE; PAST PARTICIPLE.

English The West Germanic language that first developed in England and southern Scotland, and is now spoken throughout the British Isles and in the United States, Canada, Australia, New Zealand, and the West Indies, as well as by significant communities in southern Africa, south and south-east Asia, and elsewhere.

See also BASIC ENGLISH; BBC ENGLISH; MIDDLE ENGLISH; MODERN ENGLISH; NUCLEAR ENGLISH; OLD ENGLISH; STANDARD ENGLISH.

English Grammar, An A book by Etsko Kruisinga and P. A. Erades, based on Kruisinga's **Handbook of Present-Day English*.

English Grammar: A Function-Based Introduction A functional-typological grammar in two volumes, written by the American linguist Talmy Givón in 1993.

English Transformational Grammar A description of (parts of) the grammar of English by R. A. Jacobs and P. S. Rosenbaum using early *Generative Grammar (2) as a framework, published in 1968.

enhancement *See* EXPANSION.

entail *Semantics.* Of a *sentence: to necessitate the truth of (another sentence).

• **entailment**: a relationship between two sentences such that if the first is true, the second must also be true. For example, sentence (1) entails sentence (2):

    (1) I am an only child

    (2) I have no brothers or sisters

In this particular case, sentence (2) also entails sentence (1). But such **mutual entailment** does not always obtain. For example, (1) entails (3):

    (3) I have no brothers

However, as I may have any number of sisters, (3) does not entail (1).

    Compare IMPLICATION; PRESUPPOSITION.

epicene Denoting an *animate entity of either sex without a change of *gender.

An outdated term, more usually replaced by expressions like **sex-neutral** or *dual gender.

epistemic Of *modality: concerned with likelihood, or the degree of certainty or knowledge about something. Contrasted with *deontic and *dynamic (2) modality.

Out of context, sentences containing *modal verbs are sometimes *ambiguous. The modality of *You must love your mother* is epistemic if the meaning is 'I deduce, from some information or observations, that you love her'. It is deontic if the meaning is 'You are obliged to love her'. Similarly, the modality of *Tom may keep the money* is epistemic if the meaning is 'He is quite likely to keep it', but deontic if it is 'He is allowed to keep it'.

Epistemic modality is sometimes called **extrinsic modality**.

    Compare ALETHIC.

epithet An *adjective that indicates a quality ascribed to the *noun it *modifies. Contrasted with *classifier.

Epithets include 'objective' adjectives (e.g. *green, rectangular*) and 'subjective' adjectives (*amazing, stupid*). Some can be either (*old, expensive*). This term seems to be the same as *qualitative in other models.

equational Another *word for *equative (particularly as applied to the verb *be*).

equative Denoting that one thing is equal to, or the same as, another.

The verb *be* is the primary equative *verb (or verb with an **equative function**). Such verbs are more usually described as **copular** or **copulative** (*see* COPULA).

There is also a small group of *adverbial expressions with equative meaning, such as *equally, likewise, in the same way*.

The term is sometimes used in the analysis of degrees of *comparison, where the *as X as* comparison can be described as equative. But this relationship is also often described as *equivalence.

• **equatively**.

equivalence A term referring to 'sameness' or equality from different linguistic points of view.

1. Equality from the point of view of meaning.

Comparisons taking the form *as X as* (e.g. *She is as generous as her mother*) are **comparisons of equivalence**. These are contrasted with **comparisons of non-equivalence** expressed by using *more X* (or a comparative form ending in *-er) than* or *less X than* (e.g. *She is more/less generous than her mother*).

Equivalence of *reference is a feature of strict *apposition, and may or may not be overtly signalled, e.g.

The Young Pretender, that is to say *Charles Edward Stuart*, or *Bonnie Prince Charlie*, as he is more familiarly known . . .

2. 'Sameness' from the point of view of *function (1).

Hence **functional equivalence**: having an identical or comparable function in a particular *context. In the phrases *the university press* and *this ancient press*, the *noun (phrase) *university* and the *adjective (phrase) *ancient* are functionally equivalent, since both are *modifiers.

Linguistic units that are formally different may be equivalent in function. For instance, in the examples below, the italicized strings are functionally equivalent, since they are all *adverbials:

I saw the postman *in the park* (prepositional phrase)
I lost my keys *when I got out of my car* (clause)

He ran down the hill *very quickly* (*adverb phrase)

3. 'Sameness' from the point of view of *distribution. Thus two units that are **distributionally equivalent** have the same syntactic distribution.

equivalent (*adj.*) Used to describe a linguistic unit that is semantically, functionally, or grammatically the same as another unit.

(*n.*) A linguistic unit that is semantically, functionally, or grammatically equivalent to another unit. Such a unit is sometimes described as being *X-equivalent*, where 'X' specifies a word class label.

> 1932 C. T. ONIONS A word or group of words which replaces a Noun, an Adjective, or an Adverb is called an Equivalent (Noun-equivalent, Adjective-equivalent, or Adverb-equivalent).

In more recent modern grammar this kind of label is often replaced by such terms as *nominal, nominal *group, *noun phrase, *nominal clause, and so on.

See also NOUN-EQUIVALENT.

ergative

1. This term (derived from the Greek word *ergon* 'work') is applied in languages such as Abkhaz, Eskimo, and Basque (**ergative languages**) to the *case (1) form used for the *subject of a *transitive *verb, with an **absolutive case** being used for the *direct object or for the subject of an *intransitive verb.

2. Designating a particular kind of *verb or *construction with which the same *noun (phrase) can be used as subject when the verb is intransitive, and as direct object when the verb is transitive; designating the relationship between these two uses. Compare:

My shirt has torn ~ I've torn my shirt
The door opened ~ Someone opened the door
The meat is cooking ~ I'm cooking the meat

> 1968 J. LYONS The term that is generally employed by linguists for the syntactic relationship that holds between [The stone moved] and [John moved the stone] is 'ergative': the subject of an intransitive verb 'becomes' the object of a corresponding transitive verb, and a new *ergative* subject is introduced as the 'agent' (or 'cause') of the action referred to.

Some linguists caution against this use of the term.
• **ergativity**.

erlebte Rede (German.) The same as *free indirect speech.

Essentials of English Grammar A short book by Otto Jespersen published in 1933 'embodying the principles explained in *The Philosophy of Grammar* and partly carried out in the seven volumes of my *Modern English Grammar*'.

eternal truths *See* PRESENT.

ethic(al) dative *See* DATIVE.

etymology

   1. The historically verifiable sources of the formation of a *word and the development of its *meaning; an account of these.

   2. The branch of linguistic science concerned with etymologies (in sense 1).

   2009 P. DURKIN Etymology is the investigation of word histories. It has traditionally been concerned most especially with those word histories in which the facts are not certain, and where a hypothesis has to be constructed to account either for a word's origin or for a stage in its history.

● **etymological**: of, pertaining to, based upon, etc., etymology.
● **etymologically**.

   1926 H. W. FOWLER *Saxonism* is a name for the attempt to raise the proportion borne by the originally & etymologically English words in our speech to those that come from alien sources.

●● **etymological fallacy**: the belief that the true meaning of a word is determined or implied by its provenance; for example, the idea that *awful* really means 'full of awe', 'awe-inspiring'.

   2009 P. DURKIN The etymological fallacy is the idea that knowing about a word's origin, and particularly its original meaning, gives us the key to understanding its present-day use. Very frequently, this is combined with an assertion about how a word ought to be used today: certain uses are privileged as 'etymological' and hence 'valid', while others are regarded as 'unetymological', and hence 'invalid' (or at least 'less valid').

   Compare FOLK ETYMOLOGY.

etymon (Plural **etyma**.) The *word that gives rise to a derivative or a borrowed or later form.

euphemism

   1. A circumlocutionary (often vague) expression substituted for another which is thought to be crude, offensive, painful, or unpleasant (e.g. *facilities* or *bathroom* for 'lavatory', *pass away* for 'die', *let go* for 'dismiss').

   2. The avoidance of unpleasant *words by means of such expressions.

1947 E. PARTRIDGE Euphemism may be obtained by using an extremely vague phrase, as in *commit a nuisance*.

● **euphemistic**.

eventive Of a *noun (phrase): designating an event. Contrasted with *stative.

This is not a generally used term, but it is possible to describe some nouns—often *deverbal nouns—as eventive:

The *examination* is next week (*compare*: They will examine the candidates next week)

You must do some *work* (*compare*: You must work)

Can I give you some *advice*? (*compare*: Can I advise you?)

In the first example we have an **eventive *subject**; in the second and third examples there is an **eventive *object**.

See also EVENT VERB.

event verb The same as *action verb.

exclamation

1. (In non-specialized usage.) A *word, *phrase, or *clause expressing some kind of emotion. In this sense the term is used to cover any word or group of words expressing anger, pleasure, surprise, etc. Some of these may lack normal *sentence structure, e.g. *Marvellous!, You poor thing!, How kind of you!, What a scorcher!, Woe is me!* Sometimes single word *interjections are included, e.g. *Alas!*

Compare EXCLAMATIVE.

2. (In modern grammatical analyses that distinguish *structure and *usage.) A usage label indicating the *function (2) of a *clause as expressing some kind of emotion. Contrasted with the syntactic label *exclamative. In this kind of analysis, an exclamation can be realized by various forms, e.g. by an exclamative clause (*What a nice apartment you have!*) or by an *interrogative clause (e.g. *What does he think he looks like?*, perhaps meaning 'How very oddly he is dressed'). This definition is roughly the opposite of that in 3.

Compare DIRECTIVE; QUESTION; SPEECH ACT; STATEMENT.

3. (In some popular grammatical models.) A *formal (1) and more limited *category, restricted to clauses beginning with *how* or *what* (but without the subject-auxiliary *inversion typical of interrogatives):

How difficult it all is!

What a muddle we are in!

Nowadays the label that is preferred for this type of clause is exclamative clause.

exclamative (*n. & adj.*) (A clause or sentence) denoting an exclamation (1).

As a syntactic *clause type an **exclamative clause** is typically used as an *exclamation (2). Thus, exclamative is a formal syntactic category, whereas *exclamation (2) is a category of *usage. Such clauses typically have the *wh-word *what* inside a *noun phrase in clause-initial *position, or *how* used with an *adjective or as an *adverb at the beginning of a clause, but without the subject-auxiliary *inversion typical of *interrogatives, e.g.

What a silly game these politicians are playing!

How wonderful he is!

How we sniggered at his ideas!

Compare DECLARATIVE; IMPERATIVE; INTERROGATIVE.

exclamatory Expressing or containing an *exclamation (1).

The term is used as a structure label to describe an *exclamative clause or as a *usage label to describe an *exclamation (2), either of which may be called an **exclamatory clause**. Grammarians who are careful to distinguish *structure from usage tend to confine the term to the semantic use, i.e. as the adjective corresponding to *exclamation (2).

•• **exclamatory question**: (usually) a *sentence or *clause that is *interrogative in form, but used as an *exclamation (2), e.g. *Isn't it a lovely day!*

exclusive

1. Serving to exclude an option; indicating that someone or something is excluded. Contrasted with *inclusive (1).

(i) Commonly describing the use of the first person plural pronoun *we* when the addressee is excluded, as in *We'll call for you tomorrow.*

(ii) Applied to the meaning of the word *or* in contexts indicating that one alternative rules out the other. Thus, *Are you going to have tea or coffee?* would often be interpreted as exclusive: you are expected to have one, but not both. On the other hand, *Do you take milk or sugar?* will normally have an *inclusive meaning: you can have both.

See also DISJUNCTIVE.

(iii) Applied to other elements of language which indicate exclusivity in some way. Thus, some adverbs serve to exclude all but what is specified, e.g. *alone, exclusively, merely, solely.*

2. Denoting a linguistic element whose use excludes the use of another element. Many *determinatives (1) are mutually exclusive (cf. *a the mistake*).

exhaustive conditional *See* UNIVERSAL CONDITIONAL-CONCESSIVE CLAUSE.

existential (*n. & adj.*) (A grammatically *marked *structure) typically
used to express a *proposition that someone or something exists.

An **existential *construction** (also called a ***there*-existential**) typically
conforms to the following pattern:

there + (*auxiliary/*raising verb) + *be* + *notional *subject

The unstressed *pronoun *there* is a *dummy subject called **existential
*there**. Here are some examples:

There is an emergency

There must be a God

There seems to be no solution

These are called **bare existential** *clauses, which do not have a non-
existential counterpart (cf. **An emergency is*).

An **extended existential** clause contains additional material (called
the **extension**), such as a *locative (1) or *temporal phrase, a *relative
clause, a **to-infinitive*, or an *-*ing* clause:

There is a mouse in the loft

There was a fire last week

There has been nothing in the papers about this

Can there be life on other planets?

There's one student who brings her dog to class

There is a great deal of work to do

There was a fox running down the street

Some extended existentials have a non-existential counterpart: *A fox was
running down the street.*

Existential constructions play a role in *information structuring in that
*new information is placed later in the containing clause, such that it
follows *given information.

There-existentials also occur with verbs other than *be*. This is called the
*presentational construction.

There *comes* a time in everyone's life when you leave your parents' house

Once upon a time there *lived* a beautiful princess

•• ***have*-existential**: (in CGEL) a *sentence or clause containing the
verb *have* which corresponds semantically to a *there*-existential. Thus
the following examples:

I have a hole in my pocket

My pocket has a hole in it

correspond to:

There is a hole in my pocket

Similarly:

> You have visitors waiting to see you

corresponds to:

> There are visitors waiting to see you
>
> Visitors are waiting to see you

existential *there* See EXISTENTIAL.

exocentric

1. Of a structure: without a *head. Also called **non-headed** or **unheaded**. Contrasted with *endocentric.

Some *phrases are regarded as being always exocentric in some frameworks, e.g. *prepositional phrases. *See* HEAD (1); HEADED.

2. Of a *compound: not *headed; not grammatically and/or not semantically equivalent to either of its parts.

One kind of exocentric compound is the *bahuvrihi type, which is of the same *word class as one of the members of the compound, but exhibits a significant shift of *meaning (e.g. *fathead* and *head* are both *nouns, but a *fathead* is not a kind of head). Other kinds have neither grammatical nor semantic equivalence, e.g. *pullover* (a *noun made up of a *verb + *particle (1)/*preposition), *outcome* (a noun made up of a particle/preposition + verb), *commonplace* (an *adjective made up of an adjective + noun).

> 2001 V. ADAMS The term **exocentric** describes expressions in which no part seems to be of the same kind as the whole or to be central to it. The noun *change-over* is exocentric, and so are 'verb-complement' noun compounds like *stop-gap*, along with adjective + noun and noun + noun compounds like *air-head*, *paperback*, *lowlife*.

exophora Situational *reference; a linguistic unit that derives (part of) its meaning from the *extralinguistic situation. Contrasted with *endophora.

The understanding of language in general requires a certain degree of knowledge of the world, but some language is particularly dependent for its intelligibility on the hearer's knowledge of the extralinguistic situation. For example, *There she is!* taken out of context conveys little meaning: *there* could refer to all sorts of places, and *she* can refer to a female person or animal, but it needn't.

• **exophoric**: of the nature of, or pertaining to, exophora (e.g. **exophoric ellipsis**, **exophoric reference**; the latter is the same as exophora).

expanded coordinate In CaGEL, the part of a *coordination structure that is introduced by a *coordinator, e.g.

> homes *and offices*

expansion (In *Systemic Grammar.) One of the two major logico-semantic categories held to explain the relationship between *clauses, the other being *projection.

experiencer *Semantics.* A *semantic role label applied to a *phrase that refers to the *animate entity that experiences an action, event, state, etc. expressed by a *verb.

The term comes from *Case Grammar, in which it replaces the earlier term *dative (2). A verb of involuntary perception such as *hear* or *see* can be said to have an experiencer *subject (e.g. *I heard/saw a bird*), in contrast to verbs such as *listen* or *look*, which have *agent(ive) subjects. The subjects of other verbs of perception sometimes have an experiencer role (e.g. *I smell burning*), and sometimes an *agentive role (e.g. *Smell this meat—is it all right?*).

•• **experiencer verb**: *see* PSYCHOLOGICAL VERB.

experiential

  1. Involving, or based on, experience.

  2. In *Systemic Grammar, language has three *metafunctions: *ideational, *interpersonal, and *textual. The ideational part is further analysed into two parts. One is the **experiential**, meaning 'based on experience', which contrasts with a **logical** component, meaning 'based on certain general logical relationships'.

experiential present perfect *See* PRESENT PERFECT.

expletive (*n. & adj.*) (A *word or *phrase) that serves to 'fill out' an *utterance (from late Latin *expletivus* meaning 'serving to fill out', from *ex-* 'out', and *plere* 'fill'); especially applied to a swearword.

Some expletives are *formulaic expressions of a particular type which may be grammatically *irregular in some way. For example *Damn you!* appears to be *imperative in form, but an imperative *verb is not normally followed by *you*.

•• **expletive *it***: another term for *anticipatory *it*, ambient *it*, *dummy *it*, *introductory *it*, etc.

The term indicates that this *it* fills a syntactic space.

explicit performative *See* PERFORMATIVE.

exponence

  1. The relationship between an (abstract) grammatical *feature (2), unit, *structure, etc. and an actual instance, or **exponent**, of it. Also called

simple exponence. An example is the *realization of the *past tense in English by the *inflectional ending -*ed*.

> 1964 R. H. ROBINS All categories are part of the descriptive apparatus or frame set up by the linguist to deal with the particular language, and the relation between them and the material of utterance (or, *mutatis mutandis*, of writing) is one of class and category to exponent or manifestation.

•• **extended exponence**: the phenomenon whereby a particular grammatical feature, unit, structure, etc. is realized by more than one *formative, or other kind of element. Thus in English the *perfect is realized by a form of the *auxiliary verb *have* in combination with a *past participle.

•• **multiple exponence** (also called **cumulative exponence**): the phenomenon whereby a particular formative, or other kind of element, realizes more than one grammatical feature, unit, structure, etc.

2. In *Systemic Grammar, exponence is one of three (or four) scales (*see* SCALE-AND-CATEGORY GRAMMAR), along with *rank, *delicacy, and possibly *depth.

exponent *See* EXPONENCE.

expressive

(*adj.*) *Semantics.* Designating a type of feeling-based *meaning.

Expressive meaning corresponds to some extent with *attitudinal, *emotive, and *interpersonal meaning.

See also COGNITIVE; COMMUNICATIVE MEANING; CONATIVE; CONNOTATION; DENOTATIVE; DESCRIPTIVE; ILLOCUTIONARY MEANING; REFERENTIAL MEANING.

(*n.*) A kind of *speech act, e.g. a wish, congratulation.

extended bahuvrihi *See* BAHUVRIHI.

extended existential construction *See* EXISTENTIAL.

extended exponence *See* EXPONENCE.

Extended Standard Theory *See* STANDARD THEORY.

extension

1. *Semantics.* The *referent or range of *referents covered by a particular term.

The word is taken over from logic, and contrasts with **intension**. The extension of the word *horse* would include all animals to which the word is applied. The intension of the word *horse* would cover those features and characteristics that distinguish this animal from others.

See also CONNOTATION; DENOTATION.

2. (In *Systemic Grammar.) A type of relationship between *clauses whereby one clause expands another in various kinds of ways.

Extension can be embodied in a *coordinate or a *subordinate clause. Extension adds something new to the other clause, if only by simple addition. For example, the 'extending' clause might begin (*both* ...) *and*, (*neither* ...) *nor*, *but*, *while*, *whereas*, and so on. Or the extension might add by *variation (2) (e.g. *but not*, *except* (*that*), *rather than*), or perhaps by an alternative (e.g. (*either* ...) *or*). *Apposition is also included under this heading.

● **extensional**.

See also EXISTENTIAL.

extensive

1. Of a grammatical *complement: construed as referring to someone or something other than the *referent of the grammatical *subject. Contrasted with *intensive. Thus in *Otto likes Greg*, the referent of the *direct object is not the same as the referent of the *subject.

2. In *Systemic Grammar, where the *direct object of traditional grammar is analysed as part of *complementation, the direct object may be termed the **extensive complement** to distinguish it from an *intensive complement. An **extensive verb** is therefore typically a *transitive verb taking one or two objects and an **extensive clause** is one containing such a verb and its complement(s), e.g. *They are playing our tune*.

external argument *See* ARGUMENT.

extralinguistic Referring to anything in the world outside language, but which is relevant to the *utterance.

The term is applied to the situation (sometimes called the **situational context** or **extralinguistic context**) in which language operates. Extralinguistic features of utterances often include shared knowledge, without which they might make little sense. For example, the meaning of *pronouns often depends on the situation: *Did he take them? Are they there yet? Isn't that lovely?* Extralinguistic features can also include body language, tone of voice, etc., which are called *paralinguistic features in other analyses.

Compare EXOPHORIC; METALINGUISTIC.

extraposed object *See* EXTRAPOSITION.

extraposed subject *See* EXTRAPOSITION.

extraposition The *postponement or *movement (1) of a unit, typically a *clause, to the right, involving the use of a substitute item in the position where the unit in question originated.

Extraposition is frequently found with clauses that function as *subject. In such cases the subject is moved to a *position after the *verb, and *anticipatory *it* is substituted in subject position, e.g.

It's no use *crying over spilt milk* (*compare*: Crying over spilt milk is no use)
It's disappointing *that you can't stay longer* (*compare*: That you can't stay longer is disappointing)

This displacement often takes place to satisfy the principles of *end-focus and/or *end-weight.

Some examples of 'extraposition' have no corresponding non-extraposed equivalents. In such cases extraposition is obligatory, e.g.

It seems *that they're not coming after all* (*That they're not coming after all seems)

An **extraposed subject** (exemplified above) is also called a **postponed subject**. Extraposition of *objects also occurs, and sometimes this is obligatory in the same way, e.g.

I consider *it* a shame *that you never replied to my plea*
You owe *it* to me *to explain yourself* (*You owe to explain yourself to me)

Extraposition is not to be confused with *postposition.

• **extrapose**: displace a linguistic unit by extraposition.

•• **extraposition from NP**: a process whereby a *modifying phrase, clause, etc. is moved to the right from inside a *noun phrase. In the following example the *prepositional phrase has been extraposed to the right out of its containing noun phrase:

[NP *Many reports* _] *were written* [PP *on the political situation in Scotland*]

The symbol '_' indicates where the PP was moved from.

extrinsic modality *See* EPISTEMIC MODALITY.

factitive

1. *Semantics.* Of a linguistic element, usually a *verb: expressing the notion of making something, or causing a result.

In a broad sense this term can apply to any *transitive verb with the *meaning of creating a result, e.g. the classic *kill* (if X kills Y, the result is that Y is dead). Other factitive verbs have meanings like *create, make, produce* (e.g. *make a cake*), which are usually termed *causative in more popular grammar.

The term is also sometimes used of *complex transitive verbs that have a *resultative meaning (as in e.g. *They painted the town red, They made him president*).

2. (In *Case Grammar.) Describing the *case (3) of the *noun phrase which refers to the thing made or created. In *I've been making cakes, cakes* is in the factitive case, in contrast to the same phrase in *They've eaten the cakes*, where *the cakes* is in the *objective (3) case. In later Case Grammar, this is the *result case.

See also RESULT.

factive *Semantics.*

1. (*n. & adj.*) (A *verb or a following *that-clause) relating to the *assertion of a fact.

A verb that asserts the truth of a following *clause is a **factive verb** (or **factive**), e.g.

I *know* that you were overcharged

I *regret* that you were overcharged

These verbs contrast with **non-factive** verbs which leave the *proposition open:

I *believe* that he was overcharged

and *contrafactive verbs:

He *pretends* that he was overcharged

I *wish* that he had been overcharged

The proposition that follows a factive verb is a **factive predicate** (or a **factive**). Factive predicates can also depend on other parts of speech, not only verbs, e.g.

> It is a pity that he was overcharged
> I am sorry that he was overcharged

2. (In older usage.) The same as *factitive (1).

- **factivity**: the quality of being factive.

See also FACTUAL.

factual

1. Of a *clause: referring to actual events, results, *states, etc., e.g.

> I met her last year
> I arrived late, so I unfortunately missed dinner (factual result)
> Were you late? (a factual *question, as it requires a factual answer)

This type of clause contrasts with **non-factual** clauses, as in:

> I arrived early *so that I wouldn't miss dinner* (i.e. purpose, intention).

*Imperatives, *subjunctives, and the *infinitive are said to be non-factual *moods.

Both factual and non-factual *predications (1) contrast with *counterfactual predications, where the truth is the reverse of what is said in the predication, as in:

> I wish I knew   (i.e. I don't know)
> If only I had arrived earlier!   (i.e. I did not arrive early)

Open (or real) *conditions are sometimes described as factual (*If you come at six . . .*), in contrast to remote (or unreal, hypothetical, remote) ones (*If you came at six . . .*), which are variously described as *counterfactual or non-factual.

•• **factual condition**: *see* CONDITION.

2. Of a *verb: when followed by a *that-clause containing a verb in the *indicative mood.

Factual verbs, in this formal, syntactic definition, include both *public verbs of speaking and *private verbs of thinking. Although these verbs may be generally described as referring to fact, the term is used with a rather wider meaning than the more semantically defined *factive (1), and the predication may not be factual as in sense (1). Thus factual verbs may include *allege, argue, bet, claim, pretend, realize, suspect*, and other verbs that would hardly be described as factive. Factual verbs contrast with *suasive verbs.

- **factuality**: the quality of being factual.

false cognate *See* FALSE FRIEND.

false friend A *word that has the same or a similar form in two (or more) languages, but different meanings in each.

This term is used in contrastive analysis and foreign language teaching. For example, the French adjective *sympathique* (like Italian *simpatico*) often means 'nice', 'pleasant', or 'likeable' and is therefore a false friend to English *sympathetic*. In the same way French *actuel* means 'present', not 'actual'.

Sometimes also called **false cognate** and **faux ami**.

feature

1. A distinctive characteristic of some part of the language. For example, hesitations, false starts, and the like are features of spoken language.
•• **extralinguistic feature:** a feature that is not purely linguistic, e.g. different types of body language, such as facial expressions, shrugs, and nods.

2. The atomic syntactic, semantic, and/or phonological attributes that linguistic units (e.g. *lexical items or *clauses) can be broken into, using a procedure called *componential analysis. The features are often *binary, i.e. specified as '+' or '−'. Semantic features allow us to analyse the word *bachelor* as [+ male] [+ adult] [+ human] [− married]. However, such **feature analysis** does not work equally well in all areas of the lexicon.

See also MORPHOSYNTACTIC.

feminine (*n. & adj.*) (A *noun etc.) of the grammatical *gender that mainly denotes female persons or animals. Contrasted with *masculine and *neuter.

In some languages grammatical gender distinctions of masculine and feminine (and sometimes also neuter) apply to all *nouns and related *words. In English, however, grammatical gender distinctions are found only in *third person singular personal *pronouns, where the feminine forms (*she, her, herself, hers*) contrast with the masculine ones (*he, him,* etc.) and the non-personal forms (*it, its,* etc.).

The *suffix -*ess* (e.g. in *lioness, hostess*) is a feminine marker in nouns, but its use has decreased: many people who might previously have used the word *actress* now prefer to use *actor* to refer to both male and female actors.

Some male-female pairs of words are *morphologically related (e.g. *hero/heroine, widow/widower*), but many are not (e.g. *boy/girl, duck/ drake*).

Compare COMMON; DUAL.

FG *See* FUNCTIONAL GRAMMAR.

field *Semantics*. A range or system of *referents that have some aspect of *meaning in common. Sometimes called *domain.

The theory of semantic fields asserts that the meaning of a *word depends partly on the other words it is related to in meaning. All such words together constitute a **semantic field** (or **lexical field**). In different languages the same field is often apportioned differently, with dissimilar sets of terms used for that field. Classic examples are the fields of colour and kinship. It is well known that languages divide the colour spectrum differently, but in English the meaning of, for example, *blue* is limited by the existence of *green* and *purple*, and the latter is itself further limited by the existence of, say, *mauve*. Similarly, the meanings of *brother*, *cousin*, and so on form a network of connected family terms.

field of discourse *Sociolinguistics*. The subject matter being talked or written about.

In some cases different subject matter may involve few differences other than those of *vocabulary. But some fields of *discourse are characterized by their own distinctive grammatical styles, e.g. legal language, football commentaries, advertisements, sermons.

Compare REGISTER.

filled pause The use of a hesitation noise.

Hesitation noises, inadequately represented as *eh, er, erm*, etc., are a common feature of speech; they are used to give the speaker time to think, or to prevent another speaker from taking over.

filler

1. A *word or words that can fill a particular functional *slot in a *slot-and-filler analysis of *clause structure.

Identifying functional slots, and the linguistic items that fill them, is one way of analysing clauses and *sentences. Thus *Jill/lives/on the hill* contains three slots, which are identifiable as *subject/*predicator/*adverbial. The fillers in this particular case are, formally, a *noun phrase, a *verb (phrase), and a *prepositional phrase, but these slots could be filled by other elements without changing the nature of the slots. For example, we could replace the prepositional phrase with an *adverb phrase: *Jill lives frugally*.

2. A word or larger formulaic expression, usually outside the syntax of its adjoining or containing clause, that serves to fill what might otherwise be an unwanted pause in conversation; e.g. *oh, well, you know*. Also called **pragmatic particle**.

Compare DISCOURSE MARKER.

final Designating, or occurring in, a *position at the end of a containing linguistic unit (e.g. a *phrase or *clause).

•• **final clause:** a *subordinate clause that expresses an intention or *purpose, and is typically introduced by *in order that, so that, so as to*, etc. *See also* PURPOSE.

•• **final position** (also called *end position): this is often contrasted with *initial (or *front) and *medial (or *mid) position, and the concept is used particularly in relation to *ellipsis, and to the placing of *adverbials. For any particular unit functioning as adverbial, the term does not necessarily mean 'at the very end of its containing clause', but rather 'after the *verb (and *object)'. Thus *immediately* and *without question* are both in final position in *The money was repaid immediately without question.*

final combining form *See* NEOCLASSICAL COMPOUND.

finite Carrying *tense. Contrasted with *non-finite.

*Verbs that carry tense, and by extension the *verb phrases (1/2), *clauses, and *sentences that contain them, can be described as finite.

The *third person singular *present tense -*s* form (e.g. *looks, sees*) is always finite, as is the *past (2) form (e.g. *looked, saw*), whereas the *present participle in -*ing* (e.g. *looking, seeing*) and the *past participle in -*ed/-en* (e.g. *looked, seen*) are *non-finite. The *base form (e.g. *look, see*) can be either. It is finite as a present tense form (e.g. *I <u>see</u> the coastline*), but non-finite as an *infinitive (e.g. *I can <u>see</u> the coastline*).

There is disagreement as to whether the base form in the *imperative (e.g. *<u>Stay</u> here!*) and the *subjunctive (e.g. *The boss insists that she <u>stay</u> late*) is finite or non-finite, though most accounts opt for the former view.

Although we speak of finite verb phrases, it is in fact only the first verb in a finite verb phrase that is finite, e.g.

> We *have* been wondering
> It *may* be being changed

In some recent work in linguistics the idea that verb forms are finite or non-finite has been abandoned. Instead, finiteness is regarded as a property of higher-order units such as clauses.

> 2007 I. NIKOLAEVA The development of syntactic theory starting from the 1960s led to an obvious departure from traditional assumptions. Finiteness was reanalysed as something more abstract, essentially a clausal category that is only secondarily reflected in the form of the verb.

• **finitely.**
• **finiteness:** the fact or quality of being finite.
•• **finite passive construction:** *see* PASSIVE.

finite state grammar A theoretical model of grammar discussed by the American linguist Noam Chomsky in his book *Syntactic Structures* (1957).

The model was a deliberately over-simple one that could not account for many features of real language. It was introduced in order to show the need for more elaborate theories.

Compare GENERATIVE GRAMMAR (2); PHRASE (1); TRANSFORMATIONAL.

first conditional *See* CONDITIONAL.

first language *See* LANGUAGE.

first person (Denoting, or used in conjunction with a *word referring to) the speaker or writer, in contrast to the addressee(s), or others.

First person *pronouns are *I, me, myself, my, mine* in the *singular; and *we, us, ourselves, our, ours* in the *plural. (Some of these items are regarded in some models as *determinatives (1) when they are placed before *nouns.)

Uniquely among English verbs, *be* has a distinct first person singular form in the *present tense, namely *am*.

Compare SECOND PERSON; THIRD PERSON.

Firthian (*adj.*) Of, pertaining to, or characteristic of the British linguist John Rupert Firth (1890–1960).

(*n.*) A person who subscribes to Firth's theories.

J. R. Firth, Professor of General Linguistics in the University of London (1944–56), was influential in the development of linguistics in Britain. Characteristic of his approach is the concept of **polysystemicism** (i.e. that language is not one system, but a set of systems). *Systemic Grammar is a development of his ideas.

● **Firthianism**.

1975 T. F. MITCHELL There appear to be three salient features of Firthianism . . . : (1) insistence on the centrality of meaning in all its aspects (2) adoption of a basic inductive approach to language study (3) recognition of the priority of syntagmatic analysis.

See also NEO-FIRTHIAN; SYSTEMIC GRAMMAR.

fixed Not subject to variation.

●● **fixed phrase**: a *phrase of which few if any variants are *acceptable (also called **set expression**).

In some phrases no change either of an individual *word or of the word order is likely. Examples of fixed phrases are:

knife and fork	(*fork and knife)
pay attention to	(*pay attention towards/for/at)
heir apparent	(*apparent heir)

from bad to worse	(*from good to better)
beneath contempt	(*below/under/underneath contempt)
no good, no different	(*no bad, no similar)
for the time being	(*for the time that is)
to and fro	(*to and from)
as it were	

Compare COLLOCATE; FORMULA.

•• **fixed word order**: a characteristic of some languages, whereby a change in the word order (strictly speaking: *constituent order) can change the *meaning of (a part of) a sentence.

English is, relatively speaking, a fixed word order language, since the order *subject-*verb-*object is typical, and a change can significantly affect the meaning. Compare, for instance, *The child chased the goose* with *The goose chased the child*.

See FREE WORD ORDER.

flection The same as *inflection. (Now old-fashioned.)
• **flectional, flectionless**.

focus (*n.*) The most important or contrastive part of a *sentence or *clause in terms of its information content or prominence.

In analysing a sentence in terms of the structure of its information content or 'message' (as opposed to its syntactic structure), it is common to divide it into two, applying such terms as *given and *new, *topic and *comment, and *theme and *rheme to the two parts. Focus is another label for the second term in such pairs, used as such in e.g. CGEL:

> 1985 R. QUIRK et al. There is commonly a one-to-one relation between 'given' in contrast to 'new' information on the one hand, and theme in contrast to focus on the other.

The pairs given/new, topic/comment, theme/rheme, etc. are sometimes treated as more or less synonymous, and indeed in many cases the topic or theme will be something 'given' or already known, while the second part of the sentence, the comment or rheme, will present new information. The term focus is not, however, quite the same as rheme. The former often refers to the end portion of the rheme (cf. *end-focus), rather than the entire rheme, and in speaking it roughly correlates with the final nuclear stress, as in the following example:

> The phone's still out of oRder

The focus can be shifted to a point earlier in the sentence if the information at the end of the sentence is predictable. This is called **marked focus**, e.g.

> The PHONE is ringing (i.e. not the doorbell)

In fact, the focus can be marked on any part of a sentence, by shifting the main sentence stress:

You should phone YOUR mother   (i.e. not mine)

You should PHONE your mother   (i.e. not text her)

You SHOULD phone your mother   (i.e. it's your duty)

YOU should phone your mother   (i.e. don't expect someone else to)

When written (without capitals or other marking) this sentence would normally be interpreted as having the focus at the end (i.e. as coextensive with *mother*), so special devices must be used to mark the focus at a different place.

See also CLEFT; INFORMATION STRUCTURE; MARKED; PSEUDO-CLEFT.

(*v.*) Make the focus of something, or (use to) place the focus on something.

focusing adjunct *See* FOCUSING ADVERB.

focusing adverb An *adverb that focuses on a particular part of a *sentence, *clause, *phrase, etc. Also called **focusing adjunct** and **focusing subjunct**.

Typical focusing adverbs are *even, exactly, merely, only,* e.g.

Even in old age, she was immensely active

I *merely asked* them the time

Only you would say a thing like that

The classification of adverbs is notoriously difficult, and there is considerable variety in the way it is done.

See also DEGREE; INTENSIFYING ADVERB; SUBJUNCT.

focusing subjunct *See* FOCUSING ADVERB.

folk etymology A popular modification of the form of a *word, in order to render it apparently meaningful. (Also called **popular etymology**.)

Welsh rarebit, an alteration of *Welsh rabbit,* is an example of folk etymology. It seems to be based on the belief that nobody could describe melted cheese on toast as 'rabbit'. But *Welsh rabbit* is correct: an ironical name that grew up in the days when only the better-off would be likely to eat much meat. Other examples of folk etymology are the more familiar-sounding *sparrow grass* (for *asparagus*) and *forlorn hope,* now meaning 'a faint remaining hope', but based on the Dutch *verloren hoop,* actually meaning 'lost troop' (i.e. a storming party, etc.). The *cock-* of *cockroach,* the *-wing* of *lapwing,* and the *-house* of *penthouse* all result from the attempt to make at least a part of an arbitrary word into a meaningful element (their earlier forms being *cacarootch, lappewinke,* and *pentice*).

force *See* ILLOCUTIONARY.

foreign plural A *plural form of a *noun that retains the *inflection of the foreign *word of which it is a *borrowing.

Many nouns taken from foreign languages retain their foreign plurals. This applies particularly to Greek and Latin loanwords, many of which retain **classical plurals**, e.g.

crisis, crises
phenomenon, phenomena
larva, larvae
erratum, errata

Some have alternative anglicized plurals:

candelabrums/candelabra
formulas/formulae
corpuses/corpora

And some have both types of plural, but with different *meanings (e.g. *appendixes/appendices*).

Because of its exceptional divergence in form from all other patterns of English plural formation, the Latin and Greek -*a* plural has shown a tendency to be reinterpreted as a non-*count form, or as a *singular with its own -*s* plural. This tendency has progressed furthest in *agenda*, and has met with varying degrees of acceptance in *candelabra*, *criteria*, *data*, *media*, and *phenomena*.

Examples of foreign plurals from other languages include *bureaux/ bureaus* (French), and *cherubim/cherubs*, *kibbutzim/kibbutzes* (Hebrew).

form The *shape or external characteristics of a linguistic unit; contrasted with its *meaning or *function.

1. One of the ways in which a *word can be spelt, pronounced, or inflected.

For example, all *lexical verbs have *inflectional forms (represented by a *lexeme), as do many *nouns. Thus *see* has five forms: *see*, *sees*, *seeing*, *saw*, *seen*, and many nouns have a *plural form ending in the *suffix -*s* and a *genitive form ending in -'*s*. *See also* INFLECTION.

2. Part of the internal structure of a word; the same as *morpheme (2).

Words can be made up of *free (1) forms and *bound (1) forms (or morphemes). Sometimes a bound form indicates which *word class a particular item belongs to. For example, the suffix -*ness* normally indicates that the word in which it occurs is a noun. However, the word class of many items cannot be identified in this way, and it needs instead to be identified by the *function (1) these items perform in the containing *sentence or *clause. *See* DISTRIBUTION; FORM CLASS.

3. The syntactic identity of a linguistic unit as belonging to a particular type of *phrase, clause, etc., based on its internal *structure, and on the way it behaves syntactically in a sentence. Thus in *The film ended late* we identify *the film* as a *noun phrase, because it is a string of words whose *head is a noun, and because it occurs in a typical noun phrase *position in the sentence.

Units identified in this way can be analysed further. For example, phrases can be analysed into their formal *constituent parts. Thus, a noun phrase may consist of a single noun (e.g. *people*), but often contains a *determinative (1) and/or an *adjective phrase (e.g. *the most interesting. people*) and sometimes *postmodification (*the most interesting people that I ever met*).

Form contrasts with function (1) here. 'Noun phrase' is a form category, but a noun phrase can function in various ways, for example as *subject, *direct object, prepositional *complement, or *adverbial.

formal

1. Relating to *form (3) as opposed to *function (1). Contrasted with *functional.

*Noun, *noun phrase, *verb phrase, etc. are form(al) categories, defined largely by their structural composition, irrespective of their *meaning or function in a sentence.

2. Relating to form as opposed to meaning.

Traditional grammar often defines linguistic units in *notional terms, e.g. 'A noun is the name of a person, place, or thing'. Modern grammar, seeking more formal criteria, prefers to define word classes largely by their syntactic *distribution.

3. Of language used in particular situations: characterized by a relatively impersonal, reserved attitude, and adherence to conventional social mores. Contrasted with *informal.

Formal speech and writing is characterized by the use of more complicated grammatical structures (e.g. a higher level of *subordination), by more unusual or foreign *vocabulary, and by the avoidance of contracted forms (such as *can't* and *won't*) and *colloquialisms. Thus *Patrons are requested to refrain from smoking* is more formal than *Please don't smoke* in several respects. Formal and informal are, however, at the ends of a *cline, and often language is not marked as either.

4. formal *it*: (a traditional, and now disused, label for) *dummy *it* or *anticipatory *it*.

• **formality.**

See also IMPERSONAL.

formal semantics A kind of *logical semantics.

formation The same as *word formation.

formative

1. (*n. & adj.*) (Designating) the smallest meaningful physical element used in the formation of *words. The same as *morpheme (2).

Like morpheme, the term formative can be used in a physical sense. Formatives are divided into **lexical formatives**, used in the formation of derived words (e.g. *-ful* as in *hurtful*, *spoonful*), and **inflectional formatives** (e.g. *-ing* as in *hurting*, *laughing*).

2. (Now mostly not in use.) A physical form of an abstract morpheme. The same as *allomorph.

In this use, formative is not synonymous with *morpheme (1), but denotes one of the variants of such an abstract morpheme. Thus the three regular *plural endings of English (/s/, /z/, and /ɪz/) are all formatives of the single 'plural morpheme'.

form class Generally, another term for *word class.

formula (Plural **formulae, formulas**.) An instance of stereotyped language that usually allows few or no changes in *form (1), and may not conform to current grammatical *usage.

Common formulae include:

Thank you!
How do you do? (*How does your mother do?)
See you!
No way!
You don't say!
Many happy returns!
Please God
Yours sincerely

This category overlaps with *fixed phrase and with *fossilized.

• **formulaic**: that is a formula, that uses formulae.

See also NON-SENTENCE.
Compare IDIOM.

formulaic subjunctive See SUBJUNCTIVE.

form word See GRAMMATICAL WORD (1).

forwards anaphora The same as *cataphora.

See also ANAPHOR; ANAPHORA.

fossilized Having a structure that is no longer *productive.

Fossilized *structures in English are exemplified in:

Handsome is as handsome does	(*Good is as good acts)
Come what may	(*Occur what will)
Long may it last	(*Short may it last)
How come...?	(*How happen...?)

Fossilized *phrases include *fore and aft, kith and kin, to and fro*.

Fossilized *word-formation processes include such items as the *plural *-en*, still present in *children, brethren, oxen*, but not available, except as a joke, for new *words.

This category overlaps with *archaism, *fixed phrase, and *formula. *Compare* IDIOM.

free

1. Designating a linguistic form that can be used in isolation.

•• **free form, free morpheme**: the smallest linguistic unit that can stand alone; contrasted with a *bound form. *See* MINIMUM FREE FORM.

2. Of *word order (more accurately: *constituent order) in a particular language: an order that can be varied without alteration to the basic meaning of the *sentence.

Free word order tends to be a characteristic of highly inflected languages like Latin, in which *inflections are the primary indicators of the relationships between the constituent parts of sentences, rather than word order. English, by contrast, has a fairly *fixed word order.

free direct speech *See* FREE INDIRECT SPEECH

free indirect speech Free indirect speech is a form of *indirect speech that retains the *sentence *structure of *direct speech (e.g. subject-auxiliary *inversion in *interrogatives) and usually lacks a reporting *verb, but is signalled by *backshifted verbs and by changes in *pronouns and in *time and *place references. It is popular in fiction and narrative writing for reporting both speech and thoughts. Called **erlebte Rede** in German.

Free direct speech is marked by an absence of *quotation marks, and also by *present (2) tenses that contrast with the *past (2) tenses of the rest of the narrative.

In the following extract the conversation is reported in a mixture of the author's free indirect speech (shown in italics) and the old man's free direct speech:

> As our conversation continued the old man became whiter and whiter. The dust clung to his hat, his face, his moustache, his eyelashes and his hands. He did not complain. *Who was doing all the killing?*
> —Oh, the guerillas of course. If the guerillas see you and do not know you they kill you.

And what about the army?

—The army are all right, if you greet them and have papers.

Was there enough food?

—There is enough food, but there is no business. (P. MARNHAM *So Far From God*, 1985, p.148.)

Compare DIRECT SPEECH; INDIRECT SPEECH.

free relative clause A type of *relative clause which, like many relative clauses, begins with a *wh-word (variously referred to as a **free relative pronoun** or **fused relative pronoun**) but, unlike *canonical relative clauses, has no overt *antecedent. Instead, such clauses contain the antecedent within themselves, or, to put it differently, 'the wh-element is merged with its antecedent' (CGEL).

A free relative clause can refer to things or people, as well as to abstract ideas. Examples:

You can say *what you like*   (= You can say [[that which] you like])

Whoever told you this was wrong   (= [[The person who] told you this] was
                                         wrong)

Free relative clauses are often formally analysed as *noun phrases, because they occur in typical NP positions and can display *agreement with a following *verb; hence the alternative label **nominal relative clause** (CGEL). The terms **fused relative construction** (CaGEL) and **independent relative clause** are also found.

free relative construction *See* FREE RELATIVE CLAUSE.

free relative pronoun *See* FREE RELATIVE CLAUSE.

free variation The possibility of substituting an element for another without a change in *meaning.

Free variation occurs in the spelling of some *words (e.g. *realize/realise, judgement/judgment, jail/gaol*) and in the shape of some grammatical forms of words (e.g. *hewed/hewn, leaned/leant*).

Free variation in the use of different words is normally labelled *synonymy.

See also CONDITIONING; VARIANT.

frequency

1. The term is used in its everyday sense to group together semantically related adverbs, such as *always, usually, often, sometimes, never*. These are popularly called **frequency adverbs/adjuncts**.

Rate of occurrence.

See also INDEFINITE.

2. *Linguistics*. The rate at which a particular *word in a language is used.

How commonly or rarely words are used is of special practical interest to lexicographers and educationists. With modern technology it is possible to obtain word frequencies from vast collections of texts (*corpora), in order to confirm or disprove estimates of the frequency of use of particular words. The word of highest frequency in English, according to several different corpora, is *the*.

frequentative (*n.* & *adj.*) (An *inflection, *verb, etc.) expressing frequent repetition, or intensity of action.

In some languages there are special ways of forming frequentatives from ordinary verbs, e.g. in Latin, *rogito* ,'I ask repeatedly', formed on *rogo*, 'I ask'. In English the *suffixes *-er* and *-le* have been used to produce a number of verbs of this kind, e.g. *flitter* from *flit* and *crackle* from *crack*; but this is not a regularly *productive system.

The term is also used to describe other ways of expressing repeated verbal action, and is sometimes synonymous with *iterative (1).

front (*adj.*) Of the *position of a *constituent: at, or relatively close to, the beginning of a *sentence, *clause, etc.

(*v.*) Place (a constituent) at the beginning of a sentence, clause, etc. *See* FRONTING.

•• **front position**: this is referred to especially in the description of *adverbials.

See also END; FINAL; INITIAL; MEDIAL.

fronted Of a *constituent: placed at the beginning of a *sentence, *clause, etc. *See also* FRONTING.

fronted preposition A *preposition heading a *prepositional phrase placed at the beginning of a *clause in certain types of structures, for example *interrogative clauses, as in <u>On</u> *which shelf will you store the jam pots?* (where *on* heads the prepositional phrase *on which shelf*).

Compare STRANDING.

fronting The placing of a *constituent at the beginning of a *sentence, *clause, etc., often to achieve a certain effect.

English sentences typically begin with a *subject, but other functional elements—*object, predicative *complement, *adverbial, and even part of the *predicate—can be placed at the beginning, typically for *information structuring reasons, for instance in order to mark the *topic/*theme. Examples:

Loud music I do not like	(fronted object)
Horrible I call it	(fronted object-related predicative *complement)

After half an hour, we walked out   (fronted *adverbial)

And *paint the town red* we did   (fronted *verb phrase (2))

Compare TOPICALIZATION.

FSP *See* FUNCTIONAL SENTENCE PERSPECTIVE.

full

1. Complete; conforming in every respect to a description or definition.

•• **full apposition**: *see* APPOSITION.

•• **full conversion**: designating complete and permanent *conversion from one *word class to another.

•• **full sentence/clause**: a *sentence or *clause which conforms to the standard *rules of grammar, which is not characterized by *ellipsis, and normally contains a *subject and a (*finite) *verb. This term is contrasted with a *minor, *non-finite, or *verbless sentence/clause, which may be incomplete in one or more respects.

See also COMPLETE; KERNAL.

2. full stop: (in BrE) the punctuation mark <.> used at the end of a sentence or abbreviation. Also called **full point** (BrE) and **period** (AmE).

3. full verb: another term for *lexical verb. *Compare* MAIN VERB.

4. full word: another term for *content word.

function

1. The syntactic role that a linguistic unit plays within a 'higher' unit, such as a *phrase, *clause, or *sentence; distinguished from its *form.

The five *elements of clause structure, namely *subject, *verb, *object, *complement, and *adverbial, are grammatical functions. In addition, we distinguish *predicator as the function carried by the *main verb in a clause, and *predicate as the function assigned to the portion of a clause excluding the subject.

Within phrases, certain types of units can function as *modifiers, more specifically as *premodifiers or *postmodifiers.

There is no one-to-one correspondence between functions and their possible formal *realizations. Thus the functions of subject and *direct object are often realized by a *noun phrase, but can also be realized by a clause, e.g.

That the summer will be hot is by no means certain

I believe *that the summer will be hot*

2. The pragmatic (or *discourse) role of a clause.

Clauses may be classified in terms of their pragmatic (or discourse) functions. Thus the typical pragmatic functions of the *declarative, *interrogative, *exclamative, and *imperative *clause types are to make a *statement, ask a *question, utter an *exclamation, and issue a *directive. Deviations from these typical functions are called indirect *speech acts.

See also CLAUSE TYPE; COMMUNICATIVE *function*.

3. One of the social roles for which language is used.

This sense is similar to sense 2, but it is much more general. It has been suggested that there exists a limited set of primary speech functions such as offer, command, statement, and question; and that these cover all, or most, of the purposes for which language is used.

In the teaching of English (or any other modern language) to foreign learners, the concept of function has been extended to apply to a wide variety of social uses, such as making suggestions, complaining, and sympathizing.

functional As regards function; of, in, etc. function.

●● **functional category**: *see* FUNCTIONAL CATEGORY.

●● **functional conversion**: the same as *conversion.

●● **functional equivalence**: *see* EQUIVALENCE.

●● **functional head**: *see* HEAD.

●● **functional phrase**: *see* PHRASE.

●● **functional shift**: the same as *conversion.

functional category A *category that has predominantly grammatical importance in *phrase or *clause structure. Contrasted with *lexical category.

*Grammatical words (1) are functional categories. For example, in later *Generative Grammar (2) clauses are said to be *headed by an abstract functional category 'I' (= *inflection), which functions as the head of an inflection phrase (IP), and *complementizers are said to function as the head of **complementizer phrases** (CPs).

Functional Grammar (FG) A theory of grammar developed by the late Simon Dik and his associates since 1978 in which functional notions are of chief importance at various levels of representation.

> 1997 S. DIK & K. HENGEVELD In the functional paradigm . . . a language is in the first place conceptualized as an instrument of social interaction among human beings, used with the intention of establishing communicative relationships.

Functional Discourse Grammar (FDG) is a development of FG, but differs from it in a number of ways, so that it is now considered a separate theory.

Compare SYSTEMIC GRAMMAR.

Functional Sentence Perspective (FSP) A theory of linguistic analysis developed by the *Prague School, concerned with the amount of information conveyed by different parts of a *sentence or *utterance. The theory of *theme and *rheme derives from this theory.

See also COMMUNICATIVE *dynamism.*

function word *See* GRAMMATICAL WORD (1).

functor The same as *grammatical word (1). (A rare term.)

fused determiner-head construction *See* FUSION.

fused-head construction *See* FUSION.

fused modifier-head construction *See* FUSION.

fused participle A term coined by H. W. Fowler in the early twentieth century to denote a *structure which involves the *-*ing* form of a *verb (often called a *gerund) preceded by a *noun phrase without a *genitive -'s marker, or by an *accusative *pronoun, e.g.

Were you surprised at *my father arriving* early?
Forgive *me asking*, but...

Fowler considered the following genitival versions to be more 'correct':

Were you surprised at *my father's arriving* early?
Forgive *my asking*, but...

It should be noted that the 'fused participle' form is common in spoken, and even written, English.

See also GERUND.

fused predeterminer-head construction *See* FUSION.

fused relative construction *See* FREE RELATIVE CLAUSE.

fused relative pronoun *See* FREE RELATIVE CLAUSE.

fusion

1. The merging of linguistic elements, *functions (1), or *meanings in one form.

English *verb *inflections are an example of fusion. Thus the *-s* ending (e.g. *looks, puts*) signifies '*third person' + '*singular' + '*present'. This is referred to as fused (or multiple) *exponence.

• **fusional**: exhibiting or causing fusion.

1980 E. K. BROWN & J. E. MILLER We can . . . have rules of the form: MAN + pl →
men. We call rules like this 'fusional'. Fusional rules have two morphemes on
the left-hand side of the rule matched to a single morph on the right-hand side.

2. (In CaGEL): the phenomenon whereby in a particular *noun phrase
two *functions (1) are combined: *determiner (1) + *head, *modifier +
head, or *predeterminer (1) + head. These are called **fused-head
constructions**.

In a **fused determiner-head construction** the functions of determiner
and head are combined in one item. Here are examples of **simple,
partitive**, and **special** fused determiner-head constructions:

I asked you to buy some apples, but did you buy *any*? (simple: missing head is
retrievable as *apples*)

Some of their children are at university (partitive: 'some children from among
their children')

That is unacceptable (special: missing head is not retrievable)

The **fused modifier-head construction** combines a modifier and head,
e.g. *The rich should be taxed more*; and the **fused predeterminer-head
construction** combines a *predeterminer (1) and a head, e.g. *Mike eats
half the amount I do for breakfast, but Jan eats double*.

● **fused**

●● **fused relative construction**: the same as *free relative clause.

●● **fused relative pronoun**: the same as *free relative pronoun

futurate The use of a particular *tense or *construction not normally
used for that purpose to refer to *future (1) time.

Thus the **present futurate** is a *present (2) tense used to refer to future
time, often with a time *adjunct (e.g. *Next week he flies to Kuwait*). The
past futurate is a *past (2) tense used to refer to future *situations, viewed
from a past moment in time, i.e. a *future in the past (e.g. *He left Rome in
July 1989, but only a month later he would return*). The **present progressive
futurate** is a present *progressive construction used to refer to future time
(e.g. *Tomorrow we are having pasta*), while the **past progressive futurate**
refers to the future from a past viewpoint, again using a progressive construction (e.g. *They were visiting us next week, but they've cancelled*).

future (*n. & adj.*)

1. (As a general concept.) (Designating) an *indefinite period of time yet
to unfold after the present moment.

2. (As a linguistic concept.) (Designating) the term may refer to a *tense (the
'future tense') which traditionally refers to an *inflection on a *verb encoding
*reference to a *situation in time that is yet to take place. In traditional
grammar, and in some recent work, tenses formed with *shall* and *will* are

called future tenses. More specifically, the combination *shall/will* + bare infinitive is called the **simple future tense** (sometimes **future simple**, e.g. *Greg will send you a text message later*), and *shall/will* + *be* + V-*ing* is called the **future continuous tense** or the **future progressive tense** (e.g. *They will be travelling by train*). Other tenses include the **future perfect tense** (e.g. *He will have seen your report*), the **past future perfect tense** (*She would have told you*), etc.

For some linguists the definition of tense as involving a verbal inflection entails that English has only a *present tense and *past tense, but no future tense, since there is no unique verbal inflection that encodes future time. In such frameworks it is argued that English can employ various different *constructions, each with its own meaning, to talk about future time, including the following:

the *will/shall* + *bare infinitive construction	e.g. We will close at 5 p.m.; We shall see
the *will/shall* + progressive construction	e.g. Jack will be teaching the new students
the *be going to* construction	e.g. It is going to rain
the present *futurate construction	e.g. His plane arrives at 8.33 a.m. If the plane is late … When he arrives …
the present progressive futurate construction	e.g. I am seeing Robert tomorrow
the (simple) past futurate construction	e.g. He left Rome in July 1989, but only a month he later he *would* return
the past progressive futurate construction	e.g. They *were visiting* us next week, but they've cancelled.

See FUTURATE; FUTURE IN THE PAST; TENSE; TIME.

future in the past A *construction (*tense in some frameworks) in which a future *situation is viewed from a time in the *past (1).

Traditionally this label is given to a certain type of construction containing the *model verb *would*, e.g.

They did not realize at the time that by 1914 the two countries *would* be at war

The construction (or tense) exemplified above is also called the past *futurate.

Other structures can also be used to describe what is seen as a future situation when viewed from a past perspective, e.g.

We *were* bitterly *to regret* our decision

I *was going* to tell you (when you interrupted me)

The latter is referred to as a **past progressive futurate**.

See also FUTURE; FUTURATE.

future perfect A *construction (*tense in some frameworks) formed by *shall/will* + *have* + a *past participle, expressing a **past in the future**.

In the traditional labelling of the tenses the **future perfect simple** is exemplified by:

I *will have wasted* the whole morning if they don't come soon

and the **future perfect continuous/progressive** by:

I *will have been waiting* three hours by one o'clock

A **future perfect passive** is also possible:

The best things *will have been sold* by the time you get there

In recent treatments of these constructions they are not regarded as separate tenses.

See also PAST PARTICIPLE; PERFECT.

fuzzy boundary *See* GRADIENCE.

fuzzy grammar *See* GRADIENCE.

gap A syntactic position in *clause structure associated with a *fronted *constituent, or other type of *antecedent. For example, in *What did he tell you _?* the underscore marks the position with which the *wh*-phrase *what* is associated. In some frameworks, e.g. *Generative Grammar (2), this association is treated in terms of *movement.

gapping A phenomenon caused by *medial *ellipsis (in contrast to the more usual *initial or *final ellipsis) in the second (or later) part of a *coordination, e.g.

I play golf and my brothers _ tennis
I will go by train and my friend _ by car

gender

1. A grammatical *category used for the classification of *nouns, *pronouns, and related words, partly according to natural distinctions of sex (or absence of sex).

1958 C. HOCKETT Genders are classes of nouns reflected in the behavior of associated words.

This quotation brings out that the gender of a noun in a particular grammatical configuration may be reflected on other items that are also part of the *structure in question, e.g. *adjectives. See 2 below.

See also GRAMMATICAL.

2. The property of belonging to one of such classes.

In some languages gender is an important grammatical property of nouns and related words, marked by distinct forms. In French, for example, all nouns are either *masculine (*son livre*, masculine = 'his book' or 'her book') or *feminine (*sa plume*, feminine = 'his pen' or 'her pen'). In these languages natural gender is usually, though not entirely, marked by the matching grammatical gender. In some languages (e.g. Latin, German, and Old English) there is a third gender, **neuter**, which typically marks nouns denoting inanimate objects (although many such nouns may belong to the other two genders, and some neuter nouns may refer to animate beings, e.g. *das Mädchen* 'the-NEUTER girl' in German).

In Modern English overt grammatical gender hardly exists, except in
*third person singular pronouns:

he/him/his/himself   (masculine)
she/her/hers/herself   (feminine)
it/its/itself   (often called *non-personal, rather than neuter)

Even here there can be some mismatch between natural and grammatical
gender. Inanimate countries, ships, cars, etc. are sometimes referred to by
masculine or feminine pronouns, a baby may be *it*, and animals may be
referred to by *personal or non-personal pronouns.

Natural gender distinctions are made covertly in many words referring
to males and females. Pairs of words occasionally show a *derivational
relationship (e.g. *hero/heroine*, *widow/widower*), but many male and
female noun pairs show no *morphological connection (e.g. *brother/sister*,
duck/drake).

Compare COMMON, DUAL.

general determiner *See* INDEFINITE ARTICLE; SPECIFIC.

Generalized Phrase Structure Grammar (GPSG) A linguistic
theory of grammar originating in the 1970s and offering a radical
alternative to *Generative Grammar (2).

It does not recognize *transformations, but uses 'metarules' and other
devices that result in generalized rules which were not possible in earlier
*Phrase Structure Grammar.

See also CHOMSKYAN; GENERATIVE; GOVERNMENT-BINDING THEORY;
GRAMMAR; HEAD-DRIVEN PHRASE STRUCTURE GRAMMAR; MINIMALIST
PROGRAM; PRINCIPLES AND PARAMETERS THEORY; STANDARD THEORY;
TRANSFORMATIONAL GRAMMAR.

generate (In *Generative Grammar (2) and derived frameworks.)
Produce (grammatical *structures) by the application of *rules that can be
formulated precisely.

Most grammars that have ever been written 'generate' *sentences in the
sense that the grammaticality of both existing and potential sentences can
be tested against the rules. The term in a stronger sense is derived from
one of its uses in mathematics, and was introduced into grammatical
theory by the American linguist Noam Chomsky in *Syntactic Structures*
(1957).

> 2001 T. WASOW How can we give a finite description of something infinite?
> Inspired by earlier work in mathematical logic and the foundations of com-
> puter science, Chomsky answered this question by proposing that we think of
> grammars as devices that put pieces of sentences together according to precise

rules, thereby 'generating' well-formed sentences. If some of the grammar rules can apply to their own outputs (in technical jargon, if some rules are *recursive), then it is possible for finite grammars to generate infinite languages.

• **generation**.

generative (In *Generative Grammar (2) and related frameworks.) Able to *generate grammatical structures.

• **generativist**: a person who employs the methods of *Generative Grammar (1/2).

See also GENERATE.

Generative Grammar

1. A grammar that incorporates a set of *rules capable of producing (generating) an infinite number of *grammatical (and only grammatical) sentences. This is a general sense of the term, often written with lower-case initials.

2. A theory of grammar that was first introduced by the American linguist Noam Chomsky in *Syntactic Structures* (1957). It has been developed and changed by Chomsky and others in diverging ways. It has also been challenged, but its influence on linguistic thought has been, and remains, considerable.

> 1986 N. CHOMSKY The concerns of traditional and generative grammar are, in a certain sense, complementary: a good traditional or pedagogical grammar provides a full list of exceptions (irregular verbs, etc.), paradigms and examples of regular constructions, and observations at various levels of detail and generality about the form and meaning of expressions . . . Generative grammar, in contrast, is concerned primarily with the intelligence of the reader, the principles and procedures brought to bear to attain full knowledge of a language.

The term is sometimes used as a synonym of *Transformational Grammar (or **Transformational-Generative Grammar**), but generative grammar does not necessarily contain transformational rules.

See MONOSTRATAL.

See also CHOMSKYAN; GENERALIZED PHRASE STRUCTURE GRAMMAR; GENERATIVE; GENERATIVE SEMANTICS; GOVERNMENT-BINDING THEORY; GRAMMAR; HEAD-DRIVEN PHRASE STRUCTURE GRAMMAR; MINIMALIST PROGRAM; PHRASE STRUCTURE GRAMMAR; PRINCIPLES AND PARAMETERS THEORY; STANDARD THEORY; TRANSFORM; TRANSFORMATION.

Generative Semantics A theory of grammar, associated with George Lakoff, James McCawley, John Robert Ross, and others, which was developed during the late 1960s as an alternative to the standard *generative model.

Despite its name, it is not a theory of semantics, but a grammatical model in which semantics plays an important role.

> 1991 J. LYONS The term 'generative semantics' refers to an alternative version of transformational-generative grammar—one which differs from the standard version of *Aspects* [*of the Theory of Syntax*] in that the rules of the semantic component are said to be 'generative', rather than 'interpretive'.

See also CHOMSKYAN; GENERALIZED PHRASE STRUCTURE GRAMMAR; GENERATIVE; GOVERNMENT-BINDING THEORY; GRAMMAR; HEAD-DRIVEN PHRASE STRUCTURE GRAMMAR; MINIMALIST PROGRAM; PHRASE STRUCTURE GRAMMAR; PRINCIPLES AND PARAMETERS THEORY; STANDARD THEORY; TRANSFORM; TRANSFORMATION; TRANSFORMATIONAL; TRANSFORMATIONAL GRAMMAR.

generic Relating or *referring to a whole class or *category; in contrast to *specific.

In describing the uses of the *articles, a useful distinction is drawn between the notions generic and specific which cuts across the distinction between *definite and *indefinite. In English, *the* + a *singular *count *noun can have definite and generic *meaning, as in

> *The dodo* is extinct
>
> Who invented *the wheel*?

The in combination with certain *adjectives is also used with generic (and plural) meaning:

> *The dead* are venerated in many societies
>
> *The Chinese* play a prominent role in current world affairs.

Some kinds of indefinite meaning are often labelled generic, as in

> *Unexploded bombs* are dangerous   (plural *count)
>
> *An unexploded bomb* is dangerous   (singular count)
>
> *Danger* lurks everywhere!   (*uncount)

But *see* CLASSIFYING.

Some *personal pronouns are used with the generic meaning of 'people in general' or 'mankind':

> *One* never can tell
>
> Man seems to think *he* rules the planet
>
> *You* can lead a horse to water
>
> *We* still have many diseases to conquer

genitive (*n. and adj.*) (Designating) the *case *inflection typically carried by *nouns (noun phrases), including *pronouns, when they express *possession, close association, or a range of other *meanings. (Also called the **Saxon genitive**.)

The genitive is marked by the addition of -*'s* to regular *singular nouns and to *plurals that lack *s* (e.g. *the boy's mother, the children's mother*). An *apostrophe (') only, which has no spoken realization, is added to regular plurals (e.g. *the boys' mother*).

Some grammarians argue that, although it is a relic of the earlier English case system, the genitive should no longer be described in terms of case in modern English. On this view, the English genitive is not comparable to the *inflected genitive case of Latin, but is a type of *enclitic, as evidenced by the fact that the -*'s* ending can be added to a noun phrase, e.g.

[the Prince of Wales]'s speech

[the people in the flat below]'s radio

[someone else]'s problem

This phenomenon is sometimes called the **group genitive** or **group possessive**.

'Possession' is the most central meaning expressed by the genitive form, and for this reason the distinct genitive forms of the personal pronouns are called *possessive pronouns. However, other meanings are also possible, for example 'descriptive' meaning (e.g. *a women's college, London's West End*), 'measure' meaning (e.g. *a day's work*), and 'partitive' meaning (e.g. *the car's windscreen*; i.e. the windscreen is part of the car). The genitive seen in *See you at David's* or *I got it at the chemist's* is sometimes called the **local genitive**.

Meaning, rather than *surface syntax, distinguishes the **subjective genitive** and **objective genitive**. Thus the genitive has *subjective (2) meaning in *the architect's design of the tower* (compare *The architect designed the tower*), whereas it has *objective (2) meaning in *the enemy's defeat by the army* (compare *The army defeated the enemy*).

When a possessive or similar relationship can be expressed by a postmodifying *of*-phrase (e.g. *the mother of the boys*), the term *of*-genitive is often used.

• **genitival**: belonging to the genitive case, *construction, etc.

•• **dependent genitive**: a pronoun or noun phrase in the genitive case that *modifies the head noun inside a noun phrase, e.g. *Millie's cat*, *his job*, *the Mayor of London's* policies. *See also* SUBJECT.

•• **double genitive** (also called **post-genitive** or **oblique genitive construction**): a structure consisting of a noun + *of* + a genitive noun or pronoun, as in:

> some books of Jane's
>
> that cousin of yours

This structure might appear to express 'possession' twice, but in fact it has the advantage that it can combine *indefinite and *definite meaning, whereas the single genitive can only have definite meaning (e.g. *Jane's books, your cousin*).

•• **independent genitive**: a genitive apparently standing alone as a noun phrase because the head has been *ellipted, e.g. *Tom's* in *John's results were better than Tom's.*

A comparable possessive pronoun (e.g. *mine, yours*, etc.) is sometimes called an **independent possessive pronoun**.

•• **partitive genitive**: *see* PARTITIVE.

See also OBJECTIVE, *OF*-GENITIVE; SUBJECTIVE.

genre The type of text that a piece of writing or spoken *discourse belongs to from the point of view of its purpose, setting, and conventions of language use.

Compare DOMAIN; REGISTER.

Germanic (*n. & adj.*) (Designating) a family of related Indo-European languages that includes Danish, Dutch, English, German, Icelandic, Norwegian, and Swedish, or their presumed ancestor (**Common Germanic**).

Germanic affix *See* LEVEL ORDERING (HYPOTHESIS).

gerund Traditionally the gerund is the *-*ing* form of a *verb when used in a *noun-like way, as in *The playing of ball games is prohibited*, in contrast to the same form used as a *participle, e.g. *Everyone was playing ball games.* Sometimes called **verbal noun**. Both the term gerund, from Latin grammar, and the term verbal noun are out of favour among some modern grammarians.

The noun-like and verb-like properties of the *-ing* form are on a *cline. Consider the following examples:

> He is *smoking* twenty cigarettes a day
>
> The *smoking* of cigarettes is forbidden here
>
> My *smoking* twenty cigarettes a day annoys them

In the first example *smoking* is clearly a verb, by virtue of licensing a *direct object (*twenty cigarettes*). In the second example *smoking* is a noun because it is preceded by the *definite article, and because it takes a *prepositional phrase as its *complement (*of cigarettes*). In the third example *smoking* is noun-like in being preceded by the *pronoun *my* (analysed in some grammars as a *determiner (2)), and in functioning as the *head of the phrase *my smoking twenty cigarettes a day*, which occurs in a noun phrase position as the *subject of the sentence. However, it is verb-like in taking a direct object, and in retaining verbal meaning.

When a word in *-ing* derived from a verb inflects for *plural and lacks verbal meaning, it is considered to be a noun (e.g. *these delightful drawings*).

Confusingly, different grammarians use the label gerund differently, and regard the gerund variously as a verb or as a noun, or as both at the same time, as the quotations below show. For this reason the term is perhaps best avoided.

> 1999 L. HAEGEMAN and J. GUÉRON Verbs may also end in *-ing*; this form is referred to as the present participle or the gerund.

> 2002 D. MILLER The gerund is of the category N and behaves syntactically as a noun. It is, however, a verbal noun (in traditional terms), that is, it has the internal composition of a VP. As such it is generally derived by zero-derivation or conversion.

> 2003 R. HUDSON English gerunds are indeed just what the traditional grammarians said: single words which are both verbs and nouns.

•• **gerund-participle:** a term used in CaGEL to denote the *present participle.

See also GRADIENCE; *-ING* CLAUSE; *-ING* FORM; PARTICIPLE; PRESENT PARTICIPLE.

gerundial noun (In CaGEL.) An alternative label for *gerund, i.e. a *noun that ends in *-ing*, e.g.

the *sinking* of the ships
their careless *shouting* of slogans

gerundive In Latin grammar, a gerundive (*n.*) is a form of a *verb which behaves like an *adjective, with the meaning 'that should or must be done'. There is no grammatical equivalent in English, and the term is rarely used. When it is used, it is used as an adjective, and means 'relating to the *gerund', as in e.g. **gerundive clause**. In the latter sense we also find **gerundial** and **gerundival**.

gerund-participial clause *See* *-ING* CLAUSE.

gerund-participle *See* GERUND.

get-passive A *passive construction formed by the *verb *get* (rather than *be*) + a *past participle.

The *get*-passive is sometimes considered informal, and its use has, for this reason, been discouraged. It can, however, be a useful way of making clear that the meaning of the construction as a whole involves an action or event, rather than a *state. Contrast:

> They got married
> The chair got broken

with the ambiguous

> They were married
> The chair was broken

The latter examples are *ambiguous because they can refer to the process of being married or broken, but also to the state of being married or broken. As *get* has a more *dynamic (1) meaning, the *get*-passive is often used for actions we do to ourselves (e.g. *get dressed*). When the action denoted by the verb is carried out by someone else a *get*-passive can imply that the *referent of the *subject was in some way responsible for what happened, or at any rate that there was a cause. Compare:

> He got picked up by the police
> She got involved in an argument
> *The car got found abandoned

with

> He was picked up by the police
> She was involved in an argument
> The car was found abandoned

given (*n. & adj.*) (Designating) information that is already known or familiar in a text or discourse setting, either because it has been mentioned in the *context, or through general or shared knowledge, and is therefore less important from an *information structure point of view; contrasted with *new information.

In speech, given information usually receives little prominence, while the important, new part of the message receives full prominence.

Given and new may correlate with the syntactic distinctions *subject and *predicate, as in *I'm at the end of my tether*, where *I* is given in the *situation, and is also the grammatical subject, and *(a)m at the end of my tether* is new, and also the predicate. However, the concepts in these pairs are not in a one-to-one relationship. For example, if we are already talking about Tom, then in *Tom's at the end of his tether*, *Tom* would be given. But if this were an answer to *Who did you say was at the end of his tether?* then *Tom* would be new and the rest given.

The terms given and new are often used interchangeably with *theme and *rheme; *focus; *topic and *comment, etc., but distinctions are sometimes made, e.g. in CGEL:

> 1985 R. QUIRK et al. In contrast to 'given' and 'new', which are *contextually* established and to that extent 'extralinguistic', 'theme' and 'focus' are linguistically defined, in terms of position and prosody respectively.

A somewhat different distinction is made in *Systemic Grammar:

> 2014 M. A. K. HALLIDAY & C. MATTHIESSEN The Theme is what I, the speaker, choose to take as my point of departure. The Given is what you, the listener, already know about or have accessible to you. Theme + Rheme is speaker-oriented, whereas Given + New is listener-oriented.

Glossematics A variety of *structuralism introduced by the Danish scholar Louis Hjelmslev (1899–1965) in the 1930s and 1940s, concerned especially with developing an abstract theory of the *distribution of minimal forms (called *glossemes), and their mutual relationships.

glosseme In *Glossematics, any feature in a language (e.g. of *form, order, etc.) that carries *meaning, and cannot be analysed into smaller meaningful units.

The term has not acquired general currency.

goal *Semantics*.

1. (In some specialized models of grammar.) The *semantic role carried by the affected entity in a *proposition.

In this usage, the term contrasts with *actor or *agent. Thus *dog* is the goal in both of the following:

> Man bites dog
>
> The dog was bitten by the man

The term may even include something that results from an action (*factitive or *result in other analyses), as in:

> I've built *a path*
>
> *A path* has been made

It is not normally used of mental processes.

See EXPERIENCER; SENSER.

2. A semantic role assigned to an *argument which denotes an entity that is the target of the action denoted by a *verb, or the place to which something or someone moves, e.g.

> We sent *the auditors* our accounts

In one model of *Case Grammar, goal and *patient were introduced with two contrasting semantic roles. Examples given included *I cut my foot with a rock* (*my foot* = goal) and *I cut my foot on a rock* (*my foot* = patient).

Goal, as a semantic role, is used in its more everyday sense in relation to verbs of movement (e.g. *We reached the harbour*), and as such contrasts with *source.

3. Used in semantic analyses of directional *prepositions and *adverbials.

Thus in *I always walk to the station* and *He threw the book at me*, the *prepositional phrases *to the station* and *at me* can be analysed as goal.

In a more formal *componential analysis of spatial prepositions, goal can be one of the basic components of meaning.

God's Truth (Designating) an extreme view of grammar which assumes that the 'rules' of grammar have an objective existence in the language, and that all good grammarians will therefore discover the same facts and propound the same descriptions.

Invented by Fred W. Householder (1913–1994) in 1952.

Compare HOCUS-POCUS.

govern (In traditional grammar.) Especially of *verbs and *prepositions: license a unit of a particular kind, typically a *noun phrase, and, if this NP is headed by a *pronoun, the *case (1) of the pronoun, where relevant.

The term is used in Latin and other inflected languages of *verbs and *prepositions which require the use of a particular case in a dependent noun or pronoun. Thus in *ab initio* 'from the beginning' *ab* requires the *ablative case (realized by the ending *-o* in this noun), whereas in *ad infinitum*, literally 'to infinity', *ad* requires the *accusative case (realized by *-um*).

The term is also used in relation to verbs that license a *prepositional phrase with a particular preposition as its *head, as in these examples:

They *deprived* him *of* his property

They *plied* him *with* drink

The term has been used more recently (e.g. in *Generative Grammar (2)) to refer to similar *dependencies in syntax. For example, in *Jack built this house*, the verb *build* can be said to govern the noun phrase *this house*.

See also GOVERNMENT.

government (In traditional grammar, but also in recent *Generative Grammar (2).) The property of an element (typically a *head) controlling or determining some other element (*phrase, *clause, etc.). Usually contrasted with *concord.

See also GOVERNMENT-BINDING THEORY.

Government-Binding Theory (GB Theory) A version of *Generative Grammar (2), developed primarily by Noam Chomsky and associates since the early 1980s. Chomsky himself preferred the label *Principles and Parameters Theory.

The term *government (along with the verb *govern) is taken over from traditional grammar, where, for example, a verbal *head is said to control or determine ('govern') its *object, e.g. by assigning *accusative *case to it (*saw her/*saw she*). The concept is formalized in GB Theory, and extended to embrace other elements of language.

Binding is a term taken from formal logic. In Government-Binding Theory, binding is particularly concerned with the relationship of *anaphors, *pronouns, and *referential expressions to their (grammatical) *antecedents, or directly to their *referents in the outside world. To give a simple example: in both *When Tom arrived, he unpacked the case* and *When he arrived, Tom unpacked the case* the people referred to as *Tom* and *he* may (though need not) be one and the same person, with the pronoun 'bound' to *Tom*. By contrast, in *He arrived and Tom unpacked the case* two people are involved, and the pronoun is not bound.

See also CHOMSKYAN; HEAD-DRIVEN PHRASE STRUCTURE GRAMMAR; MINIMALIST PROGRAM; STANDARD THEORY; TRANSFORMATIONAL GRAMMAR.

gradable Capable of being ranked on a scale.

The term is used in describing *sense relationships between *words, and is particularly applied to *adjectives and *adverbs.

Gradable adjectives and adverbs can take degrees of *comparison, e.g.

high, higher, highest
good, better, best
soon, sooner, soonest

and can be *intensified, e.g.

very difficult, too quickly

They contrast with **non-gradable** or **ungradable** words, e.g.

*more supreme
*very impossible
?less unique
?too occasionally
*less perfectly

Some *determinatives (1) and *pronouns are also gradable, e.g.

few, fewer, fewest
many/much, more, most
little, less, least

• **gradability**.

Compare ANTONYM.

gradience The phenomenon of categorial indeterminacy between linguistic elements on a graduated continuum (or *cline).

According to Aristotle the membership of elements in a particular *category is determined by those elements conforming to a set of defining characteristics. Categories have sharp boundaries, and their members are all equal. This so-called scholastic or classical view of categorization has been very influential in linguistics, especially in theoretical work.

More recently in *Cognitive Linguistics and related fields, the view has been taken that the boundaries between grammatical categories are not always clear-cut. *Word classes, for example, are viewed as having **fuzzy boundaries**.

Within categories there are elements that meet all the criteria for membership of a particular class. For example, some adjectives can occur in *attributive and *predicative position, have *comparative and *superlative forms, and so on. (*See* *central adjective.) Others are less adjective-like (e.g. *mere*), or share characteristics with other word classes such as *prepositions. For example, the word *exploding* in *the exploding bomb* displays both verbal and adjectival properties, and *near* displays prepositional and adjectival properties in the exhortation *sit nearer the table*. We can therefore posit gradience between the word classes of verbs and adjectives, as well as between prepositions and adjectives. Gradience within categories has been called **subsective gradience** (SG), and gradience between categories has been called **intersective gradience** (IG).

> 2007 B. AARTS SG involves a single particular class of linguistic elements, or a particular construction-type, whereas IG involves two classes of elements or construction-types. SG allows for a particular element x from category α to be closer to the prototype of α than some other element y from the same category, and recognizes a core and periphery within the form classes of language. By contrast, IG involves two categories α and β, and obtains where there exists a set γ of elements characterized by a subset of α-like properties and a subset of β-like properties.

When we have gradience between *constructions, for instance between *coordination and *subordination, we can speak of **constructional gradience**. For example, whereas the *conjunctions *and* and *or* are *coordinators, and *if* and *because* are *subordinators, other elements share some of the characteristics of coordinators and subordinators. Thus *but*, unlike *and* and *or*, cannot coordinate more than two clauses; and *for* and *so that*, unlike true subordinators, cannot be preceded by another conjunction.

Gradience is also found in semantics (e.g. *cup...mug, blue...green*) and in *grammaticality/*acceptability judgements.

•• **gradient**: (*n.*) a cline; (*adj.*) displaying gradience (e.g. *a gradient phenomenon*).

Compare CLINE.

See also DISCRETE; PROTOTYPE.

grammar

1. The system of a language, traditionally encompassing *syntax and *morphology. In some cases (e.g. the work of Jespersen), a description of the sounds of a language is also included.

2. A book containing a description of the *rules of grammar.

3. An individual's application of the rules, as in *This student's grammar is excellent.*

• **grammarian**.

There are a number of terms which refer to the different ways in which grammar can be studied:

•• **descriptive grammar**: an approach which came to fruition in the twentieth century, and is based on linguistic research into actual *usage. It thus aims to describe, rather than prescribe.

•• **pedagogical grammar** (or **teaching grammar**): a term used to refer to a grammar for (foreign) learners.

•• **reference grammar**: a term which may be restricted to referring to 'a large comprehensive descriptive work of grammar' (e.g. CGEL, CaGEL), but can be extended to include a shorter book intended primarily for reference purposes (e.g. OMEG).

•• **theoretical grammar**: an approach to syntax which is based on models of the grammatical knowledge possessed by all language users, and is mostly concerned with the notion of language in general rather than with individual languages.

•• **traditional grammar**: a term which can cover many periods, but is frequently used to mean the grammar of the eighteenth, nineteenth, and early twentieth centuries, which was often based on, or in the tradition of, Latin grammar.

Compare COMPARATIVE (2); DESCRIPTIVE (2); GENERALIZED PHRASE STRUCTURE GRAMMAR; GENERATIVE GRAMMAR (2); GOVERNMENT-BINDING THEORY; HEAD-DRIVEN PHRASE STRUCTURE GRAMMAR; PHRASE STRUCTURE GRAMMAR; PRESCRIPTIVE; STRUCTURALISM; SYSTEMIC GRAMMAR; TRANSFORMATIONAL GRAMMAR; WORD GRAMMAR.

Grammar of Contemporary English, A (GCE) A large reference
*grammar (2) published by Longman in 1972, written by Randolph Quirk, the late Sidney Greenbaum, Geoffrey Leech, and Jan Svartvik. An updated version was published in 1985 as *A *Comprehensive Grammar of the English Language*. A shorter version with a pedagogical focus was published as *A University Grammar of English* in 1973.

Grammar of Late Modern English, A A traditional *grammar (2)
published between 1904 and 1929, written by the Dutch linguist Hendrik Poutsma (1856–1936).

Grammar of Spoken English, on a Strictly Phonetic Basis, A
A pedagogical *grammar (2) of English which focuses on spoken language, written by H. E. Palmer and published in 1924.

Grammar of the English Language in Three Volumes, A
A *grammar (2) by George O. Curme published in the US between 1931 (volume 3) and 1935 (volume 2). Volume 1 on the history of the language was never published.

> 2006 A. LINN This is truly a *Great Tradition* grammar for America, embracing American as well as British literary language, and, in a way that is still quite novel in the early 1930s, 'considerable attention has been given also to colloquial speech, which in its place is as good English as the literary language is in its place'.

A shorter work by Curme entitled *English Grammar* was published in 1947.

grammatical
1. Relating to *grammar (1), determined by grammar.

In this sense, grammatical is a term relating to *form rather than to meaning, as in the terms grammatical *category, grammatical *collocation, and grammatical *hierarchy.

Grammatical *agreement contrasts with *notional agreement; grammatical *gender with natural gender; grammatical *subject with logical subject (or *psychological subject); *grammatical word (1) with *content word; grammatical *meaning with lexical meaning; and grammatical *morpheme (1) with **lexical morpheme** (*see* ROOT).

- •• **grammatical ambiguity**: *see* AMBIGUITY.
- •• **grammatical competence**: *see* COMPETENCE.
- •• **grammatical function**: the same as *function (1).
- •• **grammatical meaning**: *see* SEMANTIC; SENSE.
- •• **grammatical relation**: the same as (grammatical) *function (1).

•• **grammatical rule**: *see* RULE.
•• **grammatical subject**: *see* SUBJECT (2).
•• **grammatical word**: *see* GRAMMATICAL WORD.

2. Conforming to the (innate) *rules of grammar, particularly the syntactic rules; in contrast to *ungrammatical.

Popularly, *sentences and other *utterances are regarded as grammatical when they obey the rules of the *standard language or, more narrowly, the *prescriptive rules of *usage books, and *ungrammatical if they do not. Hence *I never said nothing to nobody* or *He were right angry*, though *acceptable in some *dialects, might be judged ungrammatical by some speakers of the standard dialect. But then so might *It's me*, or *It is essential that he checks in at Terminal 2*, which others would find acceptable.

'Grammatical' is not synonymous with 'meaningful': a sentence may be grammatical even though it is nonsensical (e.g. *'Twas brillig, and the slithy toves Did gyre and gimble in the wabe*, from Lewis Carroll's poem *Jabberwocky*). Conversely, a sentence may be meaningful but ungrammatical (e.g. *Broked he the window?*). A sentence may also be grammatical despite not being acceptable, because it is (say) too long to be comprehensible. 'Grammatical' in this sense does not entail any social value judgements.

• **grammaticality**, **grammatically**.

Compare ACCEPTABILITY; ILL-FORMED; WELL-FORMED.

grammaticalization A term, thought to have been coined by Antoine Meillet (1866–1936), which refers to the *diachronic phenomenon whereby certain items in languages acquire grammatical *functions (1).

> 2003 P. HOPPER & E. TRAUGOTT As a term referring to a research framework, 'grammaticalization' refers to that part of the study of language change that is concerned with such questions as how lexical items and constructions come in certain linguistic contexts to serve grammatical functions or how grammatical items develop new grammatical functions.

A typical example is the development of *be +going +to* into an *auxiliary-like item *be going to*.

• **grammaticalize**.

grammatical word

1. A *word that primarily has grammatical (1) importance, rather than lexical *meaning. Also called **empty word**, **form word**, **function word**, **functor**, **structural word**, or **structure word**.

In some traditional grammar, *word classes (parts of speech) are divided into grammatical words and *content words (or *lexical words). Grammatical words are mainly *closed (1) class words that glue the content words together: *auxiliary verbs, *determinatives (1), *conjunctions, *prepositions, etc. The distinction is a debatable one, since all grammatical words normally carry some meaning.

Compare EMPTY; MINOR; ORTHOGRAPHIC WORD; STRONG; WORD.

See also FUNCTIONAL CATEGORY.

2. A word considered from the point of view of the particular grammatical role it plays in a given syntactic structure. Also called **morphosyntactic word**. For example, the word *deleted* is the *past tense form of the verb *delete* in the following example:

He *deleted* the picture from his camera

but its *past participle form in

The picture has been *deleted*

The grammatical context is said to *condition the shape of grammatical words.

Compare WORD FORM.

3. (In CaGEL.) A word that conforms to the *rules of *word formation. Contrasted with **ungrammatical word**.

grammaticized preposition *See* PREPOSITION.

graph The smallest discrete unit of writing, especially a letter.

The term also includes marks of *punctuation.

The term overlaps with *allograph, which does not, however, include punctuation marks.

grapheme The smallest meaningful contrastive unit in the writing system.

The grapheme is to writing what the *morpheme (1) is to *morphology, or the phoneme to phonology. A grapheme is an idealized abstraction which can be physically written or printed in various different ways. Thus the concept of the fifth letter of the alphabet is a grapheme: each of the actual ways in which the letter may be written or printed ('E', 'e', '*e*', '*e*') is an *allograph.

• **graphemic**: of or pertaining to graphemes.
• **graphemically**.

graphemics The study and analysis of *graphemes.

graphology The (study of the) writing system of a language.

The term is formed by analogy with *morphology, phonology, etc. Graphology is concerned with *graphemes, the smallest abstract units of the writing system. It has nothing to do with the better-known meaning, namely the study of an individual's handwriting as a guide to character.

Great Tradition, the This phrase, coined by the Dutch linguist Flor Aarts, refers to the European tradition of English *grammar (2) writing.

> 1986 F. AARTS Ever since 1586 Dutch grammarians have been playing an interesting role in the history of English grammar. However, their reputation is chiefly based on a number of grammars written in the present [20th] century. These form part of what is sometimes referred to as 'The Great Tradition' . . . a series of traditional grammars of English, written in England, Germany, the Scandinavian countries and the Netherlands.

greengrocer's apostrophe The use of an *apostrophe in an ordinary *plural, where it is incorrect; e.g. *Potato's 75p per kilo.*

group A level of structure between *clause and *word.

This term is particularly used by M. A. K. Halliday and his associates in *Systemic Grammar. The main groups functioning as elements in clause structure are *nominal groups, *verbal groups, and *adverbial groups (NG, VG, AG). In *The children were singing happily*:

> *the children* = NG; *were singing* = VG; *happily* = AG

The term group often, as here, corresponds to *phrase in other analyses. It does not always do so, however, and Halliday himself uses both the terms *preposition group (roughly the *complex preposition of other analyses) and *prepositional phrase.

> 1985 M. A. K. HALLIDAY A phrase is different from a group in that, whereas a group is an expansion of a word, a phrase is a contraction of a clause.

See also WORD GROUP.

group genitive *See* GENITIVE.

group noun A *noun referring to a group of people, animals, or things, with particular grammatical characteristics.

This is usually synonymous with *collective noun, i.e. it can be followed by a *singular or *plural *verb form, as in *The committee has/have acted properly.*

group possessive *See* GENITIVE.

habitual Of a *tense or *construction: denoting a *situation that occurs regularly or repeatedly.

The term is often applied to a particular use of the *present simple and the *past simple *tenses. Thus *I always catch the 8.15 train* or *He rides his bicycle every day* are examples of the habitual present, in contrast to the *stative meaning expressed by an example like *The house belongs to his son*, or the *instantaneous present of an example like *I apologize*.

The habitual past (e.g. *He caught the same train for thirty years*) contrasts with the past used for a single event (e.g. *I caught the train just as it began to move*) or a past *state (e.g. *The house belonged to her parents*).

The habitual reading in examples like those above often comes about as a result of the use of certain *adverbials, e.g. *always, never*.

Hallidayan Designating the kind of linguistics (especially grammar) developed by the British linguist Michael A. K. Halliday (b. 1925).

Halliday's first grammatical model, developed in the 1960s, was called *Scale-and-Category Grammar, in which three scales (*rank, *exponence, and *delicacy) interacted with four *categories (*unit, *class, *structure, and *system). As the theory developed, increasing importance was attached to the category of system—and the term *Systemic Grammar (or **Systemic-Functional Grammar**) was used for later models.

Handbook of English Grammar, A A pedagogical *grammar published in a number of editions from 1945, written by the Dutch linguist Reinard Zandvoort (1894–1990).

Handbook of Present-Day English, A A traditional *grammar published between 1909 and 1932, written by the Dutch linguist Etsko Kruisinga (1875–1944).

hanging participle A *participle (*clause) that is not related grammatically to an intended *noun phrase of which it would be the *modifier; also called **dangling participle**, **unattached participle**, **unrelated participle**, or **dangling modifier**.

A participle clause often does not contain a *subject, but grammatically, if it is placed near its *superordinate clause, its subject is 'understood' to be *co-referential with the subject of that superordinate clause. Failure to observe this 'rule' results in a hanging participle, or often, more accurately, a *misrelated participle. When this happens, the participle clause is apparently grammatically attached to the subject, though according to the intended meaning, it is associated with a different *referent (which may not actually be mentioned in the *main clause). For example:

> *Speaking to her on the phone the other day*, her praise for her colleagues was unstinting (*Daily Telegraph*)

The meaning here is clear enough, but strictly grammatically speaking it is impossible to 'recover' the subject of the participle clause from its immediate *context. With regard to the following example the question arises of what is shrouded:

> *Shrouded by leaves in summer*, the coming of winter for a deciduous tree reveals the true shape of its woody skeleton (G. Durrell *The Amateur Naturalist*, 1982, p. 105)

The same rule (that the participle clause should be related to the subject) also applies when the clause is introduced by a *conjunction or *preposition. The rule is not followed in this example:

> Every afternoon, *instead of dozing listlessly in their beds*, or *staring vacantly out of a window*, there is organized entertainment (*Daily Telegraph*)

The hanging participle is generally condemned as *ungrammatical, rather than as a mere error of style. But it has long been widely used, most famously by Shakespeare:

> *Sleeping in mine orchard*, a serpent stung me (*Hamlet*, I.5)

The rule does not extend to participles that refer to the speaker's or writer's comments (e.g. *Strictly speaking, Monday is not the first day of the week*), nor to apparent participles that are accepted as *prepositions or conjunctions (e.g. *following, provided (that . . .*).

Compare MISRELATED.

hapax legomenon A *word that is used once in a *discourse, *text, or collection of texts, etc. Also simply called **hapax**. From the Greek, meaning 'said only once'.

head
1. The *word which is the principal and typically *obligatory element inside *phrases, *clauses, etc., and which designates what the whole

expression is a 'kind of'. For example, the *noun *day* designates that the noun phrase *the hot day* is a kind of day, and is hence its head.

Further examples: in the noun phrase *the ankle-deep propaganda which I waded through*, the head is the noun *propaganda*. Similarly, in the *adjective phrase *very misleading indeed* and the *adverb phrase *somewhat superficially* the heads are *misleading* and *superficially*, respectively.

2. (Less commonly.) The word which is the obligatory member of certain kinds of phrase, and which, standing alone, could perform the same grammatical *function (1) as the whole phrase of which it is part. For example, *Indian tigers are dangerous* > *Tigers are dangerous*. Note that certain kinds of phrases, such as *verb phrases and *prepositional phrases, are problematic as far as their headedness in this sense is concerned; compare *I saw her on the train* > *I saw her on.

> 2007 P. H. MATTHEWS If *girls* determines the syntactic properties of an 'NP' *tall girls*, and *tall* those of an 'AP' *very tall*, are those of 'VPs' and 'PPs' determined similarly, by a head verb or head preposition?

In *Generative Grammar (2) verb phrases and prepositional phrases are also said to have heads.

•• **functional head:** a head that does not belong to one of the major lexical *word classes, but to a *functional category. For example, in later models of *Generative Grammar (2), the clause *that he no longer works there* in the sentence *I think that he no longer works there* is regarded as a **Complementizer Phrase** (CP) which is headed by a functional category, namely the *complementizer *that*.

•• **null head:** a head without an overt realization. For example, in some frameworks, but not others, the phrase *the rich* would be regarded as a noun phrase with a noun as a non-overt null head.

•• **semantic head:** the element in a phrase, clause, etc. that is the most prominent from the point of view of *meaning, but does not function syntactically as head. For example, *dog* in the phrase *a monster of a dog* is analysed by some syntacticians as a semantic head (after all, a monster of a dog is a kind of dog, not a kind of monster), as contrasted with *monster*, which would be the syntactic head of this phrase.

head clause *See* MAIN CLAUSE.

Head-Driven Phrase Structure Grammar (HPSG) A *monostratal (non-derivational) theory of *Phrase Structure Grammar developed from *Generalized Phrase Structure Grammar in the 1990s by Carl Pollard and Ivan Sag. The model makes uses of universal principles, *rules, and schemata, and the *lexicon plays an important role.

See also CHOMSKYAN; GENERALIZED PHRASE STRUCTURE GRAMMAR; GENERATIVE; GENERATIVE GRAMMAR (2); GOVERNMENT-BINDING THEORY; GRAMMAR; MINIMALIST PROGRAM; PRINCIPLES AND PARAMETERS THEORY; STANDARD THEORY; TRANSFORMATIONAL GRAMMAR.

headed Of a *phrase or *clause: possessing a *head. Also called *endocentric.

Headed phrases contrast with *exocentric phrases, also called **non-headed** or **unheaded** phrases. Compare the italicized phrases in the examples below:

I was *very pleased*

I was *in London*

In the first example the *adjective phrase is headed by the adjective *pleased*, whereas in the second example the italicized *prepositional phrase is regarded as being non-headed in some frameworks. *See* HEAD (2). But this contrast is not made in *Generative Grammar, where all phrases must be properly headed. *See* HEAD (1).

The term is also applied to *compounds. *See* BAHUVRIHI; DVANDVA.

headlinese The grammar of newspaper headlines.

Newspaper headlines often employ grammatical conventions that differ from the norm. *Articles and other minor *words are often omitted (e.g. *Man hit by gunman 'critical'*); *present tenses are used for past events (e.g. *Designer weeps in court*); *to-infinitives refer to *future time (e.g. *UN to search for solution*); *nouns are heavily stacked in noun phrases (e.g. *Romcom movie star death mystery*); and so on.

Compare BLOCK LANGUAGE.

headword

1. The same as *head (1).

2. *Lexicography*. The word which stands at the head of a dictionary entry and which is defined within that entry.

helping verb A somewhat dated term for *auxiliary verb.

See also CATENATIVE-AUXILIARY ANALYSIS; DEPENDENT-AUXILIARY ANALYSIS.

hesitation noise A sound (or sounds) not classified as a *word, but used by speakers to keep conversation going.

Hesitation noises are somewhat inadequately indicated by such items as *er, erm, uh, um*, etc.

See also DISCOURSE MARKER; FILLER.

heterograph A *word that has a different spelling and meaning from another, but the same pronunciation, e.g. *to* (*preposition or *infinitival particle) vs *two* (*numeral).

heteronym

1. A *word having a different *meaning and pronunciation from another word, but which is identical in spelling. Examples:

alternate (verb) vs *alternate* (adjective)

bass ('type of fish') vs *bass* ('deep male voice')

lead ('cause to go') vs *lead* ('type of metal')

The term heteronym emphasizes difference.

See also ANTONYM; HETEROGRAPH; HETEROPHONE; HOMOGRAPH; HOMONYM; HOMOPHONE; HYPONYM; MERONYM; POLYSEME; POLYSEMY; SYNONYM.

2. Each of a set of morphologically different words that all have the same meaning, but are used by speakers of different *dialects or in different localities. Contrasted with *by-form, *doublet.

Such words would be synonyms if they were used in the same dialect (and may become so if one dialect—for example, *Standard English—adopts more than one of them). Examples are the numerous truce terms used by schoolchildren, each of which is characteristic of different areas of England (e.g. *pax, fainites, barley*), or the varying local terms for rubber-soled canvas shoes (e.g. *plimsolls, gym shoes, sandshoes, daps, gollies*).

3. A word that has a semantic relationship (e.g. of *antonymy, or as a translation equivalent) with another word, but is unrelated to it in form. Contrasted with *paronym.

Examples are *husband* : *wife, debtor* : *creditor* (in contrast to *widow* : *widower, mortgagor* : *mortgagee*).

Heteronym (from Greek *heteros* 'other' + *-onym* as in *synonym*, etc.) is a fairly uncommon word, and it is not clear which use prevails. Sense (2) is favoured by Continental dialectologists.

• **heteronymy**.

heterophone A *word that sounds different from another, but is spelt the same.

Since a certain similarity is the reason for considering two words together as some sort of pair (e.g. *lead* 'cause a person, animal, etc. to accompany' and *lead* 'metal', or *row* 'a line' and *row* 'a quarrel'), an alternative term would be *homograph. The term might, however, be usefully used of two forms of the same *lexeme, where both spelling and meaning are the same but the pronunciation is different, e.g. the *verb *read* /riːd/ and its *past tense and *past participle forms *read*, pronounced /red/.

See also HOMOPHONE.

hiatus (Chiefly in *historical linguistics.) A break between two vowels coming together in different syllables, as in: <u>coo</u>perate, Go<u>ya</u>esque, gu<u>ffa</u>wing, r<u>ea</u>lign.

hierarchy A system of *ranks (or classes) in which each rank includes the one below it.

The term is used in its everyday sense, and can be applied to various types of grammatical classification. Hierarchy is evident in the analysis of sentences into *subject and *predicate (1), or into *clauses, *phrases, and *words, or of words into *morphemes (1).

The concept can also be used in semantics where a series such as *furniture, chair, armchair, wing armchair* illustrates a hierarchy from the general to the particular. *See also* HYPERNYM; HYPONYM.

• **hierarchical**, **hierarchically**.

high frequency *See* FREQUENCY (2).

historical linguistics The study of language change; the same as *diachronic linguistics.

See also COMPARATIVE LINGUISTICS.

historic present The *present simple tense (or sometimes the *present progressive) when used to refer to *past (1) *time. (Also called the **narra-tive present**.) For example:

Yesterday I'm walking down the road and this woman comes up to me and she says . . .

The device is often used to make a narrative more vivid and immediate.

hocus-pocus An attitude to grammar that implies that grammarians must impose their own rules on language.

The term was coined by Fred W. Householder (1913–1994) in 1952 to denote a view of the linguist's work at one extreme, in contrast to the *God's Truth view of language.

hollow clause (In CaGEL.) A *non-finite clause in which a postverbal element is missing but is recoverable from the *context. For example, in *Kids are easy [to please _]* we interpret the direct object *gap following the verb *please* as being related to *kids*.

holonym *See* MERONYM.

holophrase A single *word used instead of a *phrase, or to express a combination of ideas.

See also HOLOPHRASIS.

holophrasis The expression of a whole *phrase, or combination of ideas, by one *word.

● **holophrastic**.

The concept originated in nineteenth-century philology. Today it is especially applied to an early stage of child language acquisition.

2011 J. M. MEISEL At around age 1:9, however, one can typically observe a spurt in the increase of the productive vocabulary from approximately fifty to over a hundred words within a short period of time; the receptive lexicon already contains significantly more items. For several months, the children remain in the holophrastic phase, that is, they use one-word utterances which, however, do not simply refer to individual objects but can normally denote complex events and actions; they thus serve similar functions as propositions in adult language.

homograph A *word that is spelt the same as another (Greek *homos* 'same') but has a different meaning and origin, and may be pronounced in the same way or differently.

Examples are:

lead ('cause to go') : *lead* ('type of metal')
routed ('defeated') : *routed* ('sent by a route')
row (as a noun: 'line'; as a verb: 'propel a boat') : *row* (as a noun and verb: 'quarrel')
slaver ('slave-trader') : *slaver* ('dribbling saliva')
slough ('swamp') : *slough* ('cast off skin')
sow ('bury seed') : *sow* ('female pig')
wound (as a noun: 'injury'; as a verb: 'cause an injury to a person, etc.') : *wound* (past form of the verb *wind*)

If in fact homographs are also pronounced the same way, the more usual term is *homonym.

See also HOMOPHONE.

● **homographic**, **homography**.

homomorph A *word that is identical to another in (written and spoken) form and shares the same meaning, but belongs to a different *word class.

1985 R. QUIRK et al. There is no standard term for words which also share the same morphological form (eg: *red* as a noun and *red* as an adjective, *meeting* as a noun and *meeting* as a verb), but it seems appropriate to adopt the term homomorph for this purpose.

● **homomorphy**: the property of being a homomorph or homomorphs.
Compare HOMONYM.

homonym A *word that has the same pronunciation and spelling as another, but is etymologically unrelated to it, and thus has a different *meaning. Examples are:

bill ('statement of charges') : bill ('beak')

fair ('just') : fair ('sale', 'entertainment')

pole ('long slender rounded piece of wood or metal') : pole ('each of the two points in the celestial sphere about which the stars appear to revolve')

pulse ('throbbing') : pulse ('edible seeds')

row (as a noun: 'line') : row (as a verb: 'propel a boat')

soil ('earth') : soil ('make dirty')

All homonyms are also *homophones.

Traditionally, homonyms of this type are treated as separate words and are given distinct entries in a dictionary (e.g. 'pole 1' and 'pole 2'), whereas more closely related meanings are treated as offshoots of the same word when this is historically justified (so 'each of the two terminals of an electric cell or battery, etc.' comes under 'pole 2'). *See* POLYSEMY.

Popularly, homonyms may or may not include pairs whose two words have the same meaning but do not belong to the same grammatical category (e.g. *red* as a *noun and as an *adjective). *See* HOMOMORPH.

 • **homonymic, homonymous, homonymy**.

See also ANTONYM; HETEROGRAPH; HETERONYM; HETEROPHONE; HOMOGRAPH; HOMOPHONE; HYPONYM; MERONYM; POLYSEME; POLYSEMY; SYNONYM.

homophone A word that is pronounced in the same way as another but has a different *meaning (or *derivation). The spelling may or may not be the same.

2009 D. MINKOVA & R. STOCKWELL The term *homophony*, useful as it is, bundles together words of the type *chair* (to sit on) – *chair* (of a department) and *corn* (on the cob) – *corn* (on toe). Yet if you look these up in the *OED*, you will find the two meanings of *chair* under one single entry, while there are two separate entries for *corn*. The term *homophony* is thus used to cover two historically distinct types of semantic identity: **homonymy** and **polysemy**.

... [A]ll homonyms are by definition also homophones.

Examples are:

bank : bank (of a river; 'financial institution')

feat : feet

hole : whole

no : know

none : nun

pupil : pupil (of the eye; 'student')

stare : stair

Some English pairs are homophones in some accents, but not in others. For example:

saw : sore
pore : pour
wine : whine

- **homophonic, homophonous, homophony.**
  Compare HETERONYM.

homophoric Of *reference: self-specifying.

Textual reference may be *anaphoric or *cataphoric. Extralinguistic reference, by contrast, is *exophoric. The term homophoric particularly describes the kind of reference that can only be to one particular person or thing in a situation. Thus use of *the doorbell* in a typical domestic situation where there is only one doorbell is homophoric in *That's the doorbell!*

hybrid

1. (*n. & adj.*) *Morphology.* (A *word) formed from words or *morphemes (1) derived from different languages.

Many *affixes in common use in English *word formation are ultimately of Latin or Greek origin (e.g. *a-, anti-, co-, ex-, in-, non-, post-, syn-; -al, -ation, -ic, -ist, -ive, -ize*), but they are so well established that they combine easily with words of *Old English, or any other, origin. Examples are:

anticlockwise	*disbelieve*	*interweave*	*refill*
eatable	*jingoism*	*starvation*	*talkative*

There is a certain resistance to mixing elements of different origins, such that there is a preference for combining a foreign *stem with a foreign affix. For example, *rational* forms *rationality* rather than *?rationalness*, *cannibalize* forms *cannibalization* rather than **cannibalizement*, and *centralize* forms *decentralize* rather than **uncentralize*. Quite a number of hybrids, generally involving longer *combining forms, were criticized when they were first introduced into English, for example *appendicitis* (Latin *appendic-* + Greek *-itis*), *speedometer* (English *speed* + Greek *-(o)meter*), and *television* (Greek *tele-* + Latin/French *vision*).

2. *Syntax.* Of a construction: a syntactic *blend.

hybrid speech The same as *free indirect speech.

hypercorrection (An example of) the use of a particular (form of a) *word, *phrase, etc. by a speaker or writer who is under the impression that this conforms to 'correct' (more prestigious) usage. (Also called **hypercorrectness**.)

> Typical instances of hypercorrection involve the use of *pronouns:
>
> That's a matter for John and *I* to decide (*me* would be expected after *for*)
>
> She mentioned some people *whom* she thought were cheating her (here the *wh*-word is the subject of the subordinate clause after *thought*, so should be in the form *who*)

Other examples involve the use of *subjunctive *were*:

> Even if his claim *were* true in 1950, it isn't now (his claim was a matter of fact, so the subjunctive is inappropriate)
>
> We didn't know if she *were* old enough (her age was a matter of fact)

A final example involves the naming of the letter *h* as /heɪtʃ/ instead of /eɪtʃ/, i.e. with the hypercorrect addition of /h/.

• **hypercorrect**: designating (use in this way of) a non-standard form.

> 1968 W. LABOV The lower middle class shows the sharpest shift towards *r*-pronunciation in formal styles, going even beyond the highest social group in this respect. This 'hypercorrect' behavior, or 'going one better', is quite characteristic of second-ranking groups in many communities.

hyperlect A *variety of language associated with the upper strata of society.

The term is intended to cover marked grammatical usage, as well as marked accent.

> 1989 J. HONEY I will call any such special variety of language, associated not with the most highly educated but with those who are socially the most highly privileged, a hyperlect, remembering that this term can cover not just their accent (which in the case of contemporary Britain I have called 'marked RP' [Received Pronunciation]) but may also refer to the complete range of accent, grammar, vocabulary, and idiom which constitute a social dialect.

Compare ACROLECT; BASILECT; MESOLECT.

hypernym *Semantics.* The *superordinate term in a set of related words; contrasted with *hyponym.

> *Animal* is a hypernym of *tiger* and *kangaroo*.
> *See also* SUPERORDINATE.

hyperurbanism The same as *hypercorrection.

hyphen (*n.*) The sign ⟨-⟩ used to join *words semantically or syntactically (as in *sister-in-law, good-natured*), to indicate the division of a word at the end of a line, or to indicate a missing or implied element (as in *over- and underpayment*).

(*v.*) Join by a hyphen, write with a hyphen. (Also **hyphenate**.)

There is considerable variation and inconsistency in the use of hyphens in words and compounds. For example, one finds *coal field*, *coal-field*, and *coalfield*.

Basically hyphens are meant to aid comprehension. One useful convention is to separate with a hyphen vowels that could otherwise be run together in a word, as in *co-occur*, but this is by no means universally followed, even though such forms as *cooccur* are rather opaque. Another useful convention is to hyphenate words that would not normally be hyphenated in order to avoid *ambiguity. Thus, a *spare room-heater* is not the same as a *spare-room heater*. Similarly, hyphens are useful for showing a close connection between words that might otherwise be understood as separate and equal (compare *a black bearded pilot* with *a black-bearded pilot*), and are employed when a sequence of words is, unusually, used in attributive position before a noun:

> Black-bearded, lazy-voiced, dressed for the weather in a great plaid lumber-jacket, the pilot roused my envy for his here-I-am, this-is-what-I-have, take-me-or-leave-me style. (J. RABAN *Hunting Mr Heartbreak*, 1990)

• **hyphenated, hyphenation**.

hypocoristic (*n. & adj.*) (Designating) a pet form of a *word; (that is or has the nature of) a pet name; e.g. *auntie*.

Compare DIMINUTIVE.

hyponym *Semantics*. A *word with a more specific *meaning than, and therefore implying or able to be replaced by, another term, typically a more general or superordinate one, called the *hypernym.

Tiger and *kangaroo* are both hyponyms of *animal*; *knives* and *forks* of *cutlery*; *diamond* and *ruby* of *gemstone*; and so on. Words that are hyponyms of the same superordinate term are *co-hyponyms*.

• **hyponymy**.

See also ANTONYM; HETERONYM; HOMONYM; HOMOPHONE; MERONYM; POLYSEME; POLYSEMY; SYNONYM.

hypotactic *See* HYPOTAXIS.

hypotaxis The *subordination of one linguistic unit to another in a relationship of inequality; contrasted with *parataxis.

• **hypotactic**: exhibiting, or in a relationship of, hypotaxis.

The relationship of a *subordinate clause to a *main clause (or *matrix clause) is hypotactic:

I'll believe it, when I see it (main + subordinate)

Although he received an email confirmation, he will check the flight details (subordinate + main)

However, the term is generally used with a much wider application than subordination. It extends to other types of *dependency or *embedding, involving not only clauses, but also single *words or *phrases. Consider the *noun phrase *a light green shirt*, which is *ambiguous. Under one reading *light* is hypotactic to *green*, i.e. the colour of the shirt is light-green. Under the second reading the two *adjectives are in a paratactic relationship, and could be overtly *coordinated, i.e. *the shirt is green and light* (in weight).

hypothetical condition *See* CONDITION.

hypothetical past *See* PAST.

ICECUP *See* SURVEY OF ENGLISH USAGE, THE.

icon A linguistic form which has a characteristic in common with the entity it signifies.

The term is derived from its more general use in *semiotics, where it means 'non-arbitrary sign'. In languages which use hieroglyphic or ideographic writing systems some of the symbols are arguably icons.

In a language such as English, *onomatopoeic words can be described as icons, although the form of such words is in fact conventional, and different from that of foreign-language equivalents. For example, English *cock-a-doodle-do* contrasts with French *cocorico*, German *kikeriki*, and Dutch *kukeleku*.

It has also been argued that various sound combinations are iconic, and that they exhibit **secondary iconicity** or **weak iconicity**. For example, the initial sequence *sn-* occurs in a number of words with unpleasant meanings, many of which are connected with the nose or mouth, e.g. *snap, snarl, sneer, sneeze, snicker, sniff, sniffle, snigger, snivel, snog, snore, snort, snot, snout, snub, snuff, snuffle*. Other words with disagreeable connotations are *sneak, snide, snob, snook, snoop, snooty*.

- **iconic**: having the nature of, or resembling, an icon.
- **iconicity**: the fact or quality of being an icon.

ideational

1. *Semantics.* Concerned with objective meaning.

2. In *Systemic Grammar, the ideational function of a *clause is the way it represents factual reality, or experience, and this is contrasted both with its *textual (2) function (how the text is organized as a message) and its *interpersonal (2) (social) function. The ideational function of a clause is said to contain an *experiential component, which is concerned with 'processes, participants, and circumstances', and a **logical** component, i.e. 'language as the expression of certain very general logical relations'.

'Ideational' is thus to some extent comparable with the labels *cognitive, *descriptive, or *referential in other analyses.

identification *See* IDENTIFY.

identifier A general semantic term that is sometimes used to refer to a particular class of *determinative (1) or *pronoun whose function is to single out an entity or individual; contrasted with *quantifier.

Definite identifiers include *the*, the demonstratives (*this*, *that*, etc.), possessives (e.g. *my*, *your*), and some pronouns (e.g. *it*, *he*, *she*, *they*). Indefinite identifiers include *a*, *an*, and *one*.

See also: IDENTIFY.

identify To single out an entity, individual, etc. uniquely.

This term and the related words **identified**, **identification**, *identifier, and especially **identifying** are used much in their everyday sense in grammar. Thus the *demonstratives (*this*, *that*, etc.) often have an identifying function, e.g. *This is my sister*.

The terms are also used in distinguishing different kinds of *complements. For example, in:

Henry's second wife was *a beautiful young woman*

or indeed in:

Ann Boleyn was *a beautiful young woman*

the complement is *ascriptive (also called *descriptive (1)), but *non-identifying. The verb is called *ascriptive *be.* By contrast

His second wife was *Ann Boleyn*

is an identifying (also called *specifying) structure, in which *Ann Boleyn* is the identifier and *his second wife* is identified. The verb *be* in this construction is called **identifying *be*** or *specifying *be.*

Similarly, the second term in an *apposition may or may not have an identifying role. Compare:

His second wife, Ann Boleyn, was beheaded (**identifying apposition**)

His second wife, a beautiful young woman, was beheaded (**non-identifying apposition**)

- **identifiability**: the property of being identifiable in a particular (discourse) setting.
- **identifiable**.
- **identifying relative clause**: the same as *defining or *restrictive relative clause.

   Compare DEFINITE; DEICTIC; DEIXIS; EQUATIVE.

identifying *be* The same as *specifying *be.*
   See also: IDENTIFY.
   Compare ASCRIPTIVE BE.

ideogram A written character symbolizing a *word or *phrase without indicating its pronunciation.

Ideograms are rather marginal to the English writing system, but include numerals and graphic symbols such as £ $ % & + −.

• **ideogrammatic**, **ideogrammic** (neither in frequent use).

Compare ABBREVIATION.

ideograph The same as *ideogram.

• **ideographic**, **ideography**.

idiolect *Linguistics* The speech (habits) of an individual person.

Speakers differ in their knowledge and use of the grammar and *vocabulary of their language, so that in some ways everyone's idiolect is different.

The term is modelled on the word *dialect, using the prefix *idio-* 'own, personal, distinct'.

• **idiolectal**, **idiolectally**.

idiom

1. A string of (more or less) fixed *words having a meaning that is not deducible from the meanings of the individual words, e.g.

over the moon
under the weather
by the skin of one's teeth
up to one's eyes in work
for crying out loud
kick the bucket
paint the town red
throw a wobbly
give in
take up
fish out of water
had better
might as well
how goes it?

Some of these phrases allow no alteration, except when used facetiously (**over the stars*, **kick the pail*); others allow some changes (*up to my/his/her/their*, etc. *eyes in work*).

Older meanings of 'idiom' in English include (i) the form of speech that is peculiar to a nation or to a limited area, and (ii) the specific character or property of a language, or the manner of expression that is natural, or peculiar, to it ('the idiom of the English tongue').

In some cases there is no very clear distinction between idiom, *collocation, and *fixed phrase.

2. A *phrase that is fairly fixed (not necessarily with opaque meaning) but which shows, or appears to show, some grammatical irregularity, e.g.

these sort of people

come to think of it

It is not unusual to find phrases such as *by car, on foot, in prison* (i.e. consisting of a preposition + a normally countable noun, but without an article) described as idioms.

● **idiomatic**: marked by the use of idioms; peculiar to the usage of a particular language.

● **idiomaticity**.

> 1973 R. QUIRK & S. GREENBAUM Like phrasal verbs, prepositional verbs vary in their idiomaticity. Highly idiomatic combinations include *go into*.., 'investigate', *come by*.., 'obtain'.

if-clause A *subordinate clause introduced by *if*.

The term is particularly applied to certain *interrogative clauses (e.g. *I don't know if she likes fish*), and to clauses introduced by *if* expressing *condition, but also covers clauses where *if* is interpreted as expressing *concessive meaning (e.g. *He's friendly, if a little bit lazy*), etc. Used loosely, the term can cover other subordinate clauses of condition (introduced by *unless, provided that, on condition that*, etc.).

ill-formed *Linguistics* Structurally *deviant.

The term is particularly used in *Generative Grammar (2), and describes any structure that cannot be generated by the rules. It contrasts with *well-formed.

● **ill-formedness**.

Compare ANOMALOUS; GRAMMATICAL; UNGRAMMATICAL.

illocution The communicative function (2), or force, of a verbal *utterance, e.g. stating, inquiring, requesting, commanding, inviting; hence **illocutionary force**.

> 1955 J. L. AUSTIN I shall refer to the doctrine of the different types of function of language . . . as the doctrine of 'illocutionary forces'.

The terminology derives from J. L. Austin's theory of *speech acts, where it contrasts with *locution and *perlocution. It is central to discussions of the social and *interpersonal meaning of language behaviour, and has gained wider currency than the other two terms.

●● **illocutionary act**: the act of asking, stating, inquiring, requesting, commanding, inviting, etc.

•• **illocutionary meaning** (or *communicative meaning): the meaning that an utterance has in a particular context. For example, in a situation in which a speaker says *I'm thirsty* the illocutionary meaning may be directing an addressee to provide a drink, rather than stating a fact.

•• **primary/secondary illocutionary force**:

2002 R. HUDDLESTON & G. K. PULLUM et al. Strictly speaking, a natural utterance of [*I promise to return the key tomorrow*] would be both a statement and a promise, though the promise is of course more important, more salient that the statement. We will speak of the promise force as **primary** and the statement as **secondary**.

See also PERFORMATIVE.

illocutionary force *See* ILLOCUTION.

immediate constituent One of the parts (*constituents) into which a linguistic unit is immediately divisible. Sometimes abbreviated as IC (analysis).

The immediate constituents of a *compound sentence or *complex sentence may be *clauses, and each clause in turn may contain a *noun phrase and a *verb phrase, or alternatively, a *subject and a *predicate, as immediate constituents. In the sentence *The cost includes air travel by scheduled services* we can say that the immediate constituents are *The cost* and *includes travel by scheduled air services*, and we can further break the predicate down into *includes* and *travel by scheduled air services*. The strings *travel by* and *scheduled air* are not constituents. This type of analysis can continue until the ultimate constituents are reached, e.g. *service* + *-s* in *services*.

Immediate constituent analysis was an important practice in *structuralism.

imperative (*n. & adj.*)

1. (Designating) a *clause type typically used for issuing *directives, syntactically characterized by a missing subject—hence **imperative clause**, e.g. *Drop that gun!*

Imperative is a formal syntactic *category, whereas directive is a category of usage. Clauses that are imperative in form can also be used to express a wish (*Enjoy yourself*) or a condition (*Come nearer and I'll scream*), or to convey an apology (*Forgive me*). These are examples of indirect *speech acts. An imperative clause can include *do* for emphasis (e.g. *Do listen!, Do be quick*) or *don't* for a negative (*Don't forget, Don't be silly*). As was noted above, in imperative clauses the subject is typically omitted (though *you* is then 'understood'), but it can be overtly expressed as well (*You listen to me, Don't you do that again*).

   Compare DECLARATIVE; EXCLAMATIVE; INTERROGATIVE.

   2. (In traditional grammar.) (Designating) the *base (1) form of a verb, regarded as an *inflectional form (the **imperative mood**; *see* MOOD), when used to express a request, command, order, exhortation, etc. (e.g. *Listen! Have fun! Be sensible!*).

● **imperatival**: pertaining to the imperative (mood).

● **imperatively**: as or in the manner of an imperative.

   Compare INDICATIVE; SUBJUNCTIVE.

   3. (Designating) a structure with *let's* where a subject cannot normally be inserted, as in *Let's go, Don't let's worry, Let's not forget that*... For some speakers a subject is permitted, as in *Let's you and I go to the movies*.

   Compare JUSSIVE.

imperfect (*n. & adj.*) (In traditional grammar.) (A *tense) denoting a past *situation that is ongoing, in progress, and not complete.

   This term was derived from the classification of tenses in Latin grammar, and has been applied particularly in English to the **past imperfect** (e.g. *They were waiting*). It is now largely superseded by the terms past *progressive or past *continuous.

   Contrast IMPERFECTIVE; PERFECT; PERFECTIVE.

   See also ASPECT.

imperfective

   1. (*adj.*) *Semantics.* Signalling imperfective meaning, i.e. viewing a *situation as it unfolds internally. In English the *progressive construction is said to signal imperfective meaning, namely 'ongoingness', e.g. *They were watching television.*

   2002 R. HUDDLESTON & G.K. PULLUM et al. With imperfective aspectuality, the situation is not presented in its totality; it is viewed from within, with focus on some feature of the internal temporal structure or some subinterval of time within the whole.

   2. (*n. & adj.*) (Designating) the grammatical *aspect that specifies how a particular situation unfolds internally. Not to be confused with *imperfect.

   Some linguists prefer to reserve this sense to languages that make extensive use of imperfective aspect, e.g. the Slavic languages.

   Compare PERFECT; PERFECTIVE.

   3. (*n. & adj.*) The same as *progressive.

impersonal Of a *construction: involving a *dummy subject, typically *it* (called **impersonal *it***).

The term is particularly applied to *verbs such as *rain* or *snow* (**impersonal verbs**) which express a *situation that is not attributable to an identifiable subject (e.g. *It is snowing*).

More widely, it is applied to other structures which have *it* as subject:

It seems that he is asleep (cf. *That he is asleep seems)

It appears that nobody knew (cf. *That nobody knew appears)

It is unacceptable that you left early (cf. That you left early is unacceptable)

In some frameworks (e.g. CaGEL) constructions involving *extraposition, as in the third example above, are not regarded as having impersonal *it* as subject, by virtue of the fact that the extraposed subject can appear in its 'original' position.

It is usually classified as a *personal pronoun, but when used with an impersonal verb or in other constructions (e.g. extraposition), different labels are also used: e.g. *anticipatory *it*, *ambient *it*, *dummy *it*, *formal (4) *it*, *introductory *it*, **non-referential *it*, preparatory *it*, ***prop *it*, and **unspecified *it***.

Compare ANIMATE; GENERIC; NON-PERSONAL.

implication *Semantics.* What is implied by an *utterance; the act of implying.

Linguists contrast implication with *entailment. Entailment is semantic: if a *proposition A entails a proposition B, then if A is true, B is also true. For example, *Jim has three brothers* entails that *Jim has three siblings*. Implication is a less clear-cut relationship, based on a mixture of logic and shared knowledge. In normal circumstances an utterance will often be understood to convey information that is not directly encoded in the words. For example, in *I brought Jim a birthday present yesterday* there is an implication that yesterday was Jim's birthday, but I could add, without contradiction, *but yesterday wasn't Jim's birthday*. Implications are cancellable. Entailments are not.

implicature A pragmatic *implication of an *utterance, i.e. an implication that arises in a particular situation but is typically not explicitly mentioned in the actual words that are uttered. Also called **conversational implicature**.

The term is taken from the philosopher H. P. Grice (1913–88), who developed the *cooperative principle. On the basis that a speaker and listener are cooperating, and aiming to be relevant, a speaker can imply a meaning implicitly, confident that the listener will understand. Thus a possible conversational implicature of *Are you watching this programme?* might be 'This programme bores me. Can we turn the television off?'

Compare PRESUPPOSITION.

See also RELEVANCE THEORY.

inanimate *See* ANIMATE.

inclusion *Semantics.* The same as *hyponomy.

inclusive

1. Designating the first *person *plural *pronoun *we* when it includes both speaker and addressee(s). Contrasted with *exclusive (1). For example:

Why don't *we* all go together? You'd enjoy it.

2. inclusive disjunction: *see* DISJUNCTIVE.

incomplete predication *See* VERB.

incomplete sentence (In traditional grammar.) A sentence lacking one or more elements that would normally be present in a *canonical structure; an *elliptical sentence.

> 1968 J. LYONS 'Incomplete' or 'elliptical' sentences . . . One must distinguish between contextual completeness and grammatical completeness.

Thus an *elliptical sentence may be incomplete in the sense that a *word or words have been omitted, but may in fact be grammatically complete, since the missing words can be readily supplied with no further context, e.g.

(Is there) anything I can do to help?

An *utterance such as *Whatever I can* may be regarded as elliptical if it follows *What are you going to do to help?*, but would be unacceptable if it followed *Are you going to help?*

Sentences may be regarded as incomplete for a variety of reasons. For sentences that are unfinished by the speaker, *see* ANACOLUTHON. For sentences that are grammatically incomplete, but complete in context, *see* ELLIPSIS. For sentences that are not full sentences according to the rules of sentence structure, *see* MINOR SENTENCE.

See also NON-SENTENCE; SMALL CLAUSE; VERBLESS CLAUSE.

indefinite Of a *word, *phrase, *construction, etc.: not having or indicating any particular identifiable *reference. Contrasted with *definite.

The word is used as part of the terms *indefinite article and *indefinite pronoun, but can also be used to describe certain other linguistic elements, as in the examples described below.

(i) Adverbs and adverbials of **indefinite frequency**, such as

generally, usually, always, repeatedly, occasionally

contrast with *adverbs and *adverbials of **definite frequency**, such as

daily, fortnightly

(ii) The *present perfect construction can refer to an indefinite time:

Have you ever read *Beowulf*?

in contrast to a *clause with a simple *past tense form which characteristically implies a definite (even if unstated) time:

I read *Beowulf* when I was 16

(iii) An **indefinite noun phrase** has an indefinite *pronoun as *head, or contains an indefinite *determinative (1) + noun:

Anyone with any sense would have realized
Some people have all the luck

(iv) Most *quantifiers are indefinite (e.g. *some*, *much*, etc.), and can be described as indefinite quantifiers by contrast with cardinal numbers, which state definite quantities.

•• **indefinite article**: *see* INDEFINITE ARTICLE.
•• **indefinite pronoun**: *see* INDEFINITE PRONOUN.

indefinite article A *word class label that is used for *a/an*, in addition to (or instead of) the label *determinative (1). *See also* ARTICLE.

Although *a* and *an* are indefinite in meaning, *reference may be general (any person or thing of that class or kind) or more particular (an actual example of the class or kind):

We don't expect letters—but send us *a postcard* (general: send us any postcard)

I've still got *a card* my grandfather sent from Kabul (specific: a particular card and no other)

Some grammarians distinguish these meanings by labelling the first meaning *classifying or *generic, and the second *specific.

But many popular models ignore the distinction, often using terms like general or specific quite differently. One model includes the indefinite article, whatever its meaning, among **general determiners**, which are said to be 'general', 'indefinite', and 'without identifying meaning'. These are contrasted with **specific determiners**, which include *the* but not *a/an*.

Another model places *a/an* in a class of **(indefinite) identifiers**, but treats *the* as a **definite identifier**.

indefinite partitive *See* PARTITIVE.

indefinite pronoun A *pronoun lacking the *definiteness (identifiability) of *reference inherent in *personal, *reflexive, *possessive, and *demonstrative pronouns, expressing a range of meanings; e.g. *any, either, enough, few, neither, none, some*. Indefinite pronouns include *compound pronouns (e.g. *anything, everybody, somebody, something*).

The pronoun *one* is often indefinite in reference, as in:

one of these days

I don't have a car—I'd like *one*

One should drink in moderation

Corresponding *determinatives (1) (*any, every, some*, etc.) also have indefinite reference.

independent Of a linguistic element (*word, *phrase, *clause, etc.): that can stand on its own, in contrast to a *dependent element.

•• **independent clause**: this is often synonymous with *main clause in contrast to *subordinate clause. However, a distinction must sometimes be made. For example, in

The more I think about it, the more I like the idea

neither clause is independent, though both are arguably main clauses. On the other hand, where two main clauses are *coordinated, with some ellipsis, as in

The plan is brilliant and the whole thing [is] excellent

some would argue that both clauses are independent, whereas others would argue that the second clause is not.

Compare MATRIX.

•• **independent genitive**: *see* GENITIVE.

•• **independent pronoun**: *see* ABSOLUTE (3).

•• **independent relative clause**: the same as *free relative clause.

indeterminacy The quality of not being clearly delimited and/or defined.

Clear-cut grammatical *categories, *rules, etc. are not always attainable, since the system of grammar is arguably subject to *gradience. The same considerations apply to the notions of 'correct' and 'incorrect' usage, since there are areas where native speakers disagree as to what is grammatically *acceptable. Indeterminacy is therefore a feature of grammar and usage.

Grammarians also speak of indeterminacy in cases where two different grammatical analyses of a particular structure are plausible.

● **indeterminate**.

See also MULTIPLE ANALYSIS.

index (Plural **indices**.) In the following examples the subscript letters are referred to as indices. Identical letters indicate *co-reference:

Wayne$_i$ likes himself$_i$ too much

In the next example, the subscript 'i/j' indicates that *she* may refer to the same person as Frederica, though this pronoun can also refer to some other female individual.

Frederica said that she$_{i/j}$ will arrive a little bit late

indicative (*n. & adj.*) (In traditional analyses. (A *verb form or *mood) that expresses factuality. Contrasted in particular with the *subjunctive.

Traditional grammar follows Latin and similar models in making a threefold mood distinction: indicative, *imperative, and subjunctive. However, the paucity of verb *inflections makes such an analysis less appropriate for Modern English than for, say, Old English.

Compare DECLARATIVE; STATEMENT.

indicator *See* MARKER (2).

indirect condition *See* CONDITION.

indirect object (IO, O^i, or O$_i$) A *noun phrase which is *licensed by a *ditransitive *verb and which typically occurs after the verb and before the *direct object, and carries the *semantic role of *recipient or *goal. When a *pronoun is used, it appears in the *accusative case. Examples:

I gave *the publisher* three manuscripts

They told *her* a lie

He never gives *me* nice presents

Although the indirect object usually precedes the direct object, there can be exceptions, e.g.

Give *me* it/?Give it *me*

The IO of an *active declarative clause can become the subject of a *passive clause:

The publisher was given three manuscripts (by me)

She was told a lie (by them)

I am never given nice presents (by him)

In traditional grammar, many phrases that express a recipient or goal are regarded as indirect objects, whatever their position, like the prepositional phrases headed by *for* and *to* in the following example:

They bought a new bicycle *for her*, and gave it *to her*

Many modern grammars (e.g. CaGEL, OMEG) do not classify such prepositional phrases as indirect objects.

There are also different analyses when only the recipient of a potentially ditransitive verb is expressed. For example, in *He told his parents*, the noun phrase *his parents* can be analysed either as an indirect object with the direct object implied (compare *He told his parents the news*), or as a direct object (compare *He informed his parents*).

Compare BENEFICIARY.

indirect question In grammars that do not make a systematic distinction between *interrogatives and *questions, and use the latter as a syntactic label: a question as reported in *indirect speech.

Indirect questions do not display subject–auxiliary *inversion, i.e. they are characterized by the use of an unmarked subject–verb *word order. Thus the reported version of

What   do   you   want?
[direct object + auxiliary + subject + verb]

becomes

I asked him [what   he   wanted]
            [direct object + subject + verb]

Indirect yes–no questions are introduced by *if* or *whether*, e.g.

I asked him *whether he will write an article for the newspaper*

Since indirect questions in the description above are defined syntactically, rather than from the point of view of usage, they are best referred to as **subordinate interrogative clauses** (or **subordinate interrogatives**).

We can then use the notion of **embedded question** to refer to a question conveyed by a subordinate interrogative.

2002 R. HUDDLESTON & G. K. PULLUM Subordinate interrogatives, like main clause interrogatives, normally express questions, but because they are embedded there is no illocutionary force associated with them . . . Subordinate interrogatives are used in reporting inquiries, as in *They asked where she was born*, but have numerous other uses too, as in *They know where she was born* or *It depends where she was born*. We refer to the questions they express as **embedded questions**, avoiding the traditional term 'indirect question'.

See also QUESTION.

indirect speech A way of reporting what someone has said, using an introductory reporting *verb and a *subordinate clause. Contrasted with *direct speech.

In indirect speech the actual words of the original speaker are usually changed, in that *pronouns, time and place *adverbials, and *tenses are adjusted to the viewpoint of the person reporting what was said (*see also* BACKSHIFT). Thus the first Duke of Wellington's advice to a new member of Parliament *Don't quote Latin, say what you have to say and then sit down* would in indirect speech become *He advised the member not to quote Latin, (but) to say what he had to say and then (to) sit down.*

The term indirect speech is often loosely used to cover the reporting of thoughts, using an introductory verb of thinking and a *that*-clause.

In general, indirect speech and *reported speech are synonymous and interchangeable, but some people make a distinction. *See* REPORTED SPEECH (2).

Compare FREE INDIRECT SPEECH.

•• **indirect speech act**: *see* SPEECH ACT.

Indo-European (*n. & adj.*) (Designating) the family of cognate languages (including English) spoken over the greater part of Europe and extending into Asia as far as northern India, or the hypothetical common ancestor of these languages (**Proto-Indo-European**).

infinite The same as *non-finite. (Now old-fashioned.)

infinitival Of, or belonging to, the *infinitive.

•• **infinitival clause**: *see* NON-FINITE CLAUSE.

•• **infinitival particle**: the element *to* used before an infinitive. Also called **infinitival marker to**, or simply **infinitival to**.

The *to* of the *to*-infinitive is historically a *preposition, but synchronically it is not, as is shown by the fact that prepositions, including *to*, cannot be followed by an infinitive, but require the *-*ing* form of a *verb; e.g.

They resorted to rudeness, and to *attacking* him physically

not:

* They resorted to rudeness, and to *attack* him physically

Infinitival *to* does not share the characteristics of any other *word class. It therefore has a label of its own.

See SYNCATEGOREMATIC.

infinitive (*n. & adj.*) (Designating) the unmarked *non-finite *base (1) form of a *verb, when used without a direct link to *time, *person, or *number.

In English when the infinitive is preceded by the *infinitival *particle *to*
we speak of a *to-infinitive (clause):

> I wanted *to help*
> *To err* is human

When the verb is used without *to* we speak of a *bare infinitive
(clause):

> Don't *apologize*
> You can't *take* it with you

Some other *non-finite *verb phrases are sometimes analysed as **complex
infinitives**:

> *To have made* a mistake is understandable (perfect infinitive)
> It was upsetting *to be questioned* (passive infinitive)
> I expected you *to be waiting* for me (progressive infinitive)

Other even more complex infinitives are also possible, e.g. (*to*) *have
been doing*, (*to*) *have been done*, (*to*) *be being done*, (*to*) *have been being
done* (rare).

Compare SPLIT INFINITIVE.

infinitive clause *See* NON-FINITE CLAUSE.

infix *See* AFFIX; TMESIS.

inflect *Morphology.* Change the form of a word by adding *inflections
in order to indicate grammatical differences of *tense, *number, *gender,
*case (1), etc.

Modern English is a relatively uninflected language. *Lexical verbs
inflect for:

> third *person singular in the *present simple *tense (*looks, sees*)
> the *past simple (*looked, saw*)
> the present *participle (*looking, seeing*)
> the past participle (*looked, seen*)

*Nouns inflect for:

> plural (*girls*)
> possessive (*girl's, girls'*)

Some *adjectives and *adverbs inflect for:

> the comparative (*nicer, hotter, sooner*)
> the superlative (*nicest, hottest, soonest*)

Inflection does not change the *word class to which a word belongs,
in contrast to *derivation, which may do so.

inflection

1. The phenomenon whereby the form of a *word is changed according to its grammatical use (e.g. whether it is used as a *plural form, *past tense form, *case (1) form, etc.). *See also* INFLECT. Contrasted with *word formation (2).

2. An *inflected form of a word (also called *inflectional form), or a *suffix or other element that is used to inflect a word.

> 1874 H. SWEET Old English is the period of full inflections ... Middle English of levelled inflections ... and Modern English of lost inflections.

- **inflectional**: pertaining to, or characterized by, inflection.
- • **inflectional class**: a *conjugation is a verbal inflectional class, whereas a *declension is a *nominal inflectional class.
- • **inflectional form**: *see* INFLECTIONAL FORM.
- • **inflectional formative**: *see* FORMATIVE (1).
- • **inflectional suffix**: *see* SUFFIX.
- • **inflection phrase (IP)**: *see* FUNCTIONAL CATEGORY; PHRASE.

The spelling *inflexion* is now considered old-fashioned.

inflectional form

The *morphosyntactic *realization of a *lexical item as determined by its syntactic position. Also called *grammatical word (2).

For example, if we wish to use the *lexeme *window* in the position indicated by '_' in the frame *those _ need to be cleaned* it must take a *plural *-s* *inflection. We refer to the item *windows* as the plural inflectional form of the *lexeme *window*.

See also SHAPE.

inflection phrase (IP)

See FUNCTIONAL CATEGORY; PHRASE.

informal

Of spoken or written style: characterized by a simpler grammatical structure and more familiar *vocabulary than *formal (3) style.

The attitude of speakers (or writers) to their audience is often reflected in different levels of formality, with formal and informal style as two extremes, and a wide range of stylistically less *marked language in between.

Compare ATTITUDINAL; COLLOQUIAL.
See also USAGE.

information content

Linguistics. The amount of information carried by a linguistic unit in a particular context.

The notion of information content is related to statistical probability. If a unit is totally predictable in a particular context then, according to information theory, it is informationally redundant and its information content is nil. This is true of the *particle (2) *to* in most contexts (e.g. *What are you going . . . do?*).

See also DUMMY.

Compare INFORMATION STRUCTURE; REDUNDANCY.

information packaging See INFORMATION STRUCTURE.

information question See QUESTION.

information structure The way in which the *constituents of a *clause or *sentence are (re)arranged so that a particular part of the 'message' receives greatest attention. Also called **information packaging**.

The term is a general one, concerned with such contrasts as *given and *new, *theme and *rheme, *topic and *comment.

See also CLEFT; EXISTENTIAL; INVERSION; PASSIVIZATION; PROPOSITION.

-ing clause A *non-finite *clause whose *verb phrase (1) contains a *verb ending in *-ing* as its *head. Also called **present participle clause**, **-ing participle clause**, and **gerund-participial clause**. Examples:

The boss hates *him always complaining about everything*
I love *working late*

Notice that the first example contains its own *subject, whereas the second example does not.

Compare BARE INFINITIVE CLAUSE; CONTENT CLAUSE; *-ED* CLAUSE; PARTICIPLE CLAUSE; *TO*-INFINITIVE CLAUSE.

-ing form A *verb form ending in *-ing*.

In traditional grammar, a distinction is made between the *gerund, regarded as a **verbal noun**, e.g.

Seeing is *believing*
Nelly's *reading* of this passage is not valid

and the present *participle, used in various *constructions in *finite and *non-finite clauses, e.g.

We'*re visiting* them tomorrow
Seeing them in that condition, I was greatly upset

See also *-ING* CLAUSE; PARTICIPIAL ADJECTIVE; PROGRESSIVE.

-ing participle See *-ING* FORM; PRESENT PARTICIPLE.

-ing participle clause See *-ING* CLAUSE.

inherent Of an *adjective: that directly characterizes the *referent of the *noun it is connected with; contrasted with **non-inherent**.

The meaning of many adjectives is not affected by their *position in a *sentence, so that *rich* means the same in *attributive position (e.g. *She's a rich woman*) as it does in *predicative position (e.g. *That woman is rich*). These are inherent adjectives.

By contrast, non-inherent adjectives do not directly characterize the referent of the noun they modify. For example, *John is a heavy sleeper* does not entail that John is heavy. Other examples of non-inherent adjectives occur in the following examples:

> an *old* friend, *pure* invention, a *complete* idiot, a *real* genius, a *generative* linguist

Non-inherent adjectives mostly only occur in attributive position.

Compare INTENSIFYING.

initial Designating or occurring in a *position at the beginning of a linguistic unit, e.g. a *phrase or *clause.

The term **initial position** (or *front position) is used in analysing various kinds of linguistic phenomena, such as the positioning of *adverbials. Since *final (or end) position in clause structure is *unmarked for adverbials, initial position is *marked. Contrast *I'm leaving tomorrow* with *Tomorrow, I'm leaving*, where *tomorrow* is marked as *topic. A manner *adjunct (3) may become a *disjunct when placed in initial position. Contrast *He spoke frankly* with *Frankly, we didn't believe him*. Initial position contrasts with final position and *medial (mid) position.

See also MOVEMENT; TOPICALIZATION.

initial combining form *See* NEOCLASSICAL COMPOUND.

initialism The use of the initial letters of a *name or expression as an abbreviation for it, each letter being pronounced separately, as in BBC, KO, RSPCA, RSVP. A type of *abbreviation.

Compare ACRONYM (2).

instantaneous Of the simple present (2) *tense: referring to a brief action beginning and ending more or less at the moment of speech; contrasted with the *habitual, *state, and *timeless uses of that tense.

This is a rather restricted use of the simple present tense. It occurs in some sports commentaries (e.g. *Wilkins takes the ball . . .*), in demonstrations (e.g. *I now add the gelatine to the hot water*), and in *performatives (e.g. *I apologize*).

Compare PUNCTUAL.

institutionalized Established as a norm.

The term is used in a fairly general way. It can be applied to (i) a distinct and acceptable variety of English such as Singaporean English or Indian English; (ii) a set expression which appears in some way to deviate from the norm (e.g. *heir apparent* rather than **apparent heir*); and (iii) a structure that is deemed unacceptable by many people (e.g. a *hanging participle), but which is prevalent, and acceptable in certain contexts.

> 1985 R. QUIRK et al. In formal scientific writing, the [hanging participle] construction has become institutionalized where the implied subject is to be identified with the *I*, *we*, and *you* of the writer(s) or reader(s):

> *When treating patients with language retardation and deviation of language development*, the therapy consists, in part, of discussions of the patient's problems with parents and teachers, with subsequent language teaching carried out by them.

instrumental

1. (*n. & adj.*) (A *noun, *phrase, *case (3), or *semantic role) that indicates the implement, or other inanimate thing, used in performing the action denoted by a *verb. Also called **instrument**.

*Old English had a few traces of an instrumental case (1), besides the four other cases marked by *inflection.

The word is now particularly used in classifying the meaning of *adverbials. Instrumental *prepositional phrases used adverbially typically begin with *with*:

> They attacked the police *with bricks*

Instrumental contrasts with *agentive:

> The officers were attacked *by the mob* with bricks

In *Case Grammar, the instrumental is extended to cover *noun phrases with a semantic role of this sort, even though syntactically they are *subjects or *objects:

> *A brick* injured the woman

> They used *riot shields* to protect themselves

2. *Semantics.* Describing the function (2) of language whereby the speaker gets the listener to do something.

Thus *directives and requests can be said to have an instrumental function. It is similar to the *conative function.

● **instrumentally**.

integrated affix See LEVEL ORDERING (HYPOTHESIS).

integrated relative clause See RESTRICTIVE.

intensifier An *adverbial that scales another element upwards
(**amplifier**) or downwards (**downtoner**) in degrees of intensity.

In the very detailed classification presented in CGEL, intensifiers
are described as a subcategory of *subjuncts, along with *emphasizers,
*focusing adverbs, and others. Intensifiers are exemplified in the
following:

> We *thoroughly* disapprove and are *bitterly* disappointed
> We *completely* agree with your assessment
> I *hardly* know them
> We were *kind of* wondering

intensify Of a *word: have a heightening (amplifying) or lowering
(downtoning) effect on the meaning of a *word, *phrase, etc.
● **intensification**: the result of having a heightening or lowering intensifying effect; the fact of being intensified.
● **intensifying**: having a heightening or lowering effect. The term is
applied to *adjectives and *adverbs. We thus have **intensifying adverbs**
(usually called *intensifiers) and **intensifying adjectives** (including
*emphasizers). The latter are exemplified in the following:

> *pure* joy, *complete* nonsense, a *firm* commitment, *utter* rubbish, *great* hopes

> Compare ATTRIBUTIVE.

intension See EXTENSION (1).

intensive Of an element, *phrase, etc.: in a *predicative (2) relationship
with another element, phrase, etc. Contrasted with *extensive.

The term can be applied to the relationship between a *subject and a
subject-related predicative *complement, and to that between an *object
and an object-related predicative complement, as well as to the identity
existing between the two terms of an *apposition:

> He seems *worried*
> You've got *me worried*
> the Queen's daughter, the Princess Royal

●● **intensive complement**: a complement of a *linking verb.
●● **intensive verb**: an alternative term for a linking verb.
> See also COPULA; COPULAR. *verb*

interjection A minor *word class whose members are outside normal
clause structure, having no syntactic connection with other words, and

generally having emotive or *interpersonal meanings. Examples are *aha, alas, eh?, mm, oops, sh!*

   Compare EXCLAMATION.

internal argument *See* ARGUMENT.

internal complement *See* COMPLEMENT.

interpersonal
   1. *Pragmatics*. Concerned with (verbal) exchanges between people; or, more specifically, concerned with the kinds of meaning(s) that may arise between people in particular circumstances—hence **interpersonal meaning**. This kind of meaning relates to its function as a connection between speaker and listener, or writer and reader. It is concerned with social exchanges, the use of language to influence behaviour, and so on. It thus shares features with *attitudinal meaning. It is sometimes called **social meaning** or *situational meaning.

   See also COMMUNICATIVE; CONATIVE; CONNOTATION; EXPRESSIVE; PROPOSITIONAL MEANING; REFERENTIAL MEANING.

   2. In *Systemic Grammar, interpersonal meaning is contrasted with *ideational (2) meaning and *textual (2) meaning.

   See also METAFUNCTION.

interpretive semantics A type of *semantics, associated especially with Noam Chomsky and Ray Jackendoff, in which the meaning of sentences is interpreted from syntactic structure (as represented in *tree diagrams).

interrogative (*n. & adj.*) (A *word or *clause) typically used in formulating a *question.

   As a *clause type, **interrogative clauses** are characterized by a *word order in which subject–auxiliary *inversion obtains (in *main clauses), and they are typically used to ask questions. Thus, interrogative is a formal syntactic category, whereas question is a category of usage, though the terms are, confusingly, often used interchangeably.
   •• **open interrogative clauses**: interrogative clauses characterized by the use of a *wh-word and by subject–auxiliary inversion (unless the *wh*-word functions as subject, e.g. *Who arrived late?*). Sometimes called **wh-interrogatives**. They can have an unlimited set of possible answers, e.g.

   What do you eat for breakfast?

•• **closed interrogative clauses** (also called **yes/no interrogatives**, a term that was probably introduced in the form 'yes-or-no question' in Jespersen (1924)): interrogative clauses characterized by subject-auxiliary inversion, which elicit 'yes' or 'no' as possible answers, e.g.

Do you like swimming in the sea?

There are of course different ways of replying to this question, for example by saying *It depends on the weather* or *Sometimes*, but these count as *responses, not as answers.

A special type of closed interrogative clauses is **alternative interrogative clauses**. These also have a limited set of answers, but not 'yes' or 'no'; e.g.

Are you happy or sad?

Interrogative clauses can also be used as *statements (e.g. *Haven't we all made mistakes at some stage?*), as *directives (e.g. *Could you please make less noise?*), or as *exclamations (e.g. *Isn't it a lovely day!*). These are examples of indirect *speech acts.

•• **interrogative tag**: *see* TAG.

•• **interrogative word**: a member of a small set of words which typically beginning with *wh*- and are used to introduce open interrogative clauses. Such words can be *adverbs (*how, why, when, where, wherever*, e.g. <u>Why</u> *did she leave?*), *determinatives (1) (*which, what*; used before nouns, e.g. <u>Which film</u> *did you see?*), or *pronouns (*what, who, whose, which*, e.g. <u>Who</u> *opened the door?*).

Compare RELATIVE PRONOUN; *WH*-WORD.

See also CLAUSE TYPE; DECLARATIVE; EXCLAMATIVE; IMPERATIVE.

intersective gradience *See* GRADIENCE.

intervening NP *See* COMPLEX CATENATIVE CONSTRUCTION.

intransitive A term used to describe a *verb which does not *license any *complements, (hence **intransitive complementation**), or a *pattern or *clause in which the verb does not license any complements, e.g.

Henrietta smirked

• **intransitively, intransitivity**.

Compare COMPLEMENTATION; COMPLEX INTRANSITIVE; COMPLEX TRANSITIVE; DITRANSITIVE; MONOTRANSITIVE; TRANSITIVE.

intrinsic modality Another term for *deontic modality.

introductory *it*

1. Another term for ambient *it*, *dummy *it*, *empty *it*, or *prop *it*.

2. Another term to describe *anticipatory or preparatory *it*.

Like all these terms, 'introductory *it*' is used by different people to cover (or exclude) different uses of the word *it*.

Compare IMPERSONAL.

invariable (*n. & adj.*) (A *word) that does not vary in form (e.g. by *inflection); contrasting with *variable (1). Also called **invariant**.

The term is applied to words that have a single (uninflected) form (e.g. *but, for, over, sheep, politics*) in contrast to words that inflect.

inversion The reversal of an *unmarked *word order (or, more accurately, *constituent order).

The term is particularly used in relation to *subjects and *auxiliary verbs (hence **subject–auxiliary inversion**). The unmarked word order subject (+ auxiliary) + *lexical verb in e.g.

> I am listening
> I have a complaint
> He understands

is changed to auxiliary + subject (+ verb) for yes/no *interrogatives (if necessary, *do* is added), e.g.

> *Are you* listening?
> *Have you* any complaints?
> *Do you* have any complaints?
> *Does he* understand?

Similar inversion occurs if a negative or near-negative adjunct is *fronted:

> <u>Never</u> *have I* seen such a ghastly sight
> <u>Hardly</u> *did I* realize how lucky I was

Inversion of subject and main verb, with no additional auxiliary, occurs in certain structures involving the fronting of an adverbial and the placing of a subject in end position, e.g.

> Here *comes the bride*

Inversion of this type typically occurs for *information structuring reasons, e.g. in order to mark a *topic/*theme.

irrealis Of a *verb, form, etc.: expressing unreality, non-factuality, extreme unlikelihood, potentiality, etc. Contrasted with **realis**.

Irrealis relates to other areas of grammar, such as *tense and *mood. For example, counterfactual *conditional clauses, which contain a past tense form (e.g. *If I <u>lived</u> to be a hundred . . .*), and so-called *subjunctive moods (e.g. *If I <u>were</u> you . . .*) describe what is extremely unlikely or totally impossible.

•• **irrealis *were***: a term used in CaGEL for *were* as a specialized non-tensed relic mood form occurring with first and third person singular subjects: *If I were you* . . . ; *If she were here* . . . Despite not carrying tense, it is regarded as a *primary (2) verb form.

> 2002 R. HUDDLESTON & G. K. PULLUM et al. In its normal use, i.e. in modal remoteness constructions, irrealis *were* does not refer to past time, and there is no synchronic reason to analyse it as a past tense form.

> 2005 R. HUDDLESTON & G. K. PULLUM et al. We include the irrealis forms among the primary forms, because there is a negative irrealis form, and also because of the close relation with preterite *was* and *wasn't*.

See also CONDITIONAL; COUNTERFACTUAL; MODALITY; MOOD.

irregular Of a linguistic form or structure: not following the rules for its *class, *paradigm, etc. Contrasted with *regular.

The term is particularly applied to *verbs that do not follow the general pattern of adding the verbal *inflectional ending -*ed* to form the *past (2) tense and the *past participle (called **irregular verbs** or *strong verbs). Thus, compare the regular verb *walk/walked/walked* with irregular *see/saw/seen* and *put/put/put*. Among *nouns, common irregular *plurals include *men, women, children, mice, teeth,* and a number of *foreign plurals.

Irregular degrees of *comparison include *good/better/best; bad/worse/worst; little/less/least; much/more/most*.

• **irregularly**.

•• **irregular lexeme**: a *lexeme which displays unpredictable inflectional forms, e.g. in the plural (cf. *ox/oxen*) or past tense (*sing/sang*).

•• **irregular sentence**: *see* MINOR SENTENCE.

See also DEFECTIVE; REGULAR LEXEME; STRONG; SUPPLETION.

Compare ANOMALOUS.

isolating The same as *analytic.

it *See* ANTICIPATORY *it*; DUMMY; EMPTY; EXPLETIVE; IMPERSONAL; INTRODUCTORY *it*; REFERENTIAL *it*.

iteration The same as *recursion.

iterative (*n. & adj.*)

1. (An expression, *construction, etc.) denoting repetition.

The term is used to describe the meaning of verbal constructions, as in

I've been walking to work for the past three weeks

where the sense is a series of repeated actions. A possible alternative term here is *habitual.

Iterative meaning is also suggested by some types of *coordination, as in

I wrote and wrote—but they didn't reply

They were running up and down the stairs

2. (A word) formed by repetition.

1961 F. G. CASSIDY In Standard English one finds three kinds of iteratives: the simple ones like *hush-hush*...; those with vowel gradation like *ding-dong*...; and the rhyming ones like *handy-dandy*.

In some cases, the meaning of such expressions is also iterative in sense (1), as in *knock-knock*, *tick-tock*. This type of *compound word is also called *reduplicative.

3. The same as *frequentative.

junction (In the work of Otto Jespersen.) The action of combining a *secondary to a *primary, forming a single *phrase containing *words of different *ranks (1). By contrast we have **nexus** when elements combine in *clauses, typically with a *verb.

> 1924 O. JESPERSEN If . . . we compare the combination of *a furiously barking dog* . . . with *the dog barks furiously* . . . there is a fundamental difference between them which calls for separate terms for the two kinds of combination: we shall call the former kind *junction*, and the latter *nexus*.

> 1933b O. JESPERSEN A junction is like a picture, a nexus is like a drama or process.

The term is virtually limited to the writings of Jespersen.

See also ADJUNCT; ADNEX.

jussive (*n. & adj.*) (A type of *verb or *clause) that expresses a command.

Jussives include not only *imperatives, as narrowly defined, but also related non-imperative clauses, including some in the *subjunctive mood:

Be sensible
You be quiet
Everybody listen
Let's forget it
Heaven help us
It is important that he keep this a secret

The term jussive is, however, used to some extent as a syntactic label, and in this use would not include commands expressed as straight declaratives, e.g. *You will do what I say*. In popular grammars, where the term is not used, such structures would be dealt with under an expanded imperative label and under the subjunctive.

See also CLAUSE TYPE; DECLARATIVE; EXCLAMATIVE; IMPERATIVE; INTERROGATIVE.

kernel Of a *phrase, *clause, etc.: formally elementary and *unmarked. Also called **canonical**.

> 1984 R. HUDDLESTON A form which is maximally basic, one which does not belong to a marked term in any system, is called a *kernel* form.

The term is derived from early *Generative Grammar (2), where the application of certain obligatory *phrase structure rules produced a set of basic structures called **kernel sentences** (or **kernel clauses**, as some grammarians prefer to call them). These are syntactically unmarked *declarative clauses, not 'optionally transformed' (e.g. by *negation, *inversion, *passivization, etc.), and *complete in themselves (i.e. not *ellipted, *coordinated, *subordinated, etc.).

kind of modality Any of the various different types of *modality that can be distinguished in language, e.g. *alethic, *deontic, *dynamic, and *epistemic.

See also DEGREE OF MODALITY; STRENGTH OF MODALITY.

King's English, the The English of the court as a model to emulate.

> D. CRYSTAL 2004 This term [was] first recorded in Thomas Wilson's *Arte of Rhetorique* in 1553, where he talks of 'counterfeiting the king's English' (p 291). It had become the Queen's English in Thomas Nashe's satirical pamphlet *Strange Newes* (1592). And responsibility varied between king and queen thereafter, along with their court, which, according to Swift, was 'the Standard of Propriety and Correctness of Speech'.

See also BBC ENGLISH; STANDARD ENGLISH.

labelled bracketing *See* BRACKETING.

LAD *See* LANGUAGE ACQUISITION DEVICE.

language

1. (In the most general sense.) A uniquely human, mentally encoded attribute principally used for written or spoken communication. When uttered by a speaker, language consists of a stream of sounds which conveys a meaning that can be decoded by a hearer.

2. A variety of this used by a particular community or nation, e.g. *the English language, the languages of the British Isles, Indo-European languages, Romance languages.*

More specifically called a **natural language** in contrast to an *artificial language or a **computer language**.
•• **first language**: the earliest language that an individual learns to speak (also called **mother tongue**), and of which he or she is a **native speaker**.

3. The style of an utterance or text; hence e.g. *bad language, graphic language, literary language, poetic language.* *See also* BLOCK LANGUAGE.

4. The *variety of language used in a particular profession or in a specialized context, e.g. *the language of advertising, legal language, religious language, scientific language.*

The language of an individual is an *idiolect; that of a region or community is a *dialect; the individual's idealized knowledge of language is his or her *competence (contrasted with **performance**); the idealized abstract concept of the language shared by a particular group of people is called *langue (contrasted with **parole**); the study of language may be over a period of time (*diachronic) or at one particular time (*synchronic).

language acquisition device (In *Generative Grammar (2).) The innate, highly abstract module of the mind that enables humans to learn *language (1). Abbreviated LAD.

The LAD forms a part of Chomsky's theory, introduced in *Aspects of the Theory of Syntax* (1965). Children do not learn language merely by repeating what they hear around them. Using the LAD they construct a grammar of their native language, and are then able to produce new utterances. The evidence for the LAD is the so-called **poverty of the stimulus**, i.e. the observation that what a child hears in its immediate environment is insufficient to learn a language, because this stimulus is corrupted in various ways (by hesitations, false starts, and so on). Chomsky's theory is controversial and has been revised considerably in recent years.

See GOVERNMENT-BINDING THEORY; MINIMALIST PROGRAM; STANDARD THEORY.

langue Language as a system. Contrasted with **parole**.

The terms langue and parole were introduced by the Swiss linguist Ferdinand de Saussure (*see* SAUSSUREAN) in order to separate two of the meanings of the word *language*. What exactly he meant has been the subject of argument, but, roughly speaking, langue is the language system of a particular language community, whereas parole is language behaviour, i.e. the way in which members of that community actually use the system.

Compare COMPETENCE.

Late Modern English A phase in the history of the English language variously described as extending from 1700 up to 1900, or from 1700 to the present. Some linguists prefer a start date of 1775 (the publication of Johnson's *Dictionary of the English Language*), 1776 (American Independence), or 1800.

Latinate affix *See* LEVEL ORDERING (HYPOTHESIS).

learned plural An older and possibly obsolete term for *foreign *plural.

left-branching *See* BRANCHING.

left dislocation *See* DISLOCATION.

level Each of the areas into which a language can be analysed, characterized by a distinct property which is the object of analysis (e.g. *form (3), *function (1), *meaning).

A very general term for the different areas of language analysis, some of which are also described under such terms as *hierarchy or *rank. At least three levels are generally recognized—grammar, phonology, and semantics—but some models of grammar recognize more. Different grammatical models relate the levels to each other in different ways. In *structuralism, analysis proceeds from the lowest level, phonetics and phonology, to progressively higher levels dealing with *morphemes, *words, *phrases, *clauses, etc. using **discovery procedures**. In other analyses, the different levels are not considered to be so clearly separable.

•• **level ordering**: see LEVEL ORDERING (HYPOTHESIS).

level of style A term referring to the *formal (3) and *informal uses of both written and spoken language.

level of usage *See* FORMAL; INFORMAL; LEVEL OF STYLE.

level ordering (hypothesis) *Morphology & Phonology.* The idea that certain *derivational and *inflectional *affixes are cyclically added to a *root or *base (2) at different levels or **strata**.

In English so-called Level I affixes (also called **Latinate affixes, non-neutral affixes**, or **integrated affixes**), which have a phonological effect when they are added (e.g. ˈgeneral – geneˈrality), are appended before Level II affixes (also called **Germanic affixes** or **neutral affixes**), which do not have a phonological effect (e.g. ˈhappy – ˈhappiness).

> 2003 I. PLAG According to the so-called **level-ordering hypothesis**, affixes can easily combine with affixes on the same level, but if they combine with an affix from another level, the level 1 affix is always closer to the base than the level 2 affix. For example, level 1 suffix -(i)an may appear inside level 2 -ism but not vice versa (cf. *Mongol-ian-ism*, but *Mongol-ism-ian). Level-ordering thus rules out many unattested combinations of affixes on principled grounds.

The hypothesis is not exceptionless, and has been criticized.

lexeme A *word in the abstract sense; an individual, distinct item of *lexis, of which a number of actual *forms (1) may exist for use in different *morphosyntactic roles. Also called **dictionary word**. This term is contrasted with the notion 'word' as an uninterruptable sequence of letters with spaces on either side (an *orthographic word).

The five **word-forms** *see, sees, seeing, saw,* and *seen* are different incarnations of the same word when we talk about lexemes.

Identical forms with unrelated meanings are treated as separate lexemes, just as they are treated as different *vocabulary items in a dictionary. Thus *see* (the area under the authority of a bishop or archbishop) is a different lexeme from *see* (discern with the eyes). *Compare* HOMONYM.

Identical forms with different meanings, which in fact have a common origin, are similarly treated. Thus *polysemous words—such as *love* with the meaning 'passion' and *love* with the meaning 'nil' (as in tennis; the relationship in this case being through the phrase *for love*, 'without stakes', 'for nothing')—are also usually considered different lexemes, even though lexicographers may treat them under one headword in a dictionary. This is a disputable area, because although some 'words' are clearly distinguishable into several 'senses' (e.g. *crane*, 'bird'; *crane*, 'lifting device'), others can be subdivided with varying degrees of refinement (e.g. *company, high, office, thing*), and the assignment of any particular schema of subdivisions to separate lexemes would be open to challenge.

The term lexeme is sometimes extended to include a sequence of words that constitute a single semantic item: e.g. *out of*, or *put off* ('postpone'). *See* MULTI-WORD LEXICAL ITEM; MULTI-WORD VERB; PHRASAL-PREPOSITIONAL VERB; PHRASAL VERB; PREPOSITIONAL VERB.

The term is occasionally used in roughly the sense of *morpheme, *root, or *stem, but this is not now usual.

> 1958 C. F. HOCKETT The lexemes in the two-word sequence *twenty-eighth* are *twenty, eight* and *-th*.

● **lexemic**: of or relating to lexemes.

● **lexemics**: the study of lexemes.

●● **compound lexeme**: a *compound word whose meaning can sometimes not be deduced from its parts (also called **word lexeme**), or a similar combination of words; e.g. *greenhouse, bucket shop*.

●● **lexeme formation**: *see* WORD FORMATION.
     See also LEXICAL ITEM; WORD.

lexical Relating to, or pertaining to, *words as units of the *vocabulary. The term is extensively used in a fairly general sense, as in **lexical factor**, **lexical recurrence** (the repetition of a word), **lexical structure** (morphology), and so on. It is also used in more specific ways (see below).

● **lexically**: as regards vocabulary.

●● **lexical ambiguity**: *see* AMBIGUITY.

●● **lexical base**: the same as *base (2).

●● **lexical blend**: *see* BLEND (1).

●● **lexical category**: a *category whose members belong to one of the major *word classes *noun, *verb, *adjective, etc.; contrasted with *functional category.

●● **lexical entry**: *see* LEXICON.

●● **lexical field**: *see* FIELD.

●● **lexical formative**: *see* FORMATIVE (1).

●● **lexical item**: *see* LEXICAL ITEM.

●● **lexical meaning**: *see* MEANING.

●● **lexical modality**: *see* LEXICAL MODALITY.

•• **lexical morpheme:** *see* ROOT.
•• **lexical verb:** *see* LEXICAL VERB.
•• **lexical word formation:** *see* WORD FORMATION (2).

Lexical-Functional Grammar A theory of grammar with two levels
(**c-structure** and **f-structure**), developed since the 1980s by Joan Bresnan
and associates, which—as its name implies—attaches more importance to
the *lexicon and grammatical *functions (1) than to purely syntactic *rules,
in contrast to *Generative Grammar (2).

lexical item The same as *lexeme, or a variant on it; an item listed in the
*lexicon. (Sometimes also called **lexical unit.**)

Although the terms lexical item and lexeme are often used interchangeably, distinctions can be made.

The former may be preferred as the more general term, with the latter
reserved for the unit which has a group of *variants (e.g. *see, saw, seen*, etc.).

> 1984 R. D. HUDDLESTON A lexical item . . . may contain more than one
> lexeme or word: these are idioms such as *bury the hatchet* 'renounce a
> quarrel'.

As the quotation above suggests, the label lexical item may be preferred for
a *word, word combination, or *phrase whose *meaning is not deducible
from the meaning of its parts: e.g. *greenhouse, bucket shop* (normally
regarded as *compounds); *bury the hatchet, show a clean pair of heels*
(normally regarded as *idioms).

The term lexical item can also be used to denote a word *form (1), such
as an *irregular *inflectional form (of a lexeme) that would be expected to
have a separate dictionary entry. For example, in addition to listing *buy*, a
dictionary might have an entry '*bought*, see *buy*'. *Bought* would then be
a separate lexical item.

lexicalize Realize as a *word or *lexical item (something that was
previously, or could conceivably be, realized in an alternative way).

A notion or practice previously expressed by a syntactic phrase may be
lexicalized for convenience and conciseness: e.g. *tailgating* (M20) for
'driving too closely behind the vehicle in front', or *doorstepping* (M20, UK)
for 'canvassing support by going from door to door'.
• **lexicalization.**

lexical modality *Modal meaning expressed by *lexical items other
than modal *auxiliary verbs (also called **lexical modals**), e.g. *probably*
(adverb), *likely* (adjective), *wish* (verb).

•• **lexical modal verb**: a *lexical verb that expresses modal meaning. *See* MODAL LEXICAL VERB.

lexical verb A *verb that expresses a particular lexical *meaning, as listed in a dictionary, and can stand alone in a *clause. (Also called **full verb**.) Contrasted with *auxiliary verb and *main verb.

Lexical verbs constitute the majority of verbs. Formally they use auxiliary verbs in the formation of *interrogative and *negative structures (e.g. *Do you understand?*, *I didn't forget*; not *Understand you?*, *I forgot not*), as well as for *emphasis (*I DID forget*) and *code (*I forgot, and so did John*). *see* NICE PROPERTIES.

The terms lexical verb and *main verb are often used interchangeably, though they can be distinguished. *See* MAIN VERB.

lexical word The same as *content word.

lexicography The art and practice of dictionary making.

lexicology The study of the *lexis.

lexicon The complete set of *vocabulary items in a language, especially considered as part of a theoretical description.

In theoretical frameworks the lexicon is a special component consisting of **lexical entries** which may contain not only semantic information about each item, but also much more complete phonological and syntactic information than ordinary dictionaries would offer. There is a lively debate about the question of how much information should be contained in the lexicon.

•• **mental lexicon**: the store of words in the mind. How it is organized is the topic of current research.

2012 J. AITCHISON The human word-store is often referred to as the 'mental dictionary' or, perhaps more commonly, as the *mental lexicon*, to use the Greek word for 'dictionary'. There is, however, relatively little similarity between the words in our minds and words in book dictionaries, even though the information will sometimes overlap.

See also LEXIS.

lexis The stock of *words in a language; the *level of language consisting of *vocabulary. Contrasted with *grammar (1) (or *syntax).

See also LEXICON.

licensing The grammatical selection of a particular type of unit (*noun phrase, *that-clause, etc.) by an appropriate lexical *head (*verb, *noun, *adjective, etc.).

For example, the adjective *fond* licenses a *prepositional phrase headed by *of*, and the verb *devour* licenses a noun phrase functioning as *direct object.
• **license**
   Compare COMPLEMENTATION; GOVERNMENT; SUBORDINATION.

ligature A written or (especially) printed character combining two letters in one, e.g. ⟨æ⟩, ⟨œ⟩.

light verb A *verb with a very general *meaning which combines with specific complements to express a more complex verbal meaning that can also be expressed by a single verb, e.g. *take a picture > photograph, give a smirk > smirk*.

limiter A name for a type of focusing *adverb with a *restrictive meaning, e.g. *just, only, merely, simply* as in *I just/only/merely/simply said it was expensive*.

limiter adjective Another name for *restrictive adjective (which is the more usual term).
   See also ATTRIBUTIVE.

limiting adjective
   1. (In traditional grammar.) Another name for *determinative (1).
   The term was used to distinguish this class of words from *adjectives proper, which were more fully called *descriptive adjectives. However, syntactically, determinatives and adjectives behave very differently, and hence this label is a misnomer.
   2. The same as *restrictive adjective.
   See also ATTRIBUTIVE.

linguist A student of, or expert in, *linguistics.
   This is nearly as old (E17) as the lay meaning 'someone fluent in several languages' (L16). To make a clearer distinction, the term **linguistician** (L19) has been suggested as the term for the student of linguistics, but it is not used by those involved in the profession.

linguistic
   1. Relating to *linguistics, e.g. *linguistic analysis, linguistic theories*.
   2. Relating to *language (1), e.g. *linguistic complexity, linguistic phenomena, linguistic properties, linguistic rules, linguistic unit. Linguistic*

knowledge is a speaker's knowledge of (typically) their native language, contrasted with *non-linguistic knowledge (i.e. encyclopaedic knowledge of the world).

•• **linguistic determinism**, **linguistic relativity**: *see* SAPIR-WHORF HYPOTHESIS, THE.

linguistic determinism *See* SAPIR-WHORF HYPOTHESIS, THE.

linguistic relativity *See* SAPIR-WHORF HYPOTHESIS, THE.

linguistics The scientific study of *language (1).

Linguistics as an academic subject has burgeoned in recent decades. Surveys of the whole field are sometimes called **general linguistics**, while more specialized areas have specific labels.

•• **applied linguistics**: the practical application of linguistic studies to certain areas, especially the teaching of foreign languages.

•• **computational linguistics**: linguistics that uses computers in the gathering, analysis, and manipulation of linguistic data (including speech synthesis, machine translation, and aspects of artificial intelligence). *See also* **corpus**.

•• **corpus linguistics**: *see* CORPUS.

•• **descriptive linguistics**: *see* DESCRIPTIVE (2).

•• **structural linguistics**: *see* STRUCTURALISM.

•• **taxonomic linguistics**: language study concerned particularly with classification; often used as a pejorative synonym for structural linguistics (*see* STRUCTURALISM) or *descriptive linguistics.

•• **theoretical linguistics**: the study of a language or languages using a theoretical model, such as *Generative Grammar (2).

See also COMPARATIVE; CONTRASTIVE; DIACHRONIC; HISTORICAL; PSYCHOLINGUISTICS; SOCIOLINGUISTICS; SYNCHRONIC; TEXT LINGUISTICS.

linker Another term for *coordinator.

Not a very widely used term, because it is too general.

linking adjunct/adverb/adverbial *See* CONJUNCT; LINKING WORD.

linking verb A *verb that syntactically and semantically joins the remainder of the *predicate, particularly a *noun phrase, or *adjective phrase, etc., functioning as subject-related predicative *complement, to the subject. Often used interchangeably with **copula** or **copular verb**.

The prime linking verb is *be*. But other verbs are used in a similar way, e.g.

> She's *become* a courier
> He's *looking* much better
> It *seemed* good at the time
> Will it *turn* cold?

Linking verbs are sometimes divided into verbs of **current meaning**, e.g.

> It *is/looks/remains* a mystery

and verbs of **resulting meaning**, e.g.

> It *became/proved* difficult

linking word (An umbrella term for) any *word that joins two linguistic units.

Linking words include:

  (i) *coordinators (e.g. *and, but*)
  (ii) *subordinating conjunctions (e.g. *that, whether*)
  (iii) *conjuncts (e.g. *however, in addition, moreover, meanwhile, nevertheless*), sometimes called **linking adjuncts** or **linking adverb(ial)s**.

link verb The same as *linking verb.

loan-shift A change in the meaning of a *word resulting from the influence of a corresponding word in a foreign language.

Examples are *arrive*, which has borrowed the sense 'achieve success' (L19) from French *arriver*, and *suspicion*, which has similarly borrowed the meaning 'slight trace or suggestion (of)' (E19) from French *soupçon*.

loan translation An expression adopted by one language from another in a more or less literally translated form; a *calque.

One of the earliest examples is *gospel* (OE *godspell*, from *god* 'good' + *spell* 'news', translating Greek *euaggelion*). The expression *lose face* is a loan translation of Chinese *tiu lien*.

loanword A word adopted or borrowed, usually with little modification, from another language.

Loanword is itself a loan translation of German *Lehnwort*.

See BORROWING.

local genitive *See* GENITIVE.

locative (*n. & adj.*)

1. (A *word, *phrase, etc.) expressing location.

Phrases that function as *adverbials of *place can be described as **locative phrases**, or as having a **locative role**.

2. *Semantics.* (In *Case Grammar.) (Designating) one of the original six *cases (3) (*semantic roles) proposed. Some *noun phrases which function as *subject or *object are classified as locatives, e.g. in:

London can be very lonely

We pounded *the pavements*

Hyde Park was the venue for the concert

locution *Semantics* An *utterance, an act of speaking.

This is a term in Speech Act Theory (*see* SPEECH ACT), and refers to the physical act of speaking, with no reference to the intention of the speaker (*illocution) or the resulting effect (*perlocution).

> 1955 J. L. AUSTIN *Locution.* He said to me 'Shoot her!' meaning by 'shoot' shoot and referring by 'her' to her.

> *Illocution*: He urged (or advised, ordered, etc.) me to shoot her.

> *Perlocution*: He persuaded me to shoot her.

●● **locutionary act.**

> 1955 J. L. AUSTIN The act of 'saying something' in this full normal sense I call . . . the performance of a locutionary act.

logical component *See* IDEATIONAL.

logical gap *See* CONDITION.

logical semantics The study of *meaning based on logic. Also called **formal semantics**.

See also MODEL-THEORETIC SEMANTICS; TRUTH-CONDITIONAL SEMANTICS.

logical subject *See* SUBJECT.

long-distance dependency *See* UNBOUNDED DEPENDENCY.

Longman Grammar of Spoken and Written English A large *corpus-based reference *grammar (2) published in 1999 by Longman, focusing on the spoken and written forms of English, and authored by Douglas Biber, the late Stig Johansson, Geoffrey Leech, Susan Conrad, and Edward Finegan. Its descriptive outlook is largely based on *A* *Comprehensive Grammar of the English Language.* A shorter version with a pedagogical focus was published as the *Longman Student Grammar of Spoken and Written English* in 2002.

long passive *See* PASSIVE.

low frequency *See* FREQUENCY (2).

lumping *See* WORD CLASS.

main clause A *clause that is not *subordinate to any other. Also called **principal clause** or **head clause**.

Main clauses are traditionally contrasted with *subordinate clauses. In *I thought that he would approve the plans*, the main clause is the whole *sentence, in which the subordinate clause *that he would approve the plans* functions as a *complement of the *verb *think*. We say that the subordinate clause is *embedded in the *verb phrase (2), and hence also in the main clause. Here the overall sentence is also a *matrix clause (1).

In *Although the paper is poorly written, it contains some excellent ideas*, the subordinate clause *although the paper is poorly written* is not a complement of a verb (or any other *head), and is analysed as an *adverbial clause (of *concession) in many frameworks. There is some disagreement as to which clause is the main clause here. In traditional accounts it is *it contains some excellent ideas*, but in recent models (e.g. CGEL, CaGEL), the main clause is the whole sentence. Whereas CGEL uses the label *matrix clause (2) for *it contains some excellent ideas*, in CaGEL this is also a main clause:

2002 R. HUDDLESTON & G. K. PULLUM et al. Note that in [*Although the paper is poorly written, it contains some excellent ideas*] *it contains some excellent ideas* is a clause contained within a larger construction (the clause that forms the whole sentence), but it has the function of head, and hence is a main clause, not a subordinate clause.

It is important to be aware of the fact that in CaGEL *although* is analysed as a *preposition which takes a subordinate clause as its complement; hence the entire string *although the paper is poorly written* is a prepositional phrase.

A main clause is often defined as a clause that can stand alone as a complete sentence, but the important criterion for a main clause is that it is not in a subordinate relationship to a higher clause. The coordinated clauses of a *compound sentence, such as *I was ten and I got the scholarship*, are also main clauses.

Compare EMBEDDING; INDEPENDENT; MATRIX CLAUSE (1); SUPERORDINATE.

main verb A *verb that can stand alone in a *clause, and functions as the *head of a *verb phrase (1). Contrasted with *auxiliary verb and *lexical verb.

Main verbs use auxiliary verbs in the formation of *interrogative and *negative structures (e.g. *Do you understand?*, *I didn't forget*; not *Understand you?*, *I forgot not*), as well as for *emphasis (*I DID forget*) and *code (*I forgot, and so did John*). *See* NICE PROPERTIES.

Main verb is basically a *function (1) label, contrasting with the functional sense of auxiliary verb. A main verb can be the only verb in a verb phrase, unlike an auxiliary verb (though note that in special constructions, e.g. *tags, auxiliaries may occur on their own). This means that if there is only one word in a verb phrase, it is the main verb, e.g.

I *know* nothing about it
What *is* the matter?

If there is more than one word in an unellipted verb phrase, the final item is the main verb (and the other verbs are auxiliaries), e.g.

Have you been *waiting* long?
It may have been *forgotten*

As the main verb function is often realized by a *lexical verb (or **full verb**), the terms main verb and lexical verb are sometimes used as synonyms.

1990 COLLINS COBUILD ENGLISH GRAMMAR **Main verb** all verbs which are not auxiliaries. Also called **lexical verb**.

This definition ignores the fact that *primary verbs (sometimes classified as auxiliaries, but never as lexical verbs) can function as main verbs in some models.

CaGEL contrasts what it calls the *catenative-auxiliary analysis in which 'there is no contrast between auxiliary verbs and main verbs', which it prefers, with the dependent-auxiliary analysis, which it does not:

2002 R. HUDDLESTON & G. K. PULLUM et al. Core auxiliaries are contrasted with **main verbs** [in the *dependent-auxiliary analysis], so that *is writing* forms a syntactic unit in which the verb *writing* is the head and the core auxiliary *is* is the dependent. As indicated by the term, core auxiliaries are never heads in the dependent-auxiliary analysis.

major Being or belonging to a group, *category, etc. that is more important, prominent, *prototypical, or frequent in occurrence than another. Contrasted with *minor.

This term is often used somewhat loosely, and not as a technical term.
•• **major word class**: one of the traditional *word classes, i.e. *noun, *verb, *adjective, *adverb, and *preposition. The **minor word classes**

(*conjunctions, *determinatives (1), *interjections, etc.) are considered to express little meaning in themselves.

Compare CLOSED (1); CONTENT WORD; GRAMMATICAL WORD (1); OPEN (1).

major sentence/clause type

1. A *structure containing at least a *subject and a *finite *verb, possibly including *imperative clauses, even though with imperatives the subject is optional (see 2).

Sentences as defined here are also called *full (3) sentences or *complete sentences. In this type of analysis, sentences that fall outside these sets of structures are variously classified as *minor, *irregular, or fragmentary.

2. (More specifically.) One of the major *clause types, namely *declarative, *interrogative, *imperative, or *exclamative.

Major Syntactic Structures of English, The A description of
English grammar written by the late Robert Stockwell, the late Paul Schachter, and Barbara Hall Partee, based on the Extended *Standard Theory of the late 1960s to early 1970s, and on Fillmore's *Case Grammar.

See also GENERATIVE GRAMMAR (2).

mandative subjunctive (clause) *See* SUBJUNCTIVE.

manner A semantic category used to describe the *meaning expressed by *adverbs or *adverbials that answer the question 'how?'.

Adverbs are traditionally classified by meaning, a fairly standard basic division being into adverbs of *place (answering the question 'where?'), *time (2) ('when?'), manner ('how?') and *degree ('to what extent?').

Single-word **manner adverbs** are often *derived from *adjectives by adding -*ly* (e.g. *brightly, stupidly, quietly*), and are felt to be *central or *prototypical adverbs. In more detailed semantic analyses of adverbials the label **manner adverbial** is more narrowly applied: such adverbials are then classified as a subclass of some larger grouping of adverbials, such as *process *adjuncts.

Some manner adverbials also occur as style *disjuncts, e.g.

Seriously, do you mean that?

Clauses of manner usually imply a *comparison:

He looked *as if he had seen a ghost*

He speaks *just as/like his father always did*

Such clauses are therefore sometimes subsumed under comparison.

marginal Of a linguistic feature or unit: not *central (2), not *prototypical, less important, less prominent, infrequent.

Sometimes applied to any of the metaphorical meanings of a *word, in contrast to the basic or central meaning.

•• **marginal adjective**: an *adjective that does not conform to one or more of the *morphosyntactic properties of adjectives, e.g. *utter*, which can only be used *attributively.

•• **marginal coordinator**: not one of the central *coordinators *and*, *or*, or *but*; e.g. *for*, *nor*, *so* (= 'therefore'), and others.

•• **marginal modal (verb)**: *see* MARGINAL MODAL (VERB).

•• **marginal noun**: a *noun that does not conform to one or more of the morphosyntactic properties of nouns, e.g. *news*, which does not have a *singular form, or *information*, which does not have a *plural form.

•• **marginal preposition**: a *preposition that shares one or more characteristics with other *word classes. For example, many marginal prepositions share certain features with *verbs or adjectives:

> He's remarkable, *considering* his age
>
> *Given* the provocation, the outcome was understandable
>
> That must be *worth* a fortune
>
> It was well written, *bar a* few trivial mistakes

Among the marginal prepositions are *less*, *minus*, *plus*, and *times*:

> What's five *times* six?
>
> He arrived *minus* a ticket.

•• **marginal subordinator**: a word, *phrase, or clause that can be followed by a *subordinate clause, but resembles another word class or sentence element:

> *Immediately* he began his speech, the crowd erupted with anger
>
> *The moment (that)* you said so, I remembered

•• **marginal verb**: *see* DEFECTIVE.

See also GRADIENCE; QUASI-.

marginal modal (verb) (*n. & adj.*) (A *verb) that is, formally, partly like a *modal verb and partly like a *lexical verb. Also called **semi-modal (auxiliary)**.

The verbs *dare* and *need* are marginal modals when they take a *bare infinitive as *complement in *negative and *inverted structures, and no *third person *singular -*s*, e.g.

> I daren't *ask Pete anything*
>
> Need I *say more?*
>
> I don't think he need *take any action*

They are *lexical verbs when they take a *to-infinitive clause as complement, and a third person singular -s ending (when appropriate), or *do-support, as in:

> She needs to leave early
>
> Did she dare to challenge her boss?

Also often classed in this category are *ought [to]* and *used [to]*, though the latter is sometimes regarded as expressing *aspectual meaning.

Ought [to] and *used [to]* are formally *past in tense, and *used [to]* is confined to past meaning.

marked Of a linguistic *feature (2): distinguished in some way from the *unmarked, more basic or central form to which it is related.

The concept was originated by the Russian linguist Nikolay Trubetzkoy (1890–1938) in relation to phonology.

•• **marked focus**: *see* FOCUS.

•• **marked order anaphora**: *see* ANAPHORA.

•• **marked predicative complement**: *see* COMPLEMENT.

See also MARKEDNESS.

markedness The condition, quality, or state of being *marked.

The concept of markedness can be applied in many areas of language. Thus a simple *declarative sentence (e.g. *I love Lucy*) is *unmarked in terms of its *constituent order (*subject - *predicator - *direct object), whereas *I don't love Lucy* is marked for *negation, and *Do you love Lucy?* is marked in having an *interrogative clause structure. Similarly, *Lucy I love* has a marked constituent order involving *topicalization.

With *nouns, *verbs, *adjectives, and other words that can be *inflected, the uninflected forms are said to be unmarked (e.g. *look, table, nice*), whereas the inflected forms (*looked, looking, looks, tables, nicer, nicest*) are marked for *past, *participle, *present, *plural, *comparative, *superlative, and so on. Similarly, the *active voice is unmarked, the *passive marked.

Markedness also applies in semantics, where *features (2) used in *componential analysis can be described in this way. Thus, *horse* is unmarked for sex, whereas *stallion* and *mare* are marked. Other words exhibit formal marking, e.g. *host* versus *hostess* (marked for 'female'), *widow* versus *widower* (marked for 'male'). In a neutral context the unmarked term in a pair is used. Thus of the pair *old* versus *young*, *old* is the unmarked term (e.g. *How old is the baby?*).

• **marking**: causing something to be marked (*see also* DOUBLE MARKING).

See also CLAUSE TYPE; CONSTITUENT ORDER.

marker

1. A *function (1) label used for certain *grammatical *words (1). Thus in *She said that her flat is for sale* the word *that* is *formally a *subordinator, and functions as a marker.

2. *Sociolinguistics.* A linguistic *feature (1) that characterizes a group of people in terms of provenance, gender, class, etc., for example the use of a particular vowel in a local variety of a language.

2011 M. MEYERHOFF Speakers show some subconscious awareness of markers, and this is made evident in the fact that they consistently use more of one variant in formal styles of speech and more of another variant in informal styles of speech. *Indicators*, on the other hand, show no evidence that speakers are even subconsciously aware of them, and speakers consistently favour one variant over another regardless of who they are talking to or where.

masculine (*n. & adj.*) (A *noun etc.) of the grammatical *gender that mainly denotes male persons and animals. Contrasted with *feminine and neuter.

In some languages grammatical gender distinctions of masculine and feminine (and sometimes also neuter) apply to all nouns and related *words. In English, however, grammatical gender distinctions are found only in *third person *singular personal *pronouns, where the feminine forms (*she, her, herself, hers*) contrast with the masculine ones (*he, him,* etc.) and the non-personal ones (*it, its,* etc.).

Compare COMMON; DUAL.

mass noun

1. An *uncount *noun (or **uncountable noun** or **non-count noun**).

In general, this is another synonym for one of the two main classes of *common nouns, the other being *count (or **countable**).

Many English nouns seem to belong to both classes:

beer, a beer   cloth, a cloth   ice, an ice
iron, an iron   paper, a paper   war, a war

One solution is to consider the words in such pairs to be two separate dictionary entries, but when the two meanings are close it seems preferable to talk of a single *lexeme with both mass and count usage. Hence terms like **mass usage**, **mass meaning**, and **mass interpretation** are sometimes introduced.

The term appears to have originated with Jespersen, who used 'mass-word' in his 1909–49 grammar.

2. (More narrowly.) A particular type of uncount noun:

1990 COLLINS COBUILD ENGLISH GRAMMAR **Mass noun** (in this grammar), a noun which is usually an uncount noun, but which can be used as a count noun when it refers to quantities or types of something; EG . . . two sugars . . . cough medicines.

This definition gives a very distinct meaning to the term mass, since it specifically includes many words that are used as countables. It excludes, however, some other nouns that can be uncount nouns when they refer to a thing in general, and count nouns when they refer to a particular instance of it. Examples of words that *Cobuild* classifies as both uncount and count (but *not* mass) are *victory* and *conflict*.

Compare BOUNDED; SINGULAR.

material process *See* PROCESS.

matrix clause

1. A *clause which contains an *embedded clause within it.

2005 R. HUDDLESTON & G. K. PULLUM Subordinate clauses characteristically function as dependent within some larger construction. The next higher clause in the structure is called the **matrix clause**.

A matrix clause may, but need not be, a *main clause.

2. (In CGEL) A *superordinate clause minus its *subordinate clause.

1985 R. QUIRK et al. For example, we have referred to the situation described in the matrix clause as contingent on that of the subordinate clause . . . :

I'll lend you some money if you don't have any money on you.

The matrix clause *I'll lend you some money* conveys an offer that is consequent on the fulfilment of the condition expressed in the subordinate clause *if you don't have any money on you.*

In CGEL, which uses the term main clause for the entire superordinate clause (*see* MAIN CLAUSE), matrix clause is thus used to distinguish the part from the whole:

[main clause [matrix clause I was ten] [subordinate clause when I got my scholarship]]

[main clause [matrix clause Nobody had expected] [subordinate clause that I would get one]]

In other frameworks (e.g. CaGEL, OMEG) the string marked as matrix clause in the second example is not a *constituent.

3. The same as *main clause (unusual).

maxims of conversation *See* COOPERATIVE PRINCIPLE.

meaning What is signified by a *word, *phrase, *clause, or longer *text. The same as *sense.

Many different types of meaning are distinguished, and different classifications are made:

Objective, factual, verifiable meaning is considered as *denotation, or as *cognitive, *descriptive (2), *ideational, *propositional, or *referential meaning.

Subjective, emotional, personal meaning is labelled *connotation, or *affective, *attitudinal, *emotive, or *expressive meaning.

Meaning as particularly involving social interaction is variously labelled *interpersonal, *situational, or *social meaning.

Meaning as derived from the context of the surrounding text is sometimes called *textual meaning. *Compare* CONTEXTUAL.

The meaning of words as given in the dictionary is called **lexical meaning** (sometimes also **dictionary meaning** or **central meaning**).

The meaning inherent in *grammar (1) (for example, the meaning of the *tenses, the relationship of *subject and *object, and the difference between *declarative and *interrogative) is called **grammatical meaning** or **structural meaning**.

Compare SPEECH ACT.

See also SEMANTIC; SEMANTICS.

means A term used in the semantic analysis of *adverbials to refer to the way that something is done or the method used to do it.

Adverbials of means (or more specifically *adjuncts of means) are usually contrasted with adverbials expressing an *agent or *instrument. Compare the first pair of sentences below, in which the italicized strings express means, with the second pair:

We came *by train*
They got in *by breaking a window*

It was stolen *by a cat burglar* (agent)
They got in *with a key* (instrument)

medial Designating or occurring in the middle of a linguistic unit (a *clause, *phrase, etc.); hence **medial position** (also called *mid-position).

The term is used in analysing *ellipsis (*see also* GAPPING), but particularly in describing the position of *adverbs (or *adverbials) in a clause. It contrasts with *initial (or *front) and *final (or *end) position. Broadly, it indicates the position between the *subject and the *verb:

The train *soon* gathered speed
I *hardly* think so

However, when there is a sequence of verbs, several positions can be called medial. A common medial position is after the first *auxiliary verb:

I have *definitely* been cheated

but other medial positions may be possible:

He *definitely* had intended to go (**initial medial**, i.e. between subject and *operator)

They must have *frequently* been investigated (**medial medial**, i.e. positioned within a sequence of auxiliaries)

It could have been *intentionally* overlooked (**end medial**, i.e. after one or more auxiliaries, but immediately before the *main verb)

This classification is found in CGEL.

• **medially**.

medial-branching *See* BRANCHING.

mediopassive A *construction (also called **middle (intransitive)**, **activo-passive**, or **passival**; though *see also* PASSIVAL) which has the structure of an *active clause, but whose *subject is interpreted in the same way as the subject in a *passive construction. That is, the subject has the *semantic role of *patient. Examples:

This book reads well

This cheese melts easily

An *adverbial of *manner is typically present.

See also MIDDLE VERB.

medium The means by which something is communicated, e.g. the spoken medium versus the written (or graphic) medium.

mental lexicon *See* LEXICON.

mental process *See* PROCESS.

mental verb *See* PSYCHOLOGICAL VERB.

meronym A *word that denotes an entity that is part of another entity.

2010 M. L. MURPHY An additional relation that has been named is the part-whole or 'has a' relation, **meronymy**. Like inclusion, this is an asymmetrical relation, so we say that *finger* is a **meronym** of *hand* and *hand* is the **holonym** of *finger*.

See also ANTONYM; HETERONYM; HOMONYM; HOMOPHONE; HYPONYM; POLYSEME; POLYSEMY; SYNONYM.

mesolect *Sociolinguistics*. A term used to describe varieties of a language in a *creole continuum. Specifically, in a particular community the mesolect is the variety (or a group of varieties) that is positioned between the *acrolect and *basilect.

metafunction (In *Systemic Grammar.) Each of the three fundamental *functions (2) that are posited for language, namely the two main kinds, the *ideational (2) metafunction ('language as reflection') and the *interpersonal (2) metafunction ('language as action'), plus a third, the *textual (2) metafunction, which is said to 'breathe relevance' into the other two.
● **metafunctional**.

metalanguage A (form of) language used to discuss language.
  Many of the terms used in this book are examples of metalanguage.
● **metalinguistic**, **metalinguistics**.

metanalysis Reinterpretation of the division between *words or syntactic units, e.g. *adder* from OE *nǣddre* by the analysis in ME of *a naddre* as *an addre*. The term was coined by Otto Jespersen.
● **metanalyse**: alter by metanalysis.

metonym A *word or expression which is used as a substitute for another word or expression with which it is in a close semantic relationship: e.g. *Whitehall* for 'the British civil service', *the Turf* for 'the racing world', *per head* for 'per person'.
● **metonymic**, **metonymy**.

mid The same as *medial.

mid-branching *See* BRANCHING.

middle (construction) *See* MEDIOPASSIVE; MIDDLE VERB.

Middle English The form of English used in Britain between circa 1150 and circa 1450; the stage in the development of the English language intermediate between *Old English and *Modern English. Abbreviated ME.

middle verb One of a small group of seemingly *transitive *verbs whose subject is not an *agent, and which do not normally occur in the *passive or *progressive.
  The term is not in very general use, but is a way of classifying verbs such as *have* (in its *possessive meaning: *We have a house* does not have a

passive version *A house is had by us), consist (of), lack, possess, resemble,* and some other verbs in certain of their meanings. Examples:

Blue suits you/*You are suited by blue

This jumper does not fit me/*I am not fitted by this jumper

Four times five equals twenty/*Twenty is equalled by four times five

The term is adapted from Greek grammar, which has a middle *voice distinct from both the *active and passive voice.

See also MEDIOPASSIVE.

middle voice *See* MEDIOPASSIVE; MIDDLE VERB; VOICE.

mid-position (*n. & adj.*) (Occupying, or typically occupying) the *position between *subject and *verb.

Used chiefly with reference to the placing of an *adverb (*adverbial), the term is a popular alternative to *medial position. For example, *frequency (1) adverbs (e.g. *always, often, sometimes, never*) can be described as usually taking mid-position, e.g.

We *always* watch the news

For this reason they are sometimes called **mid-position adverbs**, although they can in fact appear in other positions. *Modal adverbs can also appear in this position.

minimal That is, or is characterized by, a distinction based on only a single *feature (2). For example, the *articles *a* and *the* are distinguished only by the feature [±definite].

• **minimality**.

•• **minimal free form**: *see* MINIMUM FREE FORM.

Minimalist Program (MP) A programme of research (not a theory) that has developed from various versions of *Generative Grammar (2) since the mid-1990s.

See also CHOMSKYAN; GENERALIZED PHRASE STRUCTURE GRAMMAR; GENERATIVE; GOVERNMENT-BINDING THEORY; GRAMMAR; HEAD-DRIVEN PHRASE STRUCTURE GRAMMAR; PHRASE STRUCTURE GRAMMAR; PRINCIPLES AND PARAMETERS THEORY; STANDARD THEORY; TRANSFORMATIONAL GRAMMAR.

minimum free form The smallest linguistic unit that can function on its own as a complete utterance. (Also called **minimal free form**.) Contrasted with *bound forms.

In a now classic definition, the American linguist Leonard Bloomfield, in 1926, defined the word as a minimum free form. This definition is open to criticism, as Bloomfield himself realized, since it would exclude *a*, *the*, *my*, and similar forms that are generally considered to be *words, but which do not function alone. The definition largely holds, however.

There is a second objection, namely that in certain circumstances even *bound (1) forms can be used alone, e.g.

'Did you say disinterested or uninterested?'
'Dis'

But this can easily be discounted on the grounds that any speech segment, even a single sound, can be used alone as a citation form.

Compare MORPHEME.

minor Being or belonging to a group, *category, etc. that is less important, prominent, *prototypical, or frequent in occurrence than another. Contrasted with *major.

This term is often used somewhat loosely, and not as a technical term.
•• **minor word class**: *see* MAJOR.

minor sentence/clause A *sentence or *clause that does not conform to the *standard *rules of grammar in one or more respects, but is nonetheless *acceptable. Contrasted with a *regular or *full sentence/clause.

Various classifications and terms are used in the analysis of structures that do not conform to the main rules of grammar. Some grammarians use terms such as **irregular sentence** or *non-sentence.

Minor sentences/clauses occur with some frequency, and often follow their own patterns. They may include **wh*-interrogatives lacking a *verb and/or *subject:

How about a drink?
Why not forget it?

The term may also include *subordinate clauses which lack a *matrix clause (often with *exclamatory *meaning):

That you should be so lucky!
To think you were there all the time!
As if you didn't know!

Consider also:

Out with it!
The quicker the better
Not to be taken internally

Terms like minor sentence and *irregular sentence can also be extended to include sentences involving *ellipsis, *block language, *formulae, *interjections, and perhaps even the optative *subjunctive.

misrelated Not attached grammatically to the *word or *phrase intended by the meaning; either joined to the wrong word or phrase, or completely unattached.

Although misrelated and other terms such as **dangling**, *hanging, and **unattached** are most commonly applied to *participles, *verbless structures can also be misrelated. In the following example the italicized *noun phrase refers back to someone mentioned in the previous *discourse, and it refers forward to *he* in this sentence. However, grammatically it is entirely unconnected to anything in the sentence.

> *A rock-climber of some note*, there is a story, never denied, of how he tackled the treacherous Aonach Eagach ridge in Glencoe by moonlight, dressed in a dinner jacket.

In the next example the italicized *adjective phrase refers back to someone previously mentioned, i.e. the person whose parentage is mentioned. However, grammatically the phrase is misrelated to the noun phrase *the question*. Incidentally, the sentence also contains a hanging participle, namely *walking*:

> Now *nine years old*, one day out walking . . . the question of her parentage arose.

mobile Of a linguistic unit: capable of being moved to a different *position, or positions, in a *clause or *sentence.

This concept is of some importance in differentiating units according to the way they function. For example, *adverbials (*adjuncts) tend to be much more mobile than other clause constituents:

> It will be winter *soon*
> It will *soon* be winter
> *Soon* it will be winter

● **mobility**.

> 1985 R. QUIRK et al. The adverbial nature of the particle in . . . phrasal verbs . . . is generally shown by its mobility, its ability to follow the noun phrase: . . . They turned *down* the suggestion. They turned the suggestion *down*.

See also MOVEMENT.

modal

1. (*adj.*) Relating to, or expressing, *modality.

●● **modal adjective**: an *adjective that expresses *modal *meaning, e.g. *necessary, possible, probable*.

•• **modal adverb** (or **modal adverbial, modal adjunct**): an *adverb, *adverbial, or *adjunct that expresses modal meaning, such as a speaker's judgement about a *proposition, e.g. *arguably, possibly, probably, maybe, surely, apparently.*

•• **modal auxiliary, modal operator**: the same as *modal verb.

•• **modal idiom**: an expression consisting of several *words which in combination carry a modal meaning that is not predictable from its parts, e.g. *had better/best, would rather/sooner/as soon.* They syntactically behave like modal verbs to a degree: for example, they have no *third person *singular forms or *non-finite forms, and they take a *bare infinitive clause as *complement. Also included here (at least in some models) are *have got (to)* and *be (to).* The first elements of these latter combinations behave like *auxiliaries (cf. *Have we got to do this?*), and can take a third person singular form (cf. *She has got to comply with the law*). They take a *to-infinitive clause as complement.

•• **modal lexical verb** (or **lexical modal verb**): a *lexical verb that expresses modal meaning, e.g. *decree, demand, insist,* and (in some frameworks, e.g. OMEG) *have (to), be going (to).*

•• **modal noun**: a *noun that expresses modal meaning, e.g. *necessity, possibility, probability, requirement, request, resolution.*

•• **modal past**: *see* PAST (2).

•• **modal past perfect**: *see* PAST PERFECT.

•• **modal preterite (clause)**: *see* PAST (2).

•• **modal remoteness**: *see* PAST (2).

•• **modal verb**: *see* MODAL VERB.

  2. (*n.*) An abbreviation for *modal verb.

  3. (*adj.*) (Less often.) Relating to or expressing *mood.

modality The semantic concept of modality is concerned with the expression of notions such as possibility, probability, necessity, likelihood, obligation, permission, and intention, typically by *modal auxiliary verbs, but also by other linguistic means (e.g. modal *adjectives, *adverbs, and *nouns). Contrasted with the grammatical notion of *mood.

Different kinds of modality are distinguished. The main types are *epistemic modality (concerning a speaker's judgement) and *deontic modality (concerned with *obligation). A third type, *dynamic (2) modality, involves the use of certain modal verbs (especially *can/could* and *will/would*) to express subject-related meanings such as 'volition' and 'ability', or more 'circumstantial' meanings. Compare:

  You *can't* be serious (epistemic modality: conclusion)

  Can I say something, please? (deontic modality: permission)

  She *can* read Arabic (dynamic modality: ability)

See also ALETHIC; DEGREE OF MODALITY; KIND OF MODALITY; ROOT; STRENGTH OF MODALITY.

modal verb Any of a subgroup of *auxiliary verbs that express *modality. The main (*central, or **core**) modals are:

can/could	shall/should
may/might	will/would
must	

The core modal verbs share some distinct grammatical characteristics:

(i) They share with other auxiliaries the *NICE properties of *negation, *inversion, *code, and *emphasis.

(ii) Despite the fact that they are always *finite, they have no -*s* forms. Nor do they have *infinitive or *participle forms.

(iii) They are followed by a *bare infinitive (except in 'code' structures; *see* NICE properties).

There are also several verbs of disputed status that share some of their characteristics. Some grammars distinguish a set of *marginal modal verbs. Thus CGEL has *dare, need* (both used as auxiliaries), *ought (to)*, and *used (to)*. OMEG excludes from this list *used (to)*, which is regarded as *aspectual. CGEL treats *have (to)* as a *semi-auxiliary verb. In OMEG the latter is treated as a *modal lexical verb.

The meanings of the modals are often differentiated into *epistemic, *deontic, and *dynamic (2).

See also MOOD.

model An abstract representation or theory of the grammatical system or semantics of a language. Various models are proposed by linguists working in different schools of linguistics.

model-theoretic semantics A type of *truth-conditional semantics developed by Richard Montague (1930–1971; hence also **Montague Grammar**) in which the meaning of sentences is based on models of states of affairs in the world.

See also LOGICAL SEMANTICS; TRUTH-CONDITIONAL SEMANTICS.

Modern English The form of English used in Britain and other parts of the world since about 1450. Abbreviated ModE, MnE.

It is frequently divided into *Early Modern English (before 1700) and *Late(r) Modern English. The form of the language contemporaneous with the analyst may be called Present English, *Present-Day English (PDE), or Contemporary English.

Modern English Grammar on Historical Principles, A A traditional *grammar (2) published between 1909 and 1949, written by the Danish linguist Otto Jespersen (1860–1943). This work is widely regarded as one of the first grammars to describe modern English systematically and in a reasoned, sophisticated manner. It is characterized by a large number of literary examples.

modification

1. The phenomenon, or an instance, of a dependent *word, *phrase, etc. changing (i.e. affecting) the meaning of a *head, or other linguistic unit, in a relationship of *hypotaxis.

Modification is a general term. *Nouns are typically modified by *adjectives (strictly speaking, *adjective phrases, e.g. _lovely_ weather), *prepositional phrases (e.g. the food _in the fridge_), or *relative clauses (e.g. the house _that was demolished_); adjectives and *adverbs are modified by adverbs (strictly speaking, *adverb phrases, e.g. _much warmer, very warmly_); and so on.

The term is particularly used in describing *phrase structure, where it can be subdivided into *premodification and *postmodification, as in the following examples of modified *noun phrases:

the _second_ part
travels _with my father_
expensive hotels _in Paris_

•• **stacked modification** (or **stacking**): the occurrence of more than one *modifier for a particular head, e.g. _big brown bag_. In some models (e.g. *X-bar syntax), the adjective _big_ in this example modifies _brown bag_, rather than _big_ and _brown_ severally modifying _bag_.

Compare RECURSION.

•• **submodification**: *see* SUBMODIFICATION
See also QUALIFIER (1).

2. (In *Systemic Grammar.) The same as premodification.

In this model, words following the *head in a noun *group (i.e. noun phrase) are generally treated as qualification.

See also QUALIFIER (3).

3. *Morphology*. A change within a *word. Examples are:

man → men

get → got

Compare SUPPLETION.

modifier

1. A dependent *word, *phrase, *clause, etc. that affects the *meaning of another element, typically a *head, in a relationship of *modification. For example, in traditional grammar, an *adverb (or *adverbial) in *clause structure is said to be a modifier of the *verb—hence the name 'adverbial'.

A modifier in phrase structure can be a *premodifier or a *postmodifier.

•• **modifier clause**: a clause that postmodifies a head, e.g. a *relative clause.

•• **sentence modifier**: a modifier that modifies a complete *sentence or clause.

2. (In *Systemic Grammar.) A word or string of words that precedes the head in a noun group. Contrasted with *qualifier.

modify

Of a *word or similar element: affect the *meaning of (a *head or principal element).

See also MODIFICATION; MODIFIER.

modulation

A *paralinguistic feature conveying some attitude not necessarily implicit in the actual *words spoken.

> 1977 J. LYONS By the modulation of an utterance is meant the superimposing upon the utterance of a particular attitudinal colouring, indicative of the speaker's involvement in what he is saying and his desire to impress or convince the hearer.

Compare ATTITUDINAL.

module

See COMPONENT.

monolingual

(*adj.*)

1. Speaking only one language.

2. Written in one language.

(*n.*) A person who speaks only one language.

monomorphemic

Of a *word: consisting of a single *morpheme (1), e.g. *able, no, interest*.

monostratal

Of a theory: having only one *level of representation. Also called **non-derivational**.

*Head-Driven Phrase Structure Grammar is an example of a mono-stratal theory.

Contrasted with **multistratal** theories that have two or more levels of representation which are derived from each other using rules. Classical *Generative Grammar (2) is a multistratal or *derivational theory.

See also CHOMSKYAN; GENERALIZED PHRASE STRUCTURE GRAMMAR; GENERATIVE; GENERATIVE SEMANTICS; GOVERNMENT-BINDING THEORY; GRAMMAR; MINIMALIST PROGRAM; PHRASE STRUCTURE GRAMMAR; PRINCIPLES AND PARAMETERS THEORY; STANDARD THEORY; TRANSFORM; TRANSFORMATION; TRANSFORMATIONAL.

monotransitive A term used to describe a *verb which *licenses only one *object (2), namely a *direct object (hence **monotransitive complementation**), or a *pattern or *clause in which a verb licenses only one object; e.g.

> We *avoided* the traffic
> She *raises* lots of money
> They *thought* that she would be late

In CGEL the term is extended to cover *prepositional verbs (e.g. I *refer to* your letter of 4th June) and *phrasal-prepositional verbs (e.g. I won't *put up with* this sort of treatment).

Compare COMPLEX INTRANSITIVE; COMPLEX TRANSITIVE; DITRANSITIVE; INTRANSITIVE; TRANSITIVE.

Montague Grammar *See* MODEL-THEORETIC SEMANTICS.

mood

1. One of the formal grammatical *categories into which *verb forms are classified, indicating whether the *clause in which the verb occurs expresses a fact, command, hypothesis, etc. Contrasted with the semantic notion of *modality.

Traditional grammar recognizes the *indicative, *imperative, and *subjunctive moods. In modern frameworks the latter is often no longer regarded as a mood.

2. A distinction of *meaning expressed by any one of the *clause types. According to this definition, *interrogative joins *declarative and *imperative as a mood category.

Mood is an alteration, apparently in the 16th century, of the earlier *mode*, a borrowing of Latin *modus* 'manner', which was also used in this grammatical sense. The alteration may have been due to the influence of the unrelated word *mood* 'frame of mind', which has an evident semantic affinity with it.

• **analytic mood**: *see* ANALYTIC.

mood adjunct *See* MODAL *adjunct*.

morph

1. Any of the actual forms of an abstract *morpheme (1); the same as
*allomorph.

2. The actual (physical) realization of an (abstract) morpheme when
that morpheme only has one realization. For example, the *present
participle morpheme is always the morph -*ing*.

morpheme

1. The smallest meaningful unit of grammar.

According to a basically syntactic definition, the morpheme is an abstraction (comparable to *lexeme). Thus 'the *plural morpheme' is realized
in regular *nouns by phonologically *conditioned *allomorphs (/-s/, /-z/,
and /ɪz/), but also has such realizations as the change of vowel in *men* (from
man) and *mice* (from *mouse*), and *zero as in *sheep*. Similarly, we can posit a
*past participle morpheme, which has various allomorphs (-*ed*, -*en*, etc.),
and a *negative morpheme (a *prefix), again with different realizations (e.g.
in-, *im-*, *il-*, *un-*, as in *intolerable, impossible, illegible, unassailable*).

2. The smallest unit in *word formation and morphology.

In a more phonological approach, the morpheme is the smallest
meaningful part into which a word can be broken down. Thus, *stems,
*roots, and *affixes are seen as morphemes, some of them *bound and
some *free. According to this definition *looked* and *fallen* each consist of a
free morpheme and a bound morpheme (*look* + -*ed*, *fall* + -*en*). But
whereas in a syntactic definition -*ed* and -*en* are *variants (i.e. allomorphs)
of the same (abstract) past participle morpheme, in a phonological
definition -*ed* and -*en* are different morphemes.

Compare BASE.

morphemic Of or pertaining to a *morpheme.
● **morphemically**: as regards morphemes.
●● **morphemic alternant**: the same as *allomorph; *see* ALTERNANT (2).
●● **morphemic variant**: the same as *allomorph.

morphemics The study and analysis of language in terms of its
*morphemes (1).

morphology The study of the internal structure of *words.

Traditionally regarded as part of *grammar, morphology contrasts with
*syntax, the latter being concerned with the *rules that govern the way
words are put together in *sentences. Morphology itself covers *inflection
and *word formation (2). The latter in turn covers *derivation and
*compounding (and sometimes *conversion).
● **morphological, morphologically**.
●● **morphological structure**: *see* STRUCTURE.

morphosyntactic Combining morphological and syntactic properties.

Morphosyntactic properties (or **morphosyntactic features**) are the properties of a linguistic unit that have effects on both morphology and syntax. Thus *tense, *person, *number, etc. are morphosyntactic grammatical concepts.

*Plural *number, for example, morphologically requires -s in a *regular *noun (e.g. *cats*, *readers*) to be followed, syntactically, by a plural *verb form (e.g. *The cats are hungry*, not **The cats is hungry*).

• **morphosyntactically, morphosyntax.**

•• **morphosyntactic word:** *see* GRAMMATICAL WORD (2).

movement

1. In an informal sense, the displacement of a *phrase, *clause etc. to a *position other than its *canonical position. For example, in *Lamp bulbs they don't sell _*, the *noun phrase *lamp bulbs* can be said to have been moved from the *direct object position indicated by the underscore (_) to a clause-initial position. This type of displacement is known as *topicalization.

2. In the framework of *Generative Grammar (2), there are various kinds of formalized displacements such as *dislocation, **NP-movement**, as in (i), and ***wh*-movement**, as in (ii):

(i) Greg seems _ to like red wine

(ii) What did he do _ ?

See also TRACE.

multal Implying a largish number or amount, in contrast to *paucal.

In some detailed classifications of *pronouns and *determinatives (1), the label multal is given to a subset of *quantifiers (1): *many, much, more, most*.

multilingual

(*adj.*)

1. Speaking several languages.

2. Written in several languages.

(*n.*) A person who speaks several languages.

• **multilingualism.**

multiple (Used as a very general term.) Having, displaying, etc. several instances of a linguistic *feature (1/2).

•• **multiple analysis**: an analysis of a linguistic unit or string that can be made in two or more ways, when a clear-cut, right or wrong description is elusive. One classic problem concerns certain structures with the pattern *verb + *preposition + *noun phrase. Whereas the analysis of *I waited at the bus stop* is uncontroversial as *subject + verb (or *predicator) + *adverbial, the superficially similar *I relied on my family* can be analysed in two ways, namely as subject + verb (*rely on*) + *direct object (cf. *Whom did you rely on?*), or as subject + verb (*rely*) + *complement (in the shape of a *prepositional phrase; cf. *On whom did you rely?*). Also called **reanalysis** or **restructuring**.

•• **multiple apposition**: *apposition involving three or more terms, rather than the usual two.

•• **multiple coordination**: *coordination having more than two coordinated units.

•• **multiple exponence**: *see* EXPONENCE.

•• **multiple meaning**: *see* HOMONYMY; POLYSEMY.

•• **multiple negation**: a unit or structure in which three or more *negatives are combined. *Compare* DOUBLE NEGATIVE.

•• **multiple postmodification**: *postmodification involving more than one separate *postmodifier, e.g. *the lady over there by the river*.

•• **multiple premodification**: *premodification involving more than one distinct *premodifier. This can be a sequence of *adjective phrases, or a premodifier modified by another. In *poor quality leather*, *poor* premodifies *quality*, and the two together premodify *leather*. (Contrast *beautiful black leather*, where the premodifiers are simply in sequence.) *See also* STACKING.

•• **multiple sentence**: a *sentence that is a *complex, *compound, or *compound-complex sentence; the same as *clause complex in another analysis.

•• **multiple subordination**: the presence of more than one *subordinate clause within a sentence.

multiple exponence *See* EXPONENCE.

multiplier A *determinative (1) with a 'multiplying' meaning, such as *twice* the price, *three times* that amount.

multistratal *See* MONOSTRATAL.

multi-word lexical item A *lexical item composed of more than one *word.

   Compare MULTI-WORD VERB; MULTI-WORD VERB CONSTRUCTION.

multi-word subordinator *See* SUBORDINATOR.

multi-word verb A label used to describe a *verb that *licenses one or more further units in the shape of a *prepositional phrase or *particle, with or without an *object *noun phrase. In some analyses the verb and the items it licenses taken together are regarded as single verbs, and are listed as such in a dictionary (e.g. *look* NP *up*, *rely on* NP, *put up with* NP, *give way to* NP).

This is an umbrella term that covers *phrasal verbs, *prepositional verbs, and *phrasal-prepositional verbs.

multi-word verb construction An *idiomatic *verbal (1) *construction which contains a *verb that *licenses one or more units, similar to a *multi-word verb.

Examples:

break even, make clear, stand still, cut NP short (verb + (NP) + adjective)

let go, give NP to understand (verb + (NP) + verb)

put paid to, make do with (verb + verb + preposition)

mutual entailment *See* ENTAILMENT.

name *See* PROPER NOUN.

narrative present The same as *historic present.

nationality word A *noun referring to a member of a nation or ethnic group, or a related *adjective.

Grammatically these words are to some extent treated like *proper nouns, being spelt with an initial capital, but at the same time, like *common nouns, they are *countable, and can have *specific and *generic reference. The commonest type has the *singular noun identical to the adjective, and forms the *plural (both *specific and *generic) with *-s*:

> Italian (*adj.*); an Italian; Italians; the Italians
> (Similarly: Greek, Pakistani)

Those with an adjective in *-sh* or *-ch* fall into two main types:

> Danish; a Dane; Danes; the Danes
> French; a Frenchman/Frenchwoman; Frenchmen/Frenchwomen; the French

Those formed with *-ese* (and *Swiss*) are invariable in all uses:

> Chinese (*adj.*); a Chinese; Chinese; the Chinese

These patterns have numerous minor irregularities and *variations (e.g. a *Briton, Britons; a Spaniard, Spaniards, the Spanish*).

native speaker *See first* LANGUAGE.

natural gender *See* GENDER.

natural language *See* LANGUAGE.

N-bar (N′) category *See* X-BAR SYNTAX.

near negative The same as *semi-negative.

necessity A semantic term used in the description of *modality, expressed typically by certain *modal verbs, and by some other elements (e.g. *nouns, *adjectives, *adverbs). We can distinguish *deontic, *epistemic, and *dynamic (2) necessity, e.g.

> You *must* do your best (deontic; i.e. 'I oblige you to do your best')
>
> It *must* be cold in the loft in winter (epistemic; i.e. 'on the basis of what I know, I assume that it is cold in the loft in winter')
>
> We *have to* do it, whether we like it or not (dynamic; i.e. 'the circumstances are such that we must do it')
>
> It is *necessary* to close the windows at night (dynamic)

Contrast: POSSIBILITY.

negate Make (usually, a *clause or *sentence) *negative in meaning.

negation The grammatical means by which the truth of an *assertive (or *positive (1)) *sentence or *clause is denied.

Typically an English sentence or clause is negated by adding *not* or *-n't* to the *primary verb, or to the first (or only) *auxiliary verb. This is called **clausal negation**.

> This *is not* difficult
>
> He *couldn't* have been there

In the absence of an appropriate *verb to which *not* or *n't* can be added in the positive sentence, *dummy *do* is introduced:

> The bell rang > The bell *didn't* ring (not *The bell rang not/rangn't*)

Generally the **scope of the negation** extends from the negative word to the end of the clause; hence the difference in *meaning between such pairs as:

> I did*n't* ask you to go; I asked you *not* to go
>
> They are*n't* still here; They still are*n't* here

*Modal verbs behave differently with regard to the scope of negation. For example, the meaning of *deontic *must* ('obligation') is outside the scope of *not* in the following examples:

> You must not leave the platform (i.e. 'you are *obliged not* to leave the platform'; not: 'you are *not obliged* to leave the platform')

Compare this with the meaning of *deontic *may* ('permission'), which is inside the scope of negation:

> Those youngsters may not enter the premises (i.e. 'those youngsters are *not permitted* to enter the premises'; not: 'those youngsters are *permitted not* to enter the premises')

Sentences can also be negated through the use of other negative words:

> There is *nothing* to do (*Compare*: There isn't anything to do)
>
> It's *no* trouble (*Compare*: It isn't any trouble)
>
> *Nobody* told me (*Compare*: They didn't tell me/I wasn't told)

A negative *affix makes a word negative, but not the whole sentence:

> He looked worried and *uncertain*
>
> Perhaps they will sign a *non-aggression* pact

This is called **subclausal negation**.

•• **transferred negation**: the positioning of a negative in the *main clause, when logically it belongs in the associated *subordinate clause. This is often found with verbs of opinion and perception, e.g.

> I *don't* think you understand (= I think you *don't* understand)
>
> It *doesn't* look as if they're coming now (= It looks as if they are *not* coming)

See also DOUBLE NEGATIVE; MULTIPLE *negation*; NON-ASSERTIVE; SEMI-NEGATIVE.

negative (*n. & adj.*) (An *affix, *word, *clause, etc.) that expresses *negation.

negative particle A term sometimes used for the word *not*.

negative polarity item *See* ASSERTIVE.

negator A word expressing *negation, particularly the word *not*, but also e.g. *never*.

neoclassical compound *Morphology.* A *compound consisting of two *combining forms, namely an **initial combining form** and a **final combining form**, both derived from classical languages (i.e. Greek or Latin). Examples include *biology* (*bio-logy*), *monolithic* (*mono-lithic*), *endoscope* (*endo-scope*), and *telephone* (*tele-phone*). Sometimes a vowel needs to be inserted, as with *psychology* (*psych-o-logy*).

See also: COMPOUND.

neo-Firthian

(*adj.*)

1. Of, pertaining to, or characteristic of a group of linguists who continued some of the principles developed by the British linguist J. R. Firth, especially M. A. K. Halliday and his associates.

2. A term used in *corpus linguistics to refer to an approach to the use of corpora that opposes the annotation of textual databases (e.g. by *tagging or *parsing the text).

> 2012 T. MCENERY and A. HARDIE Opposition to annotation is typically associated with neo-Firthian corpus linguistics and the corpus-driven approach.

See also CORPUS-BASED; CORPUS-DRIVEN; FIRTHIAN.

(*n.*) A person belonging to the neo-Firthian group of linguists.
See also FIRTHIAN.

neogrammarian An adherent of (the views of) a loosely knit group of German scholars in the late nineteenth century who believed that sound laws (patterns of sound change which affect languages over time) must be entirely *regular and without exceptions.

It soon became apparent that this theory was overstated, but a modified version of the principle is an important tenet of *comparative and *historical linguistics. The name is a translation of the German term *Junggrammatiker.*

neologism (The coining or use of) a new *word or expression.
Neologisms have various sources. They may be the result of:

*abbreviation (e.g. HIV)
*back-formation (e.g. *ovate* from *ovation*)
*blending (e.g. *camcorder* from *camera* + *recorder*)
*borrowing (e.g. *karaoke* from Japanese)
*clipping (e.g. *cred* from *credibility*)
*compounding (e.g. *power dressing*)
*conversion (e.g. *to doorstep,* verb from noun)
*derivation (e.g. *fattism* from *fat* + *-ism*)

The term is also sometimes extended to include old words which are given new meanings (e.g. *wicked* 'marvellous').
Compare NONCE; NON-WORD.

nest (*v.*) Place (a *clause or phrase) within a larger structure (of the same kind).
See EMBEDDING; NESTING.

nesting
1. A kind of *embedding which involves the inclusion of a linguistic unit (*clause, *phrase) within another unit (of the same kind).
The views of the man in the street is a *noun phrase whose *head (*views*) is *postmodified by a *prepositional phrase (*of the man in the street*). In turn, *the man in the street* is also a noun phrase whose head (*man*) is postmodified by a prepositional phrase (*in the street*):

[NP the views [of [NP the man [in [NP the street]]]]]

In this way similarly constructed clauses or phrases are 'nested' inside each other. Nesting can be almost infinitely *recursive, as in this blurb for an article:

Why the pedestrian hates the cabby who hates the biker who hates the cyclist who hates the man who drives the coach that drives the lorry driver mad

2. (In CGEL.) Embedding in *mid (medial) position.

1985 R. QUIRK et al. Initial clauses are said to be LEFT-BRANCHING, medial clauses NESTING, and final clauses RIGHT-BRANCHING. Examples of these three arrangements:

INITIAL: *When you're ready*, we'll go to my parents' place.

MEDIAL: We'll go, *when you're ready*, to my parents' place.

FINAL: We'll go to my parents' place, *when you're ready*.

. . . Nesting (medial branching) causes the most awkwardness, if the nested clause is long and is itself complex.

See also RECURSION.

neuter *See* GENDER.

neutral affix *See* LEVEL ORDERING (HYPOTHESIS).

neutralization In general terms, the phenomenon whereby two distinct *forms (1) are blurred. More specifically, the disappearance, in a particular *context, of a grammatical distinction that is made in normal circumstances.

Contrasts of *tense and *aspect may undergo neutralization in certain circumstances. Those in the following three different statements:

She has gone
She had gone
She went

are neutralized after a *past reporting *verb: *They said she had gone.*

The lack of a distinction between the *subject and *object forms of the pronoun *you* is also a neutralization. More loosely (and controversially), so is the perceived double function of the *noun phrase in a *structure such as *We want Henry to go*, where *Henry* is, in some accounts, both the object of *want* and the subject of *go*. However, note that only an *accusative *pronoun is possible in such cases: *We want him to go.*

new (*n.* & *adj.*) (Designating) information that is not already known in a *text or *discourse setting, and is therefore the important information in an *utterance. Contrasted with *given.

See also COMMENT; FOCUS; RHEME; THEME; TOPIC.

nexus *See* ADNEX; JUNCTION.

NICE properties A term which uses an *acronym to encapsulate the four grammatical characteristics of English *auxiliary verbs that distinguish them from *lexical verbs.

<u>N</u>egation: auxiliaries can be directly *negated by *not* or by adding *-n't* to the *verb form, e.g. *will not, don't, cannot.*

<u>I</u>nversion: auxiliaries invert with the *subject in *interrogative clauses, e.g. *May I go now?*

<u>C</u>ode: auxiliaries can be used on their own to avoid repetition of the *verb phrase (2), e.g. *I will be flying to Thailand tomorrow, and so will Jane.*

<u>E</u>mphasis: auxiliaries can be stressed, e.g. *We WILL help you; I DO remember.*

node Any point in a *tree diagram from which branches lead off. The term is particularly used in *Generative Grammar (2).
•• **mother node**: *See* TREE DIAGRAM.

nominal

(*adj.*) Of (the function of) a *word, *phrase, or (in some models) *clause: *noun-like. Strictly speaking we should say 'noun-phrase-like' because the type of item in question distributes and functions like a noun phrase. *See* NOMINAL CLAUSE.

(*n.*)

1. A word or phrase that *distributes and functions like a noun phrase.
•• **nominal conjunction**: *see* CONJUNCTION.
•• **nominal group**: a term used in *Systemic Grammar that corresponds to *noun phrase in other models. It is preferred to noun phrase in that framework because of the distinction between the make-up of a *group and a *phrase (2). *See also* GROUP; WORD GROUP.
•• **nominal inflection class**: *see* DECLENSION.

2. In some versions of *Generative Grammar (2), *phrase structure grammar, and descriptive grammar (e.g. CaGEL): a *constituent of a noun phrase that is larger than a *head, but smaller than a phrase; i.e. an N-bar (N′) category.

See X-BAR SYNTAX.

nominal clause

1. A *clause that syntactically distributes and functions like a *noun phrase. (Also called **noun clause**.)

In some frameworks (e.g. CGEL) nominal clauses can be *that- clauses, *interrogative clauses, *exclamative clauses, *free relative clauses, *to-infinitive clauses, or *-ing clauses. They typically function as *subject, *direct object, or *complement in sentence/clause structure:

What happened next remains a mystery (subject)

To err is human (subject)
He alleges *(that) he doesn't remember a thing* (object)
The question is *how we should proceed* (complement)
All I did was *laugh* (complement)
It depends on *what happens next* (complement of a preposition)
He's talking about *facing the music* (complement of a preposition)

The analysis of the sentences above is controversial, and not all grammarians would analyse them as involving nominal clauses. Thus in CaGEL and OMEG many of the clauses above involve *content clauses.

2. (In some frameworks.) As for sense 1, but restricted in some way, e.g. to mean *free relative clause.

In these descriptions, different labels are used for the other nominal clauses (in sense 1), e.g. *complement clause, *that*-clause, *interrogative clause, and so on.

Compare FREE RELATIVE CLAUSE.

nominal inflection class *See* DECLENSION.

nominalize Form a *noun (or noun phrase) from an item belonging to another *word class, or from a *clause. Examples:

drive > driver
buy > buyer
accurate > accuracy
kind > kindness
examine > examinee
shrink > shrinkage
She is determined to succeed > her determination to succeed
She explained the problem > her explanation of the problem

The process often involves the use of a **nominalizing *affix**.
• **nominalizable**.
•• **nominalization**: a noun or noun phrase derived from, or corresponding to, a word from another class or a clause; the process by which such a phrase is derived.

nominal relative clause *See* FREE RELATIVE CLAUSE.

nominative *See* SUBJECTIVE (1).

nominative absolute *See* ABSOLUTE.

non-affirmative (form) *See* ASSERTIVE.

non-agentive *See* AGENTIVE, PASSIVE.

non-assertive (form) A class of forms that typically occur in
*comparative/*superlative, *conditional, *interrogative, and *negative
*contexts. Also called **non-affirmative form** or **negative polarity item**.
Contrasted with *assertive (form).

In addition to the *any*-series of *words (e.g. *any, anybody, anyone,
anything, anywhere*), which contrast with the corresponding words in the
some-series (e.g. *some, somebody, someone, something, somewhere*), other
predominantly non-assertive words include *either, ever,* and *yet*:

Jane didn't know *either* (compare: Jane knew too)

Have you *ever* had a winter holiday? (compare: I always have a winter holiday)

Haven't you finished *yet*? (compare: I have already finished)

●● **non-assertive context/territory:** *see* ASSERTIVE (FORM).

non-attributive The same as *predicative.

nonce (*adj.*) Of a *word, form(ation), etc.: deliberately coined for one
occasion.

1. (As originally used.)

1907 *New English Dictionary Nonce-word*, the term used in this Dictionary to
describe a word which is apparently used only for the nonce.

The implication of the original use was that the word in question has only
been used once (or very few times) by a single author, or possibly once
each by more than one author independently for a particular purpose.

Compare HAPAX LEGOMENON.

2. The term is now frequently used of a word that has become common,
having been coined for a particular occasion or purpose. Quite a number
of words can be traced back to their originators, although (as has been
the case with Shakespeare) some authors have been credited with
originating a word when they were merely the earliest known user, and
have lost this distinction when subsequent research has unearthed an
earlier example. But some coinages are reliably documented: T. H. Huxley
invented *agnostic*; Jeremy Bentham gave us *international*; Horace
Walpole coined *serendipity*; and more recently, Dr. M. Gell-Mann gave the
name *quark* to the subatomic particle.

3. The term is sometimes loosely used for jocular-sounding words that
seem unlikely to last long (perhaps because a word that is generally
adopted does not seem like a word for one occasion, or by association with
'nonsense').

1986 S. MORT On the matter of durability, this book can be judged only by the
reader of the 1990s. Of course, some words are probably nonce.

Examples of this kind of word might be *jocumentary*, *nepotocracy*, *oldcomer*, *trendicrat*.

(*n.*) A nonce-word.

1986 S. MORT *Private Eye*, master of the nonce, again demonstrates this kind of innovation.

Derived from the phrase *for the nonce* 'for the particular purpose; for the occasion, for the time being'. This is a Middle English *metanalysis of the phrase *for than anes* 'for the one (thing, occasion, etc.)'.

Compare NEOLOGISM; NON-WORD.

non-conclusive *See* CONCLUSIVE.

non-count Usually the same as *uncount.

See also MASS.

non-defining Of *modification or of a *modifier: giving additional, circumstantial information about the *head. Also called **non-restrictive**, **non-identifying**, **supplementary**. *See also* DEFINING; IDENTIFY; RESTRICTIVE.

●● **non-defining relative clause** (also called **non-restrictive relative clause**, **non-identifying relative clause**, **supplementary relative clause**): a *relative clause that gives additional information about the head with which it is associated, but is not a defining relative clause because the noun phrase of which it is a part is already defined and its *referent is identifiable.

A non-defining relative clause is usually separated from the rest of the sentence in which it occurs by a comma or commas, and if it is omitted, the *sentence will still make complete sense, e.g.

My mother, *who now lives alone*, does *The Guardian* crossword every day

Contrast:

A woman *I know* does six crosswords a day

Without the defining relative clause *I know*, this last example does not convey the intended sense.

Compare sentential RELATIVE CLAUSE.

non-derivational *See* MONOSTRATAL.

non-equivalence *See* EQUIVALENCE.

non-factive *See* FACTIVE.

non-factual *See* FACTUAL (1).

non-finite (*n. & adj.*) (A *verb form or a *clause) that is not marked for *tense; contrasting with *finite.

The term covers the *infinitive forms of verbs (the *to-infinitive and *bare infinitive), the *-*ing* form, and the *past participle form, as well as the associated *clauses containing these forms. Thus, a **non-finite clause** is a clause that contains one or more non-finite verbs, e.g.

> *To expect a refund* is unreasonable
>
> All he ever does is *complain*
>
> *Having said that*, I still hope he gets his degree
>
> *If consulted*, I will advise against it

A non-finite clause can perform various functions, such as *subject (as in the first example above), *complement (1) (as in the second example), or *adverbial (as in the third and fourth examples).

In some frameworks, (non-)finiteness is not defined with reference to tense. Thus in CaGEL, the italicized clause in the third example above is non-finite, but it nevertheless carries tense (namely the secondary *perfect tense).

A non-finite clause can have its own subject (notice the *objective (1) *case):

> *For him to expect a refund* is unreasonable

• **non-finitely**

•• **non-finite passive construction**: *see* PASSIVE.

Compare BARE INFINITIVE *clause*; -*ED* CLAUSE; HANGING PARTICIPLE; -*ING* CLAUSE; PARTICIPLE CLAUSE; *TO*-INFINITIVE *clause*.

non-gradable *See* GRADABLE.

non-headed The opposite of *headed; the same as *exocentric.

non-identifying The same as *non-defining.
  See also IDENTIFY.

non-inherent *See* INHERENT.

non-linguistic The same as *extralinguistic.

non-neutral affix *See* LEVEL ORDERING (HYPOTHESIS).

non-past (*n. & adj.*) (A *verb form, *clause, etc.) marked for the *present (2) (*tense).

Morphologically, English has only two tenses, called the present tense (e.g. *look(s)*, *come(s)*, *can*) and the *past (2) tense (e.g. *looked*, *came*, *could*). The label 'present' indicates one of the typical uses of that tense, namely that it can refer to present *time (1), but fails to cover its other regular *meanings. Thus the present tense can be used to indicate futurity (e.g. *If you <u>come</u> tomorrow, we'll watch a movie*), timeless *reference (e.g. *Ice <u>melts</u> when you heat it*), and so on. See PRESENT (2). For this reason, some linguists prefer the term non-past for this tense, claiming that it is better thought of as *unmarked for time rather than marked for the present.

Compare MARKED.

non-perfective *See* PERFECT.

non-personal Of the *meaning of a *noun or *pronoun: *referring to something not regarded as having human personality, including *inanimate things, abstract entities, and animals.

Non-personal nouns include all nouns other than those referring to people, but the usage with regard to pronouns is not always straightforward. Pronouns normally referring to people (e.g. *he/him, she/her, who/whom*) are sometimes used of animals, and even things (e.g. *this ship and all who sail in her*), while *it* and *which* can refer to people (e.g. *A child needs its mother; Which of my cousins do you mean?*).

Non-personal is therefore a useful semantic label when there is some apparent mismatch. It should also be noted that, of the so-called *personal pronouns, *it* is usually non-personal in meaning, while *they* and *them* can have personal or non-personal reference.

Compare IMPERSONAL.

See also GENDER.

non-plural Not *plural.

A useful term to describe the use of the demonstratives *this* and *that*, which can be used with both singular *count nouns (*this apple*) and *uncount nouns (*that food*). Unfortunately, most grammars inaccurately and confusingly use the term *singular.

Compare NON-SINGULAR.

non-predicative The same as *attributive.

non-progressive *See* PROGRESSIVE.

non-propositional meaning *See* PROPOSITION.

non-proximal *See* PROXIMAL.

non-referential *it* *See* DUMMY; IMPERSONAL.

non-restrictive The same as *non-defining.

The term usually refers to *relative clauses, but can be applied more widely:

1966 G. N. LEECH Proper nouns do occasionally combine with modifiers of non-restrictive force: 'fair Helen' . . . ; 'beautiful Britain'.

See DEFINING.

non-scalar comparison A *comparison made between entities in a *comparative clause where the comparison is absolute and not on a scale (i.e. not gradable), e.g. *His face looked the same as his brother's does.* Compare the *scalar comparison *This room is hotter than the kitchen was when we baked a cake.*

See also COMPARATIVE CLAUSE; SCALAR COMPARISON.

non-sentence A string of *words (in written or spoken language) that functions as a complete expression, but lacks a *regular *clause *structure.

Similar terms, often not very precisely defined, include *minor sentence/clause and **clause fragment**.

Non-sentences include *formulae and *interjections. Examples:

You and your headaches!

Whatever next?

Nice one, Norman!

No way!

You fool

No taxation without representation

Of all the daft things to do!

Compare FULL (3); KERNEL.

non-singular A term to describe the use of those *determinatives (1) and *pronouns that can be used with both *plural *count *nouns (*all apples*) and *uncount nouns (*all food*).

The determinative and pronoun system of English is quite complicated. Some items relate only to *count *singular (e.g. *a, each, one*); some only to *uncount (e.g. *much*); and some only to *plural (e.g. *few, many, several, these*). There are also some words that overlap two categories: *non-plural words (e.g. *this, that*) can be used for both count singular and uncount; non-singular words (e.g. *all, enough, most*) are used for both plural and uncount.

non-specific *See* SPECIFIC.

non-standard *See* STANDARD.

non-tensed verb form A form of a *verb that does not carry *tense, e.g. a *to*-infinitive, *bare infinitive, *-*en* form, or *-*ing* form.

See also FINITE; NON-FINITE.

non-word

1. A *word that is not recorded or not established.

This may be interchangeable with *nonce word, but tends to be restricted to inventions that could be unintentional errors rather than deliberate coinages:

1963 *PUNCH* The aesthetically displeasing non-word 'annoyment'.

2. A string of letters (or sounds) that is not an English word.

normative The same as *prescriptive.

Normative grammars or **normative rules** prescribe what is correct (*see* CORRECTNESS), rather than describing language as it is used. The term has largely been replaced by 'prescriptive' as a pejorative label applied to outdated or misconceived *rules.

notional Based on *meaning, e.g. *semantic roles.

1. Older traditional grammar, which defines the *word classes in terms of meaning (e.g. 'A verb is a doing word') rather than by making reference to *syntax and *distribution, is sometimes called **notional grammar**. 'Notional' in this sense contrasts with *grammatical (1) or *formal (2), and today has somewhat pejorative overtones, suggesting a lack of precision and rigour.

•• **notional subject:** a term used to contrast a grammatically defined *subject with a subject defined in terms of *semantic roles. For example, in the following *existential construction the grammatical subject is *there*, whereas the notional subject ('doer', 'agent') is *two men*:

There were two men shouting in the street (*compare*: Two men were shouting in the street)

2. In the teaching of English as a foreign language, the term notional was applied in the 1970s to syllabuses aimed at developing *communicative competence. D. A. Wilkins's *Notional Syllabuses* (1976) advocated pedagogical programmes based primarily on semantic criteria, in contrast to the older type of grammatical or 'situational' courses, although this did not exclude 'adequate learning of the grammatical system'. Suggested **notional categories** covered three areas: semantico-grammatical categories (e.g. *time and *space), *modal meaning, and *functions (3) (e.g. how to express disapproval, persuasion, or agreement). Notional in this sense still contrasts with *formal, but is a positive term with the senses 'meaningful' and 'communicative'.

In later developments in foreign language teaching, the term notional tended to be restricted to members of the first category (general concepts of time and space, etc.) which were explicitly contrasted with functions, such as agreement or suasion.

• **notionally**.

notional concord *See* AGREEMENT; GRAMMATICAL.

noun A *word that belongs to a *word class whose members can function as the *head of a *noun phrase, can inflect for *plural, and can be preceded by *determinatives (1) and *adjectives. Some nouns end in identifiable nominal *suffixes, e.g. -ness, -hood.

In traditional grammar, a noun is defined *notionally as 'the name of a person, place, or thing'. However, this definition works only partly. Thus *abstract nouns like *criticism* or *tolerance* are hardly things, and it is syntax, not *meaning, that determines that *think* is a *verb in one sentence (*I must think*) and a noun in another (*I'll have a think*). Modern grammarians therefore prefer more formal, syntactic definitions (*see* DISTRIBUTION).

Nouns are divided on syntactic and semantic grounds into *proper nouns and *common nouns. The latter are further divided into *count and *uncount (or *non-count). The division into *abstract and *concrete is notional, and cuts across that between count and uncount.

There is disagreement among different grammatical frameworks as to whether *pronouns belong to the class of nouns or not. In CaGEL pronouns are regarded as nouns, but in CGEL they form a separate word class (though they function as the heads of noun phrases).

• **nominal**: *see* NOMINAL.

•• **noun adjective**: *see* ADJECTIVE.

•• **noun substantive**: *see* ADJECTIVE.

  See also NOUN-EQUIVALENT; SUBSTANTIVE.

nounal Of or pertaining to a *noun; *nominal. (Obsolescent.)

noun clause The same as *nominal clause (1).

noun-equivalent A *word or words functioning like a *noun.

  This is a somewhat dated term, covering not only *noun phrases but also *nominal clauses.

  See also EQUIVALENT.

noun modifier

  1. A *noun in *attributive position. (Also called **noun premodifier**.).
Examples are <u>book</u> *review*, <u>sun</u> *hat*, <u>toffee</u> *apple*. Such sequences are not always easy to distinguish from *compounds.

  2. A word *modifying a noun.

  1958 W. N. FRANCIS The most common noun modifier is the adjective.

noun pattern *See* PATTERN.

noun phrase (NP) A group of *words which has a *noun (or *pronoun) as *head and performs a particular *function (1) in a *clause, such as *subject or *direct object, e.g.

The results were faked

The head of a noun phrase can be accompanied by an assortment of *dependents, including *determiner (1), *premodifiers, and *postmodifiers; e.g.

the name
an odd name
the name of the game
the name that he gave

Compare NOMINAL GROUP.

A noun phrase can also consist of a bare noun (*singular or *plural):

Statistics can be flawed

NP An abbreviation for *noun phrase.

NP-movement *See* MOVEMENT.

nuclear English A proposed simplified form of English, intended to be used as an international language.

> 1985 R. QUIRK et al. Following earlier attempts (such as 'Basic English') that were largely lexical, a proposal has also recently been made for constructing a simplified form of English (termed 'Nuclear English') that would contain a subset of the features of natural English; for example, modal auxiliaries such as *can* and *may* would be replaced by such paraphrases as *be able to* and *be allowed to*. The simplified form would be intelligible to speakers of any major national variety and could be expanded for specific purposes, for example for international maritime communication.

nucleus (In CaGEL.) A grammatical *function (1) label applied to the combination of *subject + *predicate (1).

Elements that are *dislocated are moved to the left or right of the nucleus, e.g.

Your young son [nucleus he's a good cricketer]
[nucleus He's a good cricketer] *your young son*

See also DISLOCATION; LEFT DISLOCATION; PRENUCLEUS; RIGHT DISLOCATION.

null anaphor See ANAPHOR.

null head See HEAD.

number

1. A grammatical (1) *category used in the analysis of *word classes which have contrasts of *singular and *plural.

Number contrasts in English are seen in *nouns (e.g. *boy, boys*), *pronouns (*she, they; myself, ourselves*), *determinatives (1) (*this, these*), and *verbs (*says, say; was, were*).

Compare NUMERAL.

See also AGREEMENT; COLLECTIVE; COUNT; DUAL; UNCOUNT.

2. A *numeral.

numeral (*n. & adj.*) (A *word) denoting a number (as commonly understood, e.g. *one, two, three*).

Because the term *number is also used in a specialized way to refer to a grammatical category, numeral is often the preferred term for referring to the series *1/one, 2/two, 3/three, 4/four*, etc. and *first, second, third, fourth*, etc. See CARDINAL; ORDINAL.

In traditional grammar, numerals (numbers) have been treated as a subclass of *adjectives (called **numeral adjectives**) or divided between adjectives and *pronouns. Modern grammar prefers to treat numerals as *determinatives (1), *postdeterminers, or (pro)nouns, depending on their syntactic position.

numerative (*n. & adj.*) (A *word) relating to numeration, denoting an amount or quantity.

This is used as a wider term than *numeral (*cardinal and *ordinal) to include terms for *indefinite quantity, e.g.

(a) few, (a) little, several

It also includes words related to ordinal numerals by reason of their 'ordering' function, e.g.

next, last, preceding, subsequent

In many grammars these two groups of terms belong to different word classes, e.g. *determinative (1) versus *adjective.

Compare QUANTIFIER.

See also ORDINATIVE; QUANTIFICATION; QUANTIFIER; QUANTITATIVE; QUANTITY.

O Object as an *element of clause structure.

object (*n.*)
   1. The *direct object.
   2. (In modern analyses.) One of the five elements in *sentence structure, along with *subject, *verb, *complement, and *adverbial.

In this use, both the *direct object (DO) and *indirect object (IO) are often represented simply as 'O'. Thus *She* + *gave* + *the poor dog* + *nothing* would be represented as SVOO.
•• **anticipatory object**: *see* ANTICIPATORY.
•• **object case**: *see* OBJECT CASE; OBJECTIVE (1).
•• **object complement**: *see* COMPLEMENT.
•• **object of result**: *see* RESULT.
   3. object of a preposition (also called *prepositional complement; **prepositional object**): a *phrase *licensed (*governed) by a *preposition, e.g.

   in *the box*
   look at *the sky*

object attribute *See* ATTRIBUTE.

object case The *case taken by *pronouns when in (grammatical) *object position, e.g. after a *verb or *preposition. (Also called *objective (1) case or *accusative case.)

The distinct object case forms for pronouns in modern English can be listed as follows:

   me, her, him, us, them, whom

Notice that the label 'object case' can be problematic when describing a sentence like *I want them to sing for me*. This is because in many, though not all, analyses the pronoun *them* is regarded as the *subject of the subordinate clause *them to sing for me*. For this reason some grammarians prefer the labels **nominative**, **accusative**, etc. when talking about case. *See* SUBJECT CASE.

See also SUBJECTIVE.

object complement *See* COMPLEMENT.

objective

1. Designating the *case *inflection typically carried by *pronouns when
they function as the *object of a *verb or *preposition. (Also called **object
case** or **accusative case**.)

The difference between the pronouns *I, she, he, we, they, who* (called
subjective pronouns, **subject pronouns**, or **nominative pronouns**) and
me, her, him, us, them, whom (called **objective pronouns**, **object
pronouns**, or **accusative pronouns**) can be described in terms of case.

See also GENITIVE; SUBJECTIVE (1).

2. Relating to, or referring to, an object.

In an **objective genitive** the reference is to a 'deep' object, rather than to
the object of the actual *sentence or *clause. Thus the *genitive has
objective meaning in:

Caesar's assassination by Brutus (cf. Brutus assassinated Caesar)

See also GENITIVE; SUBJECTIVE (2).

•• **objective predicative complement**: *see* COMPLEMENT.

3. (*n. & adj.*) (In *Case Grammar.) (Designating) one of six original
*cases (3).

This case is sometimes also called *affected or *patient.

objective predicative complement *See* COMPLEMENT.

object of result *See* RESULT.

object-raising *See* RAISING.

object-related predicative complement *See* COMPLEMENT.

object territory The position after a *verb, typically occupied by a
*noun phrase. Contrasted with *subject territory.

As an example, in the following (*hypercorrect) sentence the *relative
pronoun is felt to be in the object territory of *think*, but in actual fact
functions as the *subject of the following *subordinate clause, and should
hence take the form *who*:

They're looking for two men *whom* they think can help them with their
inquiries

The term was coined partly to explain the common tendency to use object
pronouns where subject pronouns are preferred by purists, e.g.

You were quicker than *me*

That's *him*

objoid *See* QUASI-.

obligation One of the main meanings of *deontic modality, along with *permission.

This covers the laying of a duty on someone (possibly oneself), e.g. *You must try harder, I must go now.*

obligatory Of a *word or structure: compulsory in a particular *context. Contrasted with *optional.

Various structures can be analysed in terms of the presence of obligatory elements, or the application of obligatory *rules or processes. For example, many *transitive verbs obligatorily take certain types of *complements, e.g. a *direct object (e.g. *He's making dinner*, but not **He's making*) or a locative complement (e.g. *He put the food on the table*, but not **He put the food*). Similarly, in non-subordinate *interrogative clauses, subject-auxiliary *inversion is obligatory (*What can they do?*, not**What they can do?*).

In earlier *Generative Grammar (2), some *rules that were needed to produce acceptable *surface structures were regarded as obligatory, while others were optional.

●● **obligatory predication adjunct**: *see* PREDICATION ADJUNCT.

oblique

1. Designating a *case other than the *subjective (1) case.

In *inflected languages, all cases (other than subjective or *vocative) of inflected *nouns, *pronouns, and *adjectives are covered by this umbrella term. In English the term is occasionally applied to the *accusative forms of pronouns that show case distinctions.

●● **oblique genitive construction**: *see* GENITIVE.

2. (*n. & adj.*) (Designating a) unit in a *clause that does not function as *subject or *object.

3. (*n. & adj.*) (By extension.) (Designating) a unit, typically a *noun phrase, that does not directly follow a particular *verb, but functions as the object of a *preposition following that verb, as in *I rely on* <u>*my neighbours*</u>, where *my neighbours* can be described as being an **oblique (object)** of *rely*. Similarly, in *The court regards these decisions as unlawful* the *adjective phrase *unlawful* is an oblique. It is called a **predicative oblique** in CaGEL, since the phrase ascribes a property to the referent of the noun phrase *these decisions*.

See also COMPLEMENT.

oblique genitive construction *See* GENITIVE.

occurrence *See* PRIVILEGE OF OCCURRENCE.

of-construction

1. A structure which conforms to the *pattern *noun + *of* + noun phrase.

This is a wider term than *of-genitive. It is often equivalent in meaning to, and interchangeable with, a *genitive construction (e.g. *the West End of London, London's West End*), but this is not always so, and *of*-constructions are sometimes preferred or essential: *the end of the road, a book of verse, an object of ridicule, a man of honour.*

2. A structure which conforms to the pattern *of* + noun phrase. Also called *of-phrase.

The term is sometimes used to distinguish a part of an *of*-construction from the whole, as when *indefinite *pronouns such as *all* or *many* are said to be able to 'take the partitive *of*-construction'.

The terms *of*-construction and *of*-phrase are both used somewhat loosely.

See also GENITIVE; *OF*-GENITIVE.

of-genitive A *genitive *construction which contains the pattern *of* + *noun phrase, corresponding closely in meaning and function to a genitive noun phrase.

For example,

George V was the grandfather *of Queen Elizabeth II*

is roughly equivalent to

George V was *Queen Elizabeth II's* grandfather

Similarly:

the mother *of my friend* = *my friend's* mother
the Lower East Side *of New York City* = *New York City's* Lower East Side
the arrest *of the student* = *the student's* arrest
the message *of the sermon* = *the sermon's* message

See also GENITIVE; *OF*-CONSTRUCTION.

of-phrase *See* GENITIVE; *OF*-CONSTRUCTION; *OF*-GENITIVE.

of-pronoun A *pronoun that can be followed by a *partitive *of*-phrase. For example:

few (of those people)
much (of the time)
some (of our problems)

-oid *See* quasi-.

Old English (OE) The form of English used in Britain from circa 450 to circa 1150; the earliest stage in the development of the English language. Also called **Anglo-Saxon**.

Although Anglo-Saxon rule came to an end with the Norman Conquest of 1066, a written form of Old English continued in use until the twelfth century.

The Old English dialects were highly *inflected. *Nouns had grammatical *gender and four *cases, *singular and *plural; *adjectives agreed with nouns; and verbs inflected for *person and *number. Most of the core *vocabulary of Present-Day English is of OE origin, e.g. *man, woman, child, be, go, come, sit, stand, young, old*, as are the remaining inflections. Without study, Old English is largely incomprehensible to modern English speakers.

Compare LATE MODERN ENGLISH; MIDDLE ENGLISH; MODERN ENGLISH.

old information *See* GIVEN.

omission of words *See* ELLIPSIS.

one-place predicate *See* PREDICATE.

onomatopoeia (The formation of) a *word denoting a sound made by an animal, object, etc.; the use of such a word. Examples:

choo-choo	cuckoo	cock-a-doodle-doo	hiss
neigh	miaow	tick-tock	

The term is sometimes extended to cover combinations in which a sound is felt to be appropriate to some aspect of *meaning, although these combinations do not necessarily denote sounds or sources of sound. Thus *sl-*, which often occurs in words with unpleasant *connotations, is sometimes cited as an example of such **secondary onomatopoeia** (e.g. *slag, slang, slattern, slaver, sleazy, slime, slop, sluggard, slurp, slut*). Other terms for onomatopoeia are **phonaesthesia** and *sound symbolism.

● **onomatopoeic**

Compare ICON.

opaque Not obvious in structure or meaning; not able to be extrapolated from *surface structure.

Contrasted with *transparent.

open

1. Of a *word class: capable of acquiring a theoretically unlimited number of new members. Also called *major word class. Contrasted with *closed (1).

The main open classes are *nouns, *lexical verbs, *adverbs, and *adjectives. Items belonging to these classes are sometimes called **open-class items**.

See also INTERJECTION; NUMERAL.

2. Of a conditional clause or sentence: *see* CONDITION.

See also CONDITIONAL.

open condition *See* CONDITION.

open interrogative clause *See* INTERROGATIVE.

operator (In some models, e.g. CGEL.) The first or only *auxiliary verb, including the *modal verbs and *do* as a *dummy verb, in *finite clauses. The verbs *be* and *have* used as *main verbs without *do-support are also included.

This item 'operates' *inversion (in *interrogative clauses) and the addition of *not/-n't* (for *negation):

They *could* have been imagining things
Could they have been imagining things?
They *couldn't* have been imagining things
He knows something
Does he know something?
He *doesn't* know anything

The verbs *be* and *have* used as main verbs can also be *operators (when there is no *do-support):

Are you ready?
I *haven't* any money
Have you any idea what you have just done?

(Note that in CaGEL *be* and *have* used in these structures are regarded as auxiliaries, not as main verbs.)

Have and *do* are not operators but main verbs when they take *do*-support:

Do you <u>have</u> any idea what you have just done?
He *doesn't* <u>have</u> a clue
I *didn't* <u>do</u> the housework
Did you <u>do</u> the dishes?

Compare NICE PROPERTIES.

optative subjunctive The same as formulaic *subjunctive.

Optimality Theory A theory of language developed by A. Prince, P. Smolensky, and associates in the 1990s in which optimal phonological, morphological, and syntactic representations are generated through a list of ordered constraints.

> 2004 A. PRINCE and P. SMOLENSKY The basic idea we will explore is that Universal Grammar (UG) consists largely of a set of constraints on representational well-formedness, out of which individual grammars are constructed.

See also GENERATIVE GRAMMAR (2).

optional Not *obligatory. The term is used to describe a *word, *phrase, etc. that can be omitted leaving a grammatical structure.

Of the five *elements of clause structure, an *adverbial is always optional (though some grammars, e.g. CGEL, allow for obligatory *predication adjuncts, e.g. *The police are here.*). *Subjects are obligatory in *finite *clause structures (**Is raining*), with the exception of *imperatives (e.g. *Go! You go!*) if these are regarded as finite. Missing subjects in *coordinated clauses are explained as being examples of *ellipsis.

• **optionality, optionally.**
•• **optional predication adjunct**: *see* PREDICATION ADJUNCT.

oral Using or pertaining to speech, as opposed to writing.

Oral competence, for example, may be contrasted with writing competence.

order of adjectives *See* ADJECTIVE ORDER.

order of words *See* WORD ORDER.

ordinal number A *word defining *position in a series (*first, second, third, fourth*, etc.). Contrasted with *cardinal number (*one, two, three, four*, etc.). Also called **ordinal numeral**.

> 1892a H. SWEET Most of the ordinal numerals are derivatives of the cardinal ones.

See also NUMBER; NUMERAL.

ordinative (*n. & adj.*) (A *numeral or *adjective) that indicates *position in an order.

This is a wider term than *ORDINAL (*number), including *words such as *next, last, preceding.*

See also NUMERATIVE.

Compare QUANTITATIVE.

or-relationship A *paradigmatic relationship. Contrasted with *and*-relationship (i.e. *syntagmatic relationship).

See also CHAIN; CHOICE; PARADIGM; SAUSSUREAN; SYNTAGMATIC; SYNTAGMATIC RELATIONSHIP.

orthographic Of, or pertaining to, spelling.
•• **orthographic word**: a *word as written or printed, i.e. with spaces on either side. This is the way that the concept of word is commonly understood, although there is variability with *compounds. There are also sometimes problems with the use of the *apostrophe. An advertisement some years ago said:

> Four little words that can cost a tobacconist £400. THEY'RE FOR MY MUM.

For many people *they're* is two words, but it is a single orthographic word, so the advertisement is correct by the definition given here.
Compare LEXEME.

orthography (The study or science of) how *words are spelt. Contrasted with *graphology.

> 1873 J. EARLE When we use the word 'orthography', we do not mean a mode of spelling which is true to the pronunciation, but one which is conventionally correct.

Spelling being largely standardized, a word normally has only one recognized orthographic form, but in a few cases there are acceptable *variants, e.g.

cipher/cypher
hallo/hello
mateyness/matiness
standardise/standardize

And there are also distinct British and American spellings:

centre/center
colour/color
sceptical/skeptical
travelling/traveling

overcorrection The same as *hypercorrection.

overgeneralize Apply a grammatical *rule, principle, etc. to inappropriate cases.
    The term is particularly used in the domain of first language acquisition. Thus a child who overgeneralizes the *plural -*s* *inflection or the *past tense -*ed* inflection might say *mans, mouses, sheeps,* or *bringed, runned,* etc.
• **overgeneralization**.

overlapping distribution *See* DISTRIBUTION.

Oxford comma *See* PUNCTUATION.

Oxford English Grammar A *corpus-based reference *grammar published in 1996, written by Sidney Greenbaum. Updated by Edmund Weiner as the *Oxford Reference Grammar* in 2000.

Oxford Modern English Grammar (OMEG) A *corpus-based reference *grammar published in 2011, written by Bas Aarts.

paradigm (Pronounced /ˈpærədaɪm/.) *Morphology*. An arrangement of the *inflectional forms of a *lexeme, according to one or more grammatical features (e.g. *case, *person, *number, *tense).

For example, *see, sees, seeing, saw, seen* constitute a verbal paradigm for the lexeme *see*.

Paradigms can be conceptualized as a series of 'slots' for the various forms of a lexeme:

> 2001 G.T. STUMP The PARADIGM of a lexeme L is a set of CELLS; each such cell is the pairing <Y, σ> of an inflected form Y of the lexeme L with a complete set σ of morphosyntactic properties for L.

The term comes ultimately from Greek *paradeigma* 'pattern, example', and is used in language teaching for a set of forms of a particular lexeme as a model for all other words which inflect in the same way. For example, for the Latin first *declension noun *puella* 'girl', we have the following paradigm for the singular:

nominative	*puella*
vocative	*puella*
accusative	*puellam*
genitive	*puellae*
dative	*puellae*
ablative	*puella*

This model can then be used to decline any other first declension noun. The term is mostly used for the description of languages which have richer inflectional systems than English.

• **paradigmatic**: forming, belonging to, or relating to a paradigm or paradigms. *See also* PARADIGMATIC RELATIONSHIP; SYNTAGMATIC RELATIONSHIP.

• **paradigmatically**.

See also CHAIN; CONJUGATION; DECLENSION.

paradigmatic relationship A relationship between two or more linguistic units that form a *paradigm or paradigms. Also called *or-relationship.

Paradigmatic (choice) relationships are contrasted with *syntagmatic (*chain) relationships. The terminology is that of Ferdinand de Saussure (1857–1913).

The English article system and pronoun system are examples of paradigms. We can say *a book* or *the book*, but not *a the book*. Similarly, we can grammatically substitute one pronoun for another in the subject position of *I told the truth* (e.g. *you/he/she/we/they/somebody*, etc.), but we cannot choose more than one pronoun, unless they are coordinated (e.g. *You and I told the truth*).

See also CONJUGATION; DECLENSION; SAUSSUREAN; SYNTAGM; SYNTAGMATIC RELATIONSHIP.

paragraph (*n.*) A distinct section of a piece of writing, beginning on a new, and often indented, line.

(*v.*) Arrange in such sections.

Although the way a text is set out on the page may be an important factor in its intelligibility, the paragraph as such has no grammatical status comparable to that of a *phrase, *clause, or *sentence.

Compare DISCOURSE.

paralanguage The *paralinguistic features of spoken language. Somewhat rare.

paralinguistic Of or pertaining to the non-verbal features of spoken language.

The term is used in a variety of ways to include or exclude certain non-verbal features of spoken communication. In analysis of non-verbal vocal phenomena, paralinguistic features are often contrasted with more measurable prosodic ones, such as intonation and stress. Paralinguistic features can thus include tone of voice, and the distinctive characteristics of an individual's voice.

Non-vocal features accompanying spoken communication, such as eye movements, nodding, or other forms of body language, are also frequently classified as paralinguistic.

There is some overlap between this term and *extralinguistic.

• **paralinguistics**: the study of paralinguistic features.

paraphrase (*n.*) A sentence or longer piece of text that expresses the same meaning as another sentence or piece of text using a different wording. However, the meaning of the 'original' and of the paraphrase are seldom exactly the same, because paraphrases often change some types of meaning in certain ways. For example, they may change the emphasis on certain units and/or the way information is structured (e.g. what the *topic is, what the *focus is), while looser paraphrases can change the level of formality, social implications, and so on.

(*v.*) Make or constitute a paraphrase of (a sentence, piece of text).

parasynthesis *Morphology*.
1. Derivation from a *compound or syntactic sequence.
An example is the formation of *red-faced* from *red face* + *-ed*.
2. The simultaneous addition of two *affixes. Also called **circumfixation**.

2003 I. PLAG [S]ome complex words with more than one affix seem to have come into being through the **simultaneous** attachment of two affixes. A case in point is *decaffeinate*, for which, at the time of creation, neither *caffeinate* was available as a base word (for the prefixation of *de-*), nor *decaffein* (as the basis for *-ate* suffixation). Such forms are called **parasynthetic** formations, and the process of simultaneous multiple affixation is called **parasynthesis**.

• **parasynthetic**: formed (by derivation) from a compound or syntactic sequence of two or more elements; or formed by the simultaneous addition of two affixes.

paratactic *See* PARATAXIS.

parataxis A relationship of grammatical equality between two linguistic units. Contrasted with *hypotaxis.

Parataxis (literally 'side-by-side arrangement') is a very general term covering various kinds of juxtaposition of units of equal status, including the *coordination of two (or more) equal words, phrases, or clauses, with or without coordinating *conjunctions, e.g.

a bus and a cab

poor but happy and optimistic

mad, bad, dangerous

Some grammarians specifically use the term for *asyndetic coordination, contrasting it with *syndetic coordination.

Others extend the term to include juxtapositions of two equal units which would not be regarded as coordination (since no conjunctions could be inserted), for example certain phrases that are contrasted with each other, *apposition, clausal linkage in *tags, or the relationship between a reporting verb and a direct quotation, e.g.

the more, the merrier

Oxford, city of dreaming spires

It's a lovely day, isn't it?

They shouted 'Go home'

The last example is certainly controversial, because many grammarians would consider *Go home* to be the *direct object of the verb *shout*, in which case this particular relationship would be hypotactic.

• **paratactic**: exhibiting parataxis.

parenthesis (Plural **parentheses**.)

1. A *word, *phrase, *clause, etc., that is inserted into a sentence as an aside, explanation, or afterthought. In writing, a parenthesis is usually marked off by brackets, dashes, or commas, e.g.

My colleagues suggested (can you believe it?) that we have a meeting every day

Tim—I haven't seen him since Sunday—doesn't want to come to dinner tonight

2. (In plural.) A pair of brackets—usually round ones, '(. . .)'—used for marking a parenthesis.

• **parenthetical**.

Compare ANACOLUTHON; COMMENT CLAUSE; SUPPLEMENT.

parole *See* LANGUE.

paronym A word derived from the same *base (2) as another, and used in a related meaning; a word formed from a foreign word with only a slight change of form (especially one used as a translation equivalent of the foreign word). Contrasted with *heteronym (3).

Examples: *wise*: *wisdom*; *preface*: Latin *praefatio* (as contrasted with *foreword*).

• **paronymous**.

• **paronymy**: the use of morphologically related words in related senses.

parse

1. Describe (a word in context) grammatically, stating for example its *inflection or relation to the rest of its containing *phrase, *clause, or *sentence.

2. Analyse a linguistic unit (sentence, clause, phrase, etc.) into its *constituent parts, and describe these grammatically.

3. (In *corpus linguistics.) Grammatically analyse a (portion of) text using an automated computational process. *Compare* TAG.

partial apposition *See* APPOSITION.

partial conversion *See* CONVERSION.

participant

1. *Linguistics.* A role that can be assigned to an individual involved in a text, discourse, etc.

Whether written or spoken, every text involves at least two people: the speaker/writer and the addressee (the listener or reader). This is true whether the participants are mentioned (*I am asking you a favour*) or not (*Keep off the grass!*). The relationship of the people involved in a text is a **participant relation** or **participant relationship**.

2. *Semantics.* The same as *case (3) or *semantic role.

The case or semantic role of a noun phrase can be called its **participant role**. For example, an *agent is an **agentive participant**; an indirect object is typically a **recipient participant**; and so on.

participial Of the nature of, of or pertaining to, a *participle.

●● **participial adjective**: *see* PARTICIPIAL ADJECTIVE.

●● **participial clause**: the same as *participle clause.

●● **participial conjunction**: a *conjunction that is a participle in form, e.g.

> You can borrow it *providing/provided (that)* you return it in good condition

●● **participial preposition**: a *preposition that is a participle in form, e.g.

> *Following* the disclosures, the chairman resigned

participial adjective An *adjective that has the same form as the *participle of the verb to which it is related, i.e. one formed with the *suffix *-ing* or *-ed/-en*. Also called **verbal adjective**. Examples:

> They are *loving* parents
> *exciting* times
> His thoughts were *alarming*

Participial adjectives are typically *gradable, e.g.

> *very* loving parents (*Compare*: They are loving every minute of it; verb + object)
> *very* exciting times
> *very* alarming thoughts

However, the attributively used participles of some verbs are best analysed as being verbal. For example, *an escaped prisoner* is 'a prisoner who has escaped', *a changing culture* is 'a culture that is changing', and *a knitted jumper* is 'a jumper that has been knitted'. Such participles cannot be modified by *very*.

*a *very* escaped prisoner
*a *very* changing culture
*a *very* knitted jumper

However, modification by an *adverb is possible in many cases:

a *recently* escaped prisoner
a *rapidly* changing culture
a *deftly* knitted jumper

In some contexts the status of a participle-like form is *ambiguous. Thus *I was annoyed* can be interpreted verbally (e.g. *I was annoyed by their behaviour*) or as an adjective (e.g. *I was very annoyed*), or perhaps even as both (*I was very annoyed by their behaviour*).

Participial adjectives also include words that are formed with a regular *-ed* or *-ing* ending, but lack a corresponding verb, e.g.

booted and *spurred*	*unexpected* pleasure
honeyed words	*wooded* slopes
talented musicians	*unconvincing* narrative

*Parasynthetic adjectives like the following are especially frequent: *able-bodied, half-hearted, one-legged, three-cornered, two-faced, white-haired*. This type (which also lack a corresponding verb) is sometimes called a **pseudo-participle**.

Some *-ing* forms in attributive position are noun-like, e.g. *dining room, planning permission*. See *-ING* FORM.

participle A *non-finite form of the *verb which in *regular verbs ends in either *-ing* or *-ed* (*-en* for *irregular verbs).

Two participles are distinguished, traditionally labelled *present participle (e.g. *being, doing, drinking, looking*; also called **gerund participle** or **-*ing* participle**) and *past participle (e.g. *been, done, drunk, looked*). Neither name is accurate, since both participles are used in the formation of a variety of complex constructions (tenses), and can be used in combination with one or more auxiliaries to refer to *past, *present, or *future *time (e.g. *What had they been doing? This must be drunk soon*). Preferred terms are *-*ing* form (which also includes the *gerund) and *-*ed* form/*-*en* form.

Compare FUSED PARTICIPLE.

participle clause A *non-finite *clause with an *-*ing* form or *-*ed* form (*-*en* form for *irregular verbs) as its principal verbal component. (Also called **participial clause**.) Examples:

Looking to neither right nor left, he marched out

Treated like that, I would have collapsed

Having been warned before, he did not do it again

A participle clause can sometimes be introduced by a *conjunction:

If treated like that, I would have collapsed.

A participle clause that contains its own subject is a type of *absolute clause.

See also BARE INFINITIVE CLAUSE; CONTENT CLAUSE; -*ED* CLAUSE; HANGING PARTICIPLE; *TO*-INFINITIVE clause.

particle

1. A neutral term to denote a word that combines with a *verb to form a *multi-word verb. Also called **adverb(ial) particle**.

Most particles are high-frequency short words which are regarded as adverbs, or as prepositions in some analyses:

She looked *up* the word/She looked the word *up*

In many grammars *look up* is treated as a *phrasal verb (2).

Contrast the example above with the following:

She looked up the road/Up the road she looked/*She looked the road up

Here most linguists would agree that *up* is a preposition that functions as the *head of the *prepositional phrase *up the road. See also* PREPOSITIONAL VERB.

2. The word *to* when used before an *infinitive. Sometimes called the *infinitival particle *to*.

To is generally a *preposition (as in *ten to six, go to Oxford*), and is sometimes regarded as an *adverb (e.g. *Brandy might bring him to*). Historically the word *to* before an infinitive is a preposition, but its grammar is different from that of the preposition *to*—most notably in that the latter, if followed by a verb, requires this verb to be an *-*ing* form, and does not permit the infinitive. Contrast:

We look forward *to* your visit

We look forward *to* seeing you } *to* = preposition

We hope *to* see you soon

*We look forward *to* see you soon } *to* = infinitival particle

3. pragmatic particle: *see* FILLER (2).

4. (Obsolete.) A member of a set of words including adverbs, prepositions, and *conjunctions.

Membership of this set varied according to different writers. It was often reckoned to include *articles, sometimes *determinatives (1), and sometimes even *affixes and *interjections.

See also NEGATIVE PARTICLE.

partition *See* PARTITIVE.

partitive (*n. & adj.*) (Denoting) (a word that is the first element in) a *phrase or *construction that expresses the relationship of a part to the whole (a **partition**), and that has the schematic form 'X of Y'. In this pattern X is a **partitive noun** (or **partitive**, or **unit noun**), e.g. *piece, bit, sort*, whereas Y is called the **partitive oblique** or **partitive genitive** (see also below).

The partitive construction often refers to a quantity or amount (**quantity partitive**):

a *piece* of paper   a *bit* of a problem
two *pieces* of paper   an *item* of clothing

but can also indicate quality (**quality partitive**):

a *sort* of clown
a different *kind* of cheese
that *type* of person

Some words that are part of the second part of the construction (e.g. *grass, bread, sheep, dirt*) combine with a specific partitive noun:

a *blade* of grass   a *loaf* of bread
a *flock* of sheep   a *speck* of dirt

Partitives are useful because they provide a means of individuating *uncount nouns:

three *slices* of bacon (*three bacons)
an interesting *piece* of information (*an interesting information)

When the second noun in a similar structure is *plural, the first noun denotes not a part, but a collection of items, individuals, animals, etc.:

a *bunch* of flowers   a *crowd* of people
a *clump* of trees   a *flock* of sheep

Some of these nouns are in fact *collective nouns, and are so classified in some grammatical models. Partitives can also denote containers:

a *packet* of cigarettes
a *sack* of potatoes
a *teaspoon(ful)* of sugar

Pronouns with *indefinite meaning in partitive constructions are sometimes labelled **indefinite partitives**. This set includes *many, few, some*, etc.

● **partitively**.

●● **partitive fused-head**: *see* FUSION.

●● **partitive genitive**: this can refer either to the *of*-phrase in the partitive construction, as above, or to a *genitive that indicates that of which something is part, rather than a possession, e.g. *the baby's eyes, the earth's surface*.

part of speech *See* WORD CLASS.

passival A now disused *progressive construction which is interpreted in the same way as a *passive construction by virtue of its subject carrying the *semantic role of *patient. Perhaps the chiefly American English *I'm hurting* (i.e. 'something is hurting me') can be viewed as a relic (or modern reincarnation) of this construction.

> 1998 D. DENISON Before it became possible to combine the progressive with the passive . . ., certain verbs could be used in the active progressive in a sense which corresponded to a passive. Visser uses the label **passival** for this notionally but not formally passive construction.

See also MEDIOPASSIVE; MIDDLE VERB.

passive (*adj.*) Of a *verb, *clause, *construction, etc.: designating an exponent of the grammatical category of *voice whereby the grammatical *subject 'undergoes', 'experiences', or 'receives' the action denoted by the verb. Contrasted with *active.

(*n.*) A construction (*verb phrase, clause, or sentence) in which the referent of the grammatical subject typically 'undergoes', 'experiences', or 'receives' the action of the verb (i.e. is its *patient). Contrasted with active.

The term is sometimes applied to the *past participle form of *lexical verbs in such constructions.

In formal terms, a passive construction contains a form of the **passive auxiliary** *be* (or *get*: see GET-PASSIVE) combined with a past participle, as in:

> The window *was shattered* by my neighbour's son

The *agent is mentioned in the *by-phrase. Passive constructions with a *by*-phrase are sometimes called **long passives**. Contrast the example above with its active counterpart:

My neighbour's son shattered the window

In some cases, mention of an agent is unlikely or impossible:

Churchill was born in 1874

A passive construction with no overtly expressed agent is called an **agentless passive**, **non-agentive passive**, or **short passive**. The agent is often omitted because it is unimportant or unknown, e.g.

Rome was not built in a day

Alternatively, the identity of the agent is deliberately concealed, sometimes for *rhetorical (1) reasons, e.g.

This church has been described as the most beautiful of its kind in Britain

The examples above involve **finite passive constructions**. The italicized clause in the following example exemplifies a **non-finite passive construction**:

He wanted *to be elected to the post*

In the *catenative-auxiliary analysis, the following examples also involve non-finite passive constructions, functioning as *complements of *modal verbs:

Dinner will *be served* by the catering staff
Trespassers may *be prosecuted* by the police
Mistakes cannot *be rectified* by the company

The active counterparts of these sentences are as follows:

The catering staff will serve dinner
The police may prosecute trespassers
The company cannot rectify mistakes

It is typically constructions headed by transitive verbs that take passive forms, since the grammatical subject of a passive construction corresponds to the object of a transitive verb in an active construction. However, not all active structures have a passive counterpart:

Blue suits you/*You are suited by blue
Those people lack confidence/*Confidence is lacked by those people

There are also passive constructions which do not have active counterparts, e.g.

They are said to be very intelligent/*People say them to be very intelligent

Some passive sentences are ambiguous. Thus *The opera house was finished in 1980*, out of context, is most likely to have an actional meaning referring to the building activity, namely 'the building work was completed in 1980'. This is called an **actional passive**. But it could also have a statal meaning, i.e. 'the building was in a finished state in 1980'. This is called a **statal passive**. In an actional passive the string *be* + past participle clearly forms a passive construction, whereas in a statal passive *be* is a *copular verb and the *-ed/-en* form is an adjective. The statal passive is sometimes called *pseudo-passive or **adjectival passive**.

• **passively, passivity**.

•• **prepositional passive**: This label is applied to the passive counterparts of constructions involving *prepositional verbs, *phrasal-prepositional verbs, and other similar constructions, e.g. *He was looked after by his grandmother*; *Such behaviour will not be put up with*; *This bed was slept in by Shakespeare*.

See also ACTIVE; AGENT; *BY*-PHRASE; DOUBLE PASSIVE; *GET*-PASSIVE; MEDIOPASSIVE; MIDDLE VERB; PASSIVAL; PATIENT; PSEUDO-PASSIVE; QUASI-; SEMANTIC ROLE; SEMI-PASSIVE; STATIVE; TRANSFORMATION; VOICE.

passive auxiliary *be* *See* PASSIVE.

passive infinitive *See* INFINITIVE.

passive participle *See* PASSIVE; PAST PARTICIPLE; VOICE.

passivize Convert into the *passive; be subject to conversion into the passive.

> 1984 F. R. PALMER We can passivize the main clause with PERSUADE, but not with WANT:

> *The doctor was persuaded to examine John*
> **The doctor was wanted to examine John*

• **passivizable, passivization**.
This group of terms was coined by Noam Chomsky.

past (*n. & adj.*)
   1. (Occurring in) the past, as in the expression *past *situation*, for example. Contrasted with *present (1).
   2. (A *tense or *inflectional form of a verb) typically expressing *anteriority. The grammatical label **past tense** is typically used of a *verb form that refers to a situation that took place in the past. However, this association can be misleading. While the past tense typically refers to past time, it can also be used hypothetically. To put it differently, it can denote **modal remoteness** (hence the alternative labels **hypothetical past**, **modal past**, and **modal preterite**), i.e. mark unreality, non-factuality, and so on:

> If I *had* my way, I would abolish this organization
> I wish I *knew*

The clause in which a modal past occurs is sometimes called a **modal preterite clause**.

The past tense can also be used for **social distancing** (the *attitudinal past):

> *Could* you lend me some money?
>
> I *wanted* to ask you something

With no further label, the phrase *past of a verb* designates the tense (the past tense), or the morphologically marked form which in regular verbs always ends in *-ed*, and which is normally listed second when verb forms are given (e.g. *complete, completed, completed*; *paint, painted, painted*). *Irregular verbs often display a vowel modification (e.g. *sing, sang, sung*), but not always (e.g. *put, put, put*).

In some frameworks the *perfect is regarded as a (secondary) past tense. *see* PRIMARY *tense*.

- **past continuous (tense)**: *see* PAST PROGRESSIVE; PROGRESSIVE.
- **past definite**: *see* DEFINITE.
- **past futurate**: *see* FUTURATE.
- **past imperfect**: *see* IMPERFECT.
- **past-in-the-future**: *see* FUTURE PERFECT; PAST PARTICIPLE.
- **past-in-the-past**: *see* PAST PERFECT.
- **past participle**: *see* PAST PARTICIPLE.
- **past perfect (tense)**: *see* PAST PERFECT.
- **past progressive (tense)**: *see* PROGRESSIVE.
- **past simple tense, simple past tense**, or **simple preterite**: this refers to a past tense form of a verb used on its own, e.g. *They <u>bought</u> a new house*.

See also BACKSHIFT; CONDITION; FUTURATE; FUTURE IN THE PAST; NON-PAST; PERFECT; PRESENT PERFECT; PRIMARY *tense*.

past participial clause *See* -ED CLAUSE.

past participle The form of a *verb which is used in *passive and *perfect *constructions, and sometimes in front of *nouns.
Examples:

> I have *looked* everywhere to find my keys
>
> The pancakes were *eaten* by my kids
>
> *lost* property

In *regular verbs the past participle ends in the same *-ed* inflection as the *past tense, and is called the *-*ed* form (or *-ed* **participle**) by some grammarians; others prefer the label *-*en* form (based on the distinctive ending of certain *irregular verbs such as *spoken, driven*), so as to distinguish it more clearly from the past tense *inflection.

The past participle is the third form listed when verb forms are given in dictionaries (e.g. *create, created, created; see, saw, seen*).

Some grammarians refer to the participle in the passive construction as the **passive participle**, even though inflectionally it is indistinguishable from the past participle.

In combination with the perfect auxiliary *have*, the past participle can signify *perfective meaning or completion (*I have finished the essay*), but is not restricted to past time; for example, *You'll have forgotten my message by this time next year* exemplifies a **past-in-the-future** (*see* FUTURE PERFECT).

•• **past participle clause**: *see* -ED CLAUSE.

•• **past participle construction**: *see* -ED CLAUSE.

Compare -ED CLAUSE; PARTICIPIAL ADJECTIVE; PARTICIPLE.

past perfect A *construction (*tense in some frameworks) formed with *had* (or *'d*) + a *past participle. Also called **before-past**, **pluperfect**, **past-in-the-past**, and **preterite perfect**.

With no further label, 'past perfect' refers to a simple active construction, e.g. *I had forgotten about the concert when Clare arrived to pick me up.*

Past perfect progressive and **past perfect passive** constructions (tenses), and combinations of the two, also occur:

We *had been wondering* about that, when the letter arrived

The matter *had been overlooked*

It *had been being compiled* by hand

In general, the past perfect refers to a time earlier than some other past reference time. But like other so-called *past (2) tenses, the past perfect in a subordinate clause may signify hypothetical or counterfactual meaning (something contrary to fact), called the **modal past perfect**:

If you *had told* me before now, I could have helped

If you *had been coming* tomorrow, you would have met my mother

The past perfect may also stress *perfectiveness or completion, as in *They waited until I had finished.*

Compare ASPECT.

See also BACKSHIFT; MODAL REMOTENESS; PAST; PLUPLUPERFECT.

past perfect passive *See* PAST PERFECT.

past perfect progressive *See* PAST PERFECT.

past progressive The *construction (*tense in some frameworks) formed with a past form of the verb *be* + an *-ing* form.

Examples:

It *was raining*

We *were waiting*

They *were being* interrogated

The last example involves a **past progressive passive** (or **past continuous passive**).

See also PROGRESSIVE.

past simple tense The *past (2) tense form of a verb used on its own, as in We <u>watched</u> a film last night. Also called **simple past (tense)** and **simple preterite**.

See PAST (2); SIMPLE (3).

past subjunctive *See* SUBJUNCTIVE; TENSE.

past tense *See* PAST.

path A *semantic role that denotes the trajectory along which an entity travels.

2002 R. HUDDLESTON & G. K. PULLUM et al. In the central case where the theme moves, as in [*She ran from the post office via the railway station to the bus-stop*], the starting-point is the **source** (*the post office*), the endpoint is the **goal** (*the bus-stop*), and the intermediate point is the **path** (*the railway station*).

patient A *semantic role assigned to an *argument which denotes an entity that is acted upon, or affected in some way by the action expressed by the verb. Also called **undergoer**, and often not distinguished from *theme (2).

In some frameworks, patient is equated with *affected.

pattern A (regular) syntactic configuration or *construction in which elements of language (*words, *phrases, *clauses, etc.) combine to form larger units.

At the syntactic level, clause structure can functionally be analysed in terms of a comparatively small set of patterns that are determined by the type of verb involved in the containing clause, as follows: *subject–*verb (SV; with an *intransitive verb), subject–verb–*object (SVO; with a *transitive verb), subject–verb–*complement (SVC; with a *linking verb), subject–verb–object–object (SVOO; with a *ditransitive verb), and subject–verb–object–complement (SVOC; with a *complex transitive verb).

Where only the verb's internal complements are concerned, we speak of *complementation patterns. Individual verbs can be said to be part of complementation patterns. For example, both *want* and *wish* can be followed by (an object +) a *to*-infinitive: *I want (you) to go, I wish (you) to* *go.* But only *wish* can be used in the pattern verb + *that*-clause. So we can say *I wish that you would go,* but not **I want that you (would) go.* Thus *want* and *wish* occur in different complementation patterns.

In a similar way we can speak of **noun patterns,** such that some nouns can be followed by clauses (e.g. *a determination to succeed, the fact that the earth is round*), by prepositional phrases (e.g. *love of money*), etc.; of **adjective patterns** (e.g. *keen to help, thoughtful of you, sorry (that) I spoke*); and so on.

Compare COLLIGATION; CONSTRUCTION; CO-OCCURRENCE.

paucal Implying a small number or amount. Contrasted with *multal.

In some detailed classifications of *pronouns and *determinatives (1), the label paucal is given to a subset of words with a *quantifying meaning: *a few, certain, fewer, fewest, a little, less, least.* The term is specifically used when describing languages that have a *number system with more categories than *singular and *plural.

P-bar (P′) category *See* X-BAR SYNTAX.

PDE An abbreviation for *Present-Day English.

pedagogical grammar *See* GRAMMAR.

perception verb One of a set of *verbs denoting the use of one of the physical senses. Also called **perceptual verb** or **verb of perception.** Grammatically, perception verbs typically occur in two *patterns:

I heard him sing

I heard him singing

Other verbs that fit both these patterns are *feel, listen (to), look (at), notice, observe, perceive, see,* and *watch.* Although it is not a perception verb, *have* also fits the pattern. Some other verbs occur in one or the other of these patterns, but not both.

perfect (*n. & adj.*) (A *construction, or a *tense in some models) that indicates that a *situation took place before some stated or implied time, implemented by a form of the perfect auxiliary *have* plus a *past participle, e.g.

He *has/had won*

I will *have finished* by next week

Having said that, . . .

The *present perfect indicates *current relevance.

Some linguists prefer to refer to this construction as **perfect aspect** (or, less felicitously, *perfective aspect) rather than tense. Perfect aspect contrasts with *progressive aspect.

Linguists who recognise **perfect tenses** often, though not always, contrast them with *progressive tenses and *simple tenses.

Contrast IMPERFECT; IMPERFECTIVE; PERFECTIVE.

See also ASPECT; FUTURE PERFECT; PAST; PAST PERFECT; PRESENT; PRESENT PERFECT; PRIMARY *tense*.

perfect auxiliary A form of the *verb *have* which is followed by a *past participle and used in the *perfect construction, e.g.

I *have* seen that film already

They believe a young girl to *have* cracked the secret code (*see* PERFECT INFINITIVE)

She will *have* been seen by the consultant

perfect infinitive A *perfect construction formed by an *infinitive form of the perfect *auxiliary *have* followed by a *past participle, e.g.

She seems to *have forgotten* what he said earlier

To *have shouted* at the children was unforgivable

You can't *have been* serious about that

See also ASPECT; PRESENT PERFECT; PRIMARY *tense*; TENSE.

perfective

1. (*adj.*) *Semantics*. Signalling perfective meaning, i.e. viewing a *situation as complete, without reference to its internal parts, e.g. *They watched television*.

2002 R. HUDDLESTON & G. K. PULLUM et al. With perfective aspectuality, the situation is presented in its totality, as a complete whole; it is viewed, as it were, from the outside, without reference to any temporal structure or segmentation.

2. (*n. & adj.*) (Designating) the grammatical *aspect that expresses a complete *situation without reference to its internal parts. Some linguists prefer to reserve this sense to languages that make extensive use of perfective aspect, e.g. the Slavic languages. Often infelicitously used interchangeably with *perfect aspect (see 3 below).

3. (In e.g. CGEL.) The same as *perfect.

• **perfectiveness**.

Compare IMPERFECT; IMPERFECTIVE.

perfect progressive *See* TENSE.

performance *See* COMPETENCE.

performative (*n. & adj.*) (Designating or belonging to) an *utterance that constitutes an action in itself.

The term is used in *Speech Act Theory (first developed by the philosopher J. L. Austin) to describe utterances or written statements that 'do' something (i.e. perform an action of some kind), e.g.

I advise you to reconsider

I promise to pay the bearer on demand the sum of five pounds

I name this ship *The Dolphin*

Performative utterances can be divided into **explicit performatives**, where the *verb specifies which action is being performed, as in the examples above, and **implicit performatives** (or **primary performatives**), where the action (e.g. promising) is merely implicit (e.g. *The bank will pay the bearer* . . .).

Performative utterances were originally contrasted with **constative statements**, which state that something is or is not the case, and which therefore, unlike performatives, have a truth-value (*see* TRUTH-CONDITIONAL SEMANTICS). Austin later realized that in a sense every utterance carries out some sort of action, and as a result is underlyingly performative. For example, when I say *It is hot today*, the underlying action is one of 'making a statement'.

In ordinary grammatical usage the term is often restricted to verbs that explicitly perform an action, e.g. *advise, apologize, beg, confess, promise, swear, warn* (**performative verbs**). The term includes verbs that in a more detailed analysis of speech acts are covered by the term **declaration** (as in *I name this ship* . . . , *I declare the meeting closed*). It is usually said that such verbs are performatives only when used in the *first person of the *present tense, and that in other contexts such verbs are merely reporting a performative act (e.g. *She advised him to reconsider*). But this may be an overly narrow definition of what constitutes a performative utterance.

Austin first used the term *performatory* (in 1949), but later substituted *performative* (in 1955).

Compare ILLOCUTION; PERLOCUTION.

period (In AmE.) The same as *full stop.

periphrasis The use of separate words to express a grammatical relationship that is also expressed by *inflection in other contexts.

Periphrasis is a common feature of *adjective and *adverb *comparison, where periphrastic phrases with *more* and *most* are an obligatory alternative to forms ending in *-er* and *-est* for longer adjectives and for most adverbs (*more beautiful, most oddly*). A choice between inflection and periphrasis is possible with some two-syllable adjectives, e.g. *It gets lovelier/more lovely every day*.

The term is sometimes applied to the formation of certain English *tenses, such as the *perfect tense, which is not expressed using a single inflected form, but through a combination of the perfect auxiliary *have* with a *past participle form of a verb. In other frameworks this combination would be called the perfect construction, rather than a tense.
- **periphrastic**.

   See also ANALYTIC (1).

perlocution The (intended or unintended) effect that a particular *speech act may have on a hearer. Contrasted with *locution and *illocution.
- **perlocutionary**: designating an act of this kind.

   1977 J. LYONS By the illocutionary force of an utterance is to be understood its status as a promise, a threat, a request, a statement, an exhortation, etc. By its perlocutionary effect is meant its effect upon the beliefs, attitudes or behaviour of the addressee and, in certain cases, its consequential effect upon some state-of-affairs within the control of the addressee . . . It is the intended perlocutionary effect that has generally been confused with illocutionary force.

•• **perlocutionary act**: a speech act that functions as a perlocution.

permanent *See* TEMPORARY.

permission One of the main meanings of *deontic modality, along with *obligation. Example:

   Can/may I go now?

person A grammatical category used, together with *number, in the classification of *pronouns (*my/mine, your/yours,* etc.), related *determinatives (1), and *verb forms, according to whether they indicate the speaker, the addressee, or a third party; one of the three distinctions within this category.

A threefold contrast between *first, *second person, and *third person is made, and is particularly distinct in the *personal pronouns. *Be* is unique among English verbs in having three distinctive person forms in the *present tense (*am, is, are*) and two in the *past tense (*was, were*). Other verbs have a distinctive form only for the third person *singular of the present tense (e.g. *has, does, wants,* etc., as opposed to *have, do, want,* etc.).
- **personal**: denoting one of the three persons.

   Compare IMPERSONAL; NON-PERSONAL.

personal pronoun A *pronoun belonging to a set that shows contrasts of *person, *gender, *number, and *case (though not every personal pronoun shows all these distinctions).

The personal pronouns are:

1st person:	I/me; we/us
2nd person:	you
3rd person:	he/him, she/her, it; they/them

*Reflexive pronouns (*myself, ourselves*, etc.) and *possessive pronouns (*mine, ours*, etc.) are also included.

Pre-nominal possessives (*my, our*, etc.) are sometimes analysed as pronouns, but more often as *determiners (2), or (infelicitously) as both. *Reciprocal pronouns (*each other, one another*) do not have different person forms, and are therefore not regarded as personal pronouns.

phase

1. In some modern terminology phase is preferred to *aspect or *tense in describing the meaning of the *perfect construction.

> 1987 F. PALMER Phase is best seen as the marker of a complex set of time relations. Though there are several possibilities, all of them share the characteristic that what is involved is a period of time that began before, but continued right up to, a point of time which may itself be present or past according to the tense used.

2. (In *Systemic Grammar.) A particular kind of semantic relationship between verbs in a sequence.

phatic *Sociolinguistics*. Of speech: used to convey general sociability, rather than any real meaning. Observations about the weather (*Nice day, isn't it?*) are often phatic.

The term is loosely derived from the anthropologist Bronislaw Malinowski's coinage *phatic communion* understood as 'speech communication used to establish social relationships' (1923), in which *phatic* has the etymological sense 'of, or pertaining to, speech'.

phenomenon *See* SENSER.

philology The science of language.

This is a traditional term, used particularly for the study of *historical linguistic change and comparison between languages. Terms favoured today include *comparative linguistics and *contrastive linguistics. In the

wider sense it has been superseded by *linguistics, though not in many
continental European universities (e.g. in Germany and Spain).
- **philological, philologically, philologist.**

  1935 J. R. FIRTH The evolutionary and comparative method had been used by
  philologists in the eighteenth century. Comparative Philology was, in fact, the
  first science to employ this method.

phrasal Consisting of, or pertaining to, a *phrase.
- **phrasally.**
- **•• phrasal adjective/phrasal-prepositional adjective:** *see* ADJECTIVE.

phrasal auxiliary verb A two- or three-part *verb based on an
*auxiliary and having some of the same grammatical characteristics, e.g.

| be able to | be about to |
| be going to | have to |

The term is an alternative to the more usual *semi-auxiliary, although
possibly not exactly synonymous.

In some models the sequences above are not regarded as verbs. For
example, in OMEG *have (to)* and *be going (to)* are analysed as *modal
lexical verbs which license a *to-infinitive as complement.

See also MARGINAL MODAL.

phrasal-prepositional adjective *See* ADJECTIVE.

phrasal-prepositional verb A *multi-word *verb consisting of a
*lexical verb, an adverb, and a preposition (with the latter two sometimes
labelled differently, e.g. as *particles, depending on the analytic framework). Also called **three-part verb or three-part word.** Examples:

  We're *looking forward to* the holidays
  You shouldn't *put up with* that sort of treatment

Some phrasal-prepositional verbs take a direct object, e.g. *it* in the
example below:

  I *put it down to* his ill-health

In other frameworks (e.g. OMEG) a 'phrasal-prepositional verb' is
simply either an intransitive verb that *licenses an intransitive PP (prepositional phrase) and a transitive PP as *complements, or a transitive verb
that licenses an NP (noun phrase), an intransitive PP, and a transitive PP
as complements:

We're *looking* [PP forward]
[PP to the holidays]
You shouldn't *put* [PP up]
[PP with that sort of treatment] } (intransitive verb with an intransitive PP and a transitive PP as complements)

I *put* [NP it] [PP down]
[PP to his ill-health] } (transitive verb with an NP, an intransitive PP, and a transitive PP as complements)

Compare MULTI-WORD VERB; PHRASAL VERB; PREPOSITIONAL VERB.

phrasal verb

1. A *multi-word *verb consisting of a verb plus one or more *particles and operating syntactically as a single unit. (Also called **compound verb**, **verb-particle construction**.)

Thus defined, phrasal verb is an umbrella term for different kinds of multi-word verb. Some analysts make metaphorical (or idiomatic) meaning a criterion for phrasal verbs, excluding combinations which have a transparent literal meaning. However, it is not always easy to draw the line. For example, *get in* seems literal when the implied object is a vehicle (e.g. *I got in and drove off*); but is it literal or metaphorical when the meaning is 'into one's own home' (e.g. *I usually get in by 7 p.m.*) or 'into Parliament' (e.g. *He got in by a tiny majority*)?

2. (In CGEL and related frameworks.) A multi-word verb consisting of a *lexical verb and a *particle (also labelled *adverb or adverb particle), regarded as operating syntactically and semantically as a unit. Contrasted with *prepositional verb and *phrasal-prepositional verb.

Phrasal verbs can be intransitive:

The plane *took off*

I don't know—I *give up*!

or transitive, where the particle (adverb) can follow the object:

Take off your coat/*Take* your coat/it *off*

I've *given up* chocolate/I've *given* chocolate/it *up*

In other frameworks (e.g. OMEG) a 'phrasal verb' is simply either an intransitive verb that *licenses an intransitive PP (prepositional phrase) as its *complement, or a transitive verb that licenses an NP (noun phrase) and an intransitive PP as its complements:

The plane took [pp off]   intransitive verb with an
I don't know—I give [pp up]   intransitive PP as complement

Take [np your coat / it]
[pp off] / Take off [pp your coat]
I've given [np chocolate / it]   transitive verb with an NP and an
[pp up] / I've given   intransitive PP as complements
[pp up] [np chocolate]

Compare MULTI-WORD VERB; PHRASAL-PREPOSITIONAL VERB;
PREPOSITIONAL VERB.

phrase

1. A linguistic unit at a level between the *word and the *clause.

In modern grammar various kinds of phrase are recognized. The most
central types are *noun phrase, *verb phrase, *adjective phrase, *adverb
phrase, and *prepositional phrase. In theoretical frameworks we also find
*determiner phrase and *determinative phrase (both abbreviated as DP),
and a further range of phrases headed by *functional categories: **inflection
phrase (IP), complementizer phrase (CP), tense phrase (TP)**, and so on.
The latter are called **functional phrases**. Phrases must be properly headed,
i.e. *endocentric, such that a phrase XP has X as its *head. Thus noun
phrases are headed by nouns, verb phrases are headed by verbs, and so on.

●● **phrase marker**: *see* TREE DIAGRAM.

●● **phrase structure grammar**: *See* PHRASE STRUCTURE GRAMMAR.

2. In *Systemic Grammar, phrases are distinguished from *groups.
A group is a *head word expanded with *modification, whereas a phrase is
a reduced clause. Thus *a small town in Germany* is a *nominal group (not
a noun phrase, as in other models) which is an expansion of *town*, but *in
Germany* is a *prepositional phrase, because it can be expanded into
a clause, namely *which is in Germany*.

See also FIXED PHRASE.

phrase structure grammar (PSG)

A cover term for *generative,
*monostratal theoretical approaches to *grammar that make use of ab-
stract representations of the structure, meaning, and phonology of sentences. *Generalized Phrase Structure Grammar and *Head-Driven Phrase
Structure Grammar are examples of phrase structure grammar.

See also CHOMSKYAN; GENERATIVE GRAMMAR (2); GOVERNMENT-BINDING
THEORY; GRAMMAR; MINIMALIST PROGRAM; PRINCIPLES AND PARAMETERS
THEORY; STANDARD THEORY; TRANSFORMATIONAL GRAMMAR.

phrase structure rule Originating in *Generative Grammar (2), these are the *rules that compose *phrases and *clauses. As an example, the following rule specifies that a *verb phrase (2) consists of a verb which may optionally be followed by one or two noun phrases.

VP → V (NP) (NP)

Also called **rewrite rule**.

phrase-word *Morphology*. A *word formed from a *phrase.

This is a term occasionally used to label a variety of *lexical items derived from phrases, especially phrases used attributively, e.g.

his *down-to-earth* manner
a *couldn't-care-less* attitude
a *once-in-a-lifetime* offer
the *carrot-and-stick* method

It may also include words derived from phrases by affixation (e.g. *up-to-dateness*) and *phrasal verbs.

pidgin A grammatically simplified form of a language, with a restricted *vocabulary taken from several languages, which is no one's and which is used as a means of communication between people not sharing a common language.

Pidgins based on various European languages developed in the heyday of colonial expansion. English-based pidgins evolved particularly on Pacific and Atlantic trade routes. A pidgin that gains a wider currency may develop into a kind of *lingua franca* for a region. A pidgin that becomes a mother tongue is called a *creole.

The term derives from **pidgin English**, the name of a trade jargon used from the 17th century onwards between the British and Chinese. It is believed to be an alteration of *business*.

pied piping The placing of a *head and its associated *complement (typically a *preposition and its *complement) at the beginning of a clause, instead of *stranding the head without its complement at the end of the clause, e.g.

To whom are you talking? (Cf. Who are you talking *to*?)
Here's the book *about which* I was telling you. (Cf. Here's the book which I was telling you *about*)

The term originates in *Generative Grammar (2), and is humorously based on the story of the Pied Piper, who, by playing a pipe, lured rats from the German town of Hamelin.

place A semantic category used especially in the classification of certain *phrases that answer the question 'where?', for example *prepositional phrases (e.g. *in the garden, by the lake*) and *adverb phrases (e.g. *here, there*; though note that some grammars, e.g. CaGEL, regard the latter as *prepositional phrases).

This is one of the traditional categories of meaning that is still used today, along with *time and *manner. An alternative label is *space.

plain case A case that is not *accusative, *genitive, or *nominative.

plain form (In CaGEL.) The *base form of a *verb when it is not a *plain present tense, e.g. in *infinitives. For example, in *He likes to <u>eat</u> pretzels* the verb *eat* is in the plain form. By contrast, in *They <u>like</u> to eat pretzels* the verb *like* is in the plain present tense.

　　Compare PLAIN PRESENT.

plain grade *See* ABSOLUTE (1).

plain present (In CaGEL.) A present *tense *verb form which occurs in the shape of the *plain form (or *base form) of a verb. For example, in *We <u>hope</u> to see you soon* the verb *hope* is a plain present tense form.

　　Compare PLAIN FORM.

pleonasm The use of more words than are needed to convey a particular meaning, e.g. *see with one's eyes, at this moment in time.*
● **pleonastic**.

　　1898 H. SWEET The pleonastic genitive, as in *he is a friend of my brother's.*

The construction described in this quotation would now be called the *double genitive.

pluperfect The same as *past perfect.
　　See also PLUPLUPERFECT.

plupluperfect (*n. & adj.*) (Designating or consisting of) a *verb phrase (1) that contains an additional, superfluous *auxiliary, and is used as an alternative to the *past perfect.

This is heard colloquially and is occasionally written, but is regarded as non-standard. The construction in full is *had have* + *past participle, but it is commonly used in shortened form:

　　If we*'d have found* an unsafe microwave oven, we would have named it
　　(advertisement in the *Daily Telegraph*, 9 December 1989)

We all take TV for granted, but if it *hadn't have been* for the pioneers at
Alexandra Palace it might never have happened (speaker quoted in the *Daily
Telegraph*, 13 December 1992)

The term was coined by I. H. Watson (1985).

1985 I. H. WATSON Please comment—however briefly—on the proliferation
of the use of the plupluperfect tense (I cannot think what else to call it).
An example is: 'If he had have gone . . .'

plural (*n. & adj.*)

1. (A *word or form) denoting more than one instance of a particular
entity. Contrasted with *singular.

The term is one of several covered by the more general term *number.
In English, plural applies to certain *nouns, *pronouns, *determinatives
(1), and *verbs. In general, *count nouns have distinct plural forms, which
in regular nouns end in *-s* or *-es*. Nouns with irregular plurals include
some of *Old English origin (e.g. *feet, children*), *zero plurals (e.g. *sheep,
deer*), and some *foreign plurals (e.g. *crises, errata*).

A few nouns are **plural only** (*see* PLURALE TANTUM). Many of these end
in *-s* (e.g. *premises, scissors*), though some are unmarked (e.g. *cattle,
people*).

Some *etymologically plural words are now increasingly used as
singulars: e.g. *The data is corrupted*, rather than *The data are corrupted*.

With certain grammatical categories, the plural versus singular contrast
leads to constraints. For example, some determinatives (1) are restricted to
use with plural nouns (e.g. *few, several*) or singular nouns (e.g. *a, every*);
and when a (pro)noun as head of a noun phrase functioning as subject is
plural, there must be *agreement between it and the verb (cf. *She is in
Chicago/They are in Chicago; The door was shut/The doors were shut*).

2. (A noun) ending in *-s/-es*. (Also called **plural in form**.)

Some grammarians, and many dictionaries, label nouns ending in *-s/-es*
'plural' or 'plural in form', even those which are never plural in syntax
(e.g. *news, measles, physics*).

Compare COLLECTIVE NOUN.

plurale tantum (Pronounced /plʊəˈreɪlɪ ˈtæntəm/. Plural **pluralia tantum**.) A noun used only as a plural.

This is sometimes defined as a noun which at least in a particular sense
is used only in the plural. Theoretically this would include words such as
people or *police*. Usually, however, it is exemplified by words with the
plural ending *-s*. They are of three types:

(i) words for tools, articles of clothing, etc. that consist of two parts: *secateurs*, *trousers*, *binoculars*;

(ii) words that are never singular: *clothes*, *riches*, *thanks*;

(iii) words that with a particular meaning are always plural, though there may be a singular form with a different meaning: *arms* = weapons, *regards* = best wishes.

Some grammarians label type (i) **binary nouns** or *summation plurals, reserving plurale tantum (or *aggregate noun or, more simply, a term such as **plural-only**) for (ii) and (iii).

Compare SINGULARE TANTUM.

pluralize Make (a word) *plural; (of a word etc.) become plural, take a plural form.
● **pluralization**.

polarity A phenomenon whereby two opposites of *positive and *negative exist.

The term is particularly applied to the difference between positive and negative *clauses, and is sometimes extended to cover more general oppositions (e.g. *good* vs *bad*, *up* vs *down*).

Non-negative (positive) clauses display **positive polarity** (e.g. *I left work late last night*), whereas negative clauses display **negative polarity** (*I didn't leave work late last night*).

●● **negative**/*see* ASSERTIVE.

●● **reversed polarity**: this occurs when a *tag added to a positive clause is negative (*They won the match, didn't they?*) or when a tag added to a negative clause is positive (*They didn't win the match, did they?*); hence **reversed polarity tag** (*see* TAG).

See also ASSERTIVE.

polyseme *Semantics*. A *word that has multiple meanings, i.e. displays *polysemy.

Many English words have several meanings which are all uses of the same word that have grown apart over time, e.g.

draw 'cause to move in a certain direction', 'produce a picture', 'finish a game with an equal score'

flat 'apartment', 'note lowered by a semitone', 'piece of stage scenery'

plain 'unmistakable', 'unsophisticated', 'not good-looking'

Theoretically, a polyseme, with meanings which are all ultimately related, is distinguished from a set of *homonyms, which are different words with distinct meanings which have all come to have the same form, e.g.

pile (i) 'heap', (ii) 'beam driven into ground', (iii) 'soft surface of fabric'

In practice it is very difficult for a person who is not a historical linguist to tell whether a word with several meanings is a case of polysemy or homonymy, or a mixture of both; and in some cases evidence is lacking by which even scholars could decide.

See also POLYSEMY.

polysemy The phenomenon of possessing multiple meanings. Also called **polysemia**.

> 2009 D. MINKOVA & R. STOCKWELL *Polysemy* refers to a single word with several different meanings. The differentiation from one into several meanings is most commonly a consequence of the change, usually over long time spans, from concrete to abstract meaning—i.e. increasingly figurative use of language.

• **polysemantic**, **polysemic**, **polysemous**: having several or multiple meanings.

> *See also* ANTONYM; HETERONYM; HOMONYM; HOMOPHONE; HYPONYM; MERONYM; POLYSEME; SYNONYM.

polysyndetic coordination A *coordination structure that contains two or more *coordinators, e.g.

> sand *and* sea *and* wind

> *See also* ASYNDETIC; SYNDETIC.

polysystemicism *See* FIRTHIAN.

popular etymology The same as *folk etymology.

> 1926 H. W. FOWLER It is true . . . that -*yard* [in *halyard*] is no better than a popular etymology corruption.

portmanteau word The same as a morphological *blend (1).

The term originates with Lewis Carroll's explanation in *Through the Looking-Glass* (1872) of the invented word *slithy* as a combination of 'lithe' and 'slimy': 'It's like a portmanteau—there are two meanings packed up into one word.'

position Any of the syntactic locations within a larger linguistic structure (e.g. a *phrase or *clause) in which a particular element can appear.

For example, we can say that *interrogative words are typically placed in clause-initial position, e.g.

> *What* did they decide?

- **positional**: of, pertaining to, or determined by position.
- **positionally**.

  Compare WORD ORDER.

  See also FINAL; INITIAL; MEDIAL.

positive (*n. & adj.*)

1. (A *word, *clause, or *sentence) that has no *negative marker. (Sometimes called *affirmative or *assertive.)

•• **positive clause:** a non-negative clause, i.e. a clause that does not contain *negation at the clausal level and typically takes a negative *tag question, e.g. *We bought some fish and chips, didn't we?* In *They were unlucky* we have negation, but it is subclausal, as is evidenced by the negative tag: *They were unlucky, weren't they?*

•• **positive polarity (item):** *see* ASSERTIVE.

  See also POLARITY.

2. The same as *absolute (1).

positive polarity (item) *See* ASSERTIVE.

possessive (*n. & adj.*) (A *word or *case) that indicates possession or ownership.

The possessive case of *nouns is also called the *genitive case, e.g. *boy's, boys', Mary's, the Smiths'.*

*Pronouns in the genitive case include the independent items *mine, yours, hers, his, ours,* etc., corresponding to *my, your,* etc. that occur before the *head in noun phrases. Some grammars include the latter items in the class of determiner (2); others regard them as **possessive pronouns**. More traditional grammars wrongly classify them as possessive *adjectives.

The basic meaning of the *verb *have* is sometimes described as possessive (as in *We have a house*) in contrast to its other meanings, especially the *dynamic (1) ones such as *have a bath, have dinner, have an operation, have a holiday, have fun.*

•• **possessive compound:** *see* BAHUVRIHI.

  See also APOSTROPHE.

possibility A semantic term used in the description of *modality, expressed typically by certain *modal verbs, and by some other elements (e.g. *nouns, *adjectives, *adverbs). We can distinguish *deontic, *epistemic, and *dynamic (2) possibility, e.g.

You *may* take a holiday later this month (deontic; i.e. 'I give you permission to take a holiday later this month')

It *may* rain later today (epistemic; i.e. 'it is possible that it will rain later today')

It *can* get hot in August (dynamic; i.e. 'it is possible for it to get hot in August')

There is a *possibility* that you will have to change your holiday plans (dynamic)

Compare NECESSITY.

Post-Bloomfieldian (*adj.*) Of, pertaining to, or characteristic of, a group of linguists who based their work on principles developed by the American linguist Leonard Bloomfield.

1993 P. H. MATTHEWS I will describe this school as 'Post-Bloomfieldian'. Many commentators have preferred to say 'Bloomfieldian', and, provided we remember that Bloomfield could have had no direct influence on its development from 1947 onwards, I have no wish to quarrel over labels.

(*n.*) A person belonging to the Post-Bloomfieldian group of linguists.

Compare BLOOMFIELDIAN.

post-creole Designating a community whose speech has developed beyond the *creole stage.

Coined by D. Decamp (1968).

postdeterminer (In CGEL.) A *determiner (2) that must follow any *predeterminer (2) or central determiner (2) in a noun phrase.

post-genitive *See* GENITIVE.

post-head adjunct (In OMEG.) A phrasal *adjunct that is positioned after a *head, e.g. *president elect*, *very happy indeed*, *quickly enough*. Also called **postmodifier**.

See also MODIFICATION; MODIFIER; POSTMODIFICATION; PRE-HEAD ADJUNCT.

postmodification The phenomenon of a dependent *phrase, *clause, etc. restricting the meaning of a preceding *head word through *modification, e.g. by ascribing a property to it. Contrasted with *premodification.

Postmodification can occur in all kinds of structures, and may take the form of phrases or clauses, e.g.

the house *on the heath* (noun postmodification by a *prepositional phrase)

That is the way *that we do things* (noun postmodification by a *relative clause)

Is that warm *enough*? (adjective postmodification by an *adverb phrase)

He speaks too quietly *for me to hear* (adverb postmodification by a *non-finite clause)

The functional label **postmodifier** is used for the italicized phrases in the examples above.

● **postmodify.**

See also MODIFIER; PREMODIFIER.

postmodifier A *modifier that follows its *head in *phrase structure, e.g. *the dog on the sofa*.

See also MODIFICATION; POSTMODIFICATION; PREMODIFICATION; PREMODIFIER.

postpone Place (a *word, *phrase, etc.) in a position further to the right in a *clause. *see* POSTPONEMENT.

●● **postponed identification**: *see* DISLOCATION.

Compare POSTPOSE.

See also CLEFT; EXTRAPOSITION; PSEUDO-CLEFT.

postponement The placing of a *word, *phrase, *clause, etc. in a position further to the right in a containing structure (typically a clause).

Postponement may occur to achieve the stylistic effect of giving *end-focus to a particular part of a message. Grammatical devices for postponement include *discontinuity, in which part of a noun phrase is postponed:

Everyone was delighted *except the chairman*

and *extraposition, which involves the displacement of a clause:

It is hardly surprising *that he did not like the architect's original plans*

In some models, *passive structures are treated as involving the postponement of an *agentive *subject to the end:

The building was opened *by the Prince*

Compare CLEFT; POSTPOSE; POSTPOSITION; PSEUDO-CLEFT.

postpose Place a *word, *phrase, etc. after the word that is being modified. *See also* POSTPOSITION.

Although *postposition is distinguished from *postponement, there is occasionally confusion between the two notions.

postposition

1. The positioning of a *word, *phrase, etc. after the word that it modifies. Any such word can be said to be **postposed** or **in postposition**:

I am a man *more sinned against than sinning*
the astronomer *royal*

2. A *word class whose members follow (rather than precede) their
*complements. Contrasted with *preposition.

In some languages (e.g. Japanese) the kinds of meaning and function
that prepositions have in English are exhibited by words that follow their
complements, and these are appropriately called postpositions (e.g. the
equivalent of *the bath in*, rather than *in the bath*). Such a class of words
does not exist in English, though some words, e.g. *ago* (as in *a month ago*),
notwithstanding (as in *his efforts notwithstanding*), and *enclitics (-*n't*, -*'s*)
are sometimes so described.

A preposition does not become a postposition just because in some
non-basic structure it apparently follows its *object or complement
(e.g. *What* are you looking *at?*).

• **postpositional**: (*n. & adj.*) (an element) that is positioned after the word
modified by it.

postpositive Characterized by *postposition; (of position) immediately
following, *postposed.

Postpositive and *postposed* are virtually synonymous, but the former is
the preferred term, to contrast with *attributive and *predicative in
describing the position of *adjectives. Postpositive position is obligatory
for adjectives modifying indefinite *pronouns and *adverbs (e.g. *nobody
special*, *somewhere quiet*), in certain set expressions (e.g. *heir apparent*,
the body politic), and with some adjectives with particular meanings
(e.g. *the members present*, *the parents involved*).

• **postpositively**.

1961 R. B. LONG Superlatives in *most* [e.g. *innermost, uppermost*, etc.] are now
felt as compounds in which a modifying auxiliary pronoun has been united,
postpositively, with a basic-form adjective head.

poverty of stimulus *See* LANGUAGE ACQUISITION DEVICE.

PP An abbreviation for *prepositional phrase or *preposition phrase.

pragmatic Of or pertaining to *pragmatics.
• **pragmatically**.
•• **pragmatic marker**: *see* DISCOURSE MARKER.
•• **pragmatic particle**: the same as *filler (2).

pragmatics The branch of *linguistics dealing with language in use.
Contrasted with *syntax and *semantics.

The term is defined in a variety of ways, but it is often used in connection with the communicative functions of language, in contrast to syntactic or semantic analysis. Thus *I've borrowed this book from the library* in different contexts may have the pragmatic implication *so I don't want to watch TV*, or *so I don't want to go out*, or even *I wasn't going to buy it*.

See also ILLOCUTION; RELEVANCE THEORY.

Prague School, the The name of a group of linguists belonging to the Linguistic Circle of Prague, founded in 1926, and others whom it has influenced, used with reference to the linguistic theories and methods initiated by them.

The effects of this school on the analysis of English have been considerable. It has been influential in the development of distinctive *feature analysis in phonology, and in the analysis of the *communicative dynamism of sentences, which is concerned with the differing amount of information that each *constituent contributes to the overall information content of a sentence.

• **Praguian**: of or pertaining to the Prague School.

See also COMMENT; FUNCTIONAL SENTENCE PERSPECTIVE; GIVEN; INFORMATION STRUCTURE; NEW; RHEME; THEME; TOPIC.

precise recoverability See RECOVERABILITY.

predeterminer

1. (In CaGEL.) A *function (1) label that is used to refer to an element that *modifies an entire noun phrase. Also called **predeterminer modifier**. Examples:

all the boats

both the governments

The form label used in CaGEL for the italicized items is *determinative (1).

2. (In CGEL.) A *form label used to refer to any *determiner (2) that precedes a *central (1) determiner in a noun phrase. The italicized items in the examples above also serve to illustrate this use of the term.

predicand (In CaGEL.) The (referent of the) *phrase of which something is *predicated.

For example, in *They appear uneasy*, the property of being uneasy is predicated of (the referent of) *they*, which is therefore the predicand.

predicate (*n.*) (Pronounced /ˈprɛdɪkət/.)

1. A *function label that refers to that part of a *sentence or *clause which is not the *subject. Formally the predicate is typically *realized as a *verb phrase (2). Examples:

subject	predicate
All good things	must come to an end
Attack	is the best form of defence
Familiarity	breeds contempt

The subject is not necessarily what the sentence is about, and the predicate is not always 'what is predicated about' the subject. For example, the grammatical subject in *It is raining* is empty of meaning, and 'is raining' is not predicated of this word.

Modern grammarians analyse predicate structure in various ways: for example, into components such as *verb, *object, *complement, and *adverbial, and into elements of *information structure such as *new (versus *given) or *comment (versus *topic). Grammatical distinctions are also made between the *operator and the rest of the *predication (2). In CaGEL the predicate is the *head of the clause. *Compare* PREDICATOR.

In some older grammar, *predicate* is used, rather than *predicative* (1), to describe an *adjective, *noun, or *pronoun when such a word is 'predicated of the subject', i.e. is used in predicative (1) position. For example:

He became mad (*mad* = predicate adjective)

Croesus was king (*king* = predicate noun)

I am he (*he* = predicate pronoun)

In modern terminology a constituent *licensed by a *linking verb is said to function as predicative *complement.

2. *Semantics.* In *logical semantics, specifically in **predicate calculus** (or **predicate logic**), the term refers to an entity (grammatically a verb, noun, adjective, etc.) that takes a number of *arguments.

Thus *fond* is an adjectival predicate which takes one argument, namely a PP-complement (a **one-place predicate**), whereas *devour* is a verbal predicate which takes two arguments, namely a subject and an object (a **two-place predicate**). The verb *tell* is a **three-place predicate**, and in *rain, snow*, etc. we arguably have **zero-place predicates**.

Grammarians who pursue this line of analysis may make this clear by using the term **syntactic predicate** when they are referring to a constituent of syntax (i.e. a predicate in sense 1).

See also ARGUMENT.

(*v.*) (Pronounced /ˈpredɪkeɪt/.) Assert (something) about a linguistic unit, typically the subject of a sentence.

predicate calculus *See* PREDICATE.

predicate logic *See* PREDICATE.

predication
1. What is predicated.

The term may be used as a rough synonym of *predicate (1), but predication is often used more theoretically to suggest the *proposition expressed by the actual words of the predicate.

2. (Specifically, in some models, e.g. CGEL.) A *predicate (1) minus its *operator.

> 1985 R. QUIRK et al. Simple sentences are traditionally divided into two major parts, a subject and a predicate . . . A more important division, in accounting for the relation between different sentence types, is that between OPERATOR and PREDICATION as two subdivisions of the predicate.

This analysis serves to emphasize that the operator and the rest of the predicate have distinct characteristics. For example, the operator is separated from the rest of the predicate in *interrogative clauses (e.g. *Are your parents flying home tomorrow?*); an operator can allow coordination of two predications (e.g. *I must [phone the airport]and [check flight times]*); and an operator can stand for a completely ellipted predication (e.g. *Yes, you should . . .*).

•• **predication adjunct**: *see* PREDICATION ADJUNCT.

•• **verb of incomplete predication**: an older term for a *linking verb.

predication adjunct
An *adjunct that applies to only part of a *sentence, namely the *predication (2) (or *predicate (1)). Also called **VP-adjunct**. Example:

> Beth ran down the street fast (*fast* applies to the way Beth ran down the street)
> *Compare* SENTENCE ADJUNCT.

•• **obligatory predication adjunct**: (in CGEL) an adjunct *licensed by a verb, e.g.

> They live *in Hong Kong*
> We are *here*

In other frameworks the italicized phrases are by definition *complements, precisely because they are obligatory.

•• **optional predication adjunct**: (in CGEL) an adjunct that is not licensed by a verb, e.g.

> They ran down the hill *recklessly*

predicative

1. Of a syntactic *position: occurring after a *linking verb. Contrasted with *attributive.

The term is particularly used in the classification of *adjectives. Most adjectives (or adjective phrases) can be used in both attributive and predicative positions (e.g. *a fine day, the day was fine; an expensive restaurant, the restaurant looks expensive*). But some adjectives are used in only one of these positions.

Among predicative-only adjectives are a group beginning with *a-* (e.g. *afraid, alone*: see A-WORD), and those that usually or always require *complementation by a *prepositional phrase (e.g. *answerable, conducive, devoid, loath*).

Predicative adjectives (as heads of adjective phrases) can also occur as *postmodifiers, e.g.

anybody *aware* of these facts (i.e. 'anybody who is aware of these facts')

people *impatient* with the slow progress (i.e. 'people who are impatient with the slow progress')

2. Of a phrase: ascribing a property to someone or something. Less commonly: occurring in the *predicate or *predication.

• **predicatively**: used of a *constituent occurring in predicative position, or used in such a way as to ascribe a property to someone or something.

•• **predicative adjunct**: an adjunct that predicates a property of the referent of one of the *constituents in the clause with which the adjunct is associated. For example, in <u>Unhappy at being insulted, Harry left the meeting</u> the property of being 'unhappy at being insulted' is ascribed to the person referred to as Harry.

•• **predicative complement**: *see* COMPLEMENT.

•• **predicative object complement**: *see* COMPLEMENT.

•• **predicative oblique**: *see* COMPLEMENT.

predicator

1. A function label used for the verb as the *head of a *verb phrase (2).

Most of the *functional constituents of clause structure (*subject, *object, *complement, *adverbial) are terminologically clearly distinguished from the *forms that these functional constituents may take. For example, an adverbial can be *realized by an *adverb phrase (e.g. *very quickly*), a *prepositional phrase (e.g. *under the table*), or a *noun phrase (e.g. *last night*). The function of predicator can only be realized by a verb. For example, the predicator in *He opened the bottle* is *open*.

Not all grammarians make use of this term:

1985 R. QUIRK et al. It is unfortunate that traditionally the word *verb* does service both for a clause element, and for the class of word which occurs as a constituent of that element. For example in the former sense *must put* in [*You must put all the toys upstairs immediately*] is a verb, and in the latter sense, *must* and *put* are verbs individually . . . The term 'predicator' has been sometimes used to replace 'verb' in the sense of 'verb element', but for lack of a familiar alternative, we shall continue to use 'verb' in both senses, distinguishing between verbs as elements and verbs as words where there is some risk of confusion.

2. (In some models.) The *verb phrase (1) (verbal group) minus the *operator.

For example, in *I would have thought so*, the predicator is *have thought*. This analysis emphasizes the fact that the operator carries *tense, and is *finite, while the predicator is concerned with other meanings such as 'secondary' time (in relation to that of the operator), *voice, and whatever 'process' (e.g. action, mental activity) is predicated of the subject.

prediction The assertion that an event or other *situation will happen in the future.

One of the meanings used in the classification of *epistemic modality, and particularly uses of the verb *will*.

predictive Relating to prediction.

•• **predictive conditional**: the commonest type of *conditional sentence, in which there is a causal link of the type 'If X, then Y', e.g. *If you drive like that, you'll have an accident*.

prefix *Morphology* (*n.*). An *affix added before a *word or *base (2) to form a new word. Contrasted with *suffix and infix (*see* AFFIX).

Prefixes are primarily semantic in their effect, changing the meaning of the base. Common prefixes include:

counter-productive (M20)	*de*frost (L19)
*dis*connect (L18)	*fore*warn (ME)
*hyper*active (M19)	*inter*national (L18)
*mini*skirt (M20)	*mal*function (E20)
non-event (M20)	*re*build (L15)
*sub*zero (M20)	*under*nourished (E20)
*un*natural (LME)	

(*v.*) Place before a word or base, especially so as to form a new word.
• **prefixation**.

> 1991 P. H. MATTHEWS Processes of affixation may then be divided into **prefixation**, **suffixation** or **infixation** ... In English the commonest processes are those of suffixation ... Examples of prefixation are found, however, in the Negative formations of *happy* → *un* + *happy* ... or of *order* → *dis* + *order*.

> *See also* DERIVATION; WORD FORMATION.

pre-head Of an *element, *phrase, etc.: positioned before the *head. For example, in the noun phrase *crazy horses* the word *crazy* is a pre-head element, namely an adjective phrase that functions as a *premodifier.

pre-head adjunct (In OMEG.) A phrasal *adjunct that is positioned before a *head, e.g. *tall building*. Also called *premodifier.

> *See also* MODIFICATION; MODIFIER; POST-HEAD ADJUNCT; POSTMODIFICATION.

premodification The phenomenon of a dependent *phrase, *clause, etc. restricting the meaning of a following *head word through *modification, e.g. by ascribing a property to it. Contrasted with *postmodification.

Premodification can occur in all kinds of structures, and can take the form of phrases or clauses, e.g.

> the *derelict* house (noun premodification by an *adjective phrase)
> an *eat-as-much-as-you-like* restaurant (noun premodification by a clause)
> the article is *too* long (adjective premodification by an *adverb phrase)
> she drives *very* fast (adverb premodification by an adverb phrase)

The functional label *premodifier is used for the italicized phrases in the examples above.

> *See also* MODIFIER; POSTMODIFIER.

premodifier A *modifier that precedes its *head in phrase structure, e.g. *the* *sleepy* *dog*.

> *See also* MODIFICATION; POSTMODIFICATION; POSTMODIFIER; PREMODIFICATION.

prenucleus (In CaGEL.) A grammatical function (1) label applied to a unit which is positioned to the left of the *nucleus of a clause, the latter being conceived of as a *subject + *predicate (1), e.g.

> (I don't know) [[prenucleus *what*][nucleus they said _]]
> [[prenucleus *Your young son* [nucleus he's a good cricketer]]

In the first example the string *what they said* is an *interrogative clause with the fronted *wh-element *what* functioning as the *direct object of *said* (as shown by the 'gap' inside the nucleus, indicated by '_'). In the second example *Your young son* is a left *dislocated noun phrase.

●● **prenucleus position**: the position before the nucleus of a clause.

The label **postnucleus (position)** for a unit placed to the right of the nucleus (e.g. right dislocated elements) does not appear to be in use.

See also DISLOCATION.

preparatory *it* *See* ANTICIPATORY; DUMMY; IMPERSONAL.

prepose Place a linguistic unit (*phrase, *clause, etc.) before another, or to an earlier *position in a containing unit.

(This type of compound element can be called a *phrase-word in *attributive position.)

●● **VP preposing**: the *movement of a *verb phrase (2) constituent to the beginning of a clause, e.g.

She said she would eat the buns, *and* [VP *eat the buns*] she did _ !

In this example the VP of the second coordinated clause has been preposed (or *fronted (2)), and is associated with the *gap after the auxiliary verb *do* (indicated by '_').

See also DISLOCATION; FRONTING; GAP; MOVEMENT; TOPICALIZATION.

preposition A word that belongs to a *word class whose members can function as the *head of a *prepositional phrase. Prepositions generally precede the constituent which they *license, typically a *noun phrase, and often relate two linguistic units to each other (frequently in a spatial sense), e.g. *(the smile)* <u>*on*</u> *your face*.

Most prepositions are simple, i.e. they are predominantly short words (e.g. *at, by, down, for, from, in, to, through, up*). There are also some longer prepositions (e.g. *alongside, into, throughout*) which can be described as *compound prepositions, and some grammars also recognize a class of *complex prepositions consisting of combinations of two or three words that function in the same way as simple prepositions (e.g. *according to, regardless of, in front of, by means of, in addition to*).

There was at one time considerable prejudice against so-called *stranded prepositions, as in

What did you do that *for*?

The problem is difficult to talk *about*

It's not to be sneezed *at*

This prejudice goes back to Latin grammar, in which the characteristic placing of the preposition is indicated by its name *praepositio*, from *praeponere* which means 'put before'. Rewording is possible in some contexts (e.g. *the word to which it belongs*), but stranded prepositions are sometimes unavoidable without major rewriting.

Prepositions bear resemblances to (some would say 'overlap with') other word classes, such as *adverbs, *particles, and *adjectives. For example, *since* is regarded in some grammars as a preposition (*since the war*), an adverb (*I haven't seen them since*), or a conjunction (*since the war ended*), and *near* behaves like an adjective in having comparative and superlative forms (*nearer* the window).

●● **grammaticized preposition**: (in CaGEL) this term refers to prepositions that acquire a meaning in particular contexts or combinations; for example, the verb *rely* is combined with the preposition *on* to yield the meaning 'be dependent on'. Such prepositions are contrasted with those that have a clear lexical content, such as *by* or *through* in their spatial senses (*on the bed, through the glass*).

●● **specified preposition**: in CaGEL this term refers to a preposition that is selected by a verb. For example, the verb *look* selects the preposition *at* in *He looked at the stars.*

See also MARGINAL PREPOSITION; PIED PIPING; POSTPOSITION (2).

prepositional Of, pertaining to, or expressed by a *preposition; formed with a preposition; serving as, or having the function of, a preposition.

prepositional adjective (In CGEL.) An *adjective that *licenses a *prepositional phrase as complement.

Examples:

I am not *averse* to his proposals

He is *fond* of opera

My camera is *inferior* to yours

prepositional adverb A lexical item that resembles both an *adverb and a *preposition in particular syntactic configurations.

Thus, the word *down* in *I fell down* is labelled a prepositional adverb by some grammarians. In other frameworks this item is classified as an *adverb, *particle, or *intransitive preposition.

> 1961 R. B. LONG Words which normally take nounal completers in some or most of their uses, and which are clearly not classifiable as verbs, can conveniently be grouped together as prepositional adverbs.

1971 D. BOLINGER For the particles that oscillate between preposition and adverb I use the term *prepositional adverb*.

prepositional complement A *phrase, *clause, etc. *licensed by a preposition. (Also called **prepositional object** or **object of a preposition**.)

A prepositional complement is typically a *noun phrase, but can be realized by other phrase types or by a clause:

in *the end* (NP)
before *the war* (NP)
from *under the table* (PP)
in *short* (AdjP)
for *sure* (AdjP)
after *he sent the letter* (*finite clause)
afraid of *being killed* (*non-finite clause)

The terms prepositional complement, object of a preposition, etc. are often used interchangeably, but some grammarians reserve the term prepositional object for complements that follow a *prepositional verb, e.g.

Listen to *this*
We depend on *his generosity*

prepositional object *See* PREPOSITIONAL COMPLEMENT.

prepositional object complement *see* COMPLEMENT.

prepositional passive *See* PASSIVE.

prepositional phrase (PP) A *phrase which takes a preposition as its *head. Also called **preposition phrase**.

Prepositional phrases can perform various functions, e.g. *subject (<u>Under the bed</u> is a dusty spot), *adverbial (e.g. *Our dog chased a squirrel <u>in the garden</u>*), and *postmodifier in noun phrases (e.g. *the clock <u>on the wall</u>*).

Compare PREPOSITION GROUP.

prepositional verb A *verb that *licenses a *prepositional phrase headed by a specific *preposition as its *complement, and sometimes also an *object.

In some grammars and dictionaries the [verb + preposition] combination is regarded as a verb in two parts, hence the label *two-part verb.

The preposition generally comes before its complement: *I am looking <u>after the children</u>/looking <u>after them</u>*, not **I am looking <u>the children after</u>/looking <u>them after</u>*. But within certain structures the complement of the preposition may be displaced: *He cannot be relied on __ ; They need looking after __*.

Prepositional verbs can be *transitive or *intransitive, e.g.

transitive	intransitive
blame NP (on NP)	look (after NP)
do justice (to NP)	rely (on NP)

Compare MULTI-WORD VERB; PHRASAL-PREPOSITIONAL VERB; PHRASAL VERB; THREE-PART VERB.

See also PREPOSITION.

preposition group (In *Systemic Grammar.) A structure consisting of a *preposition with *modification, e.g.

immediately after
right in front of

Such a *group is said to function like a preposition. It is not to be confused with a *prepositional phrase, though it can form part of one: *immediately after lunch*.

See also WORD GROUP.

preposition phrase The same as *prepositional phrase.

prescriptive Concerned with, or laying down, rules of usage. Contrasted with *descriptive.

The term is generally used pejoratively by many linguists, who then also hold up to ridicule the inappropriateness of misconceived Latin-based rules (for example 'Don't end a sentence with a preposition'; 'Say *It's I*, not *It's me*'; 'Never split an infinitive').

In reality most descriptive statements about language are also based on some value-judgement of what is acceptable and normal, however objectively descriptive they try to be.

• **prescriptivism**: the practice or advocacy of prescriptive grammar.

• **prescriptivist**.

•• **prescriptive rule**: *see* RULE.

present (*n. & adj.*)

1. (Occurring in) the time now existing. Contrasted with *past (1).

2. (A *tense or *inflectional form of a *verb) typically relating to the present time. The grammatical label **present tense** is typically used of a *verb form that refers to a *situation taking place in the present.

As applied to *tense the term can be misleading. Although the present tense is often used to refer to some sort of present time, for example to report an instantaneous event (e.g. in a sports commentary: *The keeper drops the ball*), a state (e.g. *The house is in a wooded area*), or a habit (e.g. *He reads the New York Times online*), the present tense is perhaps more accurately described as being *unmarked for time. Thus the present tense can be used for 'general', 'eternal', or 'timeless' truths (e.g. *The earth goes round the sun*), or to talk about the past, as with the *historic present (e.g. *This car comes racing down the road . . .*). It can even be used with reference to a future event that is certain, scheduled, or taken for granted (e.g. *We are leaving tomorrow; When you come next week, we will arrange everything*), referred to as the present *futurate.

•• **present continuous (tense)**: *see* PROGRESSIVE.

•• **present progressive (tense)**: *see* PROGRESSIVE.

•• **present simple tense, simple present tense**: the present tense form of a verb, used on its own, that is identical to the *base (1) form of the verb (except in the case of *be*), and adds -*s* for the third person singular, e.g. *He sings in the shower every day*.

See also NON-PAST; PAST; PRESENT PERFECT; PRIMARY *tense*.

presentational construction A *construction in which *existential *there* is followed by a verb of 'appearance', 'emergence', 'existence', etc. (such as *appear, emerge, escape, follow, grow, develop, sprout, loom, stand*). Examples:

> There appeared six falcons above the house
> There emerged three problems in the course of the day

Also called **presentative**.

See also EXISTENTIAL; INFORMATION STRUCTURE.

presentative See PRESENTATIONAL CONSTRUCTION.

present condition See CONDITIONAL.

present continuous The same as present *progressive.

Present-Day English (PDE) The English of the 20th and 21st centuries.

Compare MODERN ENGLISH.

present futurate See FUTURATE.

present participle The -*ing* form of a *verb. Also called -*ing* participle (see -ING FORM) and **gerund participle** (see GERUND).

This *participle is used in the formation of *progressive constructions, e.g.

We were *listening* (active)

The plane is *being* de-iced (passive)

It can also be used in other constructions. Among them are the following:

I love [*singing* in the shower] (the bracketed clause functions as *direct object)

[*Growing* up in London] isn't easy (the bracketed clause functions as *subject)

[*Having* seen the play twice already] I don't think I want to see it again (the bracketed clause functions as *adverbial)

The term is also applied to items that resemble both *adjectives and verbs. For example, in <u>*running*</u> *water* and <u>*rising*</u> *standards*, the underlined words resemble adjectives in being placed in *attributive position, but their form and meaning are definitely verb-like (cf. *quickly* running *water*, <u>*rapidly*</u> *rising standards*, which contain a modifying adverb). Examples such as these must be distinguished from fully adjectival *-ing* forms, e.g.

a very *interesting* book

Some modern grammars consider the various uses of participles to be on a *cline, and for this reason prefer the neutral umbrella term *-*ing* form.

See also GERUND GRADIENCE; -*ING* CLAUSE; PARTICIPIAL ADJECTIVE.

present participle clause *See* -*ING* CLAUSE.

present perfect A *construction formed by a *present tense form of the *perfect auxiliary *have* + a *past participle, regarded by some grammarians as an *aspect, but by others as a (*secondary) *tense.

The present perfect generally refers to a *situation that took place in the past, but is related in some way to the present. This is called *current relevance. Examples:

I *have known* her since she was twenty

James *has come* (i.e. he is here now)

She's *written* literally dozens of novels

Contrast the simple *past (2):

My father *knew* Lloyd George

James *came* (but perhaps is no longer here)

Ivy Compton-Burnett *wrote* 19 novels in a uniquely bizarre uncompromising style

American English often uses a simple past (e.g. *Did James come yet?*) where British English still prefers the present perfect (e.g. *Has James come yet?*).

2009 J. ELSNESS As regards today's relationship between AmE and BrE, we have seen that my corpus showed the present perfect to be more frequent in the latter variety.

In the following examples we have the **present perfect progressive** (tense) and **present perfect passive** (tense):

It's *been raining* for two days now
He *has been working* hard today/recently
She *has been told*

We distinguish a number of different uses of the present perfect:

•• **continuative present perfect**: a use of the present perfect which expresses that a situation began in the past and continues up to the moment of speaking, and possibly beyond, e.g. *We have lived in Devon since 2005*. This perfect construction is typically combined with a temporal specification indicating continuation.

•• **experiential present perfect**: a use of the present perfect which indicates that a situation obtained one or more times in a period leading up to the present, e.g. *I have eaten raw fish before*.

•• **present perfect of result**: a present perfect used to express the result of a past situation, e.g. *We have constructed a new bridge over the river*.

•• **present perfect of the recent past**: a present perfect used to express the actuality of a recent past event, e.g. *The President has released previously classified documents*. Also called the **hot news present perfect**.

See also PAST; PAST PERFECT; PERFECT; PRESENT; PRIMARY *tense*; TENSE.

present perfect of result See PRESENT PERFECT.

present perfect of the recent past See PRESENT PERFECT.

present perfect passive (tense) See PRESENT PERFECT.

present perfect progressive (tense) See PRESENT PERFECT.

present progressive (tense) See PROGRESSIVE.

present progressive passive (tense) See TENSE.

present simple tense The present *tense form of a *verb, used on its own, that is identical in shape to the *base (1) form of the verb (except in the case of *be*), and adds *-s* for the third *person singular. Also called **simple present (tense)**. For example:

I *know*, and he *knows* too

See PRESENT (2); SIMPLE (3).

present subjunctive *See* SUBJUNCTIVE.

present tense *See* PRESENT (2).

presupposition *Semantics*. An assumption underlying a *statement, *utterance, etc.

The term is taken from philosophy and logic, and is used in various ways. Thus a *sentence such as *Did you pass your driving test?* presupposes that there exists such a thing as a driving test and that the addressee took one, and a question such as *When will you stop smoking?* presupposes that the addressee smokes.

Presupposition is sometimes contrasted with *entailment, which is a logical notion. Thus *I passed my test* entails *I passed something*. Notice that *I didn't pass the test* may presuppose or imply that I tried and failed, but it does not entail this: *I didn't pass the test, because in fact I didn't take it.*

See also IMPLICATURE.

preterite (American English **preterit**). (*n. & adj.*) The same as *past (2) tense. Used, for example, in CaGEL.

primary

1. (In some frameworks, e.g. CGEL.) Applied to *verbs: designating one of three verbs which can either be a *main verb or an *auxiliary verb, namely *be*, *do*, and *have*.

Verbs are traditionally divided into main verbs and auxiliaries. But since *be*, *do*, and *have* can function as both, it can be useful to make further distinctions. Primary is used as a label for these verbs, however they are functioning.

1985 QUIRK et al. Semantically, the primary verbs as auxiliaries share an association with the basic grammatical verb categories of tense, aspect, and voice . . . In this they are broadly distinguished from the modal verbs, which are associated mainly with the expression of modal meanings such as possibility, obligation, and volition.

2. (In CaGEL.) Applied to verb forms: a **primary verb form** is principally a form *inflected for *tense. However, in CaGEL *irrealis *were* is also a primary verb form, despite the fact that it is said not to carry tense.

2005 R. HUDDLESTON & G. K. PULLUM We include the irrealis forms among the primary forms, because there is a negative irrealis form, and also because of the close relation with preterite *was* and *wasn't*. This is why we distinguish the two major subsets of inflectional forms as 'primary' vs 'secondary' rather than by the more transparent (and more usual) terms 'tensed' and 'non-tensed'.

Primary verb forms are contrasted with **secondary verb forms**, those which are not inflected for tense, i.e. *infinitives and *participles.

See also PAST; PAST PERFECT; PERFECT; PRESENT; PRESENT PERFECT.

3. (In CaGEL.) Applied to the grammatical system of tense: **primary tense** designates a tense expressed by verbal inflections, e.g. the *present tense -*s* ending or the *past tense -*ed* ending, and is hence the same as *simple (3) tense. In contrast, a **secondary tense** is marked periphrastically (e.g. the *perfect construction, which combines the perfect auxiliary *have* with a past participle, as in *Having eaten a big breakfast, Greg skipped lunch*).

> 2002 R. HUDDLESTON & G. K. PULLUM et al. The primary tense system is more highly grammaticalised than the secondary one. One obvious reflection of this is that it is marked inflectionally rather than analytically. The perfect marker ***have*** is a member of the small closed class of auxiliary verbs, so that the perfect can properly be regarded as a grammatical category, but analytic marking of this kind represents a lesser degree of grammaticalisation than inflection.

In this system, **compound tenses** combine a primary and a secondary tense, e.g. the *present perfect or the *past perfect.

See also PAST; PERFECT; PRESENT; PRESENT PERFECT; SIMPLE; TENSE.

4. (*n. & adj.*) (In some older grammar, chiefly Jespersen's.) (Designating the *rank of) a linguistic unit that is at a first level 'down' in a *phrase, group, etc. Contrasted with *secondary and *tertiary.

> 1924 O. JESPERSEN We may, of course, have two or more coordinate adjuncts to the same primary: thus in *a nice young lady*, the words *a, nice,* and *young* equally define *lady*.

See also HEAD.

primary performative *See* PERFORMATIVE.

primary tense *See* PRIMARY (3).

primary verb *See* PRIMARY (1).

primitive *Linguistics* (*n. & adj.*). (A term, *construction, etc.) that is regarded as basic and 'given', and not derived from another, but this term is not strictly defined.

> 1968 J. LYONS When the linguist sets out to describe the grammar of a language on the basis of a recorded corpus of material, he starts with a more

primitive notion than that of either the word or the sentence (by 'primitive' is meant 'undefined within the theory', 'pre-theoretical'). This more primitive notion is that of the *utterance*.

principal clause *See* MAIN CLAUSE.

principal parts Chiefly used in the description of Latin. For English, this term refers to the three forms of a *verb given in a dictionary from which all its other forms can be derived. These are the *base form, the *past form, and the *past participle form, e.g.

blow, blew, blown
come, came, come
hurt, hurt, hurt
like, liked, liked
swim, swam, swum

The only verbs outside this pattern are *have* (where we have *has* in the *third person *singular, rather than **haves*) and *be* (where we have *am/are/is*).

principle of end-focus *See* END-FOCUS.

principle of end-weight *See* END-WEIGHT.

Principle of Relevance *See* RELEVANCE THEORY.

Principles and Parameters Theory (P&P Theory) A development of *Generative Grammar (2) from the 1980s onwards, also referred to as *Government-Binding Theory.

> 1995 N. CHOMSKY Principles-and-parameters (P&P) theory is not a precisely articulated theoretical system, but rather a particular approach to classical problems of the study of language, guided by certain leading ideas that had been taking shape since the origins of modern generative grammar some 40 years ago. These ideas crystallized into a distinctive approach to the topic by about 1980.

See also CHOMSKYAN; GOVERNMENT-BINDING THEORY; GRAMMAR; HEAD-DRIVEN PHRASE STRUCTURE GRAMMAR; MINIMALIST PROGRAM; PHRASE STRUCTURE GRAMMAR; STANDARD THEORY.

private verb A *verb that expresses an intellectual state, and typically *licenses a *that*-clause. Contrasted with *public verb.

The majority of verbs introducing *that*-clauses are sometimes loosely described as **reporting verbs**. More technically, many are classified as *factual verbs and divided into two groups: those which involve a public statement, and those which refer to private thinking only, e.g. *believe, know, realize, understand.*

See also PSYCHOLOGICAL VERB.

privilege of occurrence The (functional) slot(s) in which a *word or *phrase can be used in a *construction.

Members of the same *word class, in a general way, share the same privileges of occurrence, and this is in fact one of the tests used in assigning a word to a particular class. Thus *along, back, down,* and *out* can all replace *round* in the sentence *I hurried round,* and can for that reason be assigned to the same word class (an *adverb for some, a *preposition for others).

> 1933 L. BLOOMFIELD The lexical form in any actual utterance, as a concrete linguistic form, is always accompanied by some grammatical form: it appears in some function, and these privileges of occurrence make up, collectively, the grammatical function of the *lexical* form.

Compare CO-OCCURRENCE.

PRO/pro See ANAPHOR.

process

1. A continuous action, or series of actions, events, changes, *situations, stages, etc.

The word is used in its everyday sense in the classification of the *word classes on semantic grounds.

•• **process adverbs** (or **process adverbials**): a category of *adverbs (*adverbials) that includes adverbs of manner, means, and instrument, e.g.

We went *quickly* (manner)
We travelled *by car* (means)
He walks *with a stick* (instrument)

•• **process verbs**: *dynamic (1) *verbs that indicate changing states, such as *deteriorate, grow, melt,* e.g.

The evenings are *drawing out*

2. In *Systemic Grammar, the concept of process occupies an important place in the interpretation of the clause as a 'representation of experience'.

> 1985 M. A. K. HALLIDAY A process consists potentially of three components:
> (i) the process itself;
> (ii) participants in the process;
> (iii) circumstances associated with the process.

The process itself is normally realized through a verb, the participants through *nominal groups (*noun phrases), and the circumstances through an adverbial.

proclitic *Morphology* (*n. & adj.*). (A form) pronounced with very little emphasis, usually shortened, and phonologically attached to a following host word. Contrasted with *enclitic.

This phenomenon is much rarer in English than the enclitic. Arguably, the articles (*a/an, the*) are proclitics; likewise *do* and *it* when reduced to a single consonant sound (e.g. *D'you know?*, *'Twas* the night before Christmas).

productive Describing a linguistic process that is still in use, in contrast to **unproductive**.

Many kinds of affixation are highly productive in forming new words. For example, dozens of new words are formed with *anti-*, *Euro-*, *dis-*, *un-*, *-ee*, *-ness* and so on, but few with *-dom* or *-hood*.

pro-form A *word, or word combination, that can substitute for another.

*Pronouns, as the name implies, are commonly used as pro-forms for *nouns and *noun phrases, e.g.

They bought a villa in the south of France, and they are doing *it* up now

Pro-forms can also be words such as *here*, *there*, and *then*, e.g.

All her life she dreamt of Paris, but she never got *there*

Word combinations involving *do* (e.g. *do it, do so, do that*) can replace a *predicate (1), and are called **pro-VPs**:

They said they would cancel the order, and the next day they *did/did so/did it* [i.e. cancel the order]

Also possible are *so* and *not* as pro-forms replacing *that*-clauses functioning as *direct object, e.g.

Are there any survivors? I hope *so* [i.e. I hope that there are survivors]/I fear *not* [i.e. I fear that there aren't any survivors]

A pro-form may relate to its antecedent in two grammatically different ways. Contrast:

I went to the library for a book yesterday, but they didn't have *it* (a relationship of *co-reference)

I went to the library for a book yesterday, but didn't borrow *one* (*substitution for a noun phrase)

• **proformation**: substitution by pro-forms for other words or linguistic units.

See also SUBSTITUTE.

progressive (*n. & adj.*) (Designating) an *aspectual *construction
(*tense in some frameworks) formed with the **progressive auxiliary** *be*
and the *-ing* *participle form of a *verb. (Also called the **continuous
(tense)**.)

For example:

We *are eating* our breakfast

They *were teasing* you

Most linguists classify the progressive as an aspect rather than a tense
because, rather than grammatically encoding *time, the construction
expresses how a situation unfolds over time—namely as being in progress,
and therefore often of limited duration.

We can speak of various different **progressive constructions** (tenses),
as in the examples below:

I *am staying* with friends until the 30th of May (**present progressive**,
sometimes called **present continuous**)

I *was wondering* what to do when this job cropped up (**past progressive**,
sometimes called **past continuous**)

We *will have been waiting* for two hours by then (**future perfect progressive**,
sometimes called **future perfect continuous**)

The laptop *is being repaired* (**passive progressive**, sometimes called **passive
continuous**)

The progressive construction can be used to refer to arrangements in the
near future, e.g.

I *am lunching* with Margaret tomorrow

This is an example of the **present progressive futurate** (*see* FUTURATE).

Compare IMPERFECT; IMPERFECTIVE; PERFECT; PERFECTIVE.

progressive auxiliary *be* *See* PROGRESSIVE.

progressive futurate *See* FUTURATE.

projection

1. In phrase structure this term refers to the various hierarchical levels
that *phrases are made up of.

In descriptive frameworks, the levels are the *head (i.e. a *noun, *verb,
etc.) and the phrase itself (i.e. *noun phrase, *verb phrase, etc.). In *Generative
Grammar, further levels are distinguished. *See* X-BAR SYNTAX.

2. (In *Systemic Grammar.) A type of relationship between *clauses.
Contrasted with *expansion.

Projection is largely concerned with the reporting of speaking and
thinking 'events' (dealt with under *direct speech and *indirect speech in
traditional grammar). However, the term also embraces *rankshifted

remarks and thoughts of the kind we find in *appositional clauses or in examples like the following:

The question *whether the old man would survive* did not arise

It also includes *nominal clauses:

That he was seriously ill was not disputed

pronominal Of, pertaining to, or of the nature of, a *pronoun.
• **pronominalization**: the phenomenon, or process, of replacing a *noun phrase by a pronoun.
• **pronominalize**: turn into a pronoun.
•• **pronominal adverb**: (in some traditional grammar) a term used for *adverbs of vague general meaning that share with pronouns the property of referring back to some other phrase (e.g. *here, then, there*). This category overlaps with the more general modern notion of *pro-form.

pronoun A member of a *closed class of *words that function as the *head of a phrase that can perform functions typically carried out by *noun phrases (*subject, *direct object, etc.). For this reason pronouns are often regarded as nouns (e.g. in CaGEL, OMEG). However, other grammars stress that pronouns:

  (i) show distinctions of *case (*he/him*), *person (first, second, third), and *gender (*he/she*);
  (ii) typically do not have *inflectional *plurals (with *one* being an exception);
  (iii) are very limited with regard to the *dependents they take;
  (iv) function as the head of phrases that do not have independent *reference.

For these reasons a grammar like CGEL treats pronouns as constituting a separate *word class.

The class of pronouns can be subdivided in various ways. A commonly accepted subdivision recognizes *demonstrative pronouns, *indefinite pronouns, *interrogative pronouns, *personal pronouns, *possessive pronouns, *reciprocal pronouns, *reflexive pronouns, and *relative pronouns.

Traditional grammars define pronouns as words that can replace or stand in for a noun. But this is problematic. Compare the following examples:

We have lots of *cats*, but it's a problem because my husband hates *them*

I asked *my neighbour* if *he* would cut our grass

In the first example *them* seems to replace a noun (*cats*), but in fact, as the second example shows, pronouns really replace noun *phrases*, and are for that reason perhaps best called **pro-NPs**.

There are further problems with saying that pronouns replace nouns. One is that it is hardly true to say that the first person pronoun *I* replaces a noun. Another problem is that pronouns often replace larger units such as *clauses, as in *Why did you ask that?*

Many pronouns have the same form as *determinatives (1)—e.g. *this*, *that*—but note that pronouns occur independently. Thus, *this* is a pronoun in *I like this*, but a determinative in *I like this story*. Some grammarians claim that items like *this* and *that*, which seem to belong to two classes for the reason just given, in fact nevertheless belong to one or the other class in both examples, such that in the examples cited *this* is either a pronoun or a determinative.

•• **dummy pronoun**: *see* DUMMY.

pro-NP See PRONOUN.

proper name See PROPER NOUN.

proper noun A *noun referring to a unique person, place, animal, etc. Contrasted with *common noun. (Also called **proper name**.)

The traditional distinction between common and proper nouns is both grammatical and semantic. Proper nouns do not freely allow *determinatives (1) or *number contrasts (e.g. **my Himalaya*, **that Atlantic*, **some Asias*), and *article usage tends to be invariant (e.g. *the Chilterns*, *the (River) Thames*, *Oxford*, not **Chilterns*, **Thames*, **the Oxford*).

However, the categories are not watertight. Thus, because more than one referent can share the same name, names can in some circumstances be treated like common nouns (e.g. *a Mr. Jones*, *the Smiths*). Nationality words and names of days of the week are also borderline (e.g. *three Scots*, *an Australian*, *three Mondays in succession*).

The terms proper noun and (proper) name are often used interchangeably. But a distinction is sometimes made between **names**, which can include phrase-like units (e.g. *the United States*, *New York*, *the Daily Telegraph*, *the South Downs*, *A Midsummer Night's Dream*), and proper nouns, which are then single words (e.g. *Dorchester*, *Elizabeth*, *England*).

prop *it* See DUMMY.

proportional clause One of two joined parallel *clauses involving some kind of *comparison.

As well as covering such fairly standard sentences as *As he got older, (so) he worried less*, this label also covers the more unusual pattern exemplified by the following:

The more he thought, the less he spoke

The more, the merrier

proposition *Semantics*. The specification of a *situation or state of affairs by a *declarative *sentence (or *clause) which can be said to be true or false.

• **propositional**: having the nature of a statement or *assertion about something.

•• **propositional meaning** (also called **propositional content**): the component of the *meaning expressed by a sentence, *utterance, etc. that can be said to be true or false.

> 1988 R. HUDDLESTON [P]ropositional meaning is arguably the most central part of meaning—and very often the part which can be most precisely and rigorously described, by specifying the conditions under which a sentence could be used to express a true proposition.

The latter term is often used to explain how two different sentences logically mean the same. For example, *He is hard to persuade* and *It is hard to persuade him* can be said to have the same propositional meaning. By contrast **non-propositional meaning** refers to the kinds of meanings that are 'superimposed', for instance when a sentence is uttered in a sarcastic tone of voice, or when a particular constituent of a clause is highlighted (e.g. by *topicalization). *see* INFORMATION STRUCTURE.

The terms, taken from logic, are used in a number of ways.

> 1977 J. LYONS The term 'proposition', like 'fact', has been the subject of considerable philosophical controversy . . . Further difficulties are caused by the use of 'proposition' in relation to 'sentence' and 'statement': some writers identify propositions with (declarative) sentences, others identify them with statements, and others with the meaning of (declarative) sentences; and there is little consistency in the way in which 'statement' is defined.

See also ATTITUDINAL; COMMUNICATIVE; CONATIVE; CONNOTATION; DENOTATIVE; DESCRIPTIVE; EMOTIVE; ILLOCUTION; INTERPERSONAL; REFERENTIAL MEANING.

pro-predicate, pro-predication The use of a *pro-form to stand for a *predicate or *predication.

prop word (In some traditional grammar.) The *pronoun *one* used as a *substitution *pro-form.

The pronoun *one* (plural *ones*) can be used to substitute for part or all of a *noun phrase:

> Do you have any blue leather handbags? Yes, we have some nice *ones* [i.e. blue leather handbags]. I could also show you a smart red *one* [i.e. leather handbag].

Other words or phrases (e.g. *another, the same*) can also substitute in similar ways.

The fact that the pro-form *one* can refer back to a unit that is bigger than a noun but smaller than a noun phrase is one of the motivations for the bar level category in *X-bar syntax.

The term was coined by Henry Sweet (1892b), and was much used by Jespersen.

prospective Referring to the *future (1).

A term used in some traditional grammar in the discussion of time clauses with future meaning.

protasis (Pronounced /ˈprɒtəsɪs/. Plural **protases**.) The clause expressing the *condition in a *conditional construction (typically introduced by *if*), e.g.

If we sweep the room it will be full of dust

Contrasted with *apodosis.

• **protatic** (pronounced /prəˈtætɪk/) (not common).

prototype (Originally in philosophy and psychology) the most typical exemplar(s) of a *category in terms of the defining features of that category. A prototype should not be identified with a *particular* member of a category:

> 1978 E. ROSCH By prototypes of categories we have generally meant the clearest cases of category membership defined operationally by people's judgments of goodness of membership in the category . . . To speak of a *prototype* at all is simply a convenient grammatical fiction; what is really referred to are judgments of degree of prototypicality. Only in some artificial categories is there by definition a literal single prototype . . . For natural-language categories, to speak of a single entity that is the prototype is either a gross misunderstanding of the empirical data or a covert theory of mental representation . . . Prototypes do not constitute a theory of representation of categories.

• **prototypical**.

•• **prototype theory**: the view held by many linguists, especially practitioners of *Cognitive Linguistics, that categories (linguistic or otherwise) cannot be defined by making reference to a set of defining criteria, as in the Aristotelian model. Instead, categories are viewed as having more or less prototypical members, as overlapping, and as having **fuzzy boundaries**.

See also GRADIENCE.

pro-verb The *verb *do* (*it/so/that*) used as a *pro-form, or as a *substitution item.

pro-VP *See* PRO-FORM.

proximal Indicating things that are near (to the speaker). Contrasted with *distal.

This label is sometimes applied to the *deictic words *this* and *these*.

proximity agreement, proximity concord *See* AGREEMENT.

pseudo-cleft *See* CLEFT.

pseudo-coordination An apparent *coordination of two units where the relationship between them is not one of equality, unlike in canonical coordination.

> 1985 R. QUIRK et al. When they precede *and*, members of a small class of verbs or predications have an idiomatic function which is similar to the function of catenative constructions . . . and which will be termed *pseudo-coordinations*.

Examples of this (which tend to be colloquial) include *try and come, went and complained*. Other pseudo-coordinations are found with *adjectives, e.g. *nice and warm*, and the very colloquial *good and proper*.

pseudo-participle *See* PARTICIPIAL ADJECTIVE.

pseudo-passive A *pattern (*be* + a *verb form in *-ed/-en*) that resembles a *passive construction, but does not have an *active counterpart and does not permit an *agent. Also called **adjectival passive** and **statal passive**. Example:

> My homework is finished

Here there is no active version (cf. *I finish my homework) and a *by-phrase cannot be added (cf. *My homework is finished by me*). In this example *finished* refers to a *state.

> Some passive sentences are *ambiguous, especially in the *past tense, e.g.

> The job was finished at two o'clock

If the meaning is 'By the time I arrived at two o'clock it was already finished' this example can be regarded as a pseudo-passive, with a statal interpretation. This contrasts with a *dynamic (1) central passive construction where an agent is supplied, and where the verb can be part of a *progressive construction:

> The job was finished at two o'clock by Bill

The job was being finished at two o'clock by the painters

Compare PARTICIPIAL ADJECTIVE.

See also PATIENT; SEMI-PASSIVE; VOICE.

pseudo-subjunctive A *hypercorrect use of the *were*-*subjunctive, where an indicative is acceptable, e.g. *He tried to drop in sometimes on his way to his constituency if he were alone.*

psycholinguistics The study of the cognitive aspects of language learning, production, processing, etc.

• **psycholinguist, psycholinguistic**.

psychological predicate *See* PSYCHOLOGICAL VERB.

psychological subject An older term for the *topic or *theme of a *clause, i.e. the 'subject-matter' or what the clause is about; contrasted with grammatical *subject and logical subject.

psychological verb A *verb that expresses a psychological state. Also called **experiencer verb**, **mental verb**, **psychological predicate**, **psych verb**; and **verb of psychological state**.

There are two types of psychological verb: those that have an *experiencer as *subject and a *stimulus as *object (e.g. *I felt the cold*); and those that have a stimulus as subject and experiencer as object (e.g. *The cold overpowered me*).

See also EMOTIVE.

psych verb *See* PSYCHOLOGICAL VERB.

public verb A *verb whose meaning includes or implies the idea of 'speaking', often *licensing a *that-clause expressing a *factual proposition. Contrasted with *private verb.

Examples include *affirm, announce, boast, confirm, declare*.

punctual Of a *situation expressed by a *verb: having no duration, taking place momentarily; contrasted with *durative; e.g.

The bomb exploded

He swallowed the grape

Punctual situations can be repeated:

Someone knocked at the door

Compare ATELIC; CONCLUSIVE; TELIC.

punctuation The practice or system of inserting various marks in written texts in order to aid interpretation; the division of written or printed matter into *sentences, *clauses, etc. by means of such marks.

Earlier punctuation reflected spoken delivery, marking especially the pauses where breath would be taken. Since the eighteenth century it has been based on grammatical structure, marking sentences, clauses, and some types of *phrases. Broadly speaking, it has the function either of linking items (e.g. *three potatoes, two carrots, and an onion*) or of separating them (e.g. *I don't know. Ask someone else*).

In a series of *adjectives, a comma is often used when the meanings are not linked (e.g. *a small, neat room*), but is not used when they are (e.g. *a silly little boy*). In some styles but not in others, a comma is used before a *coordinating conjunction in a list of three or more items, as exemplified by the second comma in *the flat, the landlord, and the tenant*. This is called the **serial comma** or (because it is part of the house style of Oxford University Press) the **Oxford comma**.

Various marks (brackets, dashes, and commas) are used to separate off passages that interrupt the main structure of the sentence (e.g. *This tile—despite its fresh colours—is more than two hundred years old*). See PARENTHESIS.

Punctuation in the shape of a hyphen or comma is also used to avoid grammatical or semantic *ambiguity (e.g. *a natural-gas producer* vs *a natural gas-producer*; *The quarrel over, the friendship was resumed* vs *The quarrel over the friendship was resumed*).

Grammatically complete units can be separated off by lighter punctuation than the normal full stop, either to link parallel statements (semicolon: e.g. *I wasn't going to leave; I'd only just arrived*)* or to lead from one thought to the next (colon: e.g. *I wasn't going to leave: I stood my ground*).

The *apostrophe can be said to have a quasi-morphological role in distinguishing the 'possessive' (*singular and *plural) from the plural in most nouns (e.g. *girl's, girls'*, versus *girls*).

purpose The motive, or the intention behind an action.

The term is used in its usual sense, particularly in the semantic description of *adverbials and *conjunctions, e.g.

They only do it *to annoy me* (*infinitival clause of purpose)

Similarly: *in order (not) (to), so as (not) (to)*.

A finite *adverbial clause of purpose, introduced by *so (that)* or *in order that*, normally requires a *modal verb, e.g.

They shredded the evidence so that no one *would* discover the truth

Contrast:

> They shredded the evidence so that no one discovered the truth ('result' rather than 'purpose')

Negative purpose is suggested by *lest* and *in case*.

pushdown (*n. & adj.*) (In CGEL.) (Designating) a type of *embedding in which a linguistic *constituent that is part of one *clause operates indirectly as part of another, e.g.

> What do you think happened? [i.e. *What* do you think?/*What* happened?]

•• **pushdown element**: In the sentence *Which panel is he a member of?*, the phrase *which panel* is a pushdown element: it has a function in a lower constituent, namely the *complement of the preposition *of*, and has been moved out of its containing *prepositional phrase (cf. *He is a member of which panel?*). In this particular case we can also apply the more specific label **pushdown *wh*-element**.

•• **pushdown relative clause**: exemplified by the clause *who he hoped were still alive* in the following example: *He was searching for his parents who he hoped were still alive* [i.e. *He was searching for his parents who he hoped who were still alive*].

putative *should* (In CGEL.) The *modal verb *should*, particularly as used in a *subordinate clause to refer tentatively to a possible *situation, rather than to assert a situation as fact; chiefly in British English.

The term is particularly applied to the use of *should* in subordinate clauses where it does not express *obligation, but emphasizes an emotional reaction to a possible or presumed fact. This is also called **emotive *should***, and is exemplified in the following:

> It is a pity/sad *that you should think that they are incompetent*

In this example it is not certain that that the addressee holds the view referred to. Contrast this with the *factive (1) subordinate clause in the following:

> It is a pity *that you think that they are incompetent*

Putative *should* also occurs in subordinate clauses as an alternative to the *subjunctive after expressions of suggesting, advising, etc. (In CGEL it is then called the ***should* mandative**; see SUBJUNCTIVE.):

> They insisted that I (should) stay the whole week

•• **putative *should* clause**: a **that*-clause containing putative *should*.

qualification *See* QUALIFIER.

qualifier

1. A *word (or group of words) that attributes a quality to another word, or that *modifies another word or phrase in some way.

This term (together with *qualify (1), **qualification**) is sometimes used with much the same meaning as *modifier (and the related *modify, *modification). But in much modern grammar *modifier* etc. are the preferred terms.

2. In some traditional grammar, distinctions were made between the two terms. *Qualify* etc. were largely reserved for words, especially *adjectives, that assign qualities to a *noun. *Modify* etc. were used for the way *adverbs affect *verbs. In this kind of usage, adjectives could be labelled qualifiers, whereas all or most of today's *determinatives (1) were regarded as *quantifiers.

> 1933b O. JESPERSEN *Little* is sometimes a qualifier (*a little girl*), sometimes a quantifier (*a little bread*).

3. In *Systemic Grammar, *qualifier* is contrasted with *modifier*, as in traditional grammar (see 2 above), but in a completely different way. Here *qualifier* and *qualification* describe the function of whatever follows the head in a nominal group, thus being virtually synonymous with *postmodifier and *postmodification in other models. The terms *modifier* etc. can then be used to describe modification before the head—called *premodification in other models.

qualify

1. Attribute a quality to another *word.

> 1892b H. SWEET Thus *very* in *a very strong man* qualifies the attribute-word *strong*.

The term was at one time particularly used of the way *adjectives affect *nouns, although usage could be wider, as in the quotation.

In many present-day grammatical models, the terms *qualify* etc. are often replaced by *modify* etc.

See QUALIFIER (1), (2).

2. In *Systemic Grammar, *qualify* is used to describe the effect that words following the *headword in a noun group (*noun phrase) have on that head. Such words do not, of course, have to be adjectives, but can include *relative clauses and *prepositional phrases, so in this area *qualify* has an extended meaning (i.e. it is equivalent to *postmodify in other models).

> 1972 M. L. SAMUELS *Son* is usually either modified by *my/his/her*, etc. or qualified by an *of*-group, whereas *sun* is normally preceded by the definite article.

See also QUALIFIER (3).

qualitative adjective An *adjective that is *gradable and describes a quality, in contrast to a *classifying adjective. Roughly equivalent to *epithet.

> 1990 *Collins Cobuild English Grammar* Adjectives that identify a quality that someone or something has, such as 'sad', 'pretty', 'small', 'happy', 'healthy', 'wealthy' and 'wise', are called qualitative adjectives.

The division of adjectives into qualitative and classifying is just one of the many ways in which adjectives can be categorized.

Compare ATTRIBUTIVE; GRADABLE.

quality partitive A *partitive indicating categorization by quality or kind, e.g.

> a *sort* of menu
> two *kinds* of pudding

These are distinguished from the more usual **quantity partitives**, e.g. a *piece* of cake, a *lot* of food

quantification The semantic property (of a *word, *phrase, etc.) of specifying an amount, number, or quantity.

See also QUANTIFIER; QUANTIFY; QUANTITATIVE; QUANTITY.

quantifier
1. A semantic label that can be applied to words from different *word classes (*determinative, *adjective, *adverb, etc.) which express an amount, number, or quantity.

The term normally refers to *indefinite quantity, and covers such quantifying or *quantitative words as *much, many, (a) few, (a) little, several, enough, lots (of)*, etc. It is sometimes extended to include indefinite *pronouns such as *everyone, somebody, nothing*, etc., and sometimes also to *open (1) class words such as *heaps (of), lashings (of),*

piles (of), etc. It can also be extended to include *nouns of definite
quantity, i.e. the *cardinal numbers.

2. (In one grammatical model.) A *partitive *phrase including the
word *of*.

> 1990 *Collins Cobuild English Grammar* **Quantifier**, a phrase ending in 'of'
> which allows you to refer to a quantity of something without being precise
> about the exact amount; e.g. *some of, a lot of, a little bit of.*

Compare IDENTIFIER.

See also QUANTIFICATION; QUANTITATIVE; QUANTITY.

quantify Indicate quantity. *See* QUANTIFICATION; QUANTIFIER;
QUANTITATIVE; QUANTITY.

quantitative

1. Relating to *quantity or amount as part of a *word's meaning. *See*
QUANTIFIER (1); QUANTITY.

2. (*n. & adj.*) (A word) belonging to a class consisting of (indefinite)
*quantifiers (e.g. *(a) few, several*), definite *cardinal numbers (e.g. *one,
two, three*), and measurement terms such as *a couple of, half*.

In this classification, quantitative contrasts with *ordinative, and both
are subclasses of *numerative.

See also QUANTIFICATION; QUANTIFIER; QUANTITY.

quantity Number or amount.

For number and amount as semantic categories, *see* PARTITIVE and
QUANTIFIER (1).

•• **quantity partitive**: *see* QUALITY PARTITIVE.

quasi- Appended to a descriptive label to indicate that the latter does not
apply in every single respect to a particular item.

For example, CaGEL describes the *verb *be* in such examples as *They are
to send in their passports immediately* as **quasi-modal** *be*:

> 2002 R. HUDDLESTON & G. K. PULLUM et al. The label 'quasi-modal' in-
> dicates that in spite of its one modal property (and its modal meaning) this *be*
> doesn't in fact qualify grammatically for inclusion in that class.

The *prefix *semi-* and the *suffix *-oid* have similar meanings. As a further
example, in some models of *valency grammar the postverbal noun
phrase in the following example is said to function as an **objoid**, i.e. it
functions like an *object but cannot be *passivized:

> Those shoes suit you (cf. *You are suited by those shoes)

See also GRADIENCE; MARGINAL.

Queen's English, the *See* KING'S ENGLISH, THE.

question (In modern grammatical analyses that distinguish *structure and *usage.) A usage label indicating the function of a *clause as seeking information.

Typically, *interrogative clauses (which are syntactically defined) are used to ask *questions, but other types of clauses can be used in this way as well (e.g. *declarative *You've already spent all that money?*, which is sometimes called a **declarative question**). Regrettably, not all grammars make a distinction between interrogatives and questions, using the latter (and sometimes the former) as both a *form label and a usage label.

Distinctions can be made between different types of question:

(i) A **closed question** (also called **yes-no question** is a clause (interrogative or otherwise) that is used to ask a question with *yes* or *no* as an answer (e.g. interrogative *Is Greg here?*, declarative *You are Peter?*).

(ii) An **open question** (also called *wh-* **question** or **information question**) is a clause (interrogative or otherwise) that is used to ask a question that potentially has an unlimited set of answers (e.g. interrogative *Who ate the last bun?*, declarative *You said WHAT?*). Open questions (in interrogative form) tend to be spoken with a falling intonation.

(iii) An **alternative question** is a subtype of closed question which names possible answers but does not leave the matter open. An alternative question can display subject–auxiliary *inversion, as in *Would you like coffee or tea? Are you happy or sad? Did you laugh or cry?*, or begin with a *wh*-word, as in *Which would you like—coffee, tea, or wine?* An alternative question implies that one, and only one, of the options is possible.

So-called *exclamatory questions and *rhetorical questions are in fact interrogative in form only, and are not used to ask genuine questions:

Isn't it a lovely day! (= It is a lovely day)

What's that got to do with you? (= That has nothing to do with you)

Who am I to complain? (= It is not for me to complain)

Compare ECHO UTTERANCE; TAG.

See also CLAUSE TYPE; INDIRECT QUESTION; SPEECH ACT.

question mark A *punctuation mark ⟨?⟩ chiefly used to show that the preceding *word, *phrase, *clause, or *sentence is used to ask a *question.

question tag *See* TAG.

question word *See* WH-WORD.

quotation mark A *punctuation mark ⟨ ' ' ⟩ or ⟨ " " ⟩ used as one of a pair to mark the beginning and end of a form, word, *phrase, or longer stretch of text that is being quoted by the writer from another context.

radical *Morphology* (*n. & adj.*) (Of, belonging to, connected with, or based on) the *root of a *word.

The term has a long history, but words such as *base, *root, and *stem (along with *morpheme and *minimum free form) are more usual today.

raise Move (a *noun phrase) from a position in an embedded *clause to a position in a higher clause. *See* RAISING.

raised object *See* RAISING.

raised subject *See* RAISING.

raising The displacement of a *noun phrase from a position within an *embedded clause to a position in a higher clause.

There are two kinds of raising: **subject-to-subject raising** (or simply **subject raising**; abbreviated as SSR) and **subject-to-object raising** (or simply **object raising**; abbreviated as SOR).

With SSR we have a grammatical *subject that carries a *semantic role that is associated with a *verb in a lower clause. Thus in

Henriette seems [_ to like Paul]

the subject of the *matrix clause (*Henriette*) is said to have been raised out of the bracketed clause (from the position indicated by '_'), and its semantic role, that of *experiencer, is linked with the verb *like*, not with the verb *seem* (the meaning is 'It seems that Henriette likes Paul'). The displaced subject is called a **raised subject**, and the verb *seem* is called a **raising verb** (other examples are *appear, continue, happen, prove*).

With SOR we have a grammatical *object that carries a *semantic role that is associated with a verb in a lower clause. Thus in

Jill believes Henriette [_ to like Paul]

the object of the matrix clause (*Henriette*) is said to have been raised out of the bracketed clause (from the position indicated by '_'), and its semantic role, that of experiencer, is linked with the verb *like*, not the verb *believe* (the meaning is 'Jill believes that Henriette likes Paul').

In early *Generative Grammar (2) these displacements were effected by transformations called **subject-to-subject raising** and **subject-to-object raising**, or simply raising to cover both types. In recent treatments (e.g. CaGEL, OMEG) the term raising is still used, but it does not always imply that movement has taken place.

raising verb *See* RAISING.

rank A *level of linguistic analysis.

1. In Jespersen's grammar, the term rank is used as a way of classifying units at different levels of analysis in a *phrase or *clause.

> 1933b O. JESPERSEN Take the three words *terribly cold weather*. They are evidently not on the same footing, *weather* being, grammatically, most important, to which the two others are subordinate, and of these again *cold* is more important than *terribly*. We have thus three ranks: 'weather' is Primary, 'cold' Secondary, and 'terribly' Tertiary in this combination.

2. In the *Systemic Grammar framework, grammar is seen as a system of levels or ranks, going from the 'highest' rank of *sentence, through *clause, *phrase (or *group), and *word down to *morpheme, each smaller unit being included in the larger one.

> 2014 M. A. K. HALLIDAY & C. MATTHIESSEN There is a **scale of rank** in the grammar of every language. That of English (which is typical of many) can be represented as:
> clause
> phrase/group
> word
> morpheme

rankshift (*n.*) A downward shift of a linguistic unit into a lower rank.

> 2014 M. A. K. HALLIDAY & C. MATTHIESSEN There is the potential for **rank shift**, whereby a unit of one rank may be downranked (downgraded) to function in the structure of a unit of its own rank or of a rank below.

For example, in *a street with no name* the prepositional phrase *with no name* functions as a *postmodifier in the larger noun phrase, and as such is a rankshifted phrase.

(*v.*) Assign an inferior rank to (a unit in a grammatical structure).

real condition The same as open *condition.

realis *See* IRREALIS.

reality phase *See* PHASE.

realization The overt manifestation of an abstract linguistic unit in a particular context.

Realization is applicable at all *levels of analysis. For example, in *cats and dogs* the abstract *plural *morpheme (1) is realized by /s/ and /z/. On another level, a *lexeme can have several realizations (or be realized in several ways), e.g. as *break, breaks, breaking, broke, broken*. And at *clause level we can say that the grammatical *function (1), of *subject is typically realized by a *noun phrase.

realize Cause, or be, the *realization of.

> 1980 E. K. BROWN & J. E. MILLER There is no very satisfactory way to identify part of the word *wrote* as realizing the lexeme WRITE and some other part of the word as realizing the syntactic description 'past tense': rather, the whole form *wrote*, as a unity, realizes the description 'WRITE + past'.

reanalysis See MULTIPLE ANALYSIS.

reason See CAUSE.

recipient Semantics (n. & adj.) (Indicating). the *semantic role assigned to a *noun (or *noun phrase) referring to an animate entity that is intended to 'receive' something through an action expressed by a *verb.

The role of the recipient is typically grammatically *realized by the *indirect object in a *clause, e.g.

> I bought *my cousin* a present
> I gave *him* your letter

A distinction is sometimes made between an intended (or **benefactive**) recipient (e.g. *I bought a present for him*) and an actual recipient (e.g. *I gave the letter to him*). See BENEFICIARY.

Semantically it is possible for the grammatical *subject of some verbs to be assigned a recipient role, as in *I heard a noise*, though this role may alternatively be described as *experiencer.

Compare DATIVE; GOAL (2).

reciprocal Expressing mutuality between two or more people, or between groups of people.

The term is mainly applied to the *pronouns *each other* and *one another* (**reciprocal pronouns**) when they are *licensed by certain *verbs. There is no real difference in usage between them, despite the existence of a prescriptive rule that *one another* should be used when the *reference is to more than two entities. Examples:

> The French and the German leaders haven't always liked each other

The children in Yellow Class all like one another

Occasionally the term is extended to cover other *words, such as the verbs *meet* (e.g. *James and Marilyn met*, which can be regarded as combining *James met Marilyn* and *Marilyn met James*) or *exchange* (e.g. *Ann and Frank exchanged addresses*, where Ann gave her address to Frank, and Frank gave his address to Ann).

reclassification The same as *conversion.

recover Deduce (information) not made explicit so as to make sense of an *utterance.

For example, in *We want the citizens to vote in the elections* the *subject of the *subordinate clause *to vote in the elections* can be recovered from the *main clause.

See also RECOVERABILITY.

recoverability The phenomenon whereby information can be deduced or retrieved by a hearer or reader from the *context.

The fact that certain information is recoverable enables us to make sense of otherwise incomplete *utterances, for example when *ellipsis occurs or when *pro-forms are used.

In **precise recoverability** the exact words that have been ellipted are recoverable from the surrounding context, just as the exact *referents of any pro-forms used are. Take the following example:

The doctor said she would call, but didn't

Here the pro-form (pronoun) *she* can be linked to *the doctor*, and we can recover the ellipted words *she* and *call* in the second clause from the first clause.

A distinction can be made between **structural recoverability**, which relies (as in the example above) on our knowledge of grammar, and **situational recoverability**, when we recover what is missing from some *extralinguistic context. For example, when a speaker says *Look, she's found it*, the referents of *she* and *it* will be recoverable by the hearer from the *situation.

• **recoverable**

Compare UNDERSTOOD.

recurrence Repeated or frequent occurrence, repetition.

This term is used in its everyday sense in discussing the meaning of some *verbs and *adverbials.

1985 R. QUIRK et al. Here, the type of recurrence in which we are interested depends both on the semantics of the verb and also on its aspect. Compare:

She *usually* smiles. [recurrent activity; eg 'When she sees me ...']
She is *usually* smiling. [continuous activity; eg 'Whenever one sees her ...']

recursion The phenomenon whereby a particular type of linguistic unit or structure is contained within a unit or structure of the same type.

> 2003 I. A. SAG, T. WASOW, & E. BENDER [W]e use the term recursion whenever rules permit a constituent to occur within a larger constituent of the same type.

In the following example, each PP (*prepositional phrase), except for the highest (leftmost) one, is contained in another PP:

The ring was [PP *in a bag* [PP *in a box* [PP *at the back* [PP *of a drawer* [PP *in a chest* [PP *in the corner* [PP *of the room*]]]]]]]

*Relative clauses can also be used recursively:

> 1975 F. R. PALMER The structure of language involves 'recursion' of the kind illustrated by 'This is the house that Jack built', 'This is the mouse that lived in the house that Jack built' and so on—if necessary *ad infinitum.*

- **recursive**, **recursively**, **recursiveness**.
  Compare EMBEDDING; NESTING.
  See also MODIFICATION (1).

reduce Abbreviate (a *phrase, *clause, or other linguistic form) by omitting some elements.

The concept of grammatical **reduction** embraces both *ellipsis and *substitution. Thus in reply to

You should write to your fund manager

a reduced response could be

I have (ellipsis of *written to my fund manager*)

or

I've done so (with the substitute *pro-form *do so* replacing *written to my fund manager*)

●● **reduced clause**: a shortened clause, particularly a *non-finite or *verbless clause with a *postmodifying function that can be interpreted as a *relative clause with its *relative pronoun and finite *verb omitted, e.g.

Anyone *scared of heights* is advised not to attempt to climb this tower
(= Anyone *who is scared of heights* ...)

redundancy The superfluity of a linguistic *feature (1), unit, structure, etc. due to its predictability within a containing structure.

Redundancy is to some extent a normal and necessary feature of linguistic communication, and explains why a 'message' can be understood even if there is some 'interference', for example, in spoken delivery owing to noise, or in written language owing to the occasional misspelling or the erroneous omission of a *word.

A degree of redundancy is also built into syntax. For example, in *The sun rises* there are two markers of *singular, where one might be sufficient (as indeed it is in the simple past, *The sun rose*). On the other hand, there is a counter-tendency to avoid redundancy by *reducing the use of easily *recoverable features. There are, however, grammatical limits on the avoidance of redundancy. *See* ELLIPSIS.

The concept originated in theories of information transfer and telecommunication.

• **redundant**: exhibiting, or characterized by, redundancy.

reduplicate Form (a *word, *phrase, etc.) by repetition of an element; repeat (an element) so as to form a word, phrase, etc.

> 1985 R. QUIRK et al. It is curious that analogous reduplicated phrases are virtually restricted to informal use: *for months and months, for years and years.*

• **reduplication**.

See also REDUPLICATIVE.

reduplicative (*n. & adj.*) (A *compound *word) having two identical or very similar parts, often rhyming. (Sometimes called *iterative.)

Most reduplicatives are fairly informal, e.g.

goody-goody (M19)	hugger-mugger (E16)
happy-clappy (L20)	wishy-washy (E18)
harum-scarum (L17)	

reference The relationship between an expression and what is spoken of (i.e. an entity in the world).

For example, in *Jay is a good teacher*, the *noun phrase *Jay* refers to a person with that name in the real world. It is a *referring expression. *See also* REFERENT.

Alternatively, this term can refer to the relationship between one linguistic expression and another. We can then speak of **anaphoric reference** (backward reference) and **cataphoric reference** (forward reference) within a text or discourse, which are typically brought about by means of *pro-forms:

> Henry says *he* is coming (anaphoric)
>
> Before *she* leaves, I must write to Martha (cataphoric)

A distinction must be made between reference and *substitution, although there is some overlap. *Co-referential items share the same *referent in the real world, whereas with substitution, as with *ellipsis, there is a relationship between linguistic entities. Contrast:

Is that your paper? May I borrow *it*? (reference)

Is that a cappuccino? I didn't get *one* today (substitution)

In logic and linguistics, the term reference is further used in more technical ways. Sometimes it contrasts with other kinds of meaning (*see* REFERENTIAL MEANING), and sometimes with *sense.

1977 J. LYONS Expressions may differ in sense, but have the same reference; and 'synonymous' means "having the same sense", not "having the same reference". A rather better example than Frege's [i.e. of the Morning Star and the Evening Star, both being the planet Venus] is Husserl's, 'the victor at Jena' and 'the loser at Waterloo' . . . , both of which expressions may be used to refer to Napoleon.

See also ANAPHORA; CATAPHORA; CO-REFERENCE; SENSE; UNIQUE REFERENCE.

reference grammar *See* GRAMMAR.

referent The person, entity, etc. in the real world, or in an imagined world, that is identified by a linguistic expression, typically a *noun phrase.

The noun phrases *the victor at Jena* and *the loser at Waterloo* are *referring expressions; Napoleon is the referent.

referential *it* The pronoun *it* as used to refer to an entity, e.g.

Where is my coat? Ah, there *it* is over there.

Also called **referring *it***.

Compare DUMMY IT.

referential meaning *Semantics.* That aspect of *meaning that can be expressed in terms of *referents; objective, *cognitive, *denotative meaning.

Referential meaning can be contrasted with *emotive, *connotational, and *interpersonal meaning.

See also ATTITUDINAL MEANING; COMMUNICATIVE MEANING; CONATIVE; DESCRIPTIVE; ILLOCUTIONARY MEANING; PROPOSITIONAL MEANING.

referring expression An expression (typically a *noun phrase) used to identify a person, object, place, event, etc. Also called **r-expression**.

See also REFERENT.

reflexive (*n. & adj.*)

1. (Designating) a *pronoun ending in -*self* or -*selves* (e.g. *myself, themselves*) that refers back *anaphorically to the *subject of the same *clause, as in *She likes herself too much.*

Such pronouns are not usually considered *acceptable as subject in *main clauses in standard English (e.g. **Myself isn't interested in contributing to the fund*; **James and myself intend to help*), but can be used as *emphatic reinforcement (e.g. *I myself believe that he's telling the truth, despite what the others say*).

In clauses such as *He believes himself to be a genius* there is a disagreement as to whether the reflexive is the *direct object of the main clause or the subject of the *subordinate clause. The former analysis is probably more common.

2. (A *verb, or a structure containing a verb) taking a reflexive pronoun as *direct object. English has very few verbs that require such an object. Some examples are:

absent oneself, demean oneself (usually), perjure oneself, pride oneself

Other verbs may be understood reflexively, but a reflexive pronoun as object is optional:

He washed, shaved, and dressed

- **reflexivity**: the property of being reflexive.
- **reflexivization**: the action of making reflexive; the process of becoming reflexive.
- **reflexivize**: make reflexive.

reformulation A rewording or restatement in different *words.

The expression of the second term in an *apposition (e.g. *The mayor, Mr John Morrison, will not be attending*) could be regarded as an instance of reformulation, perhaps in order to explain the first term more accurately.

●● **reformulatory conjunct**: a *conjunct that introduces a reformulation, e.g.

The city of dreaming spires, *in other words* Oxford

The Press, *that is to say* Oxford University Press

register A variety of language used in particular circumstances. This term is used somewhat differently by different linguists.

In one use it refers to a *variety of language, *text, etc. related to a level of formality, anywhere on a scale from the extremely *formal or ceremonial to the *colloquial or slangy, as manifested in syntax, *vocabulary, and, possibly, pronunciation.

It can also refer to (the linguistic characteristics of) a variety of language, text, etc. related to a particular *field of discourse, subject, or occupation: e.g. advertising language or the language of the law.

Compare DOMAIN; GENRE.

regular Of a linguistic form or structure: following the rules for its *class, *paradigm, etc. Contrasted with *irregular.

For example, a **regular verb** has a *past tense and *past participle formed by adding -*ed* to the *base (2) (or -*d* if the base ends in -*e*): e.g. *look/looked/looked, race/raced/raced*.

Similarly, regular *noun *plurals are formed by adding -*s* (or -*es*) to a *nominal (1) *base, as in *book/books, box/boxes*.

●● **regular lexeme**: a *lexeme whose *inflectional forms follow a regular *pattern (e.g. *walk/walked/walked, hand/hands*), as opposed to *irregular lexemes that display irregular inflectional forms (*sing/sang/sung, child/children*). *See also* DEFECTIVE.

●● **regular sentence/clause**: a *sentence or *clause that conforms to the standard rules of grammar; an *unmarked sentence/clause. *See also* FULL (3), and *compare* KERNEL; MINOR SENTENCE/CLAUSE.

reinforcement The strengthening of the meaning of a *word, *phrase, etc.

Reinforcement is used in its everyday sense to describe the way some expressions are used to emphasize meaning. This may be through the use of *conjuncts or by repetition:

It was expensive; *furthermore/what's more/in addition* I thought it was ugly
It's *much much* too early to decide

rejected condition The same as hypothetical *condition.

1947 E. PARTRIDGE Rejected Condition, as in 'If wishes were horses, beggars would ride'.

relation This is a very general and loosely used term describing a connection (*syntagmatic, *paradigmatic, *semantic, etc.) between units at any *level. (Also called **relationship**.)

Thus we can speak of a **constructional relation** (or a **structural relation**) between *clauses in the same sentence; of a *dependency relation between a *subordinate clause and another clause; of relations of *apposition; of the relationship between different functional elements in a clause, e.g. a subject-*predicate relationship; of *transformational relations between different structures; and so on.

1968 J. LYONS The most characteristic feature of modern linguistics—one which it shares with a number of other sciences—is 'structuralism' (to use the label which is commonly applied, often pejoratively). Briefly, this means that each language is regarded as a *system of relations* (more precisely, a system of interrelated systems), the elements of which—sounds, words, etc.—have no validity independently of the relations of equivalence and contrast which hold between them.

- **relational**: *see* RELATIONAL.
- ● ● **relation word**: the same as **relational word** (*see* RELATIONAL).

relational (*adj.*) Indicating *relation(s) or relationship(s).

This label is used of both syntactic and semantic connections.

In a general sense, many terms in linguistics express relational notions. Consider, for example, the term *head. For an element to function as head it must be the head *of something*, namely a *phrase, *clause, etc.

More specifically, in syntax, *prepositions and *conjunctions are sometimes classified as **relational words** (also: **relation words**, **relator words**), whose function is to indicate the connection(s) between *constituents.

In the discussion of *texts, the term describes ways in which *sentences and other elements are connected in grammatical, semantic, and pragmatic ways.

1985 R. QUIRK et al. But irrespective of the various purposes and general intentions of a text, there are a few relationships within texts that constantly recur, which involve particular connective devices ... They can be seen as basic relational structures.

- ● ● **relational adjective**: an *adjective that is derived from a *noun and has little semantic content other than that expressed by the related noun, e.g. *prepositional* (compare *preposition phrase* and *prepositional phrase*), *Parisian* (compare *Paris metro* and *Parisian metro*).
- ● ● **relational noun** (also called **relator noun**): a noun that expresses a kinship relationship (e.g. *father, sister*) or, more generally, any noun that can express a relationship (e.g. *director* (of a company), *manager* (of a club)).
- ● ● **relational verb**: a *verb that indicates a 'relation' of some sort, such as 'existence' (expressed by a *linking verb; e.g. *Lara is here*) or 'possession' (expressed by *have, belong, lack*, etc.; e.g. *Fran has three bicycles*). In *Systemic Grammar, such verbs are contrasted with verbs of material and mental processes.

(*n.*) (The less usual, and probably outdated, term for) a relational word.

1969 E. A. NIDA Relationals are any units which function primarily as markers of relationships between other terms e.g. *at, by, because, and, or*.

Relational Grammar A theory of grammar developed as an offshoot of *Generative Grammar (2) from the mid-1970s onwards by David Perlmutter and Paul Postal, in which *clauses are analysed as networks of functional relationships (*subject, *object, etc.) rather than in terms of *constituents.

relationship *See* RELATION.

relative (*n. & adj.*) (Designating) a *pronoun (**relative pronoun**) that introduces a **relative clause** which establishes a link with an *antecedent *head whose reference is *modified.

The **relative pronouns** are *who, whom, whose, which*, and the (invariable) *that*, although the latter is excluded from the class in some grammars (e.g. CaGEL, OMEG).

Relative clauses are of two main kinds (sometimes subsumed under the label *adnominal):

(i) *defining, in which any relative pronoun can be used, or sometimes none at all (also called **restrictive**; *see* CONTACT CLAUSE):

the woman *who/whom/that I love*
the woman *I love*

(ii) *non-defining, where a *wh*-pronoun must normally be used (also called **non-restrictive**):

Algernon, *whom I greatly admire*, has really put himself out

A third type of relative clause (though treated as non-defining in some models) is the **sentential relative clause**, which refers back to the whole or to a part of a previous clause. It is usually introduced by *which*:

The hotel is very expensive. Which is a pity.

Relative determinatives are relative words that function as determiner (1) in *noun phrases, namely *which(ever), what(ever)*, and *whose*, e.g.

I devoured [[NP *what* food] they provided]
You can eat [[NP *whatever* snacks] you like]
This is the boy [NP *whose* bike] was stolen

Note that the first two examples involve a *free relative clause, and that some grammars (e.g. CaGEL, OMEG) exclude *whose* as a determinative, since it takes *genitive *case (1), and is hence a relative pronoun.

When and *where* can be used as **relative adverbs**:

I remember very well the region *where I was born*

•• **continuative relative clause**: a non-defining relative clause that continues a narrative, e.g.

Bob had told Edwin, who passed the news to Henry, who came and told me

•• **free relative clause**: *see* FREE RELATIVE CLAUSE.

•• **relative construction**: in CaGEL this encompasses not only relative clauses, but also what the grammar calls the **fused relative construction** (*see* FREE RELATIVE CLAUSE).

See also FREE RELATIVE CLAUSE.

Compare APPOSITIVE CLAUSE; REDUCED *clause*.

relativity *See* SAPIR–WHORF HYPOTHESIS, THE.

relativized element In CaGEL, in the most typical cases, the relativized element is a *wh*-element in a *relative clause that is linked to an *antecedent *head, e.g. *which* in *The kettle, which is damaged, should not be used.*

relator

1. Syntactically, a *word or *phrase that serves to relate one part of a *sentence to another, e.g. a *conjunction or *preposition. The same as *relational word.

2. Semantically, a word or phrase that contextualizes an *utterance with regard to time and place.

Place and time relators may include words such as *here, downstairs, now* (commonly labelled *adverbs); *noun phrases (e.g. *last night*); *prepositional phrases (e.g. *to the lighthouse, before the flood*); and *adjectives (e.g. *previous, later*).

See also RELATIONAL.

relevance *See* CURRENT RELEVANCE.

Relevance Theory A theory of *pragmatics developed by Dan Sperber and Deirdre Wilson from the 1980s onwards. The theory gives prominence to the **Principle of Relevance**, developed from one of Grice's maxims of conversation.

See also COOPERATIVE PRINCIPLE; IMPLICATURE.

remote condition *See* CONDITION.

replacive (*n. & adj.*)

1. *Morphology.* (A linguistic element) that replaces, or substitutes for, something else.

The term is particularly used in the label **replacive morph** or **replacive morpheme** to explain in morphemic terms the formation of *irregular forms, such as *men* from *man* or *sang*/*sung* from *sing*, which fall outside the regular rules for the formation of *noun *plurals or *past *verb forms by the addition of *inflections.

> 1974 P. H. MATTHEWS *Men*, for example, would be said to consist of the regular allomorph *man* of the morpheme MAN plus a 'replacive morph' ('replace *a* with *e*' or '*a → e*') which was assigned as yet another allomorph of plural. The plural morpheme would thus be regarded as a class of morphs with [z] (in *seas*), [s] (in *masts*), zero (in *sheep*)... and '*a → e*' among its members... This was nonsense, of course. A process of replacement is no more a 'morph' than zero is a 'morph'.

2. *Semantics.* (A unit) that introduces a *statement replacing, or reformulating, a previous statement.

•• **replacive conjunct**: this is one among the many semantic categories applied to *conjuncts; examples include *alternatively, rather, on the other hand.*

reported command *See* REPORTED SPEECH.

reported speech

1. The same as *indirect speech.

When we report speech we can use an introductory reporting *verb (e.g. *say, tell*: He *says* that ..., She *told* us that ...). This is the usual meaning of the term; it contrasts with *direct speech.

A **reported statement** reports a statement someone made, e.g. *He said that the trains are not running today* reports someone saying *The trains are not running today;* whereas a **reported command** reports a command, e.g. *He told me to leave the job until tomorrow* reports on someone saying *Leave the job until tomorrow.*

2. (More generally.) Any of the ways in which a speaker or writer reports what someone else has said.

In this sense, reported speech includes both *direct speech and *indirect speech.

reported statement *See* REPORTED SPEECH.

reporting verb *See* PRIVATE VERB.

response What is said by way of reply to a *question. For example, in response to

What did you buy?

we can say:

I'm not sure
Mind your own business
Why do you ask?

None of these is an **answer**, narrowly conceived in some frameworks as a response in a form dictated by the type of question asked. Thus the question above (syntactically an open *interrogative) elicits a *noun phrase referring to a (concrete) entity as answer, e.g. *lasagne, a book on gardening,* etc.

restricted code *See* CODE.

restriction *See* COLLOCATION; CO-OCCURRENCE; SELECTIONAL RESTRICTION; SEMANTIC RESTRICTION.

restrictive The same as *defining. Contrasted with *non-defining, *non-restrictive.

The term is particularly applied to *relative clauses, but has wider applications.

> 1990 S. GREENBAUM & R. QUIRK Modification can be restrictive or non-restrictive. That is, the head can be viewed as a member of a class which can be linguistically identified only through the modification that has been supplied (*restrictive*). Or the head can be viewed as unique or as a member of a class that has been independently identified . . . ; any modification given to such a head is additional information which is not essential for identifying the head, and we call it *nonrestrictive*.

•• **restrictive adjective**: a member of a subcategory of *attributive *adjectives, semantically defined as restricting or limiting the meaning of the following noun (also called **limiter adjective, limiting adjective**), e.g.

a *particular* individual

the *specific* issue

The term is potentially ambiguous, because most adjectives can be used in both restrictive and non-restrictive modification.

restructuring *See* MULTIPLE ANALYSIS.

result *Semantics.* (Expressing) the outcome of an action, event, etc. The concept of result is very general, so that many language elements can be described as relating to it, and consequently usage of this term is very wide-ranging.

Result is one of the categories used in the semantic description of *subordinators and *subordinate clauses. A subordinator introducing a **result clause** is variously described as a **subordinator of result** or a **resultive/resultative subordinator/conjunction**. Examples are *so, so . . . (that), such . . . (that)*:

It was a very hot day, *so* I went for a swim

It was *so* hot (*that*) I nearly fainted

It was *such* a hot day (*that*) I nearly fainted

Result clauses are often contrasted with clauses expressing *purpose.

A grammatical *object that comes into existence only as a result of the action expressed by a *verb is sometimes called a **result object** (or **object of result**; also **effected object**), e.g.

They built *their own house*

A *conjunct with resultative meaning is called a **resultive conjunct**, e.g. *consequently, hence*.

An *infinitive with this meaning can be called an **infinitive of result**, e.g.

He arrived *to find the place on fire*

*Adverbials are sometimes said to have **resultative meaning**, e.g.

I want everyone *here* by ten (= Everyone should be back here by ten)

Some *linking verbs are described as **resulting verbs** or **verbs of resulting meaning**, and their associated subject-related predicative *complements (*president, powerful* in the examples below) are variously described as **resulting attributes**, or as showing **resultant/resulting states**, e.g.

He *became* president/powerful

Similarly, object-related predicative complements can express a result, e.g.

We painted the ceiling *pink* (i.e. the ceiling became pink as a result of our painting it)

Contrast the example above with the following example in which the object-related predicative complement expresses **depictive** meaning:

We ate the fish *raw* (i.e. the fish was raw when we ate it)

● **resultant, resultative (resultive), resulting**: expressing, indicating, or relating to result.

Compare FACTITIVE.

retrospective Expressive of looking back in time.

*Verbs such as *forget, regret, remember* are sometimes singled out as **retrospective verbs**, or verbs with **retrospective meaning**, when they are followed by an *-ing* form:

I'll never forget hearing Sutherland

I remember wondering how she did it

I regret saying that

But in fact 'looking back' is part of the meaning of many verbs when followed by an *-ing* form, in contrast to a 'forward-looking' (and hence often *modal) meaning in other verbs when a *to*-infinitive follows. Contrast *I enjoy meeting people* with *I want to meet them*.

reversed polarity (tag) *See* POLARITY; TAG.

reverse pseudo-cleft *See* CLEFT.

Revised Extended Standard Theory *See* STANDARD THEORY.

rewrite rule (In *Generative Grammar (2).) A *rule that takes the form 'rewrite X as Y', e.g.

NP → det N (where NP=*noun phrase, det=determinative (1), and N=*noun)

See also PHRASE STRUCTURE RULE.

r-expression *See* REFERRING EXPRESSION.

rhematic *See* RHEME.

rheme The second part of the structure of a *clause, in which information is given about the *theme.

The linguistic use of the terms theme and rheme comes from the *Prague School of linguists. Rheme, however, was previously used in logic.

> 1959 J. FIRBAS Those sentence elements which convey something that is known, or may be inferred, from the verbal or from the situational context . . . are to be regarded as the communicative basis, as the theme of the sentence. On the other hand, those sentence elements which convey the new piece of information are to be regarded as the communicative nucleus, as the rheme of the sentence.

> 1975 M. A. K. HALLIDAY As a message structure . . . a clause consists of a Theme accompanied by a Rheme; and the structure is expressed by the order—whatever is chosen as the Theme is put first.

It should be noted that in the first definition of theme ('something that is known, or may be inferred') the theme can be communicatively rather unimportant, corresponding to what is *given (in a given and *new analysis). The second definition is somewhat different: the theme is important, and is put first to attract the reader's or listener's attention, although even here the rheme is more important. This is more like the *topic and *comment analysis, with the topic being what the sentence is about.

Some grammarians use the term *focus rather than rheme, and so contrast theme and focus (e.g. CGEL). Theme and rheme (and some of these other terms) may coincide with the traditional syntactic binary division into *subject and *predicate, but the former are concerned with *information structure, rather than syntax.

• **rhematic**: of or pertaining to a rheme.

rhetorical

1. Pertaining to the classical study of **rhetoric**, i.e. the art of speaking well, or of persuading others of a point of view.

2. Spoken or written for effect.

When applied to a *conditional clause, rhetorical means 'not to be taken literally'. A **rhetorical conditional clause** may look like an open condition, but is actually strongly assertive, e.g.

If he wins, I'll eat my hat (= he will not win)

She's sixty, if she's a day (= she is at least sixty)

● **rhetorical question:** *see* QUESTION.

right-branching *See* BRANCHING.

right dislocation *See* DISLOCATION.

Role and Reference Grammar (RRG)

A theory of functional grammar developed by William Foley and Robert Van Valin in the 1980s that stresses the importance of meaning and language use, and denies the existence of *autonomous syntax.

> 1993 R. VAN VALIN [W]hat distinguishes the RRG conception is the conviction that grammatical structure can only be understood with reference to its semantic and communicative functions. Syntax is not autonomous.

root

1. *Morphology.* A core element which remains when all *affixes have been removed from a complex *word. (Also called **simple base**, and sometimes called *radical.)

In discussions on word structure, terms such as *base, *morpheme (1), root, and *stem are used in different ways, often confusingly. The root of a word is commonly a morpheme which cannot be further analysed, and which underlies related derivatives of the word. Thus *go* is the root of *goes*, *going*, *goer*, etc., and also of *undergo*. (In this definition, root may be contrasted with base: *undergo* is a base for *undergoes*, *undergoing*, etc.)

A root in this sense may be less than a complete word. For example, *-duce* (as in *conduce*, *deduce*, *reduce*) or *jeal-* (as in *jealous*) are roots or **root morphemes**. (But such a form has also been described as a **lexical morpheme**, a **stem morpheme**, a stem, or a base.)

Compare BASE; STEM.

2. (In *historical linguistics.) An element, either a word (a **root word**) or a root in sense 1, that is the ancestor of a more recent word. For example, Latin *magister* is the root of both *master* and *magistrate*; Latin *moneta* is the root of both *money* and *mint*.

3. The topmost *node in a *tree diagram.

root modality Any kind of *modality that is not *epistemic modality.

royal _we_ The use of _we_ by a king or queen to mean 'I'.

An example is Queen Victoria's 'We are not amused'. The style is now restricted to formal documents.

Compare EDITORIAL WE.

rule A principle regulating or determining the form or *position of *morphemes (1) in a word, *constituents in a *clause or *sentence, etc., or a regular *relation between units of grammar.

It is perhaps worth pointing out that a term such as **grammatical rule** (or **rule of grammar**) is used with two somewhat different meanings, which are often conflated in people's minds. In an ideal world, a **descriptive rule**, describing objectively how some feature of grammar works, would be the same as a **prescriptive rule** for a language user or for a foreign language learner. In reality, some prescriptive rules are based on misunderstanding, while other such rules, though useful guidelines, are oversimplifications, and are inaccurate if taken to be a complete description.

In *Generative Grammar (2), rules are viewed as predictive, often in a rather abstract or mathematical form, and are meant to be capable of generating an infinite number of grammatical structures.

See also CATEGORY; CO-OCCURRENCE RULES; REWRITE RULE; TRANSFORMATIONAL _rule_.

S

1. Subject as an *element in *clause structure.
2. Sentence (in a *tree diagram or *rewrite rule).

Sapir-Whorf hypothesis, the A theory developed by the American anthropologists and linguists Edward Sapir (1884-1939) and Benjamin Lee Whorf (1897-1941), which holds that a people's language conditions the way they view the world (**linguistic determinism**), and that different perceptual distinctions are made by different languages (**linguistic relativity**).

> *ante* 1941 B. L. WHORF Concepts of 'time' and 'matter' are not given in substantially the same form by experience to all men but depend upon the nature of the language or languages through the use of which they have been developed. They do not depend so much upon ANY ONE SYSTEM (e.g. tense, or nouns) within the grammar as upon the ways of analyzing and reporting experience which have become fixed in the language as integrated 'fashions of speaking' and which cut across the typical grammatical classifications, so that such a 'fashion' may include lexical, morphological, syntactic, and otherwise systemically diverse means coordinated in a certain frame of consistency.

Whorf illustrated his theory particularly through Hopi, an Amerindian language, which, for example, has no *tense *system (1). But this does not mean that Hopi speakers cannot talk about time, and the fact that he could explain Hopi concepts in English militates against the theory in its extremer forms. Similarly, it is often said that various *words in one language cannot be translated into another, but even though there may not be a 'one for one' equivalent, a word can always be explained in some other way, for instance by a *phrase. It has also been pointed out that language users are not totally naive: English speakers who talk of the sunrise and sunset are not flat-earthers.

Saussurean (*adj.*) Of, pertaining to, or characteristic of the Swiss linguist Ferdinand de Saussure (1857-1913) or his theories.

(*n.*) An adherent of de Saussure's theories.

De Saussure was influential particularly because of his conception of language as a *system (1) of interrelated parts that mutually affect each other. His notion of *langue contrasted with **parole**, and the distinctions *paradigmatic vs *syntagmatic and *diachronic vs *synchronic, underlie much of modern linguistics. His *Cours de linguistique générale* (1916) is based on lecture notes taken by his students and compiled after his death.

Saxon genitive *See* GENITIVE.

scalar comparison A *comparison (1) made between entities in a *comparative clause where the comparison is on a scale, i.e. *gradable:, e.g. *My sister is taller than my brother.*

See also COMPARATIVE CLAUSE; NON-SCALAR COMPARISON.

Scale-and-Category Grammar An early version of *Systemic Grammar, as developed by M. A. K. Halliday.

Scale-and-Category Grammar is so called because language is analysed as an interrelationship between four categories (units, *classes, *structures, and *systems (2)) and three (or four) scales (*rank, *delicacy, *exponence, and possibly depth).

> 1985 G. D. MORLEY Scale-and-category grammar seeks to account for any stretch of language as it actually occurs, in either written or spoken form...
> By contrast with transformational grammar, however, scale-and-category is designed to analyse structures as they appear rather than to generate them.

See CATEGORY.

scope The range or span over which a particular linguistic item meaningfully extends its grammatical or semantic influence.

Some words affect the meaning of their containing *clause or *sentence. An inverted auxiliary (see INVERSION) or a *wh-word at the beginning of a clause usually marks the whole clause as *interrogative. Similarly, a *negative word often negates everything that follows it, and may therefore necessitate *non-assertive forms, e.g.

Nobody seemed to know *anything* about *anyone*

*Adverbials vary greatly in their scope. Some apply to the entire sentence that follows:

Frankly, I don't want to talk to him

others only to part of the predication:

I dread having to talk *frankly* to him

others to just one word:

Telling him the truth is going to be *incredibly* difficult

•• **scope of negation**: *see* NEGATION.

secondary (*n. & adj.*) (In some older grammar, mainly Jespersen's.) (Designating the *rank of) a linguistic unit that is at a second level 'down' in a *phrase, *group, etc. Contrasted with *primary (3) and *tertiary.

For example, in the *noun phrase *terribly cold weather*, *cold* is a secondary: it is modified by the tertiary *terribly*, with which in combination it *modifies the *head noun *weather*.

The analysis of *verbs as secondaries in this model is controversial, since verbs are analysed in modern grammar as the most essential element in *clause structure.

> 1933b O. JESPERSEN If we compare the two expressions *this furiously barking dog* and *this dog barks furiously* ... the verb *bark* is found in two different forms, *barking* and *barks*; but in both forms it must be said to be subordinated to *dog* and superior in rank to *furiously*; thus both *barking* and *barks* are here secondaries.

•• **secondary iconicity**: *see* ICONICITY.
•• **secondary onomatopoeia**: *see* ONOMATOPOEIA.
•• **secondary predicate**: *see* SECONDARY PREDICATE.
•• **secondary tense**: *see* PRIMARY (3).
•• **secondary verb form**: *see* PRIMARY (1).

secondary predicate A *phrase which is predicated of a *constituent (typically a *subject or *direct object) that is assigned a *semantic role by the *main verb, e.g.

> He left the company *angry with his boss* (subject-related secondary predicate)
> He likes eating his eggs *raw* (object-related secondary predicate)

See also SMALL CLAUSE; VERBLESS CLAUSE.

secondary tense *See* PRIMARY (3).

secondary verb form *See* PRIMARY (1).

second conditional *See* CONDITIONAL.

second person (Denoting, or used in conjunction with a *word indicating) the *person addressed (*singular or *plural), in contrast to the speaker or writer and any other person.

The second person *pronoun in modern standard English, for *singular and *plural, *subject and *object, is *you*. The related *reflexives are *yourself*, *yourselves*, and the *possessives are *your* and *yours*.

The lack of a singular/plural distinction for the second person (except in the reflexive form) is a noteworthy feature of *Standard English; in many non-*standard forms of English this has been remedied by the creation of forms such as *yous(e)* (L19), *yez* or *yiz* (E19), *you-all* (E19), *y'all* (E20).

segregatory coordination Coordination in which the two *conjoins could be separated and still make sense. Contrasted with *combinatory coordination.

Henry and Margaret had dinner is an example of segregatory coordination, since we can reasonably say *Henry had dinner* and *Margaret had dinner*.

selectional restriction A limitation on the company particular *lexical items can keep with other lexical items.

As propounded in early *Generative Grammar (2), selectional restrictions (also called **selectional rules/features**) were said to relate to the *context in which a *word could appear. Such selectional restrictions were contrasted with what were called *subcategorization *features. However, the latter were strictly syntactic, and would stipulate, for example, that the *transitive verb *discover* *licenses a *noun phrase functioning as *object (1) (hence the deviance of **John discovered*), whereas selectional restrictions were partly based on semantic criteria, e. g. the fact that the verb *find* normally requires an *animate *subject.

Chomsky's famous sentence *Colorless green ideas sleep furiously*, presented as an example of 'failure to observe a selectional rule', is clearly *deviant in a different way from both **John discovered* and from 'clearcut cases of violation of purely syntactic rules, for example *sincerity frighten may boy the*'.

In later literature, selectional restrictions are sometimes called *semantic restrictions. They are also sometimes equated with *co-occurrence restrictions, though the latter tend to be more narrowly based on syntax. Since many restrictions are partly syntactic and partly semantic, there is considerable overlap and looseness in the use of the different terms for describing restrictions.

self-embedding *See* EMBEDDING.

semantic Relating to *meaning.

1988 W. A. LADUSAW The principal descriptive goal of semantic theory is an account of the semantic structure of a language, the properties and relations which hold of the expressions of a language in virtue of what they mean. On analogy with syntactic theory, it is an account of part of the native speaker's

linguistic competence, namely, that knowledge underlying 'semantic competence'. As such, it presumes an account of the syntax of a language and
predicts judgements of semantic relations between its expressions based upon
proposals about what they mean. Chief among the relations to be accounted
for are paraphrase (or semantic equivalence) and semantic consequence
(or entailment).

Terms such as **semantic interpretation** and **semantic representation**
belong to various theories of *Generative Grammar (1), (2). In early versions the **semantic component** had a technical status along with the
syntactic and phonological components.

    Lexical meaning, i.e. the kind of meaning conveyed by *lexical items, is
sometimes contrasted with **grammatical meaning**, i.e. the kind of
meaning conveyed by particular *grammatical words or *structures.

•• **semantic change**: *see* SEMANTIC SHIFT.

•• **semantic feature**: one of a set of meaning components (*features (2))
into which a word can be analysed. The term is part of the vocabulary of
*componential analysis, where [-male] and [-adult] could be semantic
features of the word *girl*. Note that semantic features are inherent in the
word, in contrast to semantic restrictions (see below), which require a
semantic feature to be present in another word.

•• **semantic field**: *see* FIELD.

•• **semantic restriction**: a limitation on which lexical items can combine
with a particular word, based on the latter's meaning. Semantic restrictions (also called *selectional features/restrictions/rules) are part of the
framework of *Generative Grammar (2). But the concept is of general
relevance. For example, *The student congregated* is *deviant because an
inherent feature of the *verb *congregate* requires a *noun denoting a
collection of people as *subject. Note that this requirement is different
from a strictly grammatical *rule, such as the *concord rule, which requires both subject and verb to be *plural, e.g. *They are/*is congregating*.
Other verbs may restrict the kind of subject or *object they allow in
different ways, perhaps to [+human] or [+animate] (e.g. *The cupboard
laughed*), and some *adjectives can only be paired with a *concrete noun
(cf. *an oblong suggestion*). Semantic restrictions may of course be broken
in poetry or other imaginative literature, where special effects are partly
due to violations of rules, as in Dylan Thomas's *a grief ago*.

•• **semantic role**: *see* SEMANTIC ROLE.

•• **semantic shift**: *see* SEMANTIC SHIFT.

•• **semantic structure**: *see* STRUCTURE.

•• **semantic subject**: *see* NOTIONAL.

    Compare COLLOCATIONAL RESTRICTION.

Semantic Approach to English Grammar, A As its title suggests, this grammar, written by the British linguist R. M. W. Dixon in 2005, takes semantics as the starting point in the study of English grammar.

semantic role The particular role played by an *argument of a *predicate (2). Sometimes called *case (1), *participant role, or, in *Generative Grammar (2), **thematic role** or **theta (Θ)-role**.

Different frameworks use different sets of roles, but most will include a subset of the following: *agent, *beneficiary, *causer, *dative (2), *experiencer, *factitive (2), *goal (2), *instrumental, *locative, *objective (1), *path, *patient, *recipient, *source, *stimulus, *theme.

See also CASE GRAMMAR.

semantics The study of *meaning in language.

The term is a borrowing of the French term *la sémantique* (M. Bréal 1883). An older word (now disused) with much the same meaning was **semasiology**.

> 1912 E. WEEKLEY The convenient name semantics has been applied of late to the science of meanings, as distinguished from phonetics, the science of sound.

> 1964 E. A. NIDA While semantics deals with the relationship of symbols to referents, syntactics is concerned with the relationship of symbol to symbol.

Traditionally there is a division between syntax and *word meaning, which is shown by the separation of information about language into grammar books and dictionaries. Semantics goes beyond 'word meaning' in viewing words as part of a structured *system (1) of interrelationships in *clauses and *texts.

Later versions of *Generative Grammar (2) gave rise to *Generative Semantics and *interpretive semantics. Another theory is *logical semantics, including *truth-conditional semantics and *model-theoretic semantics.

Compare PRAGMATICS.

See also FIELD; MEANING.

semantic shift A change in the *meaning of a word taking place over time. (Also called **semantic change**.)

There is a general tendency for *words to develop new meanings and to relinquish other meanings over time. This type of change does not occur in isolation, but in relation to other words whose meanings are also changing. *Meat* once meant 'food in general', while *flesh* had a wider coverage than at present, taking in both living flesh and dead flesh as food. Individually considered, each of these words has contracted its field of *reference, and when we consider them as a set it becomes clear that a certain reclassification has taken place. *Collide*, once used mainly of pairs of trains and ships in motion, has expanded its scope as a result of technological change. With this semantic shift the *verb has acquired a more general meaning, and can be used for almost any objects whose paths might cross (e.g. pedestrians, motor vehicles, aircraft, sub-atomic particles, etc.), and also for the meeting of a moving object with a static one (e.g. a car colliding with a tree).

semantic subject *See* NOTIONAL.

semasiology *See* SEMANTICS.

sememe

1. The unit of *meaning carried by a *morpheme (1).

For example, the *suffix *-ess* in *duchess, hostess, lioness* expresses the meaning 'female, feminine'.

2. A minimal unit of meaning.

An example is the grammatical meaning 'past' or 'plural', which can be realized in different ways.

1974 P. H. MATTHEWS In Bloomfield's formulation [d]/[t] would be one 'morpheme' (one phonetic form being a 'phonetic modification' of the other), and [n]/[ən] would be a different 'morpheme'; they are related only in that both could be associated with the same 'sememe' or unit of meaning. But the notion of 'sememe' is decidedly problematic (particularly for a concept such as that of the 'Past Participle').

The term was coined by the Swedish linguist A. Noreen (1904).

semi- *See* QUASI-.

semi-auxiliary (verb) (In CGEL.) A string of *words consisting of two or three parts beginning with *be* or *have*, such as *be able to, be about to, be apt to, be due to, be going to, be likely to, be supposed to, have to*, etc., often listed as such in dictionaries.

A number of these combinations, which share characteristics with *auxiliaries, cause disagreements of analysis among grammarians. Thus in alternative accounts *likely* in *be likely to* is regarded as a *modal adjective which *licenses a *to-infinitive *clause as *complement, *have* in *have to* is regarded as a *modal lexical verb, and *be going (to)* is analysed as an *idiomatic combination.

This category seems very similar to, but not quite the same as, *phrasal auxiliary verb.

See also AUXILIARY; MARGINAL MODAL; MODAL; MODAL LEXICAL VERB; MODAL VERB.

semicolon *See* PUNCTUATION.

semi-modal The same as *marginal modal.
See also SEMI-AUXILIARY.

semi-negative (*n. & adj.*) (A word) that is *negative in import, and grammatically often has the same effect as a negative word. Also called **near negative** and **approximate negator**.

A number of semi-negative *adverbs, e.g. *barely, hardly, little, scarcely*, and the *determinatives (1) *little* and *few* syntactically behave like negative words. For example, they can take positive *tags:

> It's *barely/scarcely* possible, *is it?*
> *Few* people know this, *do they?*

Similarly, *fronted semi-negative adverbs, as in the first two examples below, require subject-auxiliary *inversion in the same way that 'true' negatives do, as in the last two examples:

> *Hardly* had they arrived when the lights went out
> *Only then* [i.e. 'not before'] did we realize our mistake

> *Nowhere* have I seen such incompetence
> *Never* did I expect to see this day arrive

Compare BROAD NEGATIVE.

semiology The study of linguistic *signs and symbols.
The same as *semiotics. The term was coined (as French *sémiologie*) by Ferdinand de Saussure (1916).

semiotic (*adj.*) Relating to the use of *signs as a form of communication. (*n.*) The same as *semiotics, which is now the usual term.

> 1973 R. JAKOBSON The subject matter of semiotic is the communication of any messages whatever, whereas the field of linguistics is confined to the communication of verbal messages.

semiotics The study of *signs in language.
Semiotics is sometimes restricted to non-linguistic communication, including possibly body language and the kinds of visual signs and symbols that 'translate' into *words, e.g. traffic signs and signals, company logos, and such old established signs as a barber's pole or the three balls of a pawnbroker's sign. However, semiotics may also include language: see the quotation at *semiotic.

semi-passive (In CGEL.) A *passive construction which has both
*verbal and *adjectival properties.

  Semi-passives are like true passives in having *active counterparts, e.g.

  I *was impressed* by his fluency (*compare* His fluency impressed me)

However, the *past participles are like adjectives in a number of ways. For
example, they can be *coordinated with *central (2) adjectives:

  The whole family were *upset* and *angry*

Also, the 'participle' can be modified by *adverbs such as *more*, *most*,
quite, etc.:

  They were *quite worried* about Tom's disappearance

And finally the verb *be* can be replaced by *copular verbs such as *look*,
seem, etc.:

  Sarah didn't seem *interested* in his explanation

  Compare CENTRAL *passive*; PSEUDO-PASSIVE; *stata*/PASSIVE.

sense *Semantics*. Meaning.
  This term is used in a wide variety of ways, just like *meaning and
*reference. In semantic theory it is used to describe *lexical meaning,
which is derived partly from the meaning of other *words (**sense relations**), in contrast to the relationship of a word to the outside world, which
is reference. In an example of Husserl's the phrases *the victor at Jena* and
the loser at Waterloo have a different sense, but the same reference
(namely Napoleon). See the citation by Lyons in the entry for reference.
  Compare DENOTATION.

senser A *semantic role label applied to a *phrase that refers to the
*experiencer of an action, mental process, etc. denoted by a *verb, typi-
cally a *perception verb or *psychological verb, e.g.

  I don't like your attitude (*I* = senser; *your attitude* = the phenomenon being
  'sensed')

  It upsets me that you won't even try (*It* + *that you won't even try* =
  phenomenon; *me* = senser)

This is not a very generally used term, and experiencer is probably more
common.

sentence The largest unit of analysis in *grammar (1). Sentences usually
have a *subject and *predicate, and (when they are written) begin with a
capital letter and end with a full stop.
  Traditional definitions of the sentence are often formulated in *notional
terms, e.g. 'a set of words expressing a complete thought', but this is too

vague to be useful. However, attempts at rigorous structural definitions (as above) are not entirely satisfactory either.

One reason is that not all sentences have a subject and predicate. For example, *imperatives usually lack an expressed subject. At the same time more than one 'grammatically complete sentence' can be run together in writing with only one full stop, so that grammatical and orthographic sentences may not correspond (e.g. *I came, I saw, I conquered*). As for spoken language, it is often impossible to say where one sentence ends and another begins.

Another problem affects the definition of the sentence as 'the largest unit of analysis in grammar', since *pro-forms, *conjuncts, and *cohesive devices such as *reference and *substitution often operate over stretches of discourse larger than the sentence.

We also have to recognize the theoretical possibility of a sentence containing an infinite number of *clauses (*see* RECURSION). For this reason modern grammarians often prefer to analyse syntactic structure in terms of clauses. Sentences are categorized in modern grammar, as in traditional grammar, into *simple (2), *compound, and *complex on the basis of the number and type of clauses they contain.

Compare ABBREVIATED; CLAUSE; FULL (3); FUNCTION.

•• **sentence adjunct**: *see* SENTENCE ADJUNCT.

•• **sentence adverb**: *see* SENTENCE ADVERB.

•• **sentence adverbial**: *see* SENTENCE ADVERBIAL.

sentence adjunct An *adjunct (1) that has *scope over ('applies to' or 'relates to') a complete *sentence or *clause, rather than only a part of it, often expressing a *modal meaning. Also called **sentence modifier** and **S-adjunct**. Sentence adjuncts are typically *adverbs, and usually occur in *initial position, but can be placed elsewhere in the containing sentence:

Perhaps we need to get an engineer to come out

We will *in any case* contact you when you return

Probably you will be able to visit the US later this year

Surely that is obvious from what I have said so far

See also PREDICATION ADJUNCT; SENTENCE ADVERBIAL (1).

sentence adverb An *adverb that functions as a *sentence adjunct or *sentence adverbial (1).

1932 C. T. ONIONS *Else, only* (= 'but'), *so, accordingly, hence, also, too, likewise, moreover,* though some of them frequently come at the beginning of a sentence, are not Conjunctions at all, but Adverbs. They qualify the sentence as a whole rather than any particular part of it, and may therefore be called Sentence Adverbs. Other Adverbs which may be used thus are *truly, certainly, assuredly, verily, undoubtedly*: e.g. 'This is certainly false' (= 'It is certain that this is false').

sentence adverbial

1. An *adverbial (1) that relates to an entire *sentence or *clause.
Compare PREDICATION ADJUNCT.
See also SENTENCE ADJUNCT; SENTENCE ADVERB.
2. Another term for *disjunct only.

Sentence and its Parts, The: A Grammar of Contemporary English A *grammar (2) written by the American linguist R. B. Long in 1961 in which *grammar* is understood 'in the broad sense of the term, including word formation, phonology, spelling, and punctuation. The central interest is grammar in the narrow sense: syntax, of which inflection is here regarded as a division.'

sentence element *See* ELEMENT.

sentence structure *See* STRUCTURE.

sentence type *See* CLAUSE TYPE.

sentential Being or pertaining to a *sentence.
•• **sentential relative clause**: *see* RELATIVE.

separability The possibility of dividing a linguistic unit (*word, *phrase, etc.) by inserting an intervening element.
This is often said to be a feature of *phrasal verbs (1) in some analyses:

We *looked up our friends*
We *looked our friends up*
Compare DISCONTINUITY.

sequence of tense rule *See* BACKSHIFT.

sequent Of (the *tense of) a *verb (combination) that is used after a reporting verb in the *past tense.
Some of the tense distinctions normally available are *neutralized after a verb such as *said* or *thought*, with the result that the following (or sequent) verb has fewer options. For example, a sequent *past perfect may represent a *present perfect, a past perfect, or a *simple past in the 'original' utterance:

The neighbours said he had left

(i.e. the neighbours originally said *'He has left'*, or *'He had left (before we got here)'*, or *'He left (ten minutes ago)'*)

See also BACKSHIFT.

serial comma *See* PUNCTUATION.

set expression *See* FIXED.

SEU *See* SURVEY OF ENGLISH USAGE, THE.

sex-neutral *See* EPICENE.

-s form The third *person *singular form of *lexical verbs in the *present tense, e.g.

looks, sees, wishes

On nouns, the *-s* ending indicates *plurality.

shall/will future *See* SIMPLE (3).

shape The *realization of a particular *lexical item in writing or speech. Contrasted with *inflectional form.

2005 R. HUDDLESTON & G. K. PULLUM By shape we mean spelling or pronunciation: spelling if we're talking about written English, pronunciation if we're talking about spoken English. The preterite and past participle are different inflectional forms but they have the same shape *walked*. Similarly for the plain present and plain form, which share the shape *walk*.

shift (*n.*)

1. A change of *meaning. *See* SEMANTIC SHIFT.

2. A change from one grammatical *category to another.

1962 B. M. H. STRANG A form may have inherent rank as morpheme, word, phrase or clause, but may in special circumstances be shifted to any other rank.

See also BACKSHIFT; CONVERSION; RANKSHIFT.

(*v.*) Change phonetically, semantically, or grammatically.

short form The same as *contraction (2); a contracted form.

Short Introduction to English Grammar, A Intended as a college textbook, this grammar was written by the American linguist James Sledd in 1959. It is divided into three parts, namely the grammar itself, a glossary, and an exposition on style.

short passive *See* PASSIVE.

***should*-mandative** *See* SUBJUNCTIVE.

sign *Semantics, Semiotics.* That which conventionally stands for, or signifies, some other thing, of which linguistic units such as *words are examples, but not the only examples.

The word *sign* and related terms are used in specialized ways in linguistic discussions:

> 1977 J. LYONS The meaning of linguistic expressions is commonly described in terms of the notion of signification; that is to say, words and other expressions are held to be signs which, in some sense, signify, or stand for, other things. What these other things are ... has long been a matter of controversy. It is convenient to have a neutral technical term for whatever it is that a sign stands for: and we will use the Latin term significatum, as a number of authors have done, for this purpose.

De Saussure (1916) observed that the notion of sign generally designates only the acoustic impression, but proposed to keep the word for the combination of this and the associated concept, replacing 'concept' with *signifié* and acoustic impression with *signifiant*. Other words for *signifié* are *significatum* and *signified*; and for *signifiant* we have *significans* and *signifier*.

The study of signs is called *semiotics.

simple
   1. Of a word: not *compound or *complex.
   Steam may be described as a simple *word in contrast to *steamboat* (a compound) or *steaminess* (a complex word).
•• **simple fused head**: *see* FUSION.
•• **simple preposition**: a single-word *preposition (e.g. *from, before*), in contrast to a *complex preposition (e.g. *out of, in front of*).
   2. Of a *sentence: consisting of a single *clause (typically independent and *finite) containing a single *verb (phrase), e.g.

   Britain's role in Europe is important

Simple sentences contrast with *compound and *complex sentences.

   However, in some analyses, a sentence containing another clause may still be simple, provided that the sentence does not have a clause functioning as *subject, *direct object, *complement, or *adverbial. By this definition a sentence containing a *postmodifying *relative clause is still a simple sentence, e.g.

This presents [$_{NP}$ a choice [$_{Rel.Cl.}$ which affects every aspect of your life and future]]

The relative clause is part of a *noun phrase (which functions as direct object), so this sentence has a simple subject–verb–direct object structure.

3. Of a *tense: implemented (i.e. formed) by a verb used on its own (in sentences that are not negated).

English has two simple tenses: the *past simple (also called **simple past** or **simple preterite**, e.g. *ran*) and the *present simple (also called simple present, e.g. *run, runs*). See PAST (2); PRESENT (2).

In traditional grammar, the *shall/will* *future (e.g. *I will cook some dinner now*) is sometimes called the **simple future (tense)**, but in modern grammar this construction is not usually analysed as a tense. See FUTURE (2).

See also TENSE; PRIMARY *tense*.

4. Of a *verb phrase (1): consisting of a single verb form without ellipsis, e.g.:

'*Look!*' he *said*. 'She *blushed.*'

simple fused head See FUSION.

simple future (tense) See FUTURE (2); SIMPLE (3).

simple past (tense) See PAST (2); SIMPLE (3).

simple present (tense) See PRESENT (2); SIMPLE (3).

singular (*n. & adj.*) (Designating) a *word or form that denotes, or refers to, a single entity (person, thing, etc.).

Singular contrasts mainly with *plural in the description of *nouns, *pronouns, and *verb forms, e.g.

The girl is/looks confident (singular)

versus

The girls are/look confident (plural)

*Uncount nouns are sometimes described as singular because they take singular *verbs. But this is misleading, since singular count nouns and uncount nouns do not share the same set of *determinatives (1) (e.g. *a/ one roll* but *some/much bread*).

Invariable nouns of plural meaning which lack an -*s* ending but take a plural verb (e.g. *police*) are sometimes described as singular nouns. See COLLECTIVE NOUN.

Compare NON-SINGULAR; PLURALE TANTUM; SINGULARE TANTUM.

singulare tantum (Pronounced /sɪŋ(j)ʊˈlɑːreɪ ˈtæntəm/. Plural **singularia tantum**.) A word which has only a *singular form.

A little used term which is sometimes applied to *mass nouns (or *uncount nouns).

Compare PLURALE TANTUM.

situation

1. The extra-linguistic *context of language.

2. *Semantics.* A cover term for actions, events, states, processes, etc.

1976 B. COMRIE In discussing aspect, it is often necessary to refer to the differences between states, events, processes, etc.... However, while ordinary nontechnical language provides, with a limited amount of systematisation, a metalanguage for these various subdivisions, it does not provide any general term to subsume them all. In the present work the term 'situation' is used as this general cover-term, i.e. a situation may be either a state, or an event, or a process.

See also CONTEXT *of situation.*

situational Relating to, or determined by, the *situation.

●● **situational context**: *see* EXTRALINGUISTIC.

●● **situational meaning**: *see* INTERPERSONAL.

●● **situational recoverability**: *see* RECOVERABILITY.

slang *Words, *phrases, and uses that are regarded as very *informal, and are often restricted to special *contexts, or are peculiar to a specified profession, class, etc. (e.g. **racing slang**, **schoolboy slang**).

slot A position within a *structure that can be filled by a *filler (1).

1973 R. QUIRK & S. GREENBAUM Existential *there*... may be regarded as an empty 'slot-filler'.

See also SLOT-AND-FILLER.

slot-and-filler Designating a method of analysing *sentence or *clause structure in which various functional *slots are first identified, and the *words and *phrases that can fill them (*fillers) are then further analysed. For example, in the following sentence there are three slots:

I resist everything except temptation

These are: *subject (*I*), *predicator (*resist*), and *direct object (*everything except temptation*).

The system underlies present-day analysis into clause *elements. It also links up to some extent with the *distributional (rather than *notional) methods used in defining the *word classes. Thus the subject slot can be filled by a wide variety of *noun phrases (e.g. *you*, *the neighbours*, etc.), but all would contain a noun or *pronoun as head. Similarly, anything that can fill the second slot must be a *verb. However, the third slot could be filled by a clause: *I resist buying too many chocolates.*

Compare IMMEDIATE CONSTITUENT.

small clause (In *Government-Binding Theory.) A structure which resembles a *clause because it contains a *subject + *predicate (1), but which does not contain any *verbs. For example:

We think [*the scheme preposterous*]
I considered [*the proposal a brilliant idea*]

In many grammars such structures are not analysed as clauses. Instead, the *noun phrases *the scheme* and *the proposal* in the examples above function as *direct object, and the *adjective phrase *preposterous* and the noun phrase *a brilliant idea* function as object-related predicative *complement.

In some cases the small clause lacks a subject:

We stumbled out of the tunnel, [Ø *completely disoriented*]

Here the non-overt subject of the bracketed clause (indicated by 'Ø') is interpreted as *co-referential with the subject of the higher clause (*we*).

See also ADJECTIVE CLAUSE; COMPLEMENT.

social dialect *See* DIALECT.

social distancing The explanation given for a use of the *past tense which is attributable neither to the event being in the past nor to hypothetical meaning.

Past tenses are sometimes used where a *present tense could just as well be used, e.g.

Did you want to see me?
I *was* wondering whether you could spare me a minute?
We *were* hoping you would help
I *wouldn't* have thought so

Sometimes politeness is the motivation: it may be easier for the addressee to say 'no' to a request with a past tense verb than to a blunter request (e.g. *We are hoping you will help*); but at other times the 'distancing' may sound over-formal or cold.

social meaning The same as *interpersonal meaning.

sociolinguistics The study of language in a social setting.

Sociolinguistics is concerned with the interrelationship between language and region, language and national identity, language and peer group pressure, language and the age, sex, and social class of the user, and so on.

● **sociolinguist, sociolinguistic.**

> 1978 W. LABOV The sociolinguistic behaviour of women is quite different from that of men because they respond to the commonly held normative values in a different way.

solecism A mistake of grammar or *idiom; a blunder in the manner of speaking or writing.

This is a general term. Grammarians are more likely to speak of error, incorrect usage, *hypercorrection, etc.

● **solecistic.**

sound symbolism A (fancied) representative relationship between the sounds making up a *word and its *meaning.

Various kinds of sound and meaning correlations are said to exist; specialized terms include *iconicity and *onomatopoeia.

Usage is inconsistent. Sound symbolism can be used as a cover term for all such phenomena, but in the literature the term often seems to exclude obvious onomatopoeia such as *cuckoo* and *cock-a-doodle-doo.*

source

1. A *semantic role (or *case (3)) assigned to an *argument of a *verb, which denotes the place, location, etc. from which somebody or something originates. Often contrasted with *goal. Example:

> He comes from London

> 1975 D. C. BENNETT Three directional cases are posited: 'source', 'path' and 'goal'...A sentence such as *We went from Waterloo Bridge along the Embankment to Westminster* is considered to contain three directional expressions in its semantic representation: a source expression, a path expression and a goal expression. The source expression, realized in surface structure as *from Waterloo Bridge,* specifies the starting-point of the change of position described by the sentence.

See also PATH.

2. A general label used in classifying the meaning of *adverbials and *prepositions of *space.

3. In a model of communication, the source is the sender of a 'message'. The person who receives (or is meant to receive) the message is the **destination**.

space The three-dimensional expanse in which physical objects exist; place; used in describing the meaning of *adverb phrases, *prepositional phrases, etc., and including both position and direction, e.g. *abroad, beneath, downstairs, in the bathroom, outside.*

• **spatial**.

Compare TEMPORAL; TIME.

speaker-oriented A term used in the description of *deontic and *epistemic *modal verbs to indicate that the 'source' of the modal meaning (typically 'obligation', 'permission', etc.) is the speaker, as opposed to the *referent of the *subject of the verb.

Thus if I say *You must submit this document by Wednesday* the source of the obligation is me, as the speaker. By contrast, if I say *Lars can speak six languages* it is the referent of the subject of the sentence (Lars) who has the ability to speak six languages. In this last example the modal verb expresses *dynamic (2) modality.

Compare SUBJECT-ORIENTED.

See also MODALITY.

special fused head See FUSION.

specific Referring to a particular individual, entity, etc. and no other.

In discussions of meaning, the notion is used especially in relation to *article usage. A distinction is made between *classifying (or *generic) meaning and specific meaning, which cuts across that between *definite and *indefinite meaning. Thus specific meaning may be either definite or indefinite, e.g.

I met *an interesting man* on holiday (specific indefinite)
This man told me that he's a war veteran (specific definite)

In another model, the notion *specific* is contrasted with *general*, but the distinction that is being made is very different. All *determinatives (1) are either specific or general: thus *the* in all its uses, *demonstratives (*this, those*, etc.), and *possessives (*my, your*, etc.) are specific, whereas *a/an* (whatever the meaning) is general. Thus specific includes definite, and general equates roughly with indefinite.

Note that, since the word *specific* is in everyday use—and indeed is sometimes glossed in dictionaries as 'definite'—it is often used loosely, and the necessary distinction is frequently ignored or confused in popular grammar books.

•• **specific determiner**: see INDEFINITE.

specified preposition See PREPOSITION.

specifier (Spec) A label used in *X-bar syntax for functional elements inside *phrases that express certain types of 'specifying' meaning, e.g. *definiteness, *possession, proximity/remoteness, *intensification, etc.

For example, *the* in *the cinema* functions as specifier, as does *very* in *very bright*, and *right* in *right up my street*. Note that in other frameworks *noun phrase specifiers are called *determiners (1) or *determinatives (2), and specifiers in other types of phrases are simply analysed as *modifiers.

specifying *be* The verb *be* when it is used in a *clause whose subject-related predicative *complement identifies someone or something, e.g.

The man on the bus is my neighbour

Also called **identifying *be***.

See also ASCRIPTIVE *BE*; IDENTIFY.

speech *See* DIRECT SPEECH; INDIRECT SPEECH; REPORTED SPEECH.

speech act A social or *interpersonal act that takes place when an utterance is made.

The **theory of speech acts** (also known as **Speech Act Theory**) was popularized by J. R. Searle in his book *Speech Acts* (1969), in which he expounded and expanded the theories of the philosopher J. L. Austin. The theory propounds various important distinctions: one between *performative utterances, which are used to perform some kind of action (e.g. *I name this ship the Star of the Seas*), and **constative utterances**, which contain *propositions that are either true or false; and further distinctions between *locutions, *illocutions, and *perlocutions, and the associated *locutionary, *illocutionary, and *perlocutionary acts.

•• **indirect speech act**: a speech act in which there is a mismatch between a particular linguistic form (e.g. *declarative clause, *interrogative clause) and the typical use that is made of that form. For example, when I say *Can you close the door?* I'm not asking you a *question, but making a request.

See also CLAUSE TYPES.

speech community *Sociolinguistics*. Any social or geographical group sharing roughly the same language.

split infinitive A *to-infinitive with one or more words separating *to* from the actual infinitive, regarded as incorrect usage. The stock example is from the television series *Star Trek*:

> Space, the final frontier. These are the voyages of the starship *Enterprise*. Its
> continuing mission: to explore strange new worlds, to seek out new life and
> new civilizations, *to boldly go* where no man has gone before.

The *prescriptive grammarians' objection to the split infinitive is based on
the fact that in Latin the infinitive is a single indivisible *word.

On most occasions, and to most people, the split infinitive is perfectly
acceptable. However, avoidance may at times be wise, since a split infinitive can be stylistically awkward, and may distract a *prescriptively
minded reader from the message that a writer is trying to convey. But
avoidance also has its pitfalls, since the word(s) that 'split' the infinitive,
when moved, may become associated with another part of the sentence,
causing its meaning to change. Avoidance can thus also result in stylistic
awkwardness.

A split infinitive may be the best option in the following example:

> According to the oil company it is essential to drill on National Trust land *to
> fully exploit* a new deeper oilfield which has been found at the farm

Substituting *fully to exploit* may associate *fully* with *to drill on National
Trust land*, while substituting *to exploit fully* separates the *verb from its
*direct object. In the next example *really to unite* would be of dubious
acceptability, whereas **to unite really the country* and **to unite the country
really* are ungrammatical:

> He has promised to be the first president *to really unite* the country

splitting See WORD CLASS.

S-Structure See SURFACE STRUCTURE.

stacked modification See MODIFICATION.

standard (*n. & adj.*) (Of, pertaining to, or designating) the most prestigious *variety of a language (or, occasionally, its pronunciation).
 See also STANDARD ENGLISH.

Standard English The *variety of English employed by educated
speakers, e.g. those in the professions, the media, academia, etc.; the
English described in dictionaries, *grammars (2), and usage guides.
 The label Standard English:

(i) primarily refers to a system of grammar and *lexis, and thus to a variety
   which can be spoken in a range of different accents—Northern, Scottish,
   American, etc.;

(ii) can be applied to written and spoken English;

(iii) refers to an English norm used (with relatively minor regional variations)
   worldwide.

Standard English enjoys greater prestige than non-standard varieties, and dialects. Although non-standard varieties are popularly often felt to be the province of the less educated, linguists insist that Standard English owes its position to political and social causes, and that other varieties are not linguistically substandard.

> 2002 R. HUDDLESTON & G.K. PULLUM et al. Perhaps the most subtle concept we have to rely on is the one that picks out the particular variety of Present-day English we describe, which we call Standard English. Briefly . . . , we are describing the kind of English that is widely accepted in the countries of the world where English is the language of government, education, broadcasting, news publishing, entertainment, and other public discourse.

In addition to the basic 'common core' standard, many national standards are recognized, including American English (AmE) and British English (BrE), which have few grammatical differences, but do have an appreciable degree of lexical divergence.

standard of comparison *See* COMPARISON.

Standard Theory The model of *Generative Grammar (2) presented by Noam Chomsky in his book *Aspects of the Theory of Syntax* (1965). (Also called **Aspects Theory**, the **Aspects Model**, or the **Standard Model**.)

This model introduced the concepts of *deep structure and *surface structure, and also posited differences between a speaker's *competence and *performance. It has since been developed and radically changed by Chomsky and his associates. Later models include the **Extended Standard Theory**, **Revised Extended Standard Theory**, *Government-Binding Theory, and *Principles and Parameters Theory. The most recent model is the *Minimalist Program. *Generative Semantics is a radically different offshoot.

statal passive *See* PASSIVE.

state (Expressing) a relatively permanent or unalterable *situation. Contrasted with *action, event, happening, etc.

This term is applied to *verbs or verb combinations. For example, all the following describe states:

> They *have lived* here for twenty years (*see* PERFECT)
> They *own* their own house
> It *has* four bedrooms
> The garden *is* huge
> They really *like* it

By contrast, the following examples describe actions or events (whether single or repeated):

We *have* just *bought* a flat

They *have moved* ten times in fifteen years

They *are buying* a house

•• **state verb**: (a popular term for) *stative verb (a verb describing a state, such as *be* or *like* in the examples above).

The distinction between state verbs and *action verbs expresses broadly the same contrast as the opposition *stative vs *dynamic (1). Theoretically, therefore, state verbs are not used in the *progressive. In practice, however, some state/stative verbs are used with dynamic meaning (*We're having a party; You're being difficult*). Notice also that some state verbs may denote a brief temporary state (*I think I'll go to bed*), but this is in contrast to a temporary action (*I'm thinking about it*).

statement

1. (In non-specialized usage.) A *sentence or *utterance that states or declares.

2. (In modern grammatical analyses that distinguish *structure and *usage.) A usage label indicating the *function (2) of a *clause as stating or declaring something. Contrasted with the syntactic label *declarative.

> 1984 R. HUDDLESTON Precisely because they are semantic categories, the criteria that distinguish statement, question and directive from each other are of a quite different nature from those that distinguish the syntactic clause type categories. In performing the illocutionary act of stating, I express some proposition and commit myself to its truth: I tell my addressee(s) that such and such is the case. Statements, in the 'product' sense, are assessable as true or false; questions and directives are not.

Compare DIRECTIVE; EXCLAMATIVE; QUESTION.

static The same as *stative.

stative Expressing a *state or condition. Contrasted with *dynamic (1).

The term is mainly used, like dynamic, in the classification of *verbs, but can also be applied to other *word classes.

> 1990 S. GREENBAUM & R. QUIRK A stative adjective such as *tall* cannot be used with the progressive aspect or with the imperative: **He's being tall*, **Be tall*.

•• **stative passive**: *see* PASSIVE.

stem *Morphology*. An element in *word structure.

The terms stem, *base, and *root are sometimes used interchangeably, and sometimes in contrasting (and conflicting) ways.

Some linguists use the term stem for the primitive minimal unit of morphology, in preference to *base (see e.g. CGEL for this usage). Such a stem may be *free (1) (as in *selfish*) or *bound (1) (as in *jealous*). More complicated words are then analysed in terms of stems and bases. On this model, *pole* is the stem of *polar*, *polarize*, and *depolarize*; but in the context of *depolarize* (where no such word as **depolar* exists, and the word is formed by adding the *prefix *de-* to *polarize*), *polarize* is not a primitive stem, but a base. For other linguists, the two terms are reversed.

Other linguists avoid the term base in favour of terms such as **compound stem** and **complex stem**. Thus *self-conscious*, consisting of two **simple stems** (*self* + *conscious*), can be described as a *compound stem. If *un-* is added, we have *unselfconscious*, which in turn is a *complex stem for *unselfconsciousness*.

In Latin and Greek grammar, and in *historical linguistics, the stem is the part of the word to which *inflectional endings are attached, and is usually an extension (by means of a **thematic vowel** or a formative *suffix) of the root. For example, OE *lufode* 'loved' has the root *luf-* but the stem *lufo-*, where the root is extended by a thematic vowel *-o-* (= Latin *-a-* in *amabam*).

Compare BASE; ROOT.

stimulus A *semantic role that denotes what is being experienced. For example, in *The difficulty of the assignment surprised me* the *subject carries the role of stimulus.

See also EXPERIENCER.

strand Cause (a *word, *phrase, etc.) to become grammatically isolated, typically at the end of a *clause. The term is mostly used in *participle form (i.e. **stranded**).

*Ellipsis frequently leaves an *operator stranded, e.g.

She promised to telephone us last night, but she *didn't*

Similarly, a *subject may be stranded in a *comparison, e.g.

You play the flute so much better than George

Stranded prepositions do not immediately precede their *complement, and are also called **deferred prepositions**, e.g.

Which shelf did you put it *on*? (*compare*: On which shelf did you put it? *See* PIED PIPING)

What were you thinking *of*?

• **stranding**.

stranded preposition *See* STRAND.

Stratificational Grammar A model of grammar, developed in the 1960s by the American linguist Sydney M. Lamb, in which the various *levels of analysis are known as **strata**.

stratum *See* LEVEL ORDERING (HYPOTHESIS).

strength of modality This refers to the level of commitment that a speaker has to the *proposition which is being expressed. For example, *He must be crazy* expresses a high degree of commitment ('epistemic necessity'), whereas *He may be crazy* expresses a much weaker level of commitment ('epistemic possibility').

See also DEGREE OF MODALITY; KIND OF MODALITY.

strict subcategorization *See* SUBCATEGORIZATION.

string A sequence of linguistic elements and/or symbols.

The term is particularly used in *Generative Grammar (2). For example, a **terminal string** is the ultimate series of *lexical items in a *tree diagram after various *rules have been applied.

The term was introduced into linguistics from mathematics and computing, probably by Chomsky (1955a).

strong (In *historical linguistics and some traditional grammar.) Of a *verb or its *conjugation: forming the *past tense and *past participle through a change in vowel (e.g. *swim, swam, swum*) and without the *suffix *-(e)d/-t* (though often with the suffix *-(e)n* for the *past participle). Contrasted with **weak verbs**, which do not display a vowel change.

The distinction between strong verbs and weak verbs has been obscured since *Old English times by sound changes which, in some originally weak verbs, have introduced a variation in vowel between *present tense forms and *past tense/participle forms, or have caused the disappearance of the suffix, or both, e.g.

keep, kept (OE cep-an, cep-te)

spread, spread (OE spræd-an, spræd-de)

feed, fed (OE fed-an, fed-de)

Hence English verbs are more helpfully divided into *regular and *irregular verbs.

The terms strong and weak are a translation of the German *stark* and *schwach*, introduced by Jakob Grimm. A 'strong' verb had no need of the 'help' of a suffix to express tense.

structural Relating to (the analysis of) the component parts of (a) language, or its organization.

All grammarians take a structural approach to language, since the object of grammatical description is to reveal the *rules and systematic relationships that apply to linguistic structures.

The term is, however, associated (particularly in Europe) with the work of Ferdinand de Saussure (1857–1913; see SAUSSUREAN; STRUCTURALISM), and (more narrowly) with the American linguistic school of Leonard Bloomfield and his followers, which flourished in the 1930s, 40s, and 50s. A characteristic of the *Bloomfieldian approach was to emphasize the formal, rather than the semantic, features of language, so that the term structural often carries this sense.

> 1952 C. C. FRIES One of the basic assumptions of our approach here to the grammatical analysis of sentences is that all the structural signals in English are strictly formal matters that can be described in physical terms of forms, correlations of these forms, and arrangements of order.

●● **structural ambiguity**: see AMBIGUITY.
●● **structural conjunctive**: see CONJUNCT.
●● **structural linguistics**: see STRUCTURALISM.
●● **structural recoverability**: see RECOVERABILITY.
●● **structural semantics**: a theory of semantics which studies the meanings of *lexical items, and their relationships within sentences.
●● **structural/structure word**: the same as *grammatical word (1).

structuralism An approach to linguistics (or in some cases a theory) in which language is considered primarily as a system of *structures. (Also called **structural linguistics**.)

Narrowly, structuralism is taken to mean the theories and methods associated with the American linguist Leonard Bloomfield (1887–1949) and his followers, which emphasized form rather than meaning. Great attention was paid to what were held to be scientific **discovery procedures** by which the elements of any language at different *levels could be revealed without reference to meaning. It is this narrow structuralism that was attacked by *generative grammarians, though their debt to it was greater than is sometimes admitted.

In the European tradition, structuralism is altogether older and broader. De Saussure is generally regarded as the father of modern structural linguistics, even though some of his principles can be found in earlier writers.

> 1977 J. LYONS What must be emphasized . . . is that there is, in principle, no conflict between generative grammar and Saussurean structuralism . . .

Saussurean structuralists, unlike many of the post-Bloomfieldians, (for whom 'structural semantics' would have been almost a contradiction in terms), never held the view that semantics should be excluded from linguistics proper.

The terms structuralism and structural linguistics are broadly synonymous. Where they are differentiated today, the former tends to be confined to the Bloomfieldian type of sentence analysis, whereas the latter may then refer to a more general type of approach to linguistic structure.

● **structuralist**: (of, or characteristic of) an adherent of structuralism.

> 1970 J. LYONS Examples . . . were used by Boas to support the view that every language has its own unique grammatical structure and that it is the task of the linguist to discover for each language the categories of description appropriate to it. This view may be called 'structuralist' (in one of the main senses of a rather fashionable term).

See also SAUSSUREAN.

structure The relationships between the elements and *constituent parts of a language, and their arrangement, determining its character and organization.

The term is used in a very general way (though often more formally than the related term *construction). The analysis of **clause structure** (or **sentence structure**) is essential to any grammar.

> 2002 R. HUDDLESTON & G. PULLUM et al. To describe the sentences that belong to English we have to provide a general account of their structure that makes their form follow from **general** statements, not about particular sentences but about sentences of English quite generally. We need to bring together the principles that sentences all conform to, so that we can use those principles to appreciate the structure of new sentences as they are encountered, and see how new ones can be constructed.

See also CLAUSE.

In grammar it is equally possible to talk of **morphological structure** (e.g. in *word formation), **semantic structure** (e.g. in *lexical fields), and *information structure (the arrangement of *given and *new information, etc.).

Structure can be distinguished from *system.

> 1964 R. H. ROBINS *Structure* and *system*, and their derivatives, are often used almost interchangeably, but it is useful to employ *structure* . . . specifically with reference to groupings of syntagmatically related elements, and *system* with reference to classes of paradigmatically related elements.

In *Systemic Grammar, structure is one of the four *categories (together
with *unit, *class, and *system (2)) that contrast with scales (*see* SCALE-
AND-CATEGORY GRAMMAR).

•• **structure word**: the same as *grammatical word (1).
  Compare DEEP STRUCTURE; SURFACE STRUCTURE.

Structure of English, The Written by the American *structuralist
linguist C. C. Fries, this work is often regarded as the first *corpus-based
grammar of English.

> 1952 C. C. FRIES In the meantime, however, beginning in 1946, it became
> possible to obtain an entirely different kind of evidence. Instead of the letters
> collected and studied for the *American English Grammar* I procured the
> means and the opportunity to record mechanically many conversations of
> speakers of Standard English in this North Central community of the United
> States. Altogether these mechanically recorded conversations amounted to
> something over 250,000 running words.

style *See* STYLISTICS.

style disjunct A *disjunct that is employed by a speaker to comment on
the style and/or form of the statement to which it is attached, in contrast to
a *content disjunct; e.g.

  Seriously, I don't want to get involved
  Quite simply: she lied
  Generally speaking, little foreign aid reaches its destination

stylistics The study of the various (literary) *features (1) that characterize
a particular piece of writing, and how an interpretation of those features
can lead to an understanding of the *text in question, and situate it in a
wider (literary, social, etc.) context.

suasive verb A *verb whose *complement expresses a change of some
kind which the *referent of the verb's *subject wishes to bring about, e.g.
verbs that have a *directive meaning, or express 'suggestion', 'intention',
etc. Examples include *agree, command, decree, desire, ensure, insist, intend, order, prefer, propose, recommend, rule, urge*. They are typically
followed by a *that*-clause containing *putative *should* or a mandative
*subjunctive.

In CGEL suasive verbs contrast both semantically and syntactically with
*factual verbs. Unlike factual verbs, which take an *indicative verb form in
the *subordinate clause, suasive verbs permit a choice, e.g.

She demanded that { he returned the money
he should return the money
he return the money }

See also PUTATIVE SHOULD; SUBJUNCTIVE.

subcategorization The syntactic phenomenon whereby certain lexical
*heads create subcategories by virtue of the *complements they take. Also
called **strict subcategorization**.

For example, *verbs that take a *direct object are contained in a
subcategory of *monotransitive verbs, and verbs that take an *indirect
object and a direct object belong to a subcategory of *ditransitive verbs.
•• **subcategorization frame**: a notation that indicates the
subcategorization properties of an element, e.g. [−, NP] for the transitive
verb *devour*, and [−, NP NP] for the ditransitive verb *give*. The symbol '−'
indicates where the subcategorized element appears.

subclausal negation *See* NEGATION.

subject The *constituent in a *sentence or clause that typically comes
first, and of which the rest of the sentence is predicated. It often, though by
no means always, performs the *semantic role of *agent, and specifies the
*topic of the sentence.

The division of a sentence (or clause) into two parts, subject and
*predicate, is a long established one, and derived originally from logic and
philosophy. Latin *subjectum* translates Aristotle's *to hupokeimenon*, which
primarily means 'the material of which things are made'; hence 'the
subject of an attribute or of a predicate'.

In modern grammatical analyses the subject is one of the five possible
major formal constituents (or *elements (1)) of clause structure,
abbreviated as S. The predicate is then analysed into V (*verb), O (*object),
C (*complement), and A (*adverbial), though not all of these are always
present. In a *declarative clause the subject normally precedes the verb,
which must *agree with it in *number and *person, though agreement is
not always visible.

A **grammatical subject** is normally obligatory in English clause
structure, even when no semantic role is assigned to the subject position.
In such cases a *dummy subject is introduced (e.g. *It is raining*; *There is no
water*). *See also* ANTICIPATORY *subject*.

Subjects are, however, usually missing from *imperative sentences (e.g. *Listen!*), and may be *ellipted in an informal context (e.g. *See you soon*).

Although the grammatical subject is typically a *noun phrase, it can also be *realized by a clause or even by a *prepositional phrase, e.g.

> *That you could do such a thing* really shocks me
>
> *After nine o'clock* would be more convenient

As noted above the subject is often defined as the 'doer' or agent of the verbal action, but this definition often fails. Thus in the first example below we have a meaningless dummy subject, and in the second (*passive) sentence the subject carries a non-agentive semantic role:

> *It* is cold in this room
>
> *The match* has been cancelled

For this reason the syntactic way of defining the term is now the norm.

In traditional grammar the label subject was sometimes qualified. Thus in addition to a grammatical subject there might be a **logical subject** (= *notional subject), particularly in passive sentences. Thus in *The building was designed by my favourite architect* the grammatical subject is *the building*, but the logical subject (i.e. the agent) was said to be *my favourite architect*.

Traditional grammar also uses the notion of *psychological subject, roughly equivalent to the present-day *theme or *topic, e.g.

> *That question* I cannot answer

In this example the italicized noun phrase is grammatically the *direct object of the verb *answer*.

•• **displaced subject**: (in CaGEL) the notional subject in an *existential construction, e.g. *There is <u>a cinema</u> in the centre of town.*

•• **subject-attachment rule**: *see* ATTACHMENT RULE.

•• **subject attribute**: *see* ATTRIBUTE.

•• **subject-auxiliary inversion**: *see* INVERSION.

•• **subject case**: *see* SUBJECTIVE (1).

•• **subject complement**: *see* COMPLEMENT.

•• **subject-determiner**: (in CaGEL) an element that combines the functions of subject and *determiner (1), e.g. *Bill's* in *Bill's review of the book*, which can be contrasted with *Bill reviewed the book.*

•• **subject-operator inversion**: inversion of a subject and *auxiliary verb. *See* INVERSION.

•• **subject-oriented**: *see* SUBJECT-ORIENTED.

•• **subject–predicate relation**: *see* PREDICATE (1).

•• **subject-raising**: *see* RAISING.

•• **subject-related predicative complement**: *see* COMPLEMENT.

•• **subject territory**: the position of the grammatical subject before the verb. Contrasted with *object territory.

•• **subject-to-object raising (SOR)**: *see* RAISING.

•• **subject-to-subject raising (SSR)**: *see* RAISING.

•• **subject-verb inversion**: *see* INVERSION.

subjective

1. Designating the *case *inflection typically carried by *pronouns when they function as the *subject of a sentence or clause. (Also called **subject case** or **nominative case**.)

Only six distinct subjective pronouns (or **subject pronouns, nominative pronouns**) occur in modern English: *I, she, he, we, they*, and *who*. The difference between these and *me, her, him, us, them, whom* (called **objective pronouns, object pronouns**, or **accusative pronouns**) can be described in terms of case.

See also CASE; GENITIVE; OBJECTIVE (1).

2. Relating to, or referring to, the subject.

In a subjective *genitive the reference is to a 'deep' subject, rather than to the subject of the actual sentence or clause. Thus the genitive has subjective meaning in

the Government's abolition of tax (cf. The Government is abolishing tax)

See also GENITIVE; OBJECTIVE (2).

•• **subjective predicative complement**: *see* COMPLEMENT.

subject-oriented

A term used in the description of *dynamic (2) *modal verbs to indicate that the 'source' of the modal meaning (typically 'volition' or 'ability') is the *referent of the *subject of the sentence, as opposed to the speaker.

Thus if I say *The director will definitely let you know by the weekend* the intentional meaning imparted by the modal verb *will* originates with the person referred to as *the director*, whereas when I say *You may enter the room* the source of the 'permission' is the speaker.

Compare SPEAKER-ORIENTED.

See also DEONTIC; DYNAMIC (2); EPISTEMIC; MODALITY.

subjunct

1. (In CGEL.) A subclass of *adverbial, contrasting with *adjunct, *conjunct, and *disjunct.

This category was introduced in Quirk et al. (1985).

1985 R. QUIRK et al. We apply the term SUBJUNCTS to adverbials which have, to a greater or lesser degree, a subordinate role . . . in comparison with other clause elements.

In the authors' 1972 *Grammar of Contemporary English* such adverbials were part of the adjunct class.

In CGEL, subjuncts are distinguished syntactically from adjuncts in several ways, perhaps most obviously by the fact that whereas adjuncts function as adverbial in clause structure, on a level with other clause *elements, subjuncts do not. In the following examples, contrast *financially*, which functions as an adjunct within clause structure in the first sentence, with *technically* (meaning 'from a technical point of view'), which functions as a subjunct (more specifically a **viewpoint subjunct**) in the second sentence:

> He helped them *financially* (cf. It was financially that he helped them./How did he help them? Financially.)
>
> *Technically*, he helped them (cf. *It was technically that he helped them/*How did he help them? Technically.)

In general, subjuncts either have 'wide orientation' outside the core clause structure, by expressing a 'viewpoint' (e.g. *Politically, the idea is suicidal*) or by functioning as a 'courtesy' marker (*Kindly be seated*), or they have 'narrow orientation' by being linked to a single word or phrase (e.g. *really odd, hardly possible, too dreadful*).

●● **focusing subjunct**: *see* FOCUSING ADVERB.

See also EMPHASIZER; INTENSIFIER.

2. (In Jespersen's terminology.) A word or group of words of the third *rank (1) of importance in a *phrase or clause.

> 1909–49 O. JESPERSEN The adjunct in *perfect simplicity* is a shifted subjunct of the adjective contained in the substantive *simplicity*, cf. *perfectly simple*.

subjunctive (*n. & adj.*) Traditionally: (a *verb form or *mood) expressing hypothesis or non-factuality. Contrasted particularly with the *indicative. Also called **conjunctive**, especially in grammars describing ancient languages.

The **present subjunctive** form of a verb is *finite, and identical with the *base (1) form of the verb. Formally, it is exactly the same as the present tense indicative form, except for the *third person singular, which lacks -*s*, and for the verb *be*, whose present subjunctive form is *be*. Functionally, it can refer both to the present and to the past. The present subjunctive can be used in three different ways, described below.

First, the **mandative subjunctive** (or **subjunctive mandative**) is used in *subordinate clauses following an expression of command, necessity, suggestion, or possibility, e.g.

> I recommended that he *write* and apologize
>
> She requested that she not *be* disturbed

Notice that the negative element *not* is positioned before the verb in the second example.

It is possible to have *should* in the subordinate clause:

> I insisted that he *should* attend the meeting

This is called the **should-mandative** in CaGEL, and *putative *should* in CGEL.

Secondly, the present subjunctive can be used, rather formally, in subordinate clauses of *condition and *concession, but not with past reference, e.g.

> If that *be* the case, our position is indefensible

Thirdly, the **formulaic** or **optative subjunctive** is used in independent clauses, mainly in set expressions, e.g.

> God *save* the Queen

Some such clauses have an unusual *word order, e.g.

> *Perish* the thought!
>
> *Come* hell or high water

The so-called **past subjunctive** (also called the **were-subjunctive** or *irrealis *were*) is used in clauses of hypothetical condition. It differs from the past indicative form of *be* only in the first and third person singular, where *were* is used, though *was* is increasingly found here too. The reference is to present (or future) time, e.g.

> If I *were* you, I'd own up (*compare*: If I *was* you ...)
>
> If only my grandfather *were* alive today (*compare*: If only my grandfather *was* ...)
>
> If she *were* to come tomorrow ... (*compare*: If she *was* to ...)

The uses of ordinary indicative forms to express non-factuality, such as the use of a *past tense to refer to a present or future situation (e.g. *If you came tomorrow* ...; *see* PAST (2)), have been described as subjunctive uses—perhaps because in translation such a usage might need a subjunctive form in another language. Modern grammar considers this to be quite unjustified, and restricts the use of the term subjunctive as described above.

However, since Modern English (unlike, say, French or Spanish) has few distinct verb forms that differentiate subjunctive verb forms from indicative verb forms, the status of the subjunctive as a verbal *inflection has been challenged. Indeed, many modern frameworks prefer to speak of **subjunctive constructions** or **subjunctive clauses**. These labels then apply to the entire clause in which the 'subjunctive verb' appears.

The disappearance of the subjunctive has long been forecast:

> 1860 G. P. MARSH The subjunctive is evidently passing out of use, and there is good reason to suppose that it will soon become obsolete altogether.

But it survives, and indeed has been seen to be on the increase, especially the mandative subjunctive in British English in recent years, possibly under American influence.

•• **covert subjunctive**: a term used in CaGel to describe a construction in which an indicative verb form is used where a 'subjunctive' verb form might be expected, given the meaning of the *governing verb, e.g. *They insist that he eats his dinner* (cf. *They insist that he eat his dinner*).

　　See also PUTATIVE SHOULD.

submodification *Modification of a *modifier, as in *a very unusual result*, where *very* is a *submodifier of *unusual*. Compare this with *a large unusual house*, where both *large* and *unusual* directly modify *house*.

　　See also QUALIFIER (1).

submodifier A *word (e.g. an *adverb) which is used to *modify the meaning of another word (e.g. an *adjective or adverb) that itself functions as a *modifier, e.g.

　　a *very* unusual result

　　a *quite* extraordinarily confusing letter

Such words are called *subjuncts in CGEL, though note that subjunct is a much wider notion.

　　See also SUBMODIFICATION.

subordinate (*adj.*) (Pronounced /səˈbɔːdɪnət/.) Grammatically *dependent. Contrasted variously with *coordinate, *independent, and *superordinate.

•• **subordinate clause**: a *clause that is dependent on, or forms part of, another clause, *phrase, or sentence element. Subordinate clauses can be classified in different ways, e.g. as being *finite, *non-finite, or *verbless, e.g.

　　They think *that the swimming pool is open today* (finite *that*-clause)

　　They want *to eat pizza tonight* (non-finite *to*-infinitive clause)

　　With *you here*, things will be easier (verbless)

Traditional grammar recognized three types of subordinate clause:

　　(i) *adverbial clauses, e.g. I was surprised, *because it was so unexpected*

　　(ii) *nominal clauses, e.g. It was odd *that he didn't telephone*
　　　　This includes *nominal relative clauses, e.g. I was surprised by *what you said*

　　(iii) *relative clauses, e.g. The news (*that*) *you gave us* is very odd

In more recent frameworks (e.g. CaGEL, OMEG) three kinds of finite subordinate clause are recognized, namely *content clauses, *relative clauses, and *comparative clauses. Non-finite clauses are classified into *to-infinitive clauses, *bare infinitive clauses, *-ed clauses, and *-ing clauses.

Another kind of clause that is sometimes classified as subordinate is the *comment clause, e.g.

> We will, I think, see a lot more of him soon

•• **subordinate interrogative**: see INDIRECT QUESTION.

(v.) (Pronounced /sə'bɔːdɪneɪt/.) Make grammatically subordinate, usually by means of a *subordinator.

•• **subordinating conjunction**: see *SUBORDINATING. CONJUNCTION.

•• **subordinating correlative**: see CORRELATIVE.

subordinating conjunction The same as *subordinator.

See also CONJUNCTION.

subordination The joining of a unit, e.g. a *subordinate clause, to a higher linguistic unit, such that the former is *dependent on the latter.

Clausal subordination is often indicated formally by a *subordinator, though with some types of clauses there may be no formal marker of subordination, e.g.

> I thought (that) I had told you
>
> Having inspected the policy, I'm writing to inform you that you are covered for accidental damage

Subordination can also be signalled by *inversion:

> Had we known about the civil unrest, we would never have travelled there

It can also be indicated by the absence of major clause *elements, such as the *subject in the italicized clause in the following example:

> I would like to move to Paris

This is sometimes referred to as **desententialization**.

Independent *wh-clauses and subordinate wh-clauses are syntactically distinguishable through *constituent order, in that the former instantiate inversion, while the latter do not:

> What did he buy?
>
> I asked him what he bought.

Non-finite and *verbless subordinate clauses can be introduced by a subordinator, *zero, or a *preposition, e.g.

> I was keen for Karl to send us the money
>
> Standing on deck, Alice waved at me
>
> On hearing this, she rushed to the bank
>
> With the money under her belt, she felt better

In approaches to linguistics in which syntax does not play a prominent role subordination is often defined without reference to grammar:

> 1985 S. THOMPSON '[S]ubordinate clause' is not a grammatical category at all. That is, there does not seem to be a single function or even a group of functions that we can think of this 'category' as having been designed, as it were, to serve. So the term 'subordination' seems to be at best a negative term which lumps together all deviations from some 'main clause' norm, which means that it treats as unified a set of facts which we think is not a single phenomenon. For these reasons, we have found it more fruitful to tease it apart into its component parts and try to determine what are the discourse motivations that underlie each of these components.

> 2003 S. CRISTOFARO Subordination will be regarded as a particular way to construe the cognitive relation between two events, such that one of them (which will be called the dependent event) lacks an autonomous profile, and is construed in the perspective of the other event (which will be called the main event).

See also COMPLEMENTIZER; MULTIPLE SUBORDINATION.

subordinator A *conjunction introducing a *subordinate clause. Also called **subordinating conjunction**.

Most subordinators are single-word conjunctions, e.g. *although, because, before, for, if, since, that, whereas, whether*; but there are also multi-word subordinators, e.g. *in order that, provided (that), as long as, in case*.

Note that in recent frameworks (e.g. CaGEL, OMEG), many of these words are regarded as *prepositions, except for interrogative *if, for, that*, and *whether*.

•• **subordinator of result**: *see* RESULT.

See also MARGINAL SUBORDINATOR.

subsective gradience *See* GRADIENCE.

substance *See* FORM (4).

substandard *See* STANDARD.

substantive (In older grammar: now disused.)
   1. (*n. & adj.*) (A word) denoting a substance.
•• **(noun) substantive**: a noun.
   See also ADJECTIVE.
   2. (by extension) noun-like.
   1824 L. MURRAY Some writers are of the opinion, that the pronouns should be classed into substantive and adjective pronouns.

3. Expressing existence.

● **substantival**.

●● **substantive verb** (or **verb substantive**): the **verb* *be*.

substitute (*n. & adj.*) (A **word*, **phrase*, etc.) that is used to replace a
*constituent. Also called **pro-form* or **substitute form/word**.

This is a grammatical concept, related to **ellipsis*, and has nothing to do
with the notion of **synonym*.

(*v.*) Use (a word, phrase, etc.) as a replacement (for a constituent).

● **substitutability**:
1968 J. LYONS The notion of distribution, which is based on substitutability, is
simply not applicable to sentences.

● **substitutable**.
See also SUBSTITUTION.

substitution The use of **pro-forms* to replace a **constituent*. *See also*
SUBSTITUTE.

Substitution differs from **co-reference*. With substitution, pro-forms
replace other words, e.g.

I like *your golf umbrella*. Where can I get *one* like it?

With co-reference, the pro-form refers to the same **referent*, e.g.

I like *your golf umbrella*. May I borrow *it*?

Substitution can also be involved in replacing units other than **noun
phrases*, such as **verb phrases* (2) and **clauses*, e.g.

If you *contribute £20*, I'll *do so* too/I'll *do the same*

In this example the pro-forms *do so* and *do the same* replace *contribute £20*
(which is analysed as a verb phrase in many models).

suffix *Morphology*. (*n.*) An **affix* added at the end of a word or **base* (2)
to form a new **word*. Contrasted with **prefix* and infix (*see* AFFIX).

Suffixes, unlike prefixes, usually have a grammatical effect on the word
or base to which they are added. They are broadly of two kinds:

inflectional suffix: a suffix used to form an **inflectional form* of a
word, e.g.

look + *-s/-ed*
kind + *-er/-est*

derivational suffix: a suffix used to form a new **lexeme* from a base, e.g.

nouns:	book*let* (M19)	kind*ness* (ME)	play*er* (OE)	
adjectives:	connect*ive* (M17)	care*less* (OE)	hope*ful* (ME)	manage*able* (L16)
verbs:	idol*ize* (L16)	wid*en* (E17)		
adverbs:	pretti*ly* (LME)			

(*v.*) Add as a suffix.

- **suffixation**: the adding of a suffix.

  See also DERIVATION; INFLECTION.

summation plural A type of *noun which exists only in the *plural, and denotes a tool, instrument, article of dress, etc. that consists of two equal parts joined together, e.g. *binoculars, culottes, leggings, pliers, secateurs*. Also called **binary noun**.

  See also PLURALE TANTUM.

superlative (*adj.*) Of a *gradable *adjective or *adverb, whether *inflected (essentially, by the addition of -*est* to the *positive form) or *periphrastic (by the use of *most*): expressing the highest degree of the quality or attribute expressed by the positive degree word. Examples are *best, happiest, soonest, most beneficial, most energetically*.

- **superlative degree**: the highest degree of *comparison, above positive and *comparative.

  (*n.*) (An adjective or adverb that is in) the superlative degree.

superordinate (*n.* & *adj.*) (A linguistic unit) operating at some higher *level of analysis than another, which is *subordinate to it.

  The term is particularly applied to *clauses. In popular grammar, clauses are either *main clauses or subordinate clauses.

  But in other analyses, a main clause is said to 'contain', or *embed, one or more subordinate clauses, and is therefore superordinate to them.

  An advantage of introducing this term is that in some *complex sentences a clause that is subordinate to a particular clause may at the same time be superordinate to another. For example, in *I think that you know that I love you*, the clause *that you know that I love you* is subordinate, because it functions as *complement of the *verb *think*. However, it is superordinate to *that I love you*, which functions as complement of the verb *know*. *See also* MATRIX CLAUSE (1).

  In semantics the term is applied to a *word which has a more general meaning than, and is therefore implied by, or able to replace, other more specific terms: a *hypernym. Thus *animal* is superordinate to (is a superordinate of) *tiger* and *kangaroo*.

  See also SUPERORDINATION.

  Compare HYPONYM.

superordination *Semantics*. The relationship of being *superordinate to another linguistic unit from the point of view of meaning. Contrasted with *hyponomy.

The term is used in describing the hierarchical structure of some sets of *lexical items:

> 1977 J. LYONS Let us say, then, that 'cow' is a hyponym of 'animal'... and so on... The obvious Greek-based correlative term for the converse relation, 'hyperonymy'... is unfortunately too similar in form to 'hyponymy' and likely to cause confusion. We will use instead superordination, which, unlike 'subordination', is not widely employed as a technical term in linguistics with a conflicting sense.

supplement A term used in CaGEL for *parenthetical strings that are not integrated in *clause structure, including what are called *non-restrictive *relative clauses in other frameworks, as well as certain *adjuncts and *disjuncts.

supplementary relative clause *See* NON-RESTRICTIVE.

supplementive clause A *non-finite or *verbless clause that does not contain a *subordinator, e.g.

> *Working with the local police,* Janet tried to discover who had stolen her car

This term is not widely used.

> 1985 R. QUIRK et al. Adverbial participle and verbless clauses without a subordinator are SUPPLEMENTIVE CLAUSES... The formal inexplicitness of supplementive clauses allows considerable flexibility in what we may wish them to convey.

suppletion The occurrence of an unrelated form so as to supply a gap in a *conjugation, *declension, etc. Obvious examples are *went* as the *past tense of *go, was* and *were* as the past forms of *be,* and *good/better/best.*

• **suppletive**: designating a form used in suppletion.

surface structure

1. (In *Generative Grammar (2).) A representation of the syntactic structure of a *sentence after the application of *transformations has taken place. Later reconceptualized as **S-Structure**. *Compare* DEEP STRUCTURE.

2. Loosely, the structure of a sentence as it is spoken or written.

Survey of English Usage (SEU) An English language research unit founded by Randolph Quirk at University College London (UCL) in 1959.

At the SEU, Quirk was among the first linguists in the world to develop a *corpus for the English language (the 'Quirk Corpus') which contains a

million words of written and transcribed spoken texts. In the early years
the material was grammatically analysed manually. Technological advances over the last few decades have revolutionized corpus compilation
and analysis. As a result more recent corpora at the SEU, including the
British component of the *International Corpus of English* (ICE-GB) and the
Diachronic Corpus of Present-Day Spoken English (DCPSE), have been
electronically *tagged and *parsed (3). These corpora can be investigated
by researchers using the dedicated corpus exploration software ICECUP
(International Corpus of English Corpus Utility Program).

Recent work at the SEU includes a number of Knowledge Transfer
projects, specifically the development of apps for smartphones and tablets, and a web-based platform for the teaching and learning of English in
schools. (See www.ucl.ac.uk/english-usage.)

switching *See* CODE-*switching.*

syllepsis (Plural **syllepses.**) The use of a *word, *phrase, etc. in two
or more different ways with different *senses in the same *construction,
from the point of view of either meaning or grammar. Also called
zeugma. Example:

> She caught the train and a bad cold

Here *catch the train* has a more literal sense than *catch a cold.*

Syllepsis is grammatical when a particular *inflectional form is used
in connection with two *constituents, but can only agree with one of
them, e.g.

> Neither John nor I *agree* (*John* requires *agrees*)

The term is little used in modern grammar.

Compare AGREEMENT.

syncategorematic Not belonging to a syntactic *category; in a category
of its own. The *infinitival particle *to* is often said to be syncategorematic.

synchronic Concerned with (the analysis of) a linguistic phenomenon,
or phenomena, at a particular point in time (especially the present).
Contrasted with *diachronic.

Synchronic linguistics can theoretically be concerned with (a)
language at any point in time, but the term is often shorthand for the study
of (a) language here and now.

The term is often attributed to Ferdinand de Saussure in his
posthumously published work *Cours de linguistique générale* (1916).

Although the importance of distinguishing synchronic and *diachronic observations has seemed obvious to many for decades, more recently the distinction between synchrony and diachrony has been challenged.

1994 A. MCMAHON [I]t seems that synchrony and diachrony, or the present and the past, cannot in practice be as separate as Saussure's dictum assumes, either in language or elsewhere.

- **synchronically**.
- **synchrony**: synchronic method or treatment. *Compare* DESCRIPTIVE (1). *See also* ETYMOLOGY; SAUSSUREAN.

syncretism The realization of two or more *grammatical words (2) in a single form.

The term was originally used in *historical linguistics to refer to the merger of *inflectional categories by the transfer of the functions of one category to the form used for another. Thus in early *Middle English the functions of the *dative case of *nouns (marking the *indirect object, the *complement of certain *prepositions, etc.) were transferred to the *accusative; this had already occurred in preliterary times with several *personal pronouns (e.g. *me* = 'me', 'to me', *us* = 'us', 'to us', etc.). Thus, *bedd* ('bed') and *lif* ('life'), used as *objects of a *verb, were distinct in *Old English from the forms used after prepositions, such as *on bedde* ('in bed') and *on life* (cf. Modern English *alive*)—a distinction that had disappeared by 1500. In *Early Modern English the functions of the *subjective form of the *second person pronoun (*ye*) were transferred to the *objective form (*you*), but this did not occur with any other personal pronouns.

The term is now used in *synchronic descriptions.

1991 P. H. MATTHEWS In *He came* and *He has come* we distinguish a Past Tense *came* and a Past Participle *come*... In *He tried* and *He has tried* the first '*tried*' must again be Past Tense and the second again the Past Participle; for TRY (as for most English verbs) the two forms are identical both in spelling and in phonetics. The term **syncretism** (in origin a term in diachronic linguistics) is often applied synchronically to this situation.

syndetic Of *coordination: indicated by means of a coordinating *conjunction, e.g.

shirts *and* trousers   bicycles *or* cars

When more than one coordinator is used, we speak of *polysyndetic coordination, e.g.

wine *and* cheese *and* biscuits

Syndetic coordination is contrasted with less common *asyndetic coordination, when no coordinators are used, e.g.

> students, teachers, parents, siblings

synonym A *word or *phrase that means the same, or almost the same, as another in the same language. Contrasted with *antonym.

Strictly speaking there are few, if any, 'true' synonyms, that is, words that have exactly the same *sense and are completely and always interchangeable. But some pairs of words, for example the verbs *close* and *shut*, are sufficiently alike to rank as synonyms, even though one cannot always be substituted for the other, as the following examples make clear:

> I'm going to close my bank account
> The meeting closed with a vote of thanks
> Once he starts talking, you can't shut him up

In discussions of the meaning of linguistic units longer than a word, synonymy tends to refer to the identity of *denotational or *referential meaning, even though the emphasis or the *attitudinal meaning may be different.
- **synonymous**: in a relationship of synonymy with another word.
- **synonymy**: the property of having (almost) the same meaning.

See also ANTONYM; HETERONYM; HOMONYM; HOMOPHONE; MERONYM; POLYSEME; POLYSEMY.

Synopsis of English Syntax, A A grammar written by the American linguist Eugene Nida in 1960, based on his 1943 doctoral dissertation. '[T]he general orientation of the approach adopted in this *Synopsis* is toward the constructions in terms of immediate constituents, rather than the string of units which comprise the total frame.'

synsemantic *Semantics*. (*n. & adj.*) (A *word or *phrase) that has meaning only in a context.

See AUTOSEMANTIC.

syntactic Of or relating to *syntax.

In grammar generally, often no special need is felt to use this adjective. A **syntactic class** is usually called a *word class or simply a *class; a **syntactic function** can simply be referred to as a function; and so on.
- **syntactically**.
- **syntactic blend**: *see* BLEND.
- **syntactic predicate**: *see* PREDICATE (2).

Syntactic Phenomena of English, The. A work written by the late James McCawley in two volumes in 1988 (with a second edition in one volume in 1998). McCawley's descriptive framework is idiosyncratic, and shows signs of his earlier *Generative Semantics allegiance, but is highly insightful and original.

syntactics The same as *syntax, particularly when contrasted with *pragmatics and *semantics as a subdivision of *semiotics; the formal relationship of symbols to each other.

> 1964 E. A. NIDA While semantics deals with the relationship of symbols to referents, syntactics is concerned with the relationship of symbol to symbol; for the meaning of expressions is not to be found merely in adding up symbols, but also in determining their arrangements, including order and hierarchical structuring. For example, the constituents *black* and *bird*, when occurring in juxtaposition, may have two quite different meanings.

syntagm (Pronounced /ˈsɪntæm/.) (Also **syntagma**, pronounced /sɪn ˈtægmə/.) (A set of linguistic forms in) a linear syntactic relationship. Sometimes also called *construction (1). Contrasted with a *paradigm.

> 1959 W. BASKIN [translating F. de Saussure, coiner of the term] In discourse ... words acquire relations based on the linear nature of language because they are chained together ... The elements are arranged in sequence on the chain of speaking. Combinations supported by linearity are *syntagms*. The syntagm is always composed of two or more consecutive units.

Syntagms operate at all *levels of linguistic analysis. Thus *constituents of *words, *phrases, *clauses, etc. can form syntagms with each other. For example, *morphemes (1) can join into syntagms to produce words (e.g. *book* + *ish* = *bookish*), and phrases in a chain relationship can form clauses (e.g. *the dog* + *barked* = *the dog barked*).

> See also SYNTAX.

syntagmatic relationship A relationship between two or more linguistic units that form a *syntagm or syntagms. Also called **and-relationship**.

Syntagmatic (*chain) relationships are contrasted with *paradigmatic (choice) relationships. The terminology is that of Ferdinand de Saussure (1857–1913).

Thus in *All power corrupts*, *all* + *power* + *corrupts* are in a syntagmatic relationship with each other. The units can be analysed in terms of syntactic *form, as *determinative (1) + *noun + *verb, or in terms of *function (1), as *subject + *predicate (1).

Words that could grammatically substitute for each of the three words in the example are in a paradigmatic relationship with that particular word: thus *some, no, more*, etc. can replace *all*; a great many nouns can replace *power* (e.g. *control, strength, weakness, conversation, art*); and an indefinite number of *intransitive verbs can replace *corrupts*, as indeed can other tenses of that verb (e.g. *corrupted*).

• **syntagmatically**: in the manner of a syntagm.

> 1961 Y. OLSSON Both collocation and colligation operate syntagmatically, that is, along the line one-after-another.

See also CONJUGATION; DECLENSION; PARADIGM; SAUSSUREAN.

syntax The study of the structure of *sentences through the arrangement of *words into *phrases, phrases into *clauses, and clauses into sentences, and the codified *rules explaining this system.

The word derives from the Greek *syn-* ('together') and *tassein* ('arrange').

Traditionally syntax is regarded as part of *grammar, along with *morphology (the study of the structure of *words).

• **syntactic**, **syntactically**.

synthetic

1. *Morphology*. Designating a language in which a *word usually contains more than one *morpheme (2). Contrasted with *analytic (1).

English is an example, though not an extreme one, of a synthetic language.

Synthetic is used here in its etymological sense 'put together'. It does not mean 'artificial'.

2. *Semantics*. Designating a *proposition that is true (or false) by virtue of extralinguistic facts or circumstances, in contrast to an *analytic (2) one.

system

1. (Generally.) A network of parts in an orderly arrangement; a regular set of relationships.

With reference to this definition the English language is a system, consisting of morphological, syntactic, phonological, and semantic systems, which in turn contain other systems.

2. (Specifically.) A group of terms or *categories, particularly in a closed, *paradigmatic relationship.

> 1953 R. H. ROBINS Professor J. R. Firth has recently suggested that the terms 'Structure' and 'System' be kept apart in the technical vocabulary of linguistic description. 'Structure' might be used to refer to unidimensional, linear abstractions at various levels from utterances or parts of utterances . . . When . . .

categories have been devised by means of which the utterances of the language can be successfully described and analysed, closed systems are formed of these categories.

In *Scale-and-Category Grammar, the notion of system has a special place as one of the three (or four) categories that contrast with scales in the organization of the grammar.

> 1985 G. D. MORLEY The fourth category, system, accounts for the range of choices (classes) which are available within a unit, and any given range of possible options is known as a set of 'terms'. Thus, for example, the relations between the terms from the system of mood . . . may be set out as follows.

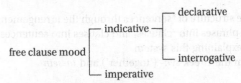

The notion of system also plays a role in *Systemic Grammar.

In some modern grammars the term is used to describe the *closed word classes, e.g. the *article system or the *pronoun system. *See* CLOSED (1). Other systems included in these grammars are simple versus non-simple sentences (which in turn have the subsystems *complex, *compound, and *compound-complex), *clause type, *number, *person, and *voice.

Systemic-Functional Grammar *See* SYSTEMIC GRAMMAR.

Systemic Grammar A theory of grammar and language use developed by M. A. K. Halliday, which is a development of *Scale-and-Category Grammar. Also called **Systemic-Functional Grammar**.

Scale-and-Category Grammar, like early *Generative Grammar (2), was much concerned with syntax and structure, but as the theory developed, the meaning and social functions of language became increasingly important.

> 1985 G. D. MORLEY During the latter half of the 1960s Halliday's work became increasingly influenced by ideas on the functional nature of language . . . and a multifunctional semantic dimension was not merely added to systemic theory but became central to it . . . At the time of this reorientation, the theory became known as systemic functional grammar, or systemic grammar for short. (Many linguists, indeed, now use the name 'systemic grammar' in referring to all work in the Hallidayan mould since 1961.)

2014 M. A. K. HALLIDAY & C. MATTHIESSEN Giving priority to the view 'from above' means that the organizing principle adopted is that of **system**: the grammar is seen as a network of interrelated meaningful choices. In other words, the dominant axis is the paradigmatic one: the fundamental components of the grammar are sets of mutually defining contrastive features ... Explaining something consists not of stating how it is structured but in showing how it is related to other things: its pattern of systemic relationships, or **agnateness** (**agnation** ...).

Confusingly, this theory is sometimes also called Functional Grammar, but is to be distinguished from Simon Dik's *Functional Grammar.

See also FIRTHIAN; NEO-FIRTHIAN.

tag (*n.*)

1. A string of *words with an *interrogative structure (*auxiliary verb + *pronoun), which is usually added to a *declarative clause, and whose form is syntactically related to the clause to which it is added. (Also called **interrogative tag**, **tag question**, or **question tag**.)

In the most usual cases, a *negative tag is added to a *positive statement, and a positive tag is added to a negative one. In other words, the *polarity is reversed (hence **reversed polarity tag**):

It's been cold this week, *hasn't it?*

You're not really going to walk all the way, *are you?*

You usually drive, *don't you?*

Said with a falling tone on the tag, the whole sentence is more like an *exclamation, assuming the listener's agreement. With a rising tone the tag becomes a *question inviting a *response. Less usual are positive statements followed by positive tags (often with an overtone of criticism):

So that's what you think, *is it?*

Question tags can also be added to imperatives and exclamations:

Keep in touch, *won't you?*

Oh, stop complaining, *will you!*

What a wonderful thing to do, *wasn't it!*

Some grammarians include short comments, answers, or fragments, sometimes added by another speaker, when these too consist of a *subject *noun phrase or *pronoun and an auxiliary verb relating to the verb of the previous utterance. For example:

It costs £1000. *Does it?/It doesn't!/So does the small one.*

That's not cheap. *Nor are the other ones.*

Shall I tell him? Yes, *do.*

Tell him to take it back, *why don't you?*

Or suppose I call them, *shall I?*

1990 J. ALGEO There are at least five uses of tag questions, some of them characteristically British, showing a progressive decline in politeness and in the degree to which they draw the addressed person into the conversation.

Algeo's five types of tag question are:

(i)   You haven't still got that map I lent you, have you? (informational)

(ii) But we wouldn't be able to use it to find the post office, would we? (confirmatory)

(iii) Took you a while to realize that, didn't it? (punctuational: i.e. similar in function to an exclamation mark)

(iv) Well, I haven't seen it before, have I? (peremptory: i.e. fending off an unwelcome remark)

(v)   You didn't exactly give me a chance to show you it, did you? (aggressive: i.e. expressing a hostile reaction)

Sometimes the term tag is used more generally to denote a short *phrase or *clause added on to an already complete utterance. This use includes, for instance, a noun phrase referring back to another phrase for emphasis, or to add an *exclamatory comment, e.g.

They use some confusing terms, *some really confusing terms*

He's won another prize, *clever man!*

In another type, perhaps more colloquial, the noun phrase occurs with a verb, e.g.

They baffle you, *do those long words*

That was the week, *that was*

Compare DISLOCATION.

2. A phrase such as *etc.*, *et cetera*, *and so on*, used to avoid further listing.

3. (In *corpus linguistics.) a *word class label assigned to a *lexical item that appears in an electronic *text, either manually or automatically using a computer, e.g. 'N' is a tag for noun, 'V' for verb, etc.

(*v.*) Assign a word class label to lexical items in electronic texts

Compare PARSE (3).

tag question See TAG.

tautology The saying of the same thing over again in different words (particularly regarded as a fault in style).

Language necessarily contains some *redundancy, and many speakers and writers repeat themselves for emphasis. Tautology, by contrast, is usually an unnecessary, and probably unconscious, repetition, as in *an unmarried young bachelor*, *one after the other in succession*, or *They shut and closed the door*.

taxis (Plural **taxes**.) Order or arrangement of words.

An outdated term; but *see* HYPOTAXIS and PARATAXIS.

taxonomic linguistics See LINGUISTICS.

telic *Semantics*. Of a *verb, *construction, *situation, etc.: expressing an inherent end point or goal, e.g.

I am redecorating the kitchen

Compare CONCLUSIVE; DURATIVE; PUNCTUAL.

See also ATELIC.

temporal Relating to *time (1). The term is particularly used in relation to the meaning of *adverbials (*in July, during the summer*).

Temporal meaning is often contrasted with *spatial meaning (e.g. *in a box, under the stairs*).

Compare TENSE; TIME.

●● **temporal noun**: a noun such as *February, summer, Sunday, today, yesterday*.

temporary Relating to an activity, attribute, *situation, etc. that lasts for a limited time. Contrasted with **permanent**.

The term temporary is particularly used in relation to verbal meaning. Thus *progressive aspect is often said to convey temporary meaning (e.g. *She's working in a bank*) in contrast to more permanent meaning (e.g. *She works in a bank*).

Similarly, temporary and permanent qualities often, though not necessarily, correlate with the *predicative and *attributive uses of adjectives. Contrast:

Those people are not *involved* (temporarily, on this occasion)

It's a long *involved* story (an inherent quality)

Compare DURATION (2); IMPERFECTIVE; PERFECTIVE.

tense Traditionally, tense is defined as a grammatical system which is used by languages to encode (or *grammaticalize) the *time (1) at which a *situation denoted by a *verb is viewed as taking place. Typically tense is realized through *inflectional endings on verbs.

Some linguists define tense semantically:

2012 I. DEPRAETERE & C. LANGFORD The criterion we use to define tense is meaning-based: a tense locates a situation in time.

In discussing tense, labels such as *present (2) tense, *past (2) tense, and *future tense are misleading, since the relationship between tense and time is often not one-to-one. Present and past tenses can be used in some circumstances to refer to future time (e.g. *If he comes tomorrow . . .*; *If he came tomorrow . . .*); present tenses can refer to the past (as in newspaper headlines, e.g. *Minister resigns*, and in colloquial narrative, e.g. *So she comes up to me and says . . .*; *see* HISTORIC PRESENT); and so on.

Some linguists define tense narrowly by form, which gives English only two tenses: the present tense, which in *lexical verbs is the same as the *base (1) form of a verb (except for the -s ending in the *third person singular); and the past tense, which in regular lexical verbs has the -ed inflection.

In terms of meaning, the present tense is then defined as the *unmarked tense, which is timeless in the sense that it can embrace any time that does not exclude the speaker's time (hence its use for general truths), and any time that the speaker does not want to distance himself or herself from. The past tense is then defined as being *marked, to express separation from the speaker's 'now', to indicate the hypothetical nature of a statement (*modal remoteness), or to convey *social distancing.

•• **compound tense**: In some frameworks (especially English Language Teaching), *verb phrase (1) combinations that incorporate features of *aspect, *mood, and *voice are treated as part of the tense system, giving such compound tenses as **past subjunctive tense** (e.g. *If I were you . . .*), **present progressive passive tense** (*Are you being served*?), **present perfect progressive tense** (*Fran has been cycling a lot recently*), and so on.

In CaGEL the term compound tense is used to describe constructions in which different kinds of tenses are combined, e.g. the *present perfect construction, which combines a *primary (3) tense with a secondary tense.

•• **tense phrase (TP)**: *see* PHRASE.

See also FINITE; FUTURATE; FUTURE; NON-FINITE; PRIMARY (3) *tense*; TENSED.

tensed Of a *verb form, *verb phrase, or *clause: having *tense, i.e. carrying a tense *inflection.

The *present and *past tense forms of the verb *sing* (*sing, sings, sang*) are tensed, whereas the *base (1) form, -ing form, and *-ed/-en form (*sing, singing, sung*) are **non-tensed**.

The notion tensed is often equated with *finite, but in some frameworks they are not the same. Thus in CaGEL a clause can be tensed but non-finite. For example, in *I'm pleased to have met you* the underlined *subordinate *to-infinitive clause carries a tense, namely the *perfect tense (*see* PRIMARY (3) *tense*). For grammarians who do not regard the perfect as a tense, the subordinate clause in this example is both non-tensed and non-finite.

tentativeness The quality of being said provisionally or experimentally; one of the meanings conveyed by *modal verbs, or by the use of the *attitudinal *past (2) tense and modal past tense, e.g.

I *might* be able to help

I *was* hoping you would come tomorrow

If you *came* at 6 p.m., you'd be able to have dinner with us

terminal Occurring at or forming the end of something; final.

Especially used in the terminology of *Generative Grammar (2), e.g.

•• **terminal element**, **terminal symbol**: any of the elements or symbols occurring in the terminal *string of a *tree diagram.

territory Used with a qualifying word to indicate the part of a sentence influenced by what the qualifying word refers to, as in **assertive territory**, **non-assertive territory** (*see* ASSERTIVE), *subject territory, and *object territory.

See also SCOPE.

tertiary (*n. & adj.*) (In some older grammar, especially Jespersen's.) (Designating the *rank of) a linguistic unit that is at a third level 'down' in a *phrase, *group, etc. Contrasted with *primary (3) and *secondary.

Thus in *terribly cold weather*, *terribly* is a tertiary: it modifies the adjective *cold*. In turn *terribly cold* modifies the *head noun *weather*.

text A piece of written or spoken language.

This is intended to be a neutral term for any stretch of language, including transcribed spoken language, viewed not so much as a grammatical entity, but as in some way a semantic or pragmatic unit.

Compare UTTERANCE.

text linguistics The study of 'communicative' *texts, rather than grammatical *sentences, as the basis for language analysis.

Text linguistics is sometimes rather similar to *discourse analysis: the aim being to observe *coherence and *cohesion over a unit larger than a sentence, though perhaps with less emphasis on inter-speaker dynamics.

textual

1. Of meaning: as structured in the *text itself.

2. In *Systemic Grammar, meaning can be analysed into three types: the *ideational (2), the *interpersonal (2), and the textual. Textual meaning is concerned with the '*clause as message', the way this is structured into *theme (1) and *rheme, and the relationship of the clause to its context.

See also METAFUNCTION.

***that*-clause** A clause beginning with *that*, or where *that* could be inserted, e.g.

That you believe such nonsense amazes me

I'm sorry *(that)* you believe such nonsense

Such clauses are analysed as *nominal clauses in many frameworks (e.g. CGEL), or as *content clauses (e.g. CaGEL, OMEG).

Although some *relative clauses begin with *that* (e.g. *What's all this nonsense that you're repeating*), they are not included in this category. Appositive clauses beginning with *that* may or may not be included: *The idea that you believe this distresses me.* (*See* APPOSITION.)

See also ZERO.

thematic Of, pertaining to, constituting, or designating the *theme (1).
• **thematically**.
•• **thematic role**: *see* SEMANTIC ROLE
   See also INFORMATION STRUCTURE; RHEME.

thematic role Used in *Generative Grammar (2): the same as *semantic role. Also called **theta role** and **Θ-role**.

theme
   1. The initial part of a *clause which establishes its subject matter or viewpoint, followed by the *rheme.
• **thematization**.
• **thematize**: convert (an element, *phrase, etc.) into the theme of a clause.
   The theme and rheme analysis is a way of looking at the *information structure of a clause, not at functional grammatical elements. Various grammatical devices are available in English to thematize different elements of a clause. One is the use of the *passive to thematize the *direct object of an *active clause:

   Trespassers will be prosecuted

   Mistakes cannot afterwards be rectified

Compare also:

   1985 R. QUIRK et al. *-ing* clauses with thematization: He's worth listening *to*.

In this example the object of the preposition *to* (cf. *It's worth listening to him*) has been turned into the theme.

   Thematizing is also called *fronting or *topicalization.
   See also TOPIC.

   2. A *semantic role assigned to a *noun phrase that refers to an entity that is moved as a result of an action or event denoted by the *verb in a clause. Often not distinguished from *patient.

theoretical grammar *See* GENERATIVE GRAMMAR (2); GRAMMAR.

theoretical linguistics *See* GENERATIVE GRAMMAR (2); LINGUISTICS.

***there*-existential** *See* EXISTENTIAL.

theta role *See* THEMATIC ROLE.

third conditional *See* CONDITIONAL.

third person (Denoting, or used in conjunction with a word indicating) the *person or people spoken about, in contrast to the speaker or addressee.

The third person *pronouns are *he, him, himself, his; she, her, herself, hers; they, them, themselves, their, theirs; it, itself, its.*

The third person *singular form of the *present tense of *lexical verbs is marked in writing by -*s* or -*es* (e.g. *writes, has, does, wants, fixes*).

Compare FIRST PERSON; SECOND PERSON.

three-part verb A *multi-word verb with two *particles (or *prepositions, depending on the analysis). (Also called **three-part word**.)

This is another way of describing a *phrasal-prepositional verb, e.g. *look down on* (= despise), *put up with* (= endure).

three-place predicate *See* PREDICATE.

time

1. In a general and everyday sense: the continuation of the existence of people, objects, *situations, etc. from the *past (1) into the *present (1) and *future (1).

For the relationship between time and tense, *see* TENSE.

2. Designating a *word, *phrase, or *clause relating to time; *temporal.

Thus in *The contractors will repair the drains next week* the *noun phrase *next week* functions as a time *adjunct. Time adjuncts are often subdivided into such categories as *duration and *frequency.

•• **time clause** (also called **temporal clause**): a *clause relating to time, and introduced by a temporal (time) *conjunction (*when, while, after, until, since, as long as,* and *once*), e.g.

After we receive the money, we will send out the orders

Note, however, that in some frameworks (e.g. CaGEL and OMEG) *after* is a preposition. Some time clauses are *non-finite or *verbless, e.g.

While smoking in bed, he had fallen asleep

While in Amsterdam he visited many museums

3. time phase: *see* PHASE.

timeless Not concerned with, or not limited by, time.

Some uses of the *present tense (e.g. *Water freezes at 0° Celsius*) are described as expressing timeless propositions.

tmesis *Morphology*. The separation of the parts of a *word by an intervening element or elements.

This is not a very productive operation in English, and is largely confined to the insertion of swearwords for greater emphasis, as in *I can't find it <u>any-blooming-where</u>*.

The phenomenon is now usually described by using the term **infix**. *See* AFFIX.

to-infinitive The *infinitive form of a *verb preceded by the *infinitival *particle *to*. Contrasted with the *bare infinitive.

The *to*-infinitive can be used:

after *catenative verbs: I want *to know*
in *subject position: *To know all* is to forgive all
in *direct object position: He loves *to eat salmon*
in *predicative position: To know all is *to forgive all*
as an *adverbial clause: Pull tab *to open*
as a *postmodifier: a book *to read*, nothing *to do*
as an adjective *complement: nice *to know*, hard *to imagine*

Strictly speaking, these are all ***to*-infinitive clauses**, i.e. clauses whose *verb phrase (1/2) contains as its *head a *lexical verb preceded by the infinitival particle *to*.

Compare BARE INFINITIVE; CLAUSE; CONTENT CLAUSE; -*ED* CLAUSE; -*ING* CLAUSE.

See also INFINITIVE.

topic That part of a sentence about which something is said. Contrasted with *comment.

The topic and comment distinction, like *theme (1) and *rheme, or *given and *new, is a way of analysing the *information structure of a sentence.

> 1958 C. F. HOCKETT The speaker announces a topic and then says something about it . . . In English and the familiar languages of Europe, topics are usually also subjects and comments are predicates.

However, although the topic frequently coincides with the *subject, and the comment with the *predicate (1), as in *The land / will be sold to the government*, the topic can be some other grammatical element, as in the following examples:

At Layhams Farm, it is now proposed to construct a ski slope (*adverbial as topic)

Recreational it may be, but no development could be more inappropriate (subject-related predicative *complement as topic)

More building we do not want in this village (*direct object as topic)

Putting the topic (or theme) at the front is variously described as *topicalization, *thematization, and *fronting.

topicalization

1. The process whereby a phrase or other element is made the *topic of a sentence.

2. Displacing a unit to the beginning of a clause from its *canonical position such that it achieves *topic prominence, e.g. *Fish I don't eat _*.
• **topicalize.**

trace In *Government-Binding Theory, and later developments of that theory, constituents that have been moved (*see* MOVEMENT) are said to leave behind a mark, called a trace, indicated by the letter 't'. Thus the sentences *Will was called by his brother* and *What did the cat eat?* involve **NP-movement** and **_wh_-movement**, respectively, both of which leave behind a trace:

Will$_i$ was called t$_i$ by his brother

What$_i$ did the cat eat t$_i$?

The subscript letter 'i' indicates *co-reference.

traditional grammar *See* GRAMMAR.

traditional orthography Standard spelling.

The term (abbreviated *t.o.*) is used by spelling reformers who would like to introduce simpler and 'more logical' spelling.

transferred negation *See* NEGATION.

transform (*n.*) (A representation of) a structure derived by the application of a *transformation. Also, occasionally, the same as *transformation.

1962 B. M. H. STRANG It is sometimes assumed that all positive and affirmative sentences have negative and interrogative transforms. This is not quite true.

(*v.*) (Cause to) change into a different, but related, structure.

See also GENERATIVE; GENERATIVE GRAMMAR (2); TRANSFORMATION; TRANSFORMATIONAL; TRANSFORMATIONAL GRAMMAR.

transformation A *rule-governed operation in older *Generative Grammar (2) that converts one structure into another, for example an *active sentence into a *passive one.

> 1955b N. CHOMSKY A sentence *X* is related to a sentence *Y* if, under some transformation set up for the language, *X* is a transform of *Y* or *Y* is a transform of *X*.

See also GENERATIVE; GENERATIVE GRAMMAR (2); TRANSFORM; TRANSFORMATIONAL; TRANSFORMATIONAL GRAMMAR.

transformational Of or pertaining to a *transform or *transformation.

In the early theory of *Generative Grammar (2) (also known as **Transformational-Generative Grammar**), **transformational rules** operated on abstract structures, and explained the systematic relationships between various types of structures.

Typical transformations produced *passive constructions from *active constructions, *interrogatives from *declaratives, and so on, and showed the regular grammatical relationships between such pairs.

An important claim for transformational *rules was that they could disambiguate structures that a purely surface grammar (using e.g. *immediate constituent analysis) cannot. Thus two superficially identical structures, such as

They need helping

They like helping

could be shown to be derived by different rules from two different underlying abstract bases (which very roughly mean 'they need + for someone to help them' and 'they like + when they help other people').

In a later development of the theory transformations were constrained in various ways, and in even later versions they were replaced by principles and parameters (*see* PRINCIPLES AND PARAMETERS THEORY).

• **transformationalism, transformationalist.**

•• **transformational component:** *see* COMPONENT.

See also GENERATIVE; TRANSFORMATIONAL GRAMMAR.

Transformational Grammar (TG) A theory of grammar in which *transformational *rules play an essential part. Such rules were first introduced by the American linguist Noam Chomsky in his book *Syntactic Structures* (1957) (although he had already treated the subject in his doctoral dissertation of 1955). Because this book also introduced the idea that the rules of a grammar should generate grammatical sentences, this type of grammar (contrasted with *structuralism and other and more traditional grammatical models) is also known as **Transformational-Generative Grammar** (TGG) and *Generative Grammar (2).

TG recognizes two levels of analysis, namely *deep structure and *surface structure, which are related by transformational rules. In later models these two levels are interpreted somewhat differently as **D-Structure** and **S-Structure**, and then dropped altogether.

See also CHOMSKYAN; GENERALIZED PHRASE STRUCTURE GRAMMAR; GENERATIVE; GENERATIVE SEMANTICS; GOVERNMENT-BINDING THEORY; GRAMMAR; HEAD-DRIVEN PHRASE STRUCTURE GRAMMAR; MINIMALIST PROGRAM; MONOSTRATAL; PHRASE STRUCTURE GRAMMAR; PRINCIPLES AND PARAMETERS THEORY; STANDARD THEORY; TRANSFORM; TRANSFORMATION.

transitional Of a word or words: indicating a change from one state, place, etc. to another.

This is not a widely used grammatical term, but is sometimes applied to *adverbials that semantically bridge a gap from the subject matter of one statement to that of another, e.g. *meanwhile, in the meantime, incidentally.*

It is also applied to the meaning of a verbal form that indicates little or no duration, with a change of state about to result (e.g. *The bus was stopping*). *See also* ATELIC; TELIC.

transitive A term used to describe a *verb (or *preposition; see below) which *licenses one or more *complements (hence **transitive complementation**), or a *pattern or *clause in which a verb licenses one or more complements. The term derives from Latin *transire*, 'go across'.

Transitive verbs can be grammatically divided into three main types:

(i) *monotransitive, with one object, e.g. *I bought a new suit*
(ii) *complex transitive, with an object and an object-related predicative complement, e.g. *I found the story unreadable, I consider her a loyal friend*
(iii) *ditransitive, with an *indirect object and a direct object, e.g. *I've bought myself a new suit*

Some verbs are virtually always transitive (e.g. *bury, devour, deny, distract*), while others are almost always intransitive (e.g. *arrive, come, digress*). However, some can be said to be transitive or intransitive in different contexts, e.g. *I was cooking* (*breakfast*). Alternatively, we can say that in its 'intransitive use' a verb like *cook* takes an implicit direct object. In other cases, the presence or absence of a direct object signals a change in meaning. Compare the following pairs of sentences:

He lodged in Cambridge; He lodged a complaint
They walked for hours on end; He walks the dog every evening

She made towards the river; He made a cake

Some normally intransitive verbs have transitive uses in which they take a *cognate object, e.g. *I dreamed a lovely dream.*

Transitive complementation is to be distinguished from *intransitive complementation, and from complementation involving *copular verbs; *see* COMPLEX INTRANSITIVE.

● **transitively, transitivity**.

●● **transitive preposition**: a preposition that takes a *complement in the shape of a *noun phrase or *clause, e.g.

[PP in *the park*] (noun phrase complement)

We'll tell you [PP after *we look at the details*] (clausal complement)

See also COMPLEMENTATION; COMPLEX INTRANSITIVE; COMPLEX TRANSITIVE; DITRANSITIVE; INTRANSITIVE; MONOTRANSITIVE.

transparent Obvious in structure or meaning; that can be extrapolated from *surface structure; that can be extrapolated from every occurrence of the phenomenon. Contrasted with *opaque.

1977 P. DOWNING A compound may be highly transparent semantically when it is coined.

tree diagram A graphical representation of the syntactic structure of a clause or other linguistic unit. Also called **phrase marker**, or simply **tree**.

Tree diagrams originated in *Generative Grammar (2), but are not tied to any particular theory of grammar. Here is an example of a tree diagram representing the simple sentence *The busker sang a Beatles tune*:

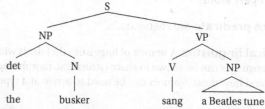

S=*sentence; NP=*noun phrase; VP=*verb phrase (2); det=*determinative (1); N=*noun; V=*verb

The **root** of the tree is at the top, i.e. S (for sentence). The other points from which lines branch off are called *nodes. The hierarchical relationships between the nodes are usually discussed using kinship terminology. Thus we say that the subject NP is the **mother node** for det and N, which are each other's **sisters**. We also observe that S *dominates NP and VP, and that VP immediately dominates both V and NP. Where the internal structure of a particular node is not at issue, triangles are used, as with the NP *a Beatles tune*. Grammatical *function (1) labels are not normally shown in trees, because functions can be read off the tree (they are said to be **configurationally defined**). Thus a *subject is defined as the first NP under S ([NP, S]); a *direct object is defined as the first NP under VP ([NP, VP]); and so on.

The way in which trees are drawn depends on the theoretical framework adopted by a particular author. In the simple tree above, the direct object NP is a daughter of VP and sister of V, the reason for this being the close bond between the verb and the direct object (the former *licenses the latter). In other frameworks (e.g. CGEL) the direct object is not part of the VP.

trigraph Three letters representing one speech sound as in *manoeuvre*, where the *oeu* is pronounced /uː/.

truth condition *See* TRUTH-CONDITIONAL SEMANTICS.

truth-conditional semantics A type of *logical semantics in which the meaning of a sentence is characterized by enumerating the set of conditions under which it is said to be true without reference to the *context of situation.

See also LOGICAL SEMANTICS; MODEL-THEORETIC SEMANTICS.

two-part verb A label that is sometimes used to describe a *multi-word verb consisting of two parts, e.g. a *phrasal or *prepositional verb. Also called **two-part word**.

two-place predicate *See* PREDICATE.

typological linguistics A branch of linguistics that deals with the way in which languages can be shown to share (structural, morphological, etc.) *features, and how those features can be used to arrive at a typology of languages.

> 1990 W. CROFT The broadest and most unassuming linguistic definition of 'typology' refers to a classification of structural types across languages. In this second definition, a language is taken to belong to a single type, and a typology of languages is a definition of the types and an enumeration or classification of the languages into those types. We will refer to this definition of typology as **typological classification**.

typology *See* TYPOLOGICAL LINGUISTICS.

ultimate constituent *See* IMMEDIATE CONSTITUENT.

unacceptable *See* ACCEPTABLE.

unanalysable *See* ANALYSABLE.

unattached participle *See* HANGING PARTICIPLE.

unbounded dependency A link between two *positions in a sentence that crosses one or more *clause-boundaries, e.g.

[What [do you think [that Graham believes [his sister likes _]]]]?

Here the *wh*-word *what* (the direct object of the verb *like*) is linked with the position marked by '_' across several clause boundaries.

Also called **long-distance dependency**.

•• **unbounded dependency word**: used in CaGEL as a cover term for *wh*-exclamative, *wh*-interrogative, and *wh*-relative words.

unconditioned *See* CONDITIONING; VARIANT.

uncount Designating a *noun that has no *plural form, and cannot be used with numerical values. Contrasted with *count. (Also called **uncountable, non-count**.)

Grammatically, uncount nouns are distinguished by the fact that they can be used without an *article or *determinative (1), and with certain determinatives that are exclusive to them (e.g. *much*). Uncount nouns often refer in a rather general way to substances and abstract qualities, processes, and states (e.g. *china, petrol, poverty, rain, welfare*), rather than to discrete units. But the uncount versus count distinction is grammatical, not semantic, and a number of English uncount nouns (e.g. *information, luggage, news, traffic*) have countable equivalents in other languages.

Uncount is generally synonymous with *mass*; but *see* MASS NOUN for a distinction that is sometimes made.

uncountable (*n. & adj.*) (A noun that is) *uncount.

See UNCOUNT.

undergoer *See* PATIENT.

underlying Designating (abstract) *deep structure grammatical or semantic *features posited to explain various relationships or meanings in the actual language (i.e. the *surface structure realization).

In *Generative Grammar (2), concepts such as **underlying form/ structure/phrase-marker/string** are part of the apparatus of the theory. Underlying structures are used, among other things, to explain why we sometimes have to interpret similar structures in different ways, while two very different structures may be understood to mean the same thing.

Underlying structures are often said to contain elements not present in the 'surface' language. For example, in early *Transformational Grammar the underlying structure of an imperative sentence like *Sit down* was posited to be *You will sit down*. From this underlying structure the surface structure *Sit down* was derived by the application of transformational rules that deleted *you* and *will*.

In a less technical way (without involving transformational rules) various structures may be explained in terms of some underlying structure. Thus a *prepositional phrase functioning as a *postmodifier to a *noun, as in *the man in the iron mask*, could be said to be underlyingly clausal (i.e. *who was in the iron mask*). Or a *genitive may be labelled *subjective (2) or *objective (2) on the basis of its meaning, e.g.

the hair of the dog (subjective: *the dog* has hair)

love of money (objective: someone loves *money*)

The concept of underlying structure can be seen as a more abstract extension of the *concept understood of traditional grammar.

• **underlyingly**.

understood Of a *word or words: deducible.

The term *'you' understood* is sometimes used to describe the *subject that is missing from most *imperatives, but clearly implicit, as shown by the fact that it can be inserted, or added in a *tag, e.g.

(You) do as you're told

(You) be quiet

Don't (you) forget

Sit down, won't you

Understood is not entirely synonymous with *recoverable. The latter is usually applied to words that could, with little or no change of form, be inserted in the *text. *Understood* may relate more abstractly to *underlying meaning. Thus a *non-finite *clause following a *catenative verb has an

understood subject that is usually the same as the subject of the catenative, e.g.

They tried to telephone us

but occasionally different, as in the informal *We said not to worry*. In neither of these cases could we insert the understood words (cf. **They tried they to telephone us, *We said they not to worry*).

See also UNDERLYING.

unfulfilled condition The same as unreal *condition.

ungradable See GRADABLE.

ungrammatical Not conforming to the rules of some grammatical system; syntactically *deviant. Contrasted with *grammatical.

More generally, grammaticality is judged in relation to what is considered a *standard, but standards vary. *I never said nothing to nobody* is ungrammatical in *Standard English, but conforms to the rules of its own *dialect.

For many linguists grammaticality is a phenomenon that is subject to *gradience, as are grammaticality judgements.
•• **ungrammatical word**: *see* GRAMMATICAL.

Compare ACCEPTABILITY; ILL-FORMED; WELL-FORMED.

unheaded The same as *exocentric.

uninflected See INFLECTED.

unique Pertaining to something of which there is only one.
• **uniqueness**.
•• **unique reference**: a concept invoked to explain the use of the *definite article (*the*) in various contexts where, although the *referent may not have been mentioned before, its uniqueness (or *identifiability) can be assumed. Sometimes the referent really is unique (e.g. *the Earth*); more often it is unique in the context of a particular place or time (e.g. *the Pope, the Queen, the Head of Department*), or even in some much smaller situational context (e.g. *I'm going to the post office*, Please *shut the windows*).

Uniqueness may also be due to other factors. Thus the phrase *the day after tomorrow* can refer to only one particular day at the time it is uttered, and the phrase *the best man* in *May the best man win* can refer to only one man.

unit A general term to denote a discrete building block of linguistic analysis at any *level, e.g. a *word, *phrase, or *clause. Also called **linguistic unit**.

unit noun A unit *noun is a *word that allows us to break up an *uncountable noun into *countable parts, e.g.

a *pat* of butter

two *pieces* of toast

The same as a *partitive noun.

universal (*n. & adj.*) (A grammatical *feature (1)) that is common to all natural languages.

Features of English which seem basic to grammar, such as *tense distinctions and *prepositions, are non-existent in some languages. **Language universals**, i.e. grammatical characteristics which feature in all languages, tend to be rather general: e.g. all languages have *nouns and *verbs, have ways of talking about *time (1) and *place, and distinguish speaker and addressee.

universal conditional-concessive clause (In CGEL.) A type of *conditional clause with an element of *concessive meaning that signifies a condition that offers an unlimited choice, regardless of the circumstances, e.g.

Whatever you do, don't tell him that you are not a plumber (i.e. 'no matter what you do . . .')

Other items that occur in such clauses are *whoever, whichever, wherever*, and *however*. In CaGEL this is a type of **exhaustive conditional**.

See also ALTERNATIVE CONDITIONAL-CONCESSIVE CLAUSE; CONDITION; CONDITIONAL.

unmarked Of a linguistic *feature or structure: that is more basic, *central, or usual than the *marked form to which it is related.

1985 R. QUIRK et al. 'Measure' adjectives . . . have two terms for the opposite ranges of the scale (*old/young, deep/shallow, tall/short*), but use the upper range as the 'unmarked' term in measure expressions.

For example, normal unmarked questions about age and height are:

How *old* is the baby?

How *tall* is your little girl?

•• **unmarked order anaphora**: see ANAPHORA.

See also MARKEDNESS.

unmodalized *See* DEGREE OF MODALITY.

unproductive *See* PRODUCTIVE.

unreal condition *See* CONDITION.

unrelated participle *See* HANGING PARTICIPLE.

unspecified *it* *See* DUMMY; IMPERSONAL.

untensed *See* TENSED.

usage Established and customary ways of using language.

Usage is a somewhat wider and somewhat vaguer term than *grammar or *syntax. In one sense, usage is what people generally say and write, how they actually use their language. Ideally therefore, *usage* should (i) include grammar and (ii) be objective and *descriptive, rather than *prescriptive.

In practice, usage guides deal cursorily with consensual core grammar, and pay most attention to areas of disputed usage, giving guidance that veers towards prescription (which is doubtless what most users of such books want). Grammatical usages discussed include such matters as *If I were* versus *If I was*, or *used not to* versus *didn't use to*. Other areas are *word formation and spelling (e.g. *blamable* versus *blameable*), pronunciation (*haRASSment* versus *HArassment*), and *vocabulary (*flout* versus *flaunt*; *disinterested* versus *uninterested*; and the meaning of *decimate*).

Questions of usage are complicated by the fact that accepted usage may vary from one *speech community to another, according to different national, regional, or social *varieties, and such factors as who is writing or speaking to whom about what.

Many dictionaries employ **usage labels** to indicate whether particular senses, *words, or *phrases are *formal (3), *informal, British, American, dialectal, dated, *slang, offensive, *euphemistic, and so on.

A distinction is sometimes made between usage in the sense of what is grammatically and linguistically correct and *acceptable (and of avoiding what is disputed), and **use**, i.e. what is appropriate to communication between people in an actual *situation (1).

use *See* USAGE.

utterance An uninterrupted sequence of spoken language.

This is intended to be a neutral term pertaining to language use, unlike the grammatically defined terms *clause and *sentence. It is sometimes contrasted with *text, and sometimes included in it.

See also ECHO UTTERANCE; SPEECH ACT.

V Verb as an *element (1) in *clause structure.

valency (A specification of) the number and type of *arguments that a particular *predicate (typically a *verb) *licenses.

> 2008 T. HERBST & S. SCHÜLLER The fundamental idea of valency theory, which developed out of Tesnière's model of dependency theory, is that the structure of a sentence is largely determined by the verb.

See also ARGUMENT.

value judgement A judgement attributing merit or demerit to an action, event, *situation, etc.

This is one of many meaning categories assigned to *disjuncts. Thus in *Foolishly, Greg didn't ask for a receipt*, the *adverb *foolishly* expresses the speaker's judgement on what happened (in this case that it was foolish of Greg not to ask for a receipt). It does not describe the manner of asking.

Compare VIEWPOINT ADJUNCT.

variable

1. (*n. & adj.*) (A *word) having more than one form (or *variant). Contrasted with *invariable.

Variable words include *count *nouns (with *singular and *plural forms); *verbs (with *third person singular *present tense, *present participle, *past, and (in some verbs) *past participle forms; e.g. *know, knows, knowing, knew, known*); and some *gradable *adjectives and *adverbs (with *comparative and *superlative forms; e.g. *fine, finer, finest; soon, sooner, soonest*).

2. A word with variable *reference, i.e. a word whose meaning is largely dependent on *context.

For example, although personal *pronouns convey meanings such as 'singular' (e.g. *he, it*) or 'plural' (e.g. *we, they*), 'masculine' (e.g. *him*) or feminine (*her*), their *referents are largely conditioned by the *context. Thus the word *he* can refer in a particular context to any male person, but this is not part of the dictionary meaning of the word. And, indeed, *he* is not necessarily confined to male persons (outside politically correct circles).

> 1984 R. HUDDLESTON *He* is used by many speakers as a 'variable' ranging over a set containing both males and females (normally human) as in . . . *If any student wishes to take part in the seminar, he should consult his tutor.* The semantic distinction male vs female is here neutralised, and the fact that *he* is used makes it the semantically unmarked member of the pair *he/she.* As we noted earlier, *they* has long been used as an alternative to *he* in this sense.

3. An element that substitutes for one or more others. For example, we can talk about 'XP'—where 'X' denotes the *word class categories N, V, A, or P (*noun, *verb, *adjective, *preposition)—to designate NP, VP, AP, or PP.

4. Any factor that contributes to differences between language *varieties, e.g. regional or social variables.

variant (*n. & adj.*) (Designating) one of the forms in which a *variable element can appear.

Such forms may be determined by the *context in which they appear. For example, the *indefinite article appears as *an* when it is placed before a *word that begins with a vowel. As such its shape is *conditioned by the following word. **Unconditioned** variants are not determined in this way; for example, the two variants of the *past participle of *show* are *showed* and *shown.*

See also FREE VARIATION; INVARIABLE.

variation

1. (The existence of) differences between *varieties of English.
Often used with a distinguishing word, such as *regional* or *stylistic.*

2. The existence of alternative linguistic forms within a single variety of English.

See also CONDITIONING; FREE VARIATION; VARIANT.

variety A distinct form of a language, as used for example by a particular (national or regional) group, or in a particular context.

The terms variety and *variation are especially used in the analysis of different kinds of English. Thus we can talk of regional and social varieties (or variation); varieties according to the *field of discourse; varieties consistent with spoken or written mediums; and 'stylistic' varieties, due to different degrees of *formality, the attitude of the speaker, and so on.

Compare ATTITUDINAL.

V-bar category (V′ category) *See* X-BAR SYNTAX.

verb

1. A member of a major *word class which is normally essential to
*clause structure (though *see* SMALL CLAUSE) and which can show
(sometimes in combination with other syntactic elements) contrasts of
*tense, *aspect, *mood, *voice, *number, and *person.

In traditional grammar, the verb is sometimes defined notionally as a
'doing' word, but modern grammar prefers a *distributional
(i.e. *morphosyntactic) definition of the kind given above.

Verbs are usually subdivided first into:

  (i) *lexical (or *full, or *main) verbs
  (ii) *auxiliary verbs

Lexical verbs are further classified syntactically, depending on whether
any accompanying elements are obligatory or permissible. The major
types include *transitive, *intransitive, and *linking verbs (or *copular
verbs). Auxiliary verbs are sometimes divided into *primary and *modal
verbs, though other classifications are also possible, e.g. by distinguishing
the *aspectual auxiliaries *be* and *have*, *dummy *do*, and *passive *be*.

In some recent accounts (e.g. CaGEL, OMEG) auxiliary verbs are
regarded as main verbs. *Compare* CATENATIVE-AUXILIARY ANALYSIS;
DEPENDENT-AUXILIARY ANALYSIS.

•• **verb group**: a sequence of verbs that contains a lexical verb in addition
to one or more auxiliaries. The same as *verb phrase (1). The term is used
in *Systemic Grammar; *see* GROUP; WORD GROUP.

•• **verb of psychological state**: *see* PSYCHOLOGICAL VERB.

•• **verb of resulting meaning**: *see* RESULT.

See also COPULA; LEXICAL VERB; LINKING VERB; MAIN VERB; MULTI-WORD
VERB; PHRASAL VERB; PHRASAL-PREPOSITIONAL VERB; PREPOSITIONAL
VERB; RAISING; REGULAR; TWO-PART VERB.

2. A major, and usually essential, *element of clause structure.

In the representation of the functional elements of clause structure,
V stands for *verb phrase (1). Thus both *I bought oranges* and *I have been
buying oranges* are SVO sentences. The verb element (V) is the only
element that must always be filled by items that belong to the same word
class, namely verb.

•• **verb of incomplete predication**: (an old-fashioned term for)
a *linking verb (or a *copular verb), especially the verb *be*, so-called
because such a verb is 'incomplete' without a *complement.

See PREDICATOR.

verbal

1. Of, relating to, or derived from a *verb.

•• **verbal adjective**: *see* PARTICIPIAL ADJECTIVE.

•• **verbal conjunction**: *see* CONJUNCTION.

•• **verbal group**: (in *Systemic Grammar) the same as *verb phrase (1).

•• **verbal noun**: *see* GERUND; *-ING* FORM.

2. Relating to words, particularly when spoken, as in *verbal ability*, *verbal abuse. Compare* ORAL.

Linguists usually try to avoid using this sense of the word *verbal*, particularly when *oral* is more accurate (e.g. *oral communication*).

verbal idiom

1. An *idiom based on a *verb, e.g. *hit the road* ('leave'), *kick the bucket* ('die').

2. Used in CaGEL for *phrasal verbs and *phrasal-prepositional verbs, though not for *prepositional verbs.

verbal inflection class *See* CONJUGATION.

verbless Of a *sentence or *clause: lacking a *verb.

Verbless clauses are not usually recognized as such in traditional grammar, where they are more likely to be regarded as *phrases. They have some of the semantic and structural features of clauses. For example, some are introduced by a *conjunction, e.g.

When in Rome, do as the Romans do

Come early *if possible*

Others have a *subject preceded by *with* or *without*:

With the exam behind her, she felt able to enjoy the holiday (Compare *The exam being behind her ...*)

Without you here, I don't know what I'd do (Compare *If you were not here ...*)

Other examples have neither a conjunction nor a subject, but a paraphrase suggests a clausal, rather than a phrasal, interpretation, e.g.

Unhappy at the result, she decided to try again (compare *Because she was unhappy ...*)

Notice the existence of a subject–*predicate (1) relation in (the paraphrases of) all these examples.

•• **verbless sentence**: any type of *minor sentence lacking a verb. *Compare* SMALL CLAUSE.

verb of emotion *See* PSYCHOLOGICAL VERB.

verb of psychological state *See* PSYCHOLOGICAL VERB.

verb-particle construction *See* MULTI-WORD VERB; PHRASAL-PREPOSITIONAL VERB; PHRASAL VERB; PREPOSITIONAL VERB.

verb phrase (VP)

1. A *phrase consisting either of a single-word *verb on its own, or of a group of verbs which functions in the same way as a single-word verb. Called **verb(al) group** in *Systemic Grammar. Examples:

> went
> will go
> will have gone
> must be forgotten
> must have been forgotten
> must have been being forgotten
> having been forgotten

> 1987 F. R. PALMER Sequences of verb forms such as *has been running, may have run, keeps wanting to run* will all be referred to as 'verb phrases'.... One way of treating a form such as *has taken* is to say that it is the perfect form of the verb lexeme TAKE. That assigns to the two-word sequence the same kind of grammatical status as that of single words in another language (*eg* Latin *amavi* 'I have loved').

A verb phrase can be *finite or *non-finite. In a finite verb phrase, the first word is the only word that is finite, i.e. carries *tense. The last word in both finite and non-finite verb phrases is a *main verb. If a finite verb phrase consists of a single word, then it must be a main verb that carries tense (e.g. *goes, went*).

See also COMPLEX VERB PHRASE.

2. (In theoretical grammar and recent descriptive grammars such as CaGEL and OMEG.) A sequence of words normally containing a *lexical verb together with any *complements and *adjuncts, but excluding the *subject. (In *Generative Grammar (2) *auxiliary verbs are also excluded from VP because they are placed under 'Aux', or an equivalent node.) In this sense, verb phrase is the formal counterpart of *predicate (1), and forms, with the constituent that is its subject (if there is one), a clause or sentence.

See also TREE DIAGRAM.

viewpoint adjunct A subcategory of *adjunct (3), typically in the shape of an *adverb phrase, that qualifies the contents of a *clause from a particular point of view, e.g.

> *Morally*, the tax had much to commend it, but *politically* it was madness

This kind of adjunct can be expanded:

> Morally speaking..., but politically speaking...
> From a moral point of view..., but from a political point of view...

In classifications that distinguish adjuncts from *subjuncts, the label used is **viewpoint subjunct**.

viewpoint subjunct *See* SUBJUNCT; VIEWPOINT ADJUNCT.

vocabulary The entire set of *words (1) in a language.

In most approaches to grammar, vocabulary as such does not feature very prominently. Such frameworks tend to focus on syntax and morphology, leaving word meanings to the dictionary. However, in recent decades there has emerged an interest in the study of the (mental) *lexicon, and there is an increasing interest in the interrelationship between the lexicon and the components of grammar.

In applied linguistics, *vocabulary* is used in its everyday sense as a set of words. There are many books for foreign learners that are devoted to learning vocabulary, and most general coursebooks have chapters or sections on vocabulary.

With regard to *lexicography, many modern dictionaries (especially learners' dictionaries such as the *Oxford Advanced Learner's Dictionary*) provide a considerable amount of grammatical information, for example by marking verbs as *transitive or *intransitive, or by specifying in which patterns they can be used.

●● **vocabulary size**: It is not easy to say how many words there are in the English language, partly because the notion of word is difficult to define, and partly because of problematic issues such as whether to include obsolete or dialect words, slang, words in recognized *varieties of English (e.g. Indian English, New Zealand English), and so on. A typical desk dictionary may define about 100,000 vocabulary items, while the *Oxford English Dictionary* lists more than 600,000.

As for how many words an individual English-speaking adult knows or uses, estimates vary greatly. Figures published in 1940 reporting on tests conducted with American college students claimed they know around 150,000 items, while tests published in 1978 claimed a figure of no fewer than 250,000. Both figures have been challenged on various grounds, not least because it is not clear what it means to 'know' a word. However, the figure is likely to be many tens of thousands.

Recent computer surveys tell us that around 1,000 common words account for over 70 per cent of everyday speech and writing.

vocative (*n. & adj.*) (An optional element in *clause structure) denoting a person or entity addressed.

In *inflected languages (e.g. Latin) the vocative is a *case (1) form taken by a *noun phrase denoting an addressee. In English the vocative is not marked by *inflection, but by intonation. Vocatives can include *proper nouns (e.g. *Mary, Grandpa*) and titles (e.g. *Sir, Mr President, Doctor, Waiter, Nurse*), as well as *epithets and general nouns, both polite and otherwise (e.g. *darling, chums, bastard, friends, liar, mate*). Some of these can be expanded (e.g. *Mary dearest, my dear friends, you silly fool*).

Inanimate entities can also be addressed, but this tends to be in fairly formal or literary contexts, and involves a degree of personification, e.g.

I vow to thee, my country…

Come, friendly bombs, and fall on Slough! (from the poem *Slough* by John Betjeman)

voice A grammatical *category which provides two different ways of presenting a particular *situation, namely as *active or *passive.

In many frameworks active and passive *clauses are viewed as *constructions, so that the notion voice is applicable to *verb phrases, *clauses, and *sentences. The concepts active and passive are linked to meaning in that the *subject of an active clause is typically the *actor, or 'doer' of the action expressed by the verb, as in *The bird caught the worm*, whereas the *object typically 'undergoes' the action expressed by the verb. In a passive construction these roles are reversed: now the subject is 'acted upon', and the agent appears in a *by*-phrase, as in *The caught by the bird*.

Some languages (e.g. Greek) also have a **middle voice**, which includes verbs of *reflexive meaning.

See also AGENT; PATIENT; SEMANTIC ROLE.

volition A semantic notion that denotes 'willingness', as expressed typically by *verbs (*want, desire*, etc.).

The *modal verbs *shall* and *will* carry little meaning other than indicating 'futurity', although often an element of 'intention', 'promise', or other shade of volition is blended in, e.g.

We *shall* do all we can to help

I *will* not forget

Along with 'ability', the notion of 'volition' is an exponent of *dynamic (2) modality, which is said to be typically *subject-oriented, in contrast to *deontic and *epistemic modality, which express *speaker-oriented meanings (e.g. 'permission').

• **volitional**.

Compare PREDICTION.

VP Abbreviation for *verb phrase.

•• **VP-adjunct:** *see* PREDICATION ADJUNCT.

VP-preposing *See* PREPOSE.

weak iconicity *See* ICONICITY.

weak verb *See* STRONG.

well-formed In harmony with (or generated by) the *rules of a particular linguistic system, especially grammar; thus often taken to mean *grammatical. Contrasted with *ill-formed.

In earlier *Generative Grammar (2), a **well-formed utterance** is one generated according to the rules of syntax, semantics, and phonology. It is a wider term than grammatical, which often has a more strictly syntactic sense.

In later work Chomsky denies that the notion plays a role in linguistic theory.

> 1994 (2000) N. CHOMSKY The class of expressions generated by the (I-)language L should not be confused with a category of well-formed sentences, a notion that has no known place in the theory of language, though informal exposition has sometimes obscured the point, leading to much confusion and wasted effort.

● **well-formedness**.

Compare ACCEPTABILITY; GRAMMATICAL.

were-subjunctive *See* SUBJUNCTIVE.

wh A symbol representing the *exclamative, *interrogative, or *relative quality of *wh-words. Probably introduced by the American linguist Noam Chomsky.

Wh is often prefixed to another word, indicating the quality (exclamative, interrogative, relative, etc.) of the item which it combines with:

●● *wh*-**clause**: a neutral term for *exclamative, *interrogative, and *relative clauses that involve *wh*-words. *See also* MOVEMENT.

●● *wh*-**cleft**: *see* CLEFT CONSTRUCTION.

●● *wh*-**element**: *see* WH-ELEMENT.

●● *wh*-**interrogative (clause)**: *see* INTERROGATIVE.

•• *wh*-**item**: *see* WH-ELEMENT.

•• *wh*-**movement**: *see* MOVEMENT; TRACE.

•• *wh*-**phrase**: *see* MOVEMENT; WH-ELEMENT.

•• *wh*-**question**: *see* MOVEMENT; QUESTION; WH-ELEMENT.

•• *wh*-**relative**: a *relative pronoun that begins with *wh*-.

•• *wh*-**word**: *see* WH-WORD.

See also MOVEMENT.

***wh*-element** A single **wh*-word, or a phrase containing such a word. Also called **wh*-form**, **wh*-item**, **wh*-phrase**.

In the sentence *What happened?* the *wh*-element is the word *what*. But often the *wh*-element is longer, e.g.

Which pictures do you like best?

Tell me *what kind of pasta* you bought

See also MOVEMENT; WH.

Whorfian Designating, or characteristic of, the theories of B. L. Whorf.

•• **Whorfian hypothesis**: the same as the *Sapir-Whorf hypothesis.

***wh*-word** One of a small class of *interrogative or *relative *words most of which begin with *wh*-.

The main *wh*-words are *what, which, who, whom, whose; when, where, why*, and *how*.

Wh-words are sometimes intensified by adding *ever*, often written as a separate word (always after *why*), e.g.

Who ever would have guessed?

Why ever didn't you say?

This usage is grammatically distinct from the similar-looking compounds *whatever, whoever*, etc. (e.g. *Whatever you do, don't tell him the truth*). See FREE RELATIVE CLAUSE; UNIVERSAL CONDITIONAL-CONCESSIVE CLAUSE.

The *wh*- spelling does not correctly represent any present or past pronunciation. In modern pronunciation the sound is /w/. An older (but never, since *Old English times, universal) pronunciation, still current in Scottish and Irish English, and in the United States and Canada, is /hw/. In Old English the spelling *hw*- was used, but the letters were reversed in *Middle English by analogy with *ch*-, *ph*-, *sh*-, and *th*-.

See also MOVEMENT; WH; WH-ELEMENT.

***will*-condition** See CONDITIONAL.

wishing The verbal expression of a wish.

Wishing is sometimes singled out in grammatical description because the *verb of a *subordinate clause after an expression of wishing must be in the *past (2) tense, and as such is used to express *modal remoteness, e.g.

I wish I *knew/had* known what to say

If only I *knew/had* known

Such expressions when referring to *present (1) or *past (1) time denote what is contrary to fact; for example, *I wish I knew/had known* implies *I don't/didn't know*. With reference to the *future (1), wishing implies something that may be unlikely, but is not necessarily impossible. For example:

I wish you would come tomorrow

does not rule out your coming, though my remark is more diffident than *I hope you come/will come tomorrow*.

See PAST (2); SUBJUNCTIVE.

word

1. A meaningful unit of speech which is normally not interruptable, and which, when written or printed, has spaces on either side (also called **orthographic word**).

Native speakers intuitively recognize words as distinct meaningful grammatical units of language. It is words whose meanings and very existence are catalogued in dictionaries, and which combine to form larger units such as *phrases, *clauses, and *sentences.

Grammarians recognize smaller meaningful units in the grammatical hierarchy, such as *morphemes, but words have distinct characteristics. As has been noted, they are normally uninterruptable, and they are cohesive in the sense that their parts cannot be rearranged in the way that words in a sentence often can. Contrast *unhappiness* (in which no reordering is possible; e.g. *nesshappiun*) with *This sentence can be rearranged*, which can be changed to *Can this sentence be rearranged?*

Another characteristic of words, which would probably seem obvious to native speakers, is enshrined in Bloomfield's definition of them as 'minimal free forms', i.e. the smallest units that can reasonably constitute a complete utterance, as in

Do you accept? *Yes/Maybe/Naturally*

However, some words fail this test, e.g. *a/an* and *the*.

The characteristic of being 'complete in itself' is supported by the writing convention that separates one word from another, but there are problems with this. Opinions vary as to whether certain *compounds are in fact one word or two (e.g. *half way, half-way, halfway*), and whether such forms as *don't* and *I'll* are single words or not.

2. A word, as listed in a dictionary, together with all its variants. Distinguished from sense (1) as *lexeme. Also called **dictionary word**.

Although this is a more abstract sense of the notion word, it is a common meaning; thus e.g. *see, sees, seeing, saw, seen* are all part of the same 'word' *see*.

•• **grammatical word**: *see* GRAMMATICAL WORD.

word blend *See* BLEND.

word class A category of *words that syntactically *distribute in the same way, and predominantly share the same *morphosyntactic characteristics.

The classification of words into word classes (sometimes called **form classes**) is much the same as the more traditional classification of words into **parts of speech**, but the former favours more rigorous *distributional definitions and disfavours *notional ones.

There is no single correct way of analysing words into word classes. Generally recognized are *nouns, *verbs, *adjectives, *adverbs, *conjunctions (*coordinators and *subordinators), *prepositions, and *interjections. In recent times the set of word classes has expanded to include items such as *complementizer, *determinative (1), and *determiner (2).

Grammarians disagree about the boundaries between the word classes (*see* GRADIENCE), and it is not always clear whether to **lump** subcategories together or to **split** them. For example, in some grammars (e.g. CaGEL) *pronouns are classed as nouns, whereas in other frameworks (e.g. CGEL) they are treated as a separate word class.

In some recent theoretical frameworks, word classes are regarded as *feature complexes (*see* PHRASE STRUCTURE GRAMMAR) or as constructions (*see* *CONSTRUCTION GRAMMAR).

Compare MAJOR WORD CLASS.

word complex *See* WORD GROUP.

word ending *See* SUFFIX.

word form
  1. The form that a particular *word can assume in speech or writing. *Compare* GRAMMATICAL WORD (2).
  2. Any variant of a *lexeme. (Also called **form of a word**.)
The term is used as a way of avoiding the ambiguity of *word*. For example, *see, sees, seeing, saw*, and *seen* are word forms of (or forms of) the lexeme *see*.

word formation

1. The subdiscipline of linguistics covered by *morphology, including *inflection, *derivation, and *compounding.

2. (More narrowly.) The formation of *lexemes through *derivation and *compounding (and sometimes *conversion). Also called **lexical word formation**.

In this model, inflection is handled as part of syntax.

3. (More narrowly still.) Derivation only.

Word Grammar (WG) A grammatical theory, developed by the British linguist Richard (Dick) Hudson since the 1980s, in which the notion of *dependency is central. It claims that the *word—rather than, say, the *phrase or *clause, or *levels of structure—is the most important element in language.

> 1990 R. HUDSON a. WG is *lexicalist* because the word is central—hence the name of the theory. Grammars make no reference to any unit larger than the word (except for the unit 'word-string', which as we shall see is used only in coordinate structures and is very different from the 'phrase' and 'clause' of other theories). b. WG is *wholist* because no distinction is recognized between the grammar 'proper' and the lexicon. The grammar includes facts at all levels of generality, all of which are handled in the same way.

> 2010 R. HUDSON Word Grammar is a theory of language structure based on the assumption that language, and indeed the whole of knowledge, is a network, and that virtually all of knowledge is learned. It combines the psychological insights of cognitive linguistics with the rigour of more formal theories.

word group (In *Systemic Grammar.) A *head (1) together with other words that may complement or modify it. Also called **word complex**.

Word groups occupy a special place in Systemic Grammar, because a *group (1) is syntactically defined as the expansion of a head, and is distinguished from a *phrase (2), which is viewed as a reduced *clause. Word groups therefore have a distinct *rank (2) in this kind of grammar. The groups recognized are *nominal group, *verb(al) group, and *adverbial group (corresponding to *noun phrase, *verb phrase, and *adverb phrase in other models), plus *conjunction group (e.g. *even if, if only*) and *preposition group (e.g. *right behind, in front of*). The latter is distinguished from *prepositional phrase.

> 2014 M. A. K. HALLIDAY & C. MATTHIESSEN A **phrase** is different from a group in that, whereas a group is an expansion of a word, a phrase is a contraction of a clause. Starting from opposite ends, the two achieve roughly

the same status on a rank scale, as units that lie somewhere between the rank of a clause and that of a word.

word order The order in which *words (more precisely, *constituents; see below) are arranged in *sentences and *clauses.

In *inflected (varieties of) languages, such as *Old English or Latin, word order may be comparatively free, because the function of a word (or *phrase) is often indicated by an *inflectional form. Modern English, having few inflections, has a much more fixed word order. The basic (*unmarked) order of the main clause *elements in English is SVO (subject-verb-object).

In grammatical models in which words are grouped into phrases, clauses, etc., it is more accurate to speak of constituent order.

Compare ADJECTIVE ORDER; INFORMATION STRUCTURE.

***would* condition** *See* CONDITIONAL.

***would have*-condition** *See* CONDITIONAL.

X-bar syntax A model of *syntax, introduced by the American linguist Noam Chomsky into *Generative Grammar (2), that treats all *phrases as having the same skeletal hierarchical structure, as shown in the following *tree diagram:

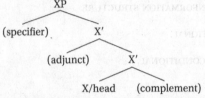

XP stands for a *phrase headed by X (the obligatory *head), where X stands for *N(oun), *V(erb), *A(djective), or *P(reposition), and sometimes *Adv(erb). In this representation X′ (read 'X bar') is called a **bar level category**, i.e. a category that is intermediate between XP and X. Optional *adjuncts are linked by *adjunction to the left of the lower X′ in the tree above (e.g. [$_{V'}$ *quickly* [$_{V'}$ *opened the door*]]), but they can also be adjoined to the right ([$_{V'}$ [$_{V'}$ *opened the door*] *quickly*]). The adjunct and the lower X′ are sisters (i.e. they share the same *node immediately above them). The *specifier position is occupied by various kinds of elements in different phrases, for example by *determinatives (1) in *noun phrases (e.g. *these lectures*), intensifying adverbs in *adjective phrases (e.g. *very kind*), etc. *Complements, if present, are sisters of the head X. The various levels inside phrases are regarded as *projections of the head.

yes-no interrogative/question *See* INTERROGATIVE; QUESTION.

Z element *See* ELEMENT.

zero An abstraction, often symbolized by 'ø', representing the absence of any *realization, where there could theoretically be, or in comparable grammatical contexts there is, a morphological or syntactic realization.

The concept of *zero* is used as a way of making *rules more comprehensive and consistent than they would otherwise be.

It is not generally used in relation to *elliptical structures, where the symbol [∧] is sometimes preferred.

•• **zero allomorph**: *see* ALLOMORPH.

•• **zero anaphor**: *see* ANAPHOR.

•• **zero article**: a unit posited before an *uncountable *noun or a *plural *count noun when either is used with an *indefinite meaning, e.g. ø *food*, ø *vegetables*.

•• **zero genitive**: the realization of the *genitive *inflection without an additional *s* in *words that already end in -*s*. This is the usual genitive with regular plural nouns, as in *the athletes' achievements*, where the form is identical in pronunciation with the ordinary plural form (*athletes*), and differs only in having an *apostrophe added to the written form. The zero genitive also occurs with some *singular words, particularly foreign names ending in /z/, e.g. *Aristophanes' plays*. By contrast, *irregular plurals not ending in -*s* show a contrast of form between the plural *common *case (e.g. *men*) and the plural genitive (e.g. *the men's achievement*), just like their singular forms (e.g. common case *man*; genitive *man's*).

•• **zero-place predicate**: *see* PREDICATE.

•• **zero plural**: a plural form of a count noun that is not distinct from the singular. Some count nouns have no distinct plural form (e.g. *sheep*, *cod*, *deer*). Other nouns for animals can have zero plurals or *regular plurals (e.g. *fish/fishes*, *pheasant/pheasants*).

•• **zero relative pronoun**: a phonetically unrealized *relative pronoun in a relative clause, e.g.

The books ø I bought yesterday

The girl ø I was talking to

Such relative clauses are called *contact clauses.

•• **zero *that*-clause**: a *clause which could be introduced by *that*, but from which it is absent, e.g.

He said Ø he was sorry (= that he was sorry)

The use of *zero* in synchronic linguistics was introduced in Bloomfield (1926).

zeugma *See* SYLLEPSIS.

References

Aarts, B. (2007). *Syntactic gradience: the nature of grammatical indeterminacy.* Oxford: Oxford University Press.

Aarts, B. (2011). *Oxford Modern English grammar.* Oxford: Oxford University Press.

Aarts, F. (1986). 'English grammars and the Dutch contribution: 1891–1985' in Leitner, G. *The English reference grammar: language and linguistics, writers and readers,* 363–386. Tübingen: Max Niemeyer.

Adams, V. (1988). *An introduction to Modern English word-formation.* London: Longman.

Adams, V. (2001). *Complex words in English.* Harlow: Pearson Longman.

Aitchison, J. (2012). *Words in the mind* (edn. 4). Oxford: Wiley-Blackwell.

Algeo, J. (1990). 'It's a myth, innit? Politeness and the English tag question' in Ricks, C. & Michaels, L. *The state of the language,* 443–450. Berkeley and Los Angeles: University of California Press.

Austin, J. L. (1955). Lectures published in: *How to do things with words* (1962). Oxford: Oxford University Press.

Baker, M. (2003). *Lexical categories: verbs, nouns and adjectives.* Cambridge: Cambridge University Press.

Baskin, W. (1959). Translation of F. de Saussure's *Course in general linguistics.* New York: The Philosophical Library, Inc.

Bennett, D. C. (1975). *Spatial and temporal uses of English prepositions: an essay in stratificational semantics.* London: Longman.

Biber, D., Conrad, S., & Leech, G. (2002). *Longman student grammar of spoken and written English.* Harlow: Pearson Education.

Biber, D., Johansson, S., Leech, G., Conrad, S. & Finegan, E. (1999). *Longman grammar of spoken and written English.* London and New York: Longman.

Bloomfield, L. (1926). 'A set of postulates for the science of language' in Hockett, C. F., ed. *Leonard Bloomfield anthology* (1970), 128–138. Bloomington: Indiana University Press.

Bloomfield, L. (1933). *Language.* New York: Holt, Rinehart and Winston.

Bolinger, D. (1971). *The phrasal verb in English.* Cambridge, MA: Harvard University Press.

Bolton, W. F. (1975). *The English language.* Sphere History of Literature in the English Language, volume 10. London: Sphere Books.

Brinsley, J. (1612). *The posing of the parts.* London: Thomas Man.

Brown, E. K. & Miller, J. E. (1980). *Syntax: a linguistic introduction to sentence structure.* London: Hutchinson.

Carter, R. & McCarthy, M. (2006). *Cambridge grammar of English.* Cambridge: Cambridge University Press.

Cassidy, F. G. (1961). *Jamaica talk: three hundred years of the English language in Jamaica.* Cambridge: Cambridge University Press.

Catford, J. C. (1959). 'The teaching of English as a foreign language' in Quirk, R. & Smith, A. H., eds. *The teaching of English,* 164–189. London: Secker and Warburg.

Chalker, S. (1984). *Current English grammar.* London and Basingstoke: Macmillan.

Chalker, S. (1995). *Little Oxford dictionary of English grammar.* Oxford: Oxford University Press.

Chomsky, N. (1955a). *The logical structure of linguistic theory* (microfilm, Massachusetts Institute of Technology).

Chomsky, N. (1955b). *Transformational analysis* (Ph.D. dissertation, University of Pennsylvania).

Chomsky, N. (1957). *Syntactic structures.* The Hague: Mouton.

Chomsky, N. (1965). *Aspects of the theory of syntax.* Cambridge, MA: MIT Press.

Chomsky, N. (1986). *Knowledge of language: its nature, origin and use.* New York: Praeger.

Chomsky, N. (1994). 'Naturalism and dualism in the study of language and mind' in *International Journal of Philosophical Studies* 2: 181–200. (Reprinted in Chomsky, N. (2000). *New horizons in the study of language and mind,* 75–105. Cambridge: Cambridge University Press.)

Chomsky, N. (1995). *The minimalist program.* Cambridge, MA: MIT Press.

Chomsky, N. & Halle, M. (1968). *The sound pattern of English.* New York: Harper and Row.

Collins Cobuild English grammar (1990). London: Collins.

Comrie, B. (1976). *Aspect.* Cambridge: Cambridge University Press.

Comrie, B. (1985). *Tense.* Cambridge: Cambridge University Press.

Cristofaro, S. (2003). *Subordination.* Oxford: Oxford University Press.

Croft, W. (1990). *Typology and universals.* Cambridge: Cambridge University Press.

Crystal, D. (2004). *The stories of English.* London: Penguin.

Curme, G. O. (1931/1935) *A grammar of the English language in three volumes* (2 vols.). Boston and London: Heath.

Curme, G. O. (1931). *Syntax, a grammar of the English language,* volume 3. Boston: Heath.

Curme, G. O. (1947). *English grammar.* New York: Barnes and Noble.

Decamp, D. (1968). 'The field of Creole language studies' in *Latin American Research Review* 3:35–46.

Depraetere, I. & Langford, C. (2012). *Advanced English grammar.* London: Continuum.

de Saussure, F. (1916). *Cours de linguistique générale.* Paris: Lausanne.

de Saussure, F. (1959). See Baskin (1959).

Dik, S. (with Hengeveld, K.) (1997). *The theory of functional grammar. Part 1: The structure of the clause* (edn. 2). Berlin and New York: Mouton de Gruyter.

Dixon, R. M. W. (2005). *A semantic approach to English grammar* (edn. 2). Oxford: Oxford University Press.

Downing, P. (1977). 'On the creation and use of English compound nouns' in *Language* 53: 810–842.

Durkin, P. (2009). *The Oxford guide to etymology.* Oxford: Oxford University Press.

Earle, J. (1873). *The philology of the English tongue* (edn. 2, revised). Oxford: Clarendon Press.

Elsness, J. (2009). 'The present perfect and the preterite' in Rohdenburg, G. & Schlüter, J. *One language, two grammars: differences between British and American English,* 228–245. Cambridge: Cambridge University Press.

Fillmore, C. J. (1968). 'The case for case' in Bach, E. & Harms, R. T., eds. *Universals in linguistic theory,* 1–90. New York: Holt, Rinehart and Winston.

Firth, J. R. (1935). 'The technique of semantics' (*Transactions of the Philological Society*) in Firth, J. R. (1957), *Papers in linguistics 1934–1951,* 7–33. London: Oxford University Press.

Firth, J. R. (1951). 'Modes of meaning' (*Essays and Studies*) in Firth, J. R. (1957), *Papers in linguistics 1934–1951,* 190–215. London: Oxford University Press.

Fowler, H. W. (1926). *Modern English usage.* Oxford: Clarendon Press.

Francis, W. N. (1958). *The structure of American English.* New York: Ronald Press Co.

Fries, C. C. (1940). *American English grammar.* New York: Appleton-Century-Crofts.

Fries, C. C. (1952). *The structure of English: an introduction to the construction of English sentences.* New York: Harcourt, Brace and Company; London: Longmans, Green and Company, 1957.

Givón, T. (1993). *English grammar: a function-based introduction* (2 volumes). Amsterdam and Philadelphia: John Benjamins.

Goldberg, A. (2006). *Constructions at work: the nature of generalization in language.* Oxford: Oxford University Press.

Greenbaum, S. (1996). *Oxford English grammar.* Oxford: Oxford University Press.

Greenbaum, S. (2000) (ed. E. S. C. Weiner). *Oxford reference grammar.* Oxford: Oxford University Press.

Greenbaum, S. & Quirk, R. (1990). *A student's grammar of the English language.* London: Longman.

Greenwood, J. (1711). *An essay towards a practical English grammar.* London: Keeble, Lawrence, Bowyer, Bonwick and Halsey.

Haegeman, L. (1994). *Introduction to Government and Binding Theory* (edn. 2). Oxford: Blackwell.

Haegeman, L. & Guéron, J. (1999). *English grammar: a generative perspective.* Oxford: Blackwell Publishers.

Halliday, M. A. K. (1985). *An introduction to functional grammar.* London: Edward Arnold.

Halliday, M. A. K. & Hasan, R. (1976). *Cohesion in English.* London: Longman.

Halliday, M. A. K. & Matthiessen, C. (2014). *An introduction to functional grammar* (edn. 4). Abingdon: Routledge.

Harris, Z. S. (1951). *Methods in structural linguistics.* Chicago: University of Chicago Press.

Herbst, T. & Schüller, S. (2008). *Introduction to syntactic analysis: a valency approach.* Tübingen: Gunter Narr.

Hockett, C. F. (1958). *A course in modern linguistics.* New York: Macmillan.

Hoey, M. (1991). *Patterns of lexis in text.* Oxford: Oxford University Press.

Honey, J. (1989). *Does accent matter?* London: Faber and Faber.

Hopper, P. J. & Traugott, E. C. (2003). *Grammaticalization* (edn. 2). Cambridge: Cambridge University Press.

Householder, F. W. (1952). Review of Z. S. Harris, *Methods in structural linguistics*, in *International Journal of Applied Linguistics* 18:260–268.

Huddleston, R. D. (1976). *An introduction to English transformational syntax.* London: Longman.

Huddleston, R. D. (1984). *Introduction to the grammar of English.* Cambridge: Cambridge University Press.

Huddleston, R. D. (1988). *English grammar: an outline.* Cambridge: Cambridge University Press.

Huddleston, R. & Pullum, G. (2005). *A student's introduction to English grammar.* Cambridge: Cambridge University Press.

Huddleston, R. & Pullum, G. et al. (2002). *The Cambridge grammar of the English language.* Cambridge: Cambridge University Press.

Hudson, R. A. (1980). *Sociolinguistics.* Cambridge: Cambridge University Press.

Hudson, R. A. (1990). *English word grammar.* Oxford: Blackwell.

Hudson, R. A. (2003). 'Gerunds without phrase structure' in *Natural Language and Linguistic Theory* 21. 3: 579–615.

Hudson, R. A. (2010). *An introduction to Word Grammar.* Cambridge: Cambridge University Press.

Jacobs, R. A. & Rosenbaum, P. S. (1968). *English transformational grammar.* Waltham, MA: Blaisdell Publishing Company.

Jakobson, R. (1973). *Main trends in the science of language.* London: Allen and Unwin.

Jespersen, O. (1909–49). *A modern English grammar on historical principles* (7 volumes). Copenhagen: Ejnar Munksgaard; Heidelberg: Carl Winters Universitätsbuchhandlung; London: George Allen and Unwin.

Jespersen, O. (1924). *The philosophy of grammar.* London: George Allen and Unwin.

Jespersen, O. (1933a). *The system of grammar.* London: George Allen and Unwin.

Jespersen, O. (1933b). *Essentials of English grammar.* London: George Allen and Unwin.

Johnson, S. (1755). *A dictionary of the English language.* London: Longman.

Kruisinga, E. (1909–32). *A handbook of present-day English* (4 volumes).

Utrecht: Kemink en zoon; Groningen: P. Noordhoff.

Kruisinga, E. & Erades, P. A. (1941). *An English grammar*. Groningen: P. Noordhoff.

Kuryłowicz, J. (1936). 'Dérivation lexicale et dérivation sémantique'. Contribution à la théorie des parties de discours. In *Bulletin de la Société de Linguistique de Paris* 27:79–92.

Labov, W. (1968). *The study of nonstandard English* (revised edn., 1978). Urbana: National Council of Teachers of English.

Ladusaw, W. A. (1988). 'Semantic theory' in Newmeyer, F. J., ed. *Linguistics: the Cambridge survey* I. Cambridge: Cambridge University Press.

Latham, R. G. (1841). *The English language* (edn. 3). London: Taylor, Walton, and Maberley.

Leech, G. N. (1966). *English in advertising*. London: Longmans.

Leech, G. N. & Svartvik, J. (1975). *A communicative grammar of English*. London: Longman (3rd edn. 2003).

Leech, G. N., Deuchar, M., & Hoogenraad, R. (1982). *English grammar for today*. London and Basingstoke: Macmillan Press in conjunction with the English Association.

Linn, A. (2006). 'English grammar writing' in Aarts, B. & McMahon, A., eds. *The handbook of English linguistics*, 72–92. Malden, MA and Oxford: Blackwell.

Long, R. B. (1961). *The sentence and its parts: a grammar of contemporary English*. Chicago: The University of Chicago Press.

Lyons, J. (1968). *Introduction to theoretical linguistics*. Cambridge: Cambridge University Press.

Lyons, J. (1970). *Chomsky*. London: Fontana/Collins.

Lyons, J. (1977). *Semantics* (2 volumes). Cambridge: Cambridge University Press.

Lyons, J. (1991). *Chomsky* (edn. 3). London: Fontana.

McArthur, T. (1992) (ed.). *The Oxford companion to the English language*. Oxford: Oxford University Press.

McCarthy, M. (1991). *Discourse analysis and language teachers*. Cambridge: Cambridge University Press.

McCawley, J. (1998). *The syntactic phenomena of English* (edn. 2). Chicago: University of Chicago Press.

McEnery, T. & Hardie, A. (2012). *Corpus linguistics*. Cambridge: Cambridge University Press.

McMahon, A. (1994). *Understanding language change*. Cambridge: Cambridge University Press.

Malinowski, B. (1923). 'The problem of meaning in primitive languages' in Ogden, C. K. & Richards, I. A. *The meaning of meaning*, 451–510. London: Kegan Paul, Trench, Trubner and Co. Ltd.

Marsh, G. P. (1860). *Lectures on the English language*. London: John Murray.

Matthews, P. H. (1974). *Morphology*. Cambridge: Cambridge University Press.

Matthews, P. H. (1991). *Morphology* (edn. 2). Cambridge: Cambridge University Press.

Matthews, P. H. (1993). *Grammatical theory in the United States from Bloomfield to Chomsky*. Cambridge: Cambridge University Press.

Matthews, P. H. (2007). *Syntactic relations: a critical survey*. Cambridge: Cambridge University Press.

Matthews, P. H. (2014). *The concise Oxford dictionary of linguistics* (edn. 3). Oxford: Oxford University Press.

Meisel, J. M. (2011). *First and second language acquisition*. Cambridge: Cambridge University Press.

Meyerhoff, M. (2011). *Introducing sociolinguistics* (edn. 2). Abingdon: Routledge.

Miller, D. G. (2002). *Nonfinite structures in theory and change*. Oxford: Oxford University Press.

Minkova, D. & Stockwell, R. (2009). *English words: history and structure* (edn. 2). Cambridge: Cambridge University Press.

Mitchell, T. F. (1975). 'Syntax (and associated matters)' in Bolton (1975), 135–213.

Morley, G. D. (1985). *An introduction to systemic grammar*. London and Basingstoke: Macmillan.

Morris, R. (1872). *Historical outlines of English accidence*. London: Macmillan.

Mort, S. (1986). *Longman Guardian new words*. Harlow: Longman.

Murphy, M. L. (2010). *Lexical meaning*. Cambridge: Cambridge University Press.

Murray, L. (1824). *English grammar* (edn. 38). London: Longman, Hurst, Rees, Orme, Brown and Green.

New English dictionary (1884–1928). (*Oxford English dictionary*, edn. 1). Oxford: Clarendon Press.

Newmeyer, F. J. (1986). *Linguistic theory in America* (edn. 2). San Diego, Calif.: Academic Press.

Nida, E. A. (1948). 'The analysis of grammatical constituents' in *Language* 24: 168–177.

Nida, E. A. (1960). *A synopsis of English syntax*. Norman, OK: Summer Institute of Linguistics of the University of Oklahoma.

Nida, E. A. (1964). *Toward a science of translating*. Leiden: E. J. Brill.

Nida, E. A. (1969). 'Science of translation' in *Language* 45: 483–498.

Nikolaeva, I. (2007). 'Introduction' in Nikolaeva, I., ed. *Finiteness: theoretical and empirical foundations*, 1–19. Oxford: Oxford University Press.

Noreen, A. (1904). *Vårt språk, Nysvensk grammatik i utförlig framställing*. Lund: C. W. K. Gleerup.

Olsson, Y. (1961). *On the syntax of the English verb*. Gothenburg Studies in English 12. Göteborg: Acta Universitatis Gothoburgensis.

Onions, C. T. (1932). *An advanced English syntax* (edn. 6). London: Routledge and Kegan Paul.

Palmer, F. R. (1975). 'Language and languages' in Bolton (1975).

Palmer, F. R. (1984). *Grammar* (new edn.). Harmondsworth: Penguin.

Palmer, F. R. (1987). *The English verb* (edn. 2). London: Longman.

Palmer, H. E. (1924). *A grammar of spoken English, on a strictly phonetic basis*. Cambridge: Heffer.

Partridge, E. (1947). *Usage and abusage* (UK edn.). London: Hamish Hamilton.

Payne, J., Huddleston, R. & Pullum, G. K. (2010). 'The distribution and category status of adjectives and adverbs' in *Word Structure* 3.1: 31–81.

Plag, I. (2003). *Word-formation in English*. Cambridge: Cambridge University Press.

Platt, J. T. (1977). 'The sub-varieties of Singapore English: their sociolectal and functional status' in Crewe, W. ed. *The English language in Singapore*. Singapore: Eastern Universities Press.

Poutsma, H. (1904–29). *A grammar of late modern English* (5 volumes). Groningen: P. Noordhoff.

Prince, A. and Smolensky, P. (2004). *Optimality theory: constraint interaction in generative grammar*. Malden, MA: Wiley-Blackwell.

Puttenham, G. (1589). *The arte of English poesie* (ed. Arber, 1869). London: Edward Arber.

Quirk, R. (1988). Introduction in Greenbaum, S. & Whitcut, J., eds. *Longman guide to English usage*, iii–xii. Harlow: Longman.

Quirk, R. & Greenbaum, S. (1973). *A university grammar of English*. London: Longman.

Quirk, R., Greenbaum, S., Leech, G., & Svartvik, J. (1972). *A grammar of contemporary English*. London: Longman.

Quirk, R., Greenbaum, S., Leech, G., & Svartvik, J. (1985). *A comprehensive grammar of the English language*. London and New York: Longman.

Robins, R. H. (1953). 'Formal divisions in Sundanese' in *Transactions of the Philological Society*, 52 (1): 109–141.

Robins, R. H. (1964). *General linguistics: an introductory survey*. London: Longmans.

Robins, R. H. (1990). *A short history of linguistics* (edn. 3). London: Longman.

Rosch, E. (1978). 'Principles of categorization' in Rosch, E. & Loyd, B., eds. *Cognition and categorization*, 27–48.

Hillsdale, NJ: Lawrence Erlbaum Associates.

Ross, A. S. C. (1958). *Etymology: with especial reference to English*. London: Andre Deutsch.

Sag, I. A., Wasow, T., & Bender, E. (2003). *Syntactic theory: a formal introduction* (edn. 2). Stanford: CSLI Publications.

Samuels, M. L. (1972). *Linguistic evolution with special reference to English*. Cambridge: Cambridge University Press.

Siegel, J. (2008). *The emergence of pidgin and creole languages*. Oxford: Oxford University Press.

Spencer, A. & Luís, A. R. (2012). *Clitics: an introduction*. Cambridge: Cambridge University Press.

Stockwell, R., Schachter, P., & Partee, B. H. (1973). *The major syntactic structures of English*. New York and London: Holt, Rinehart and Winston.

Strang, B. M. H. (1962). *Modern English structure*. London: Edward Arnold. (3rd edn. 1968).

Strang, B. M. H. (1970). *A history of English*. London: Methuen.

Stump, G. T. (2001). *Inflectional morphology: a theory of paradigm structure*. Cambridge: Cambridge University Press.

Sweet, H. (1874). *A history of English sounds*. London: English Dialect Society.

Sweet, H. (1892a). *A short historical English grammar*. Oxford: Clarendon Press.

Sweet, H. (1892b). *A new English grammar*, Part 1. Oxford: Clarendon Press.

Sweet, H. (1898). *A new English grammar*, Part 2. Oxford: Clarendon Press.

Thompson, S. (1985). ' "Subordination" in formal and informal discourse' in Schiffrin, D., ed. *Meaning, form, and use in context: linguistic applications*. Proceedings of the 1984 Georgetown University Roundtable on Linguistics, 85–94.

Washington DC: Georgetown University Press.

Ullman, S. (1962). *Semantics*. Oxford: Blackwell.

Vachek, J. (1964). 'Notes on the phonematic value of the Modern English [ŋ]-sound' in Abercrombie, D. et al., eds. *In honour of Daniel Jones: Papers contributed on the occasion of his eightieth birthday*, 191–205. London: Longmans.

Vanderveken, D. (1990). *Meaning and speech acts*, volume 1. Cambridge: Cambridge University Press.

Van Valin, R. (1993). 'A synopsis of Role and Reference Grammar' in Van Valin, R., ed. *Advances in Role and Reference Grammar*, 1–164. Amsterdam and Philadelphia: John Benjamins.

Van Valin, R. & LaPolla, R. J. (1997). *Syntax: structure, meaning and function*. Cambridge: Cambridge University Press.

Wasow, T. (2001). 'Generative grammar' in Aronoff, M. & Rees-Miller, J., eds. *The handbook of linguistics*, 295–318. Malden, MA and Oxford: Blackwell.

Watson, I. H. (1985). Letter to the editor. In *English Today* 1.4: 3.

Weekley, E. (1912). *The romance of words*. London: John Murray.

Weiner, E. S. C. & Delahunty, A. (1994). *The Oxford guide to English usage*. Oxford: Oxford University Press.

Whorf, B. L. (*ante* 1941). 'The relation of habitual thought and behavior to language' in Carroll, J. B., ed. *Language, thought and reality: selected writings of Benjamin Lee Whorf* (1956), 134–159. Cambridge: MIT Press.

Wilkins, D. A. (1976). *Notional syllabuses*. Oxford: Oxford University Press.

Zandvoort, R. W. (1945). *A handbook of English grammar*. Groningen: Wolters-Noordhoff.

Useful Web Links

SEE WEB LINKS

This is a web-linked dictionary. To access the websites, go to the dictionary's web page at www.oxfordreference.com/page/enggram.

EAW: English for Academic Writing

- An app for mobile devices (Apple and Android phones and tablets) which offers guidance for improving your academic writing.

The Electronic World Atlas of Varieties of English

- A database on grammatical variation in a wide range of different varieties of English, compiled at the University of Freiburg, Germany.

ESP: English Spelling and Punctuation

- An app for mobile devices (Apple and Android phones and tablets) which offers a complete approach to improving your spelling and punctuation.

Glossary of Linguistic Terms

- A glossary of linguistics produced by SIL International.

Glottopedia

- A freely editable encyclopaedia of linguistics.

iGE: the interactive Grammar of English

- A grammar app for mobile devices (Apple and Android phones and tablets), developed at University College London.

The Internet Grammar of English

- An online course in English grammar written by linguists at University College London.

Lexicon of Linguistics

- A glossary of linguistics compiled at Utrecht University.

Longman Dictionary of Contemporary English Online

- An online dictionary covering British and American English.

Macmillan Dictionary Online

- An online dictionary with an option to select British or American English.

Merriam Webster Online

- An online dictionary of American English.

Oxford Advanced American Dictionary Online

- An online dictionary of American English.

Oxford Advanced Learner's Dictionary Online

- An online dictionary covering British and American English.

Oxford Dictionaries Online

- An online dictionary with an option to select British & World English or American English.